THE New Age Baby Name BOOK

SUE BROWDER

Handwritten notes:

Samanta — Matthew
sthephania — christopher.
Lindsey. — brandon.
Leslie.
Kerry.
Kasandra
Andrea
Linette.
Rachel.
Jessica.

WORKMAN PUBLISHING · NEW Y[...]

For Walter,
who taught me the distance between the stars

★

Library of Congress Cataloging-in-Publication Data

Browder, Sue.
The new age baby name book / by Sue Browder.—3rd ed., completely rev.
p. cm.
ISBN 0-7611-0232-9 (pb)
1. Names, Personal—United States—Dictionaries.
2. New Age movement—Miscellanea. I. Title.
CS2377.B72 1998 929' .4'4—dc21 97—53250 CIP

Cover illustration: Mary Engelbreit

Workman books are available at special discounts when purchased in bulk for
premiums and sales promotions as well as for fund-raising or educational use.
Special editions or book excerpts can also be created to specification. For details,
contact the Special Sales Director at the address below.

Workman Publishing Company, Inc.
708 Broadway
New York, NY 10003-9555

Manufactured in the United States of America

First printing May 1998
10 9 8 7 6 5 4 3 2 1

C O N T E N T S

✦ ☾ ✦

GIRLS' NAMES   49

✶ ☾ ✶

BOYS' NAMES 227

INTRODUCTION: WHAT'S A "NEW AGE" BABY NAME BOOK?

Naming your baby should be one of the happiest experiences of your entire pregnancy. Now's the time to kick off your shoes, settle into a cozy chair or warm bath with a cup of herbal tea, and let your imagination flow. If your baby is a girl, do you want a cheerful-sounding name like Merry or Holly? Or would something more serious, like Allison or Reagan, sound better? Should your son be named after a relative? Or would you rather he have a name that's distinctively his? Ichabod is definitely out; but what about Jordan, Michael, or Taylor? Close your eyes, relax, and daydream for twenty minutes about your new baby. Who do you imagine she'll look like? What day do you think he'll be born? The possibilities for names are endless.

Of course, you'll have countless questions. What are the pros and cons of giving your baby a traditional name like Deborah or David instead of a less traditional one like Tiara or Trevor? Can the name you choose affect your baby's personality? Are some names more intelligent-sounding than others? Will a gender-free name like Kendall or Sydney help your daughter break through the glass ceiling in the corporate world? What unspoken messages can you send with a name? Which common myths should you ignore? How soon will your baby know her own name? You'll find answers to all these questions in this book, as well as news about important naming trends, curious stories, legends, and many fun facts about names.

Why is this called the *"New Age" Baby Name Book?* When this book was first written in the early 1970s, I was pregnant and my husband and I were wondering what to name our own baby.

Yet all the baby name books at the time contained only names we've all heard a thousand times, such as Mary, Susan, and John. Since we knew our baby would be special (as all babies are), we wanted a name that would be a little less common. Something unique and trendy, yet also meaningful. A name with a bit of flair.

We wanted the name to contain a lovely hidden meaning, but we also wanted it to sound melodic. Although we were eager to explore names from many cultures, we didn't want anything *too* unusual. A name like Intwasahlobo ("spring") or Mafileokaveka ("good-looking conqueror"), while fine for a child in Nairobi or Polynesia, simply wouldn't do for our daughter or son in first grade. That's when I began collecting the most musical names I could find from all over the world.

Every culture has its rhythms. Every name has its music. The names in this book were chosen mostly for their music. There are many beautiful names from other countries that don't match America's rhythms; for instance, Jyotishmati is a Hindu name with a beautiful meaning—"the night illuminated by the stars" (referring to a peaceful state of mind in yoga philosophy). It sounds lovely in India but long and awkward in America—not because it's a "bad" name, but simply because our rhythms are different.

When choosing a name for my baby, I believed it important to consider all the traditional favorites like Sarah, Matthew, and John. But whenever I came across one of these timeless classics, I always tried to find something extra-special about it. Sometimes I came upon a bit of hidden "magic" in a name, such as an unusual mythological or spiritual meaning. Other times I'd find that a traditional name had a fascinating legend buried deep in its history. My personal interest quickly grew into a passion, and before long I had enough names for a book.

I finally called my new baby Erin Kimberly Browder. But what should I call the book? At the time, many people believed we were approaching a "New Age"—a time when prejudice and fear would at last melt away and people of all races, nationalities, and creeds would live side by side in mutual respect, understanding, and peace. I realized that, symbolically, the names I'd collected were already reflecting this harmonious New Age.

Maru (a Japanese name meaning "round") sat comfortably beside Mary; Jamal (Arabic for "handsome") peacefully preceded James. These names were already as richly mixed and blended as the children in many kindergarten classrooms. The dream of a day when all children would live together without prejudice or fear seemed a lovely idea to reflect in a book about babies, who are always our best hope for the future. Thus, *The New Age Baby Name Book* was born.

That peaceful New Age envisioned years ago still hasn't arrived, of course. Many would say we're far from it. But as the Internet connects millions of us daily with people all over the world, the dream is alive in ways it never has been before.

In a very real way, the names we choose for our babies reflect how we feel about ourselves. When our identities as a people shift, so do the names we prefer. In Germany, parents who've grown weary of conventional German favorites such as Hans, Anna, and Klaus are now giving their babies names with more international character, like Jennifer, Julia, Tamara, Daniel, and Alexander. South African researchers report that Zulu parents (who once chose from a very traditional pool of names) are now giving their children contemporary "Western" names to reflect their new worldview of themselves. Ethnic names are also flourishing—not only in the United States, but worldwide. In tradition-bound Britain, the name Mohammed recently became more popular than John.

Meanwhile, in this country we've witnessed an explosion of new names that were unheard-of just a few decades ago. Names like Chanda, Kaylee, Lakeisha, Richelle, and Tiana for girls; and Deston, Jerone, Jalen (pronounced JAY-len), Teryl, and Tevin for boys, have all recently been coined by imaginative American parents. Gender-free names like Blair, Cameron, Cassidy, Jordan, Mackenzie, Payton, and Taylor are also becoming quite trendy. As we reinvent ourselves, often the names that worked so well in the past no longer seem just right—so we find new ones.

This revised, better-than-ever third edition of *The New Age Baby Name Book* has been greatly expanded to include thousands of new names from all over the world, including many created by inventive American parents. Yet even as this book continues to grow (with an additional 10,000 names), its unifying vision remains the same. This collection of richly meaningful names are still the best ones I could find for the continuing advent of the New Age.

As Pulitzer Prize-winning novelist James Agee once said, "In every child who is born, under no matter what circumstances, and of no matter what parents, the potentiality of the human race is born again."

Have a delightful time choosing a special name for your baby!

C H A P T E R 1

Choosing a Name for the Twenty-First Century

✶ ✶ ✶

The Yoruba-speaking people of Nigeria have a proverb: "Consider the state of your life before you name a child." And that's what more and more American parents are doing nowadays as they seek distinctive names for their children.

In this book you will find meanings and pronunciations (when useful) for thousands of names used in this country from cultures all over the world—African, Arabic, Asian, Eskimo, Hawaiian, Hindu, Irish, Native American, and Russian, to name only a few. In addition, Americans are constantly creating new names, which reflect not only our independence and creativity but also our changing cultural consciousness; in fact, many of these newly created names have been collected from newspaper birth announcement columns.

You may want to use the names in this book exactly as they are listed, or you may decide to use them as a springboard to create new, personalized names. In that case, the chapter "Twelve Fun, Easy Ways to Create a Name" (pages 21–25) will give you some good ideas to begin.

TRENDY NAMES

When choosing a contemporary name, you'll probably want to consider a few of the current fashions. Seeking out slightly unusual names for our babies is one popular trend. To find special names, some Americans are creating their own, but many are dipping into traditional name pools from other cultures. Today's babies are being given names that weren't even listed in American baby name books thirty years ago—names such as Liam (an Irish form of William), Tamika (traditionally Japanese), Tanisha (which comes from Africa), and Hans (the German form of John).

Another trend is to choose what were once last names as first names. Names like Madison, Jordan, Taylor, Murphy, and Kelsey are gaining popularity for both boys and girls.

Many names that were once only nicknames are now being bestowed as full given names. Newspaper records show that Randy has become more popular than Randolph or Randall, and Stacy is used more than Anastasia. You will find many of these "shortened" names listed in this book as independent names. This trend toward using nicknames may be the result of Americans' characteristic informality and also a loss of the superstitions that created nicknames in some cultures in the first place. Nicknames were originally used (and still are in a few remote parts of the world) to hide one's real name from evil spirits, the idea being that—as in the fairy tale "Rumpelstiltskin"—one has only to know another's name to gain control over him. Believing this, people in some relatively primitive tribes still consider it quite rude to ask someone his or her name, and when asked their own name will often simply reply, "I forgot it" or "I have none."

Another modern development is using what were formerly exclusively boys' names for girls. Many traditionally masculine names—Bailey, Kendall, and Sydney—are more popular today for girls than for boys, probably the result of the reduced emphasis on traditional male and female stereotypes. For this reason, traditional boys' names that have been widely adopted by girls are also listed in the girls' section.

UNIQUE CHOICES

We are also seeking names with deep personal meaning for us as well as for our children. Years ago, parents rarely knew that Barbara meant "stranger," and even if they did, the meaning was just an interesting bit of trivia having nothing personally to do with them or their child. But since the early 1970s parents of all heritages, from African to Irish, have increasingly sought names with more personal meaning. This trend, though relatively recent to the United States, is traditional in many other cultures where a child's name is considered part of his soul and has profound personal significance.

A Hopi Indian called Quoiavama, or "Sunrise," once told me his name was a picture. "It means," he said, "the golden sun coming up over the misty mountains and glimmering on hazy smoky-blue waters, while the morning birds chirp in the rustling green trees." Once, Sunrise recalled, he rose before dawn to take photos from the floor of the Grand Canyon, and when he showed the pictures to his clansmen, they said, "That is your name." The modern return to heritage, or cultural, names is one attempt to regain lost meaning. In this book I've tried wherever possible to get beyond a name's literal meaning to show the "picture"— the connotations and traditions—that brought the name into being.

Names are listed by nationalities, so that you may choose a name to reflect your family heritage. If your last name were Leibowitz, for example, you might want to give your little girl the pretty Polish name Melcia instead of the English equivalent Amelia, or Henka rather than Harriet. Or perhaps you would like to name your baby after a favorite relative, but somehow his name (John, for instance) seems too ordinary. You might consider one of the many variations of John, such as Ivan (Russian), Shane or Sean (Irish), or Jens (Swedish). Today, fewer babies are named "junior" than fifty years ago, perhaps because many parents feel that each child deserves a unique, individual name of his own (see Dad Jr?, page 19). If the father's name is Daniel, you might call the baby Dani, a modern Israeli form of Daniel, used for both boys and girls. If the baby is a girl, you could name her Daniela or one of the modern or international forms of Daniela: Dana, Danett, Dania, Danice, Danit, or Danya.

There are about twenty commonsense rules telling you how to pick a name for your baby; they all boil down to this: The name should sound pleasant and should avoid leaving possibilities open for embarrassing or derogatory nicknames like Piggy or Fatso. The old rules that a name should clearly designate gender and not be too unusual, as I have pointed out, have all but disappeared. Generally, for the sake of a pleasing sound, it is suggested that children with two- or three-syllable family names should receive two given names, one with one syllable and the other with two syllables. One-syllable family names (Smith and Jones, for example) often go best with two- or three-syllable given names. Avoid rhyming your child's first name with his or her last. And watch out for embarrassing initials. Superstition has it that if your child's initials spell out a word, she'll be lucky. But a little girl whose initials spell MUD or RAT may not feel blessed. The composer Arthur Seymour Sullivan (of the Gilbert and Sullivan musical team) always found his initials mortifying—with good reason.

How Many Are Enough?

How many names should your baby have? Most parents believe that because of society's increasing complexity, a middle name is practically essential. If you have a common surname, you may even want to select three given names for your child to avoid identity mix-ups. It's not uncommon in other parts of the world (in China, for example) for a child to have as many as ten names, each bestowed to commemorate an important event, such as entering school, graduating, getting married, and so forth. Some Americans, of course, have been given long strings of names for other reasons. Years ago, Mr. Jackson Ezekiel David James Nathaniel Sylvester Willis Edward Demosthenes Henderson of Charlotte, North Carolina, was so named because his mother hoped one of her son's rich-uncle namesakes would remember the boy in his will. Unfortunately for J. E. D. J. N. S. W. E. D. H., the wealthy old men all died without giving him a cent. Which brings us to the last rule: You can't please everyone, so simply pick the name you and your mate like best.

CHAPTER 2

The Psychology of Naming Your Baby

✱ ✱ ✱

Af/fter working hard to build her career as an attorney, my friend Joanne was about to have her first baby at age thirty-five. Not content with just one book, she'd bought half a dozen and had even dug out several magazine articles telling how to choose the best name for her baby. Unfortunately, the more she read, the more uncertain she felt. "Several articles say the name I choose can affect the grades my child will get in school," Joanne told me one day. "I honestly don't see how a child's name alone could affect how her teachers treat her . . . but, still, I do worry. Also, if my baby's a girl, I was thinking of calling her Kayla or Shanna, but then I read about a psychologist who said unusually named kids are unpopular and have emotional problems. Maybe I should just listen to my mother. She wants me to call the baby Kathy or Michael."

People like Joanne are hardly alone. Many thoughtful, loving parents-to-be are concerned about the psychological impact a particular name may have on their baby's future. Clearly, our names are important to us. Scientists have observed that when you hear your own name spoken—even when you're asleep— your brain waves become twice as active as when you hear someone else's name. The well-known Harvard psychologist Gordon Allport contended that a child's name is the focal point around which he organizes his self-identity throughout life. But what does modern psychological research tell us about choosing the very best name for a baby? What are the pros and cons, for example, of giving your baby an unusual name like Nia rather than a common one like Kathy? Can the name you choose affect your baby's future school grades or emotional development (as some so-called experts ominously warn)? Should you play it safe and opt for an ordinary name like Tom or Jane?

When trying to answer such complex questions, it's not enough to simply glance at findings from one or two poorly designed name studies. One has to examine dozens of carefully designed studies to see what they really reveal. While frequently interesting, findings from a scientific study done in a lab don't always translate directly and easily to hard-and-fast naming "how-to's" in the real world. So let's analyze the latest scientific findings about the psychology of names to see what this research tells you (if anything) about how to choose the very best name for your special baby.

WILL YOUR CHILD'S NAME DETERMINE HOW OTHERS SEE HER?

Articles about names often note that, whether you like it or not, others will judge and stereotype your child by her name. Depending on the particular study, you'll be told that people generally consider Bertha a "fat" name, Brian "macho and dynamic," Justin "vigorous," Rebecca "sweet," April "spritely," Kevin "popular and virile," and Harvey "something of a klutz." Percy is reportedly a "weak" name, whereas Eric is perceived as "very strong."

In a very old but still quoted 1963 study reported in the *British Journal of Psychiatry,* a British psychologist found that John is nearly always thought to be trustworthy, Robin young, and Tony sociable. Agnes and Matilda were considered unattractive, Ann passive. The most unusual name in this study—Grizelda—received the largest number of mixed ratings, a phenomenon the researcher chalked up to the fact that people probably had no views either way. When asked whether Grizelda was trustworthy, sociable, or kind, respondents jotted down "yes" or "no" more or less at random. This finding suggests that unusual and rare names are less quickly stereotyped. In other words, a child with a distinctive name may be able to "write her own meanings" more easily than a child given a common name about which people already have many preconceived notions.

The box on the facing page gives some stereotypes. What can you make of these and other pairings? A few researchers still imply that giving your baby an unpopular name like Bertha or Harold may handicap your child for life. They argue that we tend to see ourselves as others see us, and so a name with negative connotations can hamper a child's emotional development. Such warnings can generate real anxiety for parents who take them too seriously. Fortunately, most careful social scientists now realize that the dire warnings of the past were overblown. Certainly, you want to carefully consider any name you choose. But naming your baby should be fun.

Here's why you should avoid taking name stereotypes too seriously.

First, overly simplified stereotypes reveal only how one small group of people (usually college students) viewed these names on average. When you look at the research more closely, you'll find that nearly every name had both advocates and detractors. In the 1963 *British Journal of Psychiatry* study, for example, only 35 percent of the people polled thought a boy named William would be good-looking. But let's face it: Anytime any of us has a trait, talent, or ability, if one in three people applauds, we're doing pretty well.) Also, stereotypes usually apply only to names written down on a list; once someone actually meets bright-eyed, perky, adorable baby William, any negative ideas about his looks will vanish. Let's remember that our perceptions change over time. Now that Britain has a Prince William, a lot more people will probably view the name as "handsome."

A second reason not to let such findings make you nervous is that stereotypes can vary considerably, depending on how the name is spelled (which suggests these generalities about names are hardly set in stone). Intriguingly, 90 percent of those in the British study thought a girl named Ann would be young. But when an *e* was added, changing the name to *Anne,* the number who considered her young dropped to 78 percent. Would Lynda be rated as "feminine and energetic," as Linda has been? Would Caren, Caryn, Karen, and Karin each be stereotyped in exactly

NAME THAT STEREOTYPE
Other common names and their stereotypes include:

Girls' Names

AMANDA: cultured

AMY: active

ANGELA: attractive and a bit willful

ANN: ladylike and honest but rather plain

EMILY: a wallflower

JENNIFER: young but old-fashioned

JESSICA: beautiful and ambitious

KATHARINE: determined, strong-willed, and pretty

LISA: popular but frail

MARGARET: trustworthy and kind but a bit dowdy

MARY: womanly, active, and wholesome

PATRICIA: plain-looking

VICKY: very sexy and popular

Boys' Names

ANTHONY: tall, thin, and elegant

BENJAMIN: not to be trusted

CHARLES: popular and masculine but not very athletic

CHRISTOPHER: intelligent and hardworking

CYRIL: old and unattractive

DAVID: good, strong, wise, serious, sociable, masculine

HAROLD: weak, foolish, passive, and humorless

IAN: young and honest but unaggressive

JAMES: an all-around winner

KEVIN: virile and quite popular

ROBERT: shy and lacking in confidence

WILLIAM: honest but unattractive and unassertive

the same ways? If the findings of this study are any indication, probably not.

How people stereotype a name also depends on whether they perceive the bearer as upper, middle, or lower class. Dr. Richard L. Zweigenhaft, a psychologist at Guilford College in Greensboro, North Carolina, asked his psychology students to judge a number of names, including McKinley and Talmadge. McKinley was generally rated as "upper class," "overconfident," "intolerant," and "cold." In contrast, Talmadge was considered "lower class," "bad," "weak," "stupid," "uncertain," "weak-willed," and "cowardly." But the ratings for these names changed dramatically when the baby's father's class status was stated. If the father was a physician, the name McKinley was rated as more "good," and Talmadge considered more "strong" and "strong-willed" than if the student believed the father was unemployed.

Also, name stereotyping studies rarely—if ever—take into account the effect of nicknames. How, for example, would the stereotypes of McKinley's name change if all his friends just called him Mack? Or what if Talmadge was often called just Tal?

As you can see, there are countless subtle aspects to consider before you can say with any certainty that Harold is a "bad" name and David is a "good" one. In fact, so many elements contribute to stereotyping that it's really not worth worrying too much about. Certainly, if you read that a certain name—Cyril, for example—was rated very negatively by everyone (as, unfortunately, Cyril was in one study), you might want to think twice about that name or consider using an alternative spelling or a shorter version, such as Cyrill or Cy. Generally, though, most names get such mixed reviews that the findings are of more use to psychologists trying to devise more name studies than they are to you as a parent. No one yet has ever found that calling a baby Cyril or any other so-called "undesirable" name will doom him to an unhappy life, or that calling a boy David will guarantee his future success.

Do Names Affect
Your Child's Grades in School?

Y ou'll occasionally still read of a study done by psychologists John W. McDavid and Herbert Harari, which supposedly "proved" you'd better give your child a popular name if you want her to do well in school. "What exactly *is* a popular name?" you might ask. No one really knows. The plain fact is, name fads shift—often quite dramatically—from year to year.

Let's examine this study more closely to see what was actually found. McDavid and Harari asked eighty elementary school-teachers to grade short paragraphs written by fifth- and sixth-graders. The eight essays were all on the topic "What I Did All Day Last Sunday." Supposedly, the only difference in these "comparable" essays was that four names on the tests (David, Michael, Lisa, and Karen) were "popular" among the teachers, whereas the other four names (Elmer, Hubert, Adelle, and Bertha) were "unpopular." Papers by Michael or David received a full grade higher than those by Elmer or Hubert. Karen and Lisa were given a grade and a half higher than the supposedly outcast, unpopular Bertha.

Before taking such findings too seriously, however, you should know there were major problems with this study.

First, one of the so-called undesirable names—Adelle—actually received the highest grade of all. This finding, if reported at all, is generally skipped over with the lame excuse that the teachers probably considered the name Adelle "scholarly" and "academic." But the fact that Adelle did get a better grade than the popularly named kids leaves the often-drawn conclusion that kids with uncommon or out-of-vogue names do poorly in school open to question.

Second, what if this study—which has been cited ad nauseam as "proof" against unpopular names—was, in fact, flawed? Suppose Lisa's essay really was subtly better in some way than Bertha's, and Lisa's higher grade had little, if anything, to do with her first name. Writers who cite this study seldom bother to tell you that the essays were *not* the same. David wrote about "The

Store," Michael about "Tarzan," Elmer about "The Anniversary," and Hubert about "Kites." Adelle wrote about "Shopping" and Lisa about "Walking the Dog." Bertha's topic was "Planting Seeds" (hardly the liveliest subject). As researchers Louisa Seraydarian and Thomas V. Busse point out in the *Journal of Psychology*, not only is it possible that the essays *weren't* comparable, but the teachers in the McDavid-Harari study also weren't given any specific criteria for grading the essays. The vaguer and more unspecified a task, Drs. Seraydarian and Busse note, "the more likely it is that irrelevancies (e.g., first names) might affect the task."

Third, to be accepted as scientific "fact," a study has to be reproduced—and the same results found—by other teams of scientists. Yet in 1981, when Drs. Seraydarian and Busse, then at Temple University, tried to duplicate the McDavid-Harari findings, they couldn't. In the Temple University study—which involved 60 children's names, 10 essays, and 180 teachers—popular or unpopular names had no effect at all on the marks fifth-graders received. Though the children's names were prominently displayed on the papers, many teachers later admitted they hadn't even noticed them.

Experts frequently warn parents about the "dire" consequences of names so that we won't select one that definitely *would* be a lifelong handicap, such as Lout, Moron, or Killer (all real names that have actually been used). Their goal may be admirable, but their warnings only create unnecessary fear. As a loving, thoughtful parent, you're obviously not going to choose a mean-spirited name like Killer or a peculiar name like Last Chance, No More, or Truck Stop (once given to a baby born in one). Since psychologists have never proved that any "normal" first name can seriously affect a child's grades in school, it does seems wisest—and certainly less angst-provoking—just to choose the name you like best.

SHOULD IT BE KIANA OR KATHY?
UNUSUAL VS. ORDINARY NAMES

Years ago, scientists thought an unusual, distinctive name would make a child unpopular in school and harm her emotional development. It was also thought that children with uncommon names like Risa or Blair would have fewer friends than children with "ordinary" names like Susan or David. Happily, these ideas have gone by the wayside. The most recent research reveals that, far from being a handicap, an attractive but slightly unusual name can be quite an advantage.

Clinical psychologist C. R. Snyder, coauthor of *Uniqueness: The Human Pursuit of Difference,* argues that a child's name is one of his or her "uniqueness" traits. "To have self-esteem," says Dr. Snyder, "all human beings have to feel special. If you make people too similar to others, you threaten their uniqueness, and their self-esteem will take a nose-dive." Dr. Snyder points out that any name helps a child establish a unique identity. But a distinctive name that makes a child stand out a little more from the crowd may actually help the child in his or her struggle to feel individual and special.

Sports heroes, singers, and Hollywood stars have long recognized the publicity value of having a distinctive name. Would Yogi Berra have been as memorable on and off the baseball diamond if he'd gone by his real name—Lawrence Peter Berra? Would Cary Grant have been a sex symbol as Archie Leach? Or would Bo Derek have rated a "10" had she stayed Mary Cathleen Collins? Probably not.

An unusual name may be especially advantageous to a child born in the upper-middle or upper class. As Guilford College psychologist Richard Zweigenhaft notes in a *Journal of Social Psychology* article, a child already privileged by birth may see his distinctive name as just another positive way he stands out. Research on upper-class children who go on to fulfill their promise of birth strongly supports this theory. To see whether an unusual name had any effect on later success, Dr. Zweigenhaft chose 436 male names at random from *The Social Register,* which has been called the "best guide to membership of the national upper class." Half the men had unusual first names like Urie and Cornell, whereas the other half had common names like William and John. Of those thirty men who actually went on to become listed in *Who's Who,* twenty-three—or a whopping 77 percent—came from the group with unusual names.

Past studies showed that children with unusual names did worse on IQ tests and had lower self-esteem. Again, more recent studies have not supported this. Indeed, another study reported in the *Journal of Social Psychology* found unusually named college women actually scored higher on many variables, including capacity for status, sociability, social presence, and self-acceptance, than did women with ordinary names.

You also need not worry that giving your child an unusual name will make her unpopular. One often-cited 1966 study did suggest that kids with uncommon names might be less popular with their peers. But that study included only fifty-nine children (all Jewish) who knew one another. In a much more extensive study done in 1979, Dr. Busse looked at 1,548 children from many racial, ethnic, and religious backgrounds. Comparing kids with ordinary names to those with unusual ones, he found no relation between a child's first name and his or her popularity. In fact, a pretty or distinctive name like Kala or Jared will likely just help a child feel more special.

GENDER-FREE NAMES

Another outmoded naming rule that's faded is the notion that your child's name should clearly denote his or her gender. The old idea was that if you gave your child an ambiguous name (like Robin, Lee, Dana, or Harper), he or she would have trouble establishing a sexual identity and would likely suffer serious psychological problems (a phenomenon known as the "boy-named-Sue syndrome").

This notion has now been discarded. In carefully controlled studies at Wesleyan University, Dr. Zweigenhaft compared students with sexually ambiguous or misleading names (such as

Dana, Leslie, and Ronnie) with students whose names were decidedly masculine or feminine. All the students had taken the California Psychological Inventory (CPI), which tests psychological health on eighteen scales. Students with gender-free names were just as psychologically healthy as students whose names clearly denoted their gender. As a matter of fact, girls with gender-free names scored higher than other girls on "capacity for status," whereas boys with these names scored higher than other boys on the "well-being" and "good impression" scales. Dr. Zweigenhaft's conclusions are very clear. He writes, "There is no evidence in these data to support the dire prediction for the 'boy-named-Sue syndrome.'"

Dad Jr?

What about naming your son after his father, with "Jr." attached? Research has generally shown this isn't such a good idea. Most studies have found boys intensely dislike being given their father's name (although Dr. Busse did find in one study that boys with their father's name liked their names and also got along well with other boys). Dr. Zweigenhaft found in his 1980 studies that "juniors" scored significantly lower than other boys on a number of psychological measures, including capacity for status, well-being, responsibility, tolerance, and intellectual efficiency.

It's important to remember, of course, that such findings are for juniors *on average.* Any one specific junior (yours, for example) may actually score way above other boys in these areas. If you do name a son Junior, the most important thing is to instill in him a sense of individuality. Thus, if a boy is named Thomas Jones, Jr., it's advisable to give him a distinctive-sounding nickname (like T. J., for example) to emphasize the fact that he's still unique and special.

Intriguingly, when Dr. Zweigenhaft looked at the psychological scores of boys named after their fathers but whose junior status was designated with Roman numerals rather than "Jr.", (as in John Smith II or John Rockefeller III), he found these boys were as well-adjusted as those not named for their fathers. Dr. Zweigenhaft suggests that a boy with a II, III, or IV after his name may see himself as one link in a long chain of respected, admired high achievers, and may therefore see himself as quite special. "In contrast," he writes, "the person with Jr. attached to his name may or may not be part of a long line of many. His title reminds us, and him, that he is younger, most likely smaller (at least for the first 15 years of his life), and lesser in status than the real thing, the person he was named after." This may be an important point you'll want to consider.

In general, the latest scientific research has shown that choosing the perfect name for your child is a lot less perilous—and a lot more fun—than overly simplified stereotypes from the past would have you believe.

CHAPTER 3

Twelve Fun, Easy Ways to Create a Special Name

✦ ✦ ✦

*"A self-made man
may prefer a self-made name."*

—JUDGE LEARNED HAND

Creating a totally original name for a child is a tradition in many cultures. The Chinese have few "common" first names because each child is believed too special to be given a name many others have used before. The same is true of some Native Americans, who believe a person's name is his soul. In fact, it was said of many an Indian paradise that you had only to tell the gods your name to be admitted. Among these Indians, then, if two people accidentally ended up with the same name, one of them would choose a new one. The Purim Kukis, a tiny Tibeto-Burmese tribe in China, actually have clan monopolies on names. If anyone takes a name from another clan, he is fined a pig and a pot of rice brew, but allowed to keep the name.

In many cultures original names are created from an event in the father's life. The Miwok name Lipetu, for example, means "bear going over a man hiding between rocks," referring to a close call the father had with the animal. Or the child might be named for an event at birth; for instance, the Miwok girl called Huyana ("rain falling") was probably born during a rainstorm. Another favorite custom is to name children for the first object one of the parents sees after the birth, which accounts for some pretty unusual-sounding names like the Zuni Indian Taci ("wash-tub") and Tiwa ("onions").

Methods for creating a name are limited only by your imagination. Here are twelve delightful ways to begin.

NUMBER 1: USING ANAGRAMS

If you love playing Scrabble, you'll have fun with this. Take a name or word that has special meaning for you and switch the letters until you produce a new name you like. Playing around with the letters in Marian, for example, you might come up with Mirana or Ramina. Or you could turn "earth" into Retha or Thera. (Secret: starting with a word that has several vowels makes it easier.)

NUMBER 2: TELESCOPING FROM CELEBRITIES OR FAMOUS NAMESAKES

Simply drop letters from a word until you arrive at a suitable name. If you want to telescope from the name of a person you admire—Martin Luther King Jr., for example—you might shorten the name to Marin. Or Kahlil Gibran can be changed to Kabran. You can also telescope and then juggle letters to create a name. Hence, Golda Meir might be shortened to (Go)lda Me(ir), which can then become Melda.

NUMBER 3: TELESCOPING FROM TRENDS

This process simply involves using the first letters of words to create a name. You might create a "world peace" telescope from the words "peace," "interdependence," "enlightenment," and "trust," producing the name Piet. Or you might create the "unspoiled nature" telescope Tesa from the words "trees," "earth," "streams," and "air." Another possibility is to use first letters from a favorite saying, book, movie, or song title.

NUMBER 4: INVERSIONS

To create a name by inversion, you switch the syllables in a familiar name. Examples are Mary to Ryma, the flower name Dahlia
to Liadah, Marco to Comar, the Spanish *blanco* to Coblan, and
Donald to Alddon.

NUMBER 5: NAMES FROM THE FATHER'S NAME

A boy, of course, can easily be named after his father by adding
"junior" or a Roman numeral, or by shortening the father's name.
Donald might name his son Donal or Doni. Similarly, a girl can be
named after her father by adding one of dozens of feminine suffixes. The combinations are virtually endless. For example, from
the name John a girl might be called Jonalee, Jonanne, Jonetta,
Jonette, Joney, Joni, Jonica, Jonia, Jonie, Joniki, Jonille, Jonine,
Jonisa, Jonit, Jonitka, Jonitsa, Jonitta, Jonitte, Jonsay, Jony, or Jonya
to name only a few. These, in turn, could be spelled with John
in place of Jon (Johnille), two n's instead of one (Jonnisa), and
so forth.

NUMBER 6: NAMES FROM THE MOTHER'S NAME

The most popular way to name a boy after his mother (especially
in the upper classes) is to use her maiden name. Thus, a boy
might be named Cole, Davis, Grey, Johnson, Parker, Potter,
Richardson, Ross, Sanders, Taylor, or Ward. The mother's name
can also be shortened and used with male suffixes. Hence, the
name Mary, transformed into a boy's name, could become Mar-
ald, Mardy, Marle, Marley, Marick, Marnand, Marnett, Marrand,
Marren, Marris, Marsin, Marson, Marston, Marten, Marton, Marty,
Marwin, and so forth. In the same way, Maria could become a
feminine Mari, Marica, Marine, Marisa, or Martisa, to name but
a few.

NUMBER 7: COMBINATION USING BOTH PARENTS' NAMES

This method of making up names is practically self-explanatory. The parents' first or first and middle names are written down, and letters are dropped, added, or juggled until a pleasant name is formed. Joseph and Ellen might name their little girl Joselle, or Daniel and Susan might call their boy Dansan. The first letters of the parents' names could also be used to form a new name. For instance, Gerald and Ida Adams might call their daughter Gia.

NUMBER 8: APHERISIS

Apherisis involves dropping unaccented syllables from the beginning of a name. This has already been done with familiar names (Tilda from Matilda, Beth from Elizabeth). So if you want to create a new name using this method, you'll probably have to choose an unusual name to start with. Examples of apherisis using unusual names are the Hebrew Arella to Rella, the Russian Amaliya to Maliya or Liya, and the Native American name Aponi to Poni.

NUMBER 9: APOCOPATION

Apocopation is apherisis reversed. You drop unaccented last syllables to create a new name. Again, we have familiar examples, such as Elisa from Elisabeth or Nicol from Nicholas. You might shorten the Swahili Azizi to Azi, the Irish Delano to Delan, or the Russian Lidiya to Lidi.

NUMBER 10: DIMINUTIVES

After using apocopation, you might choose to create a diminutive by adding a pet ending. For example, you might drop the final syllable of Arna and add the suffix -ette to produce Arnette (just as mothers in the past changed Susan into Susette). The more common Sharon becomes Shari, Sharie, Shary, Shareen, Sharette, Sharita, and so forth. The examples under "Names from the Mother's Name" (see page 23) give you typical masculine endings to get you started, whereas a few common feminine endings are listed under "Names from the Father's Name" (also on page 23).

NUMBER 11: COMBINATIONS

Combinations are made almost exactly like names invented by combining those of the parents, except that you go a step further and create a new name with a specific, personal meaning. For instance, Avra could be created by combining the two Hebrew names Avirice, meaning "air" or "atmosphere," and Burura, meaning "clean" or "pure." The name Avra might express your hope for the future—a clean atmosphere with pure, fresh air.

NUMBER 12: GENDER SWITCHES AND RESPELLINGS

Gender switches and respellings are becoming increasingly common today. Just a few examples of boys' names now being used for girls are Brooke, Kendall, Cameron, Gari from Gary, and Doni from Donald. Respelling usually involves changing *i* to *ie* or *y* or vice versa, *k* to *c* or the reverse, or *e* to *i* or *y,* producing examples like Caren, Carin, Caryn, Karin, Karyn, Ellyn, Kari, Karie, Kary, Robyn, and so forth. Another possibility is to capitalize a letter in the middle of a name, creating names like MacKenzie, MariAnne, and LaMonde, or to hyphenate a name like Amber-Lee or Anna-Lisa.

C H A P T E R 4

Choosing a Name
from a Special Culture

✳ ✳ ✳

Y ou may want to choose a name that reflects your own roots. Giving your baby a traditional African, Arabic, Irish, Japanese, or Jewish name can be a wonderful way to proclaim your identity and honor your family's traditions. On the other hand, you may want to follow a growing new trend and choose a name from *another* culture. Encountering people from all walks of life—whether it's on the Internet, on trips abroad, or simply in our large cities—has sparked a definite American fascination with names that once seemed quite "foreign." Intriguing choices like Caitlin, Jared, Kenya, and Tamika are now more popular in some circles than Edward or Jane.

This chapter will give you a general overview of naming customs around the world, so if you want a name that crosses cultural lines—whether it's African, French, Japanese, or Irish—you'll know how to find one.

AFRICAN

N aming customs vary greatly in Africa, but the types of names most commonly found denote the time of birth ("born on Sunday"), the order of birth ("first-born daughter"), a physical characteristic, or a recent family incident. Because of Africa's relatively high infant mortality rates, mothers in Ghana and many other countries do not name a child until it has survived seven days. Some children are, in fact, believed to be reincarnated spirits who quickly enter and leave this world, and such infants are given special "born-to-die" names to prevent their returning to the spirit world. Kaya, a common Ghanaian name, means "stay and don't go back."

Some of the most fascinating African names come from Yoruba and Umbundu proverbs. Examples are Cilehe, from "just let it stink, let it be," meaning if you bother it, you will make it worse; Kanene, from "a little thing in the eye is big"; and Ayondela, "a little tree bends and bends, as we all bend toward death." Among the Ibo-speaking people of Nigeria, short-sentence names are popular and include those such as Dumaka ("help me with your hands") and Nnamdi ("my father is alive").

Other common African names are inspired by the spirit. The Ibo god Chi, for instance, gives rise to such names as Chinelo ("thought of Chi"), Cinese ("Chi is protecting") and Cis (which simply means "Chi"). Chi, a personal god thought to stay with a person from conception until death, is believed to be the cause of myriad misfortunes as well as successes.

Included in this book are Bari, Hausa, Ibo, Swahili, Umbundu, Yoruba, and other African names. Many names reflecting African roots can also be found among Arabic entries.

Arabic and Moslem

The fact that Arabic and Moslem names have remained virtually unchanged for over two thousand years may account for their strongly felt influence on names in many other cultures. Nearly every country has a version of the Arabic Leila ("born at night"), and a high percentage of Swahili names are simply slight variants of the Arabic.

Many popular Arabic names come from the ninety-nine qualities of God listed in the Koran: Hakeem ("wise"), Kadar ("powerful"), Kamil ("perfect"), Karim ("generous"), and Nasser ("victorious"). In addition, these are often prefixed with Abdul, Abdel, or Abd, each meaning "servant of." Abdel Nasser, as an example, means "servant of the victorious one." Moslem names, on the other hand, are usually derived from those of the Prophet Muhammad's descendants or immediate family: Ali, Hashim, and

Hussein for boys, and Aisha (also spelled Ayasha), Fatma, and Hinda for girls. The Prophet's name, with its estimated five hundred variations, is often considered the most popular name in the world, and a pious Moslem saying goes, "If you have a hundred sons, name them all Muhammad."

Following religious names in popularity are those describing an abstract quality or virtue. Girls are named Amineh ("faithful"), Marid ("rebellious"), and Zarifa ("graceful"), whereas boys are called Nabil ("noble"), Sharif ("honest"), and Zaki ("intelligent"). Similar are Rafi ("exalting") and Yasar ("wealth"), names which, according to Orthodox Moslems, Muhammad disdained because they were too proud.

Although less common than a century ago, animal names are also used today. Typical are Hamal ("lamb") and Numair ("panther"). Nature names like Rabi ("fragrant breeze") and occupation names, such as Harith ("plowman"), are also common.

To avoid having one's name used too casually—something Arabs consider extremely rude—an Arab often attaches a prefix to his or her name. In this way, Sharif's father might be called Abu Sharif ("father of Sharif") and his mother Um Sharif ("mother of Sharif") instead of by their own given names. Similarly, Bin, Binte, or Ibn ("daughter of" or "son of") followed by the father's name are often used in place of a child's true given name.

CHINESE

China is currently undergoing a crisis because they have too few last names (see box, page 281). But when it comes to first names, the Chinese have one of the most elaborate systems on earth.

First, about a month after birth, a child is given a "milk" name. This name often consists of two elements that "go together," such as Lien-Hua ("lotus blossom") or Mei-Zhen ("beautiful pearl"). Frequently, parents also believe the names of their children should "match." Thus, Precious Jade's sisters might be called Precious Jewel and Precious Peace. A name with a good meaning lends a child social status, and milk names for girls are usually quite pretty. The name Xiao-Xing (pronounced Zhou-Zhing), for example, means "morning star," whereas Jing Wei means "small bird."

In the past, parents of boys sometimes chose the most repulsive milk names they could think of, hoping that evil spirits would be fooled into thinking the child was unloved and would leave him alone. Two of these names translate into "swine urine" and "cat vomit."

Once the child goes to school, a newly selected "school name" is bestowed. Meanwhile, at home, the child is often known by a name like Zhong ("middle or second brother") to reflect his or her position in the family.

When a man marries, starts a business, or enters government service, he acquires yet more names. And as he grows older— and presumably wiser—he adopts yet other names to reflect his character. It is said in China that "A shallow scholar has too many names," meaning he often thinks himself wiser than he truly is.

Since Chinese names are designed by the parents, giving your baby a true Chinese name means creating your own. Elements you can use to get you started include: Bo ("precious"); Hua ("flower"); Jin ("gold"); Jun ("truth"); Lee ("plum"); Li ("strong"); Ling ("delicate or dainty"); Lok ("happy"); Ming ("shining"); Quon ("bright"); Shen ("a deep thought"); Tao ("peach"); Wing ("glory"); and Yuke ("jade"). However, you'll probably also want to use a good Chinese-English dictionary. When studying Chinese names, don't forget that Chinese surnames are written first and the given names last.

FRENCH

When naming their babies, French parents have surprisingly little freedom. The name must "sound French" and be spelled in a "French way." If not, the local registrar, who has a special list of acceptable names, can actually refuse to record the baby's birth—and often does. Saints' names, of course, are always acceptable; but after that, it gets tricky. Henry must be spelled

Henri (although an occasional Henry reportedly slips through). And one mother was actually denied the right to name her child Samuel, even though it comes from the Bible.

Why are the French so rigid about naming? The custom goes back centuries—first to the 1500s, when names had to be approved by a local priest, then to an 1803 imperial decree by Napoleon limiting babies' names to those on the church calendar. In 1957 the old Napoleonic law was more strictly enforced when the French Justice Ministry declared that babies had to have common French names spelled in the "French way"—not as they would be, say, by foreigners in Ireland or the United States. In 1966, French president Charles de Gaulle also banned what he called "ridiculous" names. Not only did he prevent Jewish people from using Hebrew names that went back thousands of years, but he put a stop to anyone who wanted to give their baby the first name De Gaulle.

From time to time, the lists of "permissible" names have been expanded, and now French parents can choose names of mythological figures and pet names like Colas (short for Nicolas), as well as common names in foreign languages. Cindy, Jennifer, Vanessa, Anthony, and Kevin—all pronounced in the French way—now regularly appear on French birth certificates.

Still, lists of the most frequently bestowed names tend to sound like characters in *Les Misérables*. Girls are named Anne, Catherine, François, Jeanne, Marie, Nicolette, and Sylvie; boys today are commonly called André, François, Jacques, Jean, Pierre, and René.

Many French parents are angry about their country's restrictions on naming, and some have even gone to court for the right to give their babies more unusual names. Though French judges have rejected such "ice-cream flavor" names as Cerise (cherry) and Vanille (vanilla), one judge did allow a mother and father to call their baby boy Sinbad.

If you want an authentically French name yet still want one that's a bit different, you might want to consider a common pet form. Just keep in mind that the French tend to create nicknames and diminutives differently than we do. Whereas we often drop the last part of a name (so that Benjamin becomes Ben,

Alexander becomes Alex, and Thomas becomes Tom), the French tend to drop the *first* syllable or two (just as our Elizabeth sometimes becomes Beth), so that Benjamin becomes Jamin and Thomas becomes Mas. This isn't a strict rule of thumb, though. A favorite pet form of Monique, for example, is Mique, and Alice often becomes Aliz. Further, if you decide to shorten Nicolette to Colette, Josephine to Fifi, or Stephanie to Fanette, you'll be following a time-honored Gallic, or ancient French, tradition.

GERMAN

For years—centuries, actually—the Germans only "exported" names to other cultures. Many of our most time-honored names, like Arnold, Frank, Frederick, Gerald, Herman, Richard, and Roger, spring from Teutonic, or Germanic, roots. Yet despite their enormous influence on names in other languages, until recently the Germans refused to use any names from "foreign" sources. Early Germans frequently gave their babies names that described their social status or feats in war and peace. Richard, for example, means "powerful ruler"; Roger was "famous spear"; and Gerald was "spear strong" or "spear brave." Even Hilda was a "battle maiden."

Under Hitler, Nazis made it illegal to give a child a name that wasn't on an "approved" list; German Jews, who had previously been required to take "Jewish-sounding" last names, were forced to give up their traditionally Hebrew first names. Even when German parents chose an "accepted" first and middle name, they had to specify which one they planned to use on a regular basis. Nicknames—except for a few familiar ones like Klaus from Nikolaus and Hans for Johannes—were also strictly forbidden.

As late as the 1960s, the most popular names in Germany all sounded Germanic. Among the favorites for boys were Erich, Ernst, Franz, Frederich, Johannes, Karl, Kurt, Max, Otto, Richard, and Wilhelm. Favorites for girls were the traditional Anna, Elsa, Frieda, Gretchen, Hedwig, and Wilhelmine.

Whether it was the demise of the Berlin Wall or simply a change of consciousness among the German people, nobody knows. But the names preferred by German parents seem to be changing. Saints' names remain favorites in parts of the country where the Catholic Church still has a strong influence; but foreign names are also becoming quite popular. If you want a distinctly German name for your baby, you can still go with one of the German classics like Hans, Klaus, Otto, Wilhelm, or Wolfgang for boys, or Erna, Gudrun, Hildegarde, Inga, or Winifred for girls. But if you want to follow current trends in Germany, you may want to opt for Folke, Jens, or Sebastien for boys or Rebekka, Monika, or Katya for girls.

HAWAIIAN

Many contemporary Hawaiian names are adaptations of English or Biblical names. Some are similar to the English names, such as Dorisa for Doris, whereas others have been changed more significantly (Akoni for Anthony, for example). Although Hawaiians have many short names, they also have some of the longest in the world, and the custom of giving a child an English first name with a Hawaiian middle name sometimes produces fascinating combinations. One example is David Kekoalauliionapalihauliuliokeekoolau Kaapuawaokamehameha, nicknamed Kekoa Kaapu. While such names often seem amusing to outsiders, they usually have melodic, picturesque meanings, the above being "the fine-leafed koa tree on the beautiful green ridges of the Koolau (mountains)." The same boy's sister was named Kapualehuaonapalilahilahiokaala, or "the lehua flower blooming on the steep ridges of Mount Kaala."

Included here are shorter names with similarly pretty meanings. Alaula ("light of early dawn" or "sunset glow") and Aolani ("heavenly cloud") are typical and can be given to both boys and girls.

Many pretty Hawaiian names are created by the parents from an incident at birth. For instance, if a father looked up and saw a seagull shortly after his daughter was born, he might name her Iwalani ("heavenly seabird") or perhaps Iulani ("the highest point of heaven"). The names listed in this book are only samples of the many names you can create yourself. Some of the most commonly used elements in Hawaiian names include: Iao ("name of a star"), Ipo ("darling"), Kapu ("sacred"), Lani ("sky" or "heavenly"), Lei ("wreath or "child"), Malu ("peace"), Mele ("a song" or "poem"), Nani ("beautiful"), Ola ("life" or "health"), Olu ("gentle"), and Pua ("flower"). Two common names, in fact, are combinations from this list: Pualani, which means "heavenly flower," and Puanani, "beautiful flower." Another example: Melei, from Mele plus Lei, meaning "song child."

HINDU

I n India, Hindu naming rules laid down by early lawgivers were basically the same as they are in most other cultures today. Basically, the name should be easily pronounced, have a clear meaning, and be charming, lucky, or contain a hidden blessing. The only rule of thumb not shared by other cultures was the idea that a girl's name should have an odd number of syllables and end with a long *i* or *a,* whereas a boy's name should begin with a consonant and have an even number of syllables. Today, of course, most Hindu parents choose any name they please. However, many of the old traditions are still reflected in the names they choose.

Many powerful Hindu names, for example, come from the Hindu gods, who are all, in reality, manifestations of the One God. It's commonly believed that frequently pronouncing the holy name of God leads to health, happiness, and good fortune in this world and spiritual bliss in the next. Common boys' names include Hanuman, Kistna, Narain, Ram, Ravi, Siva, and Valli, while Devaki, Devi, Rama, Rati, and Sita are common girls' names.

Although members of high castes were once legally forbidden to marry anyone with a "plebian" nature name, girls today are often named after rivers, flowers, trees, animals, and stars. River names include Ganga, Kaveri, Krishna, Narmada, and Yamuna. As is true in some regions of China and Africa, a few superstitious Hindu parents still believe an ugly name will trick demons into thinking the child is not worth notice. Such parents may name a child Klesa ("pain") or Kirwa ("worm").

The many suffixes added to Hindu names make the combinations and variations on one name almost endless. For example, in the Punjab, where children are named after common words, Nath ("lord") may become Natha, Nathan, Nathi, Nathi Mall, Natho, Nathu, and Nathu Rai, to name only a few variations. Since most of the entries in this book are simple forms of Hindu names, to create a name for your own baby you might add any of about sixty suffixes used today, some of which can be considered names themselves. The more common ones are Ananda ("bliss"), Autar ("incarnation"), Das or Dasa ("slave"), Datta ("gift"), Guha ("secret"), Gupta ("protector), Ji ("soul" or "life"), Lal ("cherished"), Mall or Sena ("warrior"), Pandita ("scholar"), Putra ("son"), Rai ("prince"), Ram ("god"), Sagara ("ocean"), Singh or Simha ("lion"), Tirtha ("ford"), Vala ("mine" or "from"), and Varma ("shield"). For example, to come up with your own contemporary name, you might take Kali, which is another name for the goddess Shakti, and add the suffix -das to create Kalidas, meaning "slave of Kali" or "devoted to Kali." Or, since it's a common practice in India to split one long name in two, you might choose one of the above elements as a middle name.

IRISH AND SCOTTISH GAELIC

Some names we consider "Irish" in this country aren't really Irish at all. Names like Erin, Molly, and Colleen (Irish for "girl"), for example, aren't even used in Ireland. Megan, which many people consider Irish, actually comes from Wales, where it's a pet form of Marged, or Margaret. The currently trendy Caitlin *is* authentically Irish; but the way it's usually pronounced in this country—KATE-lin—is strictly American. In Ireland, it's pronounced *Kathleen*.

So what should you do if you want to give your baby a name that's *truly* shamrock green? One good way is to check the name lists throughout this book. You'll find authentic Irish variations of many traditional names—from Mary and Margaret to Robert, William, and John. A second great source of Irish first names are those of the saints. Unlike the familiar Matthew, Mark, Luke, and, John, Irish saints' names have a distinctively Gaelic flavor. Many of us don't think of Brendan, Kevin, Kiernan, Brigit, or Tara as saints—but they are.

Yet another trend, and a very popular recent development in this country, is to take an Irish last name like Blaine, Kelsey, or Murphy, and use it as a first name for either a boy or girl. You can often tell an Irish last name just by looking at the first few letters. If a name starts with *O'*, such as O'Bryan, O'Connor, or O'Hara, it's Irish for sure. The *O*, which comes from an old Gaelic word *eu*, means "descended from" or "grandson." Other Irish names start with *Mac*, meaning "son of." Strictly speaking, Mackensie means "*son* of the wise leader," even though it's currently used in this country for girls.

What are the most popular baby names among parents in Ireland? Old Gaelic names—particularly those borne by saints, such as Aiden, Hugh, Kilian, Lorcan, and Malachy—are especially favored for boys. Other popular names, such as Maeve and Una for girls, and Ronan for boys, come from Irish myths and legends.

As for Scottish names, they've become so much a part of our American culture that they don't even sound Scottish to us anymore. The royal Stuart family popularized Charles and James, for example, whereas other "Scottish" names include Craig, Gary, Gordon, Donald, and Douglas.

The most popular baby names in Scotland have stayed basically the same for over one hundred years. Agnes, Aileen, Carol, Catherine, Heather, Margaret, Megan, and Moira (a form of the Virgin Mary) are common for girls, whereas Adam, Angus, Charles, Colin, Donald, Ian, James, and John are big favorites for boys. If you want a name that truly sounds Scottish and is still used in Scotland, you might want to consider these: Calum (name of an Irish saint who helped convert Scotland to Christianity); Cameron and Campbell (both famed Highland clan names); Conall; Duncan; Parlan (the Scottish form of Bartholomew); and, of course, Stuart. Girls' names with a Scottish flair include Fiona; Morag (Gaelic for Sarah); Seonaid, pronounced SHO-nah (a form of Janet); and Sine, or SHEE-nah (a Scottish-Gaelic form of Jane). You'll find many others in the name lists.

JAPANESE

The most typical Japanese girls' names denote virtue, with examples being Setsu ("fidelity"), Shizu ("quiet" or "clear"), and Sumi ("the refined"). Similarly, many other names have an implied virtue meaning. For example, Umeko, meaning "plum-blossom child," also connotes wifely devotion, whereas a name from the lotus blossom implies all the Buddhist concepts of a heaven where immortal souls sleep enveloped in lotus buds until they are admitted to paradise.

The Japanese also use order-of-birth and number names for children. Hence, we find Ichi, meaning "one," all the way up to Man, or "ten thousand." The smaller numbers often indicate order of birth, the higher ones, such as eighty, a hope for longevity; very large round numbers, such as ten thousand, were once considered good omens. Numeral names, of course, leave opportunities for whimsy, as in the family of children with names meaning "Ten Dollars," "One Hundred Dollars," and "One Thousand Dollars," or the boy called "1-2-3-4-5-6-7-8-9-10."

Girls' names include Chika or Chikako ("near"), Kiku ("chrysanthemum"), Suzu ("little bell"), and Taka or Takako ("lofty"). Boys' names include Taro ("first male"), Jiro ("second male"), Saburo ("third male"), and Akio ("bright boy").

You can create your own boys' names by using any of a number of prefixes, the most common of which are Masa ("good"), Michi ("righteous way"), Shin ("faithful"), Toku ("virtue"), Yu ("courage"), and Zen ("just" or "benevolent"). Masataro, for example, means "good first-born male," and so forth. You will find other major elements to use with these prefixes in the regular name lists. Similarly, you can create your own girls' name by adding the suffixes -ko, -yo, or -e to regular name elements. Thus, Kiku and Suzu might become Kikuko and Suzuyo.

JEWISH

According to Jewish tradition, a child should be given two first names, one purely Hebrew (the *shem hakodesh,* or holy name) and the other secular. In America, the holy name, when it's given, is often used only in the synagogue.

If you're Jewish, how names were traditionally bestowed in your family probably depended on your family's roots. Among Orthodox Ashkenazic Jews (who hailed from Germany, Austria, Poland, and Russia), it was once considered bad form to name a child after a living relative. This taboo sprang from an ancient belief that naming a baby after a living person would rob the original namesake of a full life and could upset the spirit of the dead. It was considered especially poor judgment to name a baby after an older relative; it was believed the angel of death might confuse the two names and, when it was time for the older relative to die, might take the baby by mistake. Even today when some Orthodox Ashkenazic Jewish parents name a child after a favorite relative, they'll choose the name of someone who's deceased. Often they'll borrow only the first letter of the relative's name; thus it's understood that Michael is named in Uncle Murray's honor.

Conversely, among Sephardic Jews (from France, Italy, Spain, and Portugal), it was and still is customary and quite common to name a baby after a living relative.

In Israel, it has become popular to choose a name that sounds unmistakably Israeli, yet is easy for Gentiles to pronounce and remember. Names of this type often end in "-n" and have no more than four consonants: Doron, Givon, Rimon, and the like. In Israel, as in the United States, the trend is toward shortened names. Zlatopolsky becomes Paz, and Taranto, Tal. Other formerly long names include Dan, Gal, Kol, Nir, Niv, and Ziv. At one time, animal names like Lieb, or "lion" were widely used, but the modern trend is toward plant and flower names, such as the feminine Nurit, meaning "little yellow flower."

Hebraizing names by rearranging the letters is popular in Israel and was recommended by the late Moshe Sharett as well as other leaders. Thus, Kleinman becomes Kenan, Neurath becomes Nur, and so forth. You will find many of these shortened forms in the name list, as well as longer names you may want to abbreviate yourself. (Of course, names from the Torah and Bible also have Hebraic roots.)

Native American

Today, Native Americans may very well be named John, Robert, or William. But traditional Indian names are far more impressive and often contain hidden stories. The Miwoks, one of the largest groups of Indians in California, had in their heritage many extremely expressive names, which revealed much about traditional Indian life, as well as their close partnership with the natural world. These names often imply far more than their literal meanings. To a person who understands Moquelumnan (the Miwok language), the name Memtba simply means "to taste." But if you'd ask a person named Memtba what his name really meant, he might say, "tasting farewell-to-spring seed after it has been mashed with the pestle, but while it's still in the mortar." Probing deeper, you might find that the name described what Memtba's mother was doing when she felt her first labor pain. To a stranger, the name Luyunu simply means "to shake the head sideways." But to Luyunu's friends, his name is really "bear taking off a leg or arm of a person while eating him," implying the child has the strength of a vicious bear.

The complexity of their meanings has often led Native American names to be misunderstood. A Native American name that translated into English as "sweaty blanket" did not indicate that its bearer had a dirty bed, but that he was a tireless rider.

Many imaginative ecological names, taken from plants, animals, the stars, the moon, and other natural phenomena, come to us from Native Americans. It's because of their detailed observations and close associations with nature that we have such names as Taipa, meaning "valley quail spreading its wings as it alights" and Tiponya, "great horned owl sticking her head under her body and poking an egg that is hatching." Such names may refer to an actual event or to a dream one of the baby's parents had.

Because of a strong belief in each person's individuality and unique soul, a Native American following traditional practices would seldom take one of his parents' names. Instead, his name might mirror a proud event in his grandfather's or great-grandfather's life. Wakiza ("desperate fighter") may refer to a battle won without weapons, and Kijika ("walks quietly") to a time the older man noiselessly sneaked up on a deer in the forest. Similarly, a child born during a storm might be given an imposing name such as Shappa ("red thunder") or a whimsical name like Lokni ("rain coming through a small hole in the roof").

In contrast (though the practice has diminished over time), some Eskimos still believe that they must give a newborn a recently deceased relative's name, since the dead return to this world only through their names. In the same Eskimo families, however, it is taboo to name a child after a living relative, because the name would then be saddled with two bodies, one of which it is believed would have to die.

Because of the tendency to create new names, there are no "most common" Native American names. The most typical names, however, are nature names, magical names taken from religious beliefs, war and peace names, and names that simply have pretty meanings, such as Halona ("happy fortune") and Onida ("the looked-for one").

In addition to giving him one deeply meaningful name at birth, many Native Americans will change or add to a boy's name at each important event in his life.

RUSSIAN

Back when there was a Soviet Union, Russians were urged to give their children Russian-sounding names like Ivan, Vladislav, Vladlen, Anna, Sofia, and Vera. In fact, foreign-sounding names were ridiculed—the *Russian Gazette* noted that names like Azalia, Ella, Alfred, and Henry were not only unpatriotic but ludicrous. An article in the daily *Pravda* reported that the four most popular names for girls in Russia were Yelena, Natalya, Olga, and Irina, while the big favorites for boys were Sergei, Aleksei, Aleksandr, and Oleg. Alexander and the feminine equivalent Alexandra (both of which are commonly shortened to Sasha), were so popular that one Russian remarked, "If you yell 'Sasha' on a Moscow street, twenty men and a couple of women will look around."

Unlike people in many other nations, the Russians seldom named their children after political figures for fear the child's namesake would fall out of favor. Many women named Stalina hastened to change their name after Stalin was posthumously denounced in 1956, and again in 1961. One man named Melsor (a telescope name from Marx, Engels, Lenin, Stalin, and October Revolution) actually went so far as to drop the "s" from his name and became simply Melor. Other Russians have kept their names from bygone days. Some elderly women born in the 1920s still bear names like Oktabrina ("October Revolution"), and many babies born when the former Soviet Union first conquered space were called Yuri and Valentina (after cosmonauts Yuri Gagarin and Valentina Tereshkova).

The latest trend in Russia? Now that the Soviet Union is gone, Czarist names are back in style. Yekaterina (after Catherine the Great) and Yelizaveta (for the Empress Elizabeth) are popular for girls. Favorites for boys include Dmitri and Yaroslav, the names of ancient Slavic princes.

Perhaps no other people in the world use pet forms, variations, and nicknames as much as the Russians. A man named Ivan Ivanovich Ivanov (the Russian equivalent of John Johnson), for example, might be called by any of forty or fifty different names, including Ivanyshka, Vanechka, Vanek, Vanka, Vanko, Vanushechka, Vanushka, Vanya, Vanyashka, Vanyatka, Vanykha, and Yanka. Likewise, the Russian equivalent of the English Agnes can be called Agnesa, Agnita, Agnya, Ahniya, Gusya, Nessa, Nyusha, Nyushka, and Nessia, all of which are in a sense the same name. In addition, each pet name has an implied meaning. Names ending in -ka, for instance, are used in anger, while those ending in -usha or -ya are special terms of endearment.

SCANDINAVIAN

Many Scandinavian names refer to leadership in battle, to bravery, or to Norse mythology. The Swedish Lars means "crowned with laurel," a victory symbol; Akin is "descent of the eternal king"; and Bodil means "commanding." You'll rarely find peace names from Scandinavia, the few exceptions being names that start with Fred (such as Fredrik, meaning "peaceful ruler," often shortened to Frits).

The Scandinavians have given the world a number of individualistic names, such as Hamar ("a symbol of man's ingenuity") and Einar ("individualist" or "nonconformist"). These northern countries are also great sources of short, masculine names—Alf, Alrik, Arens, Arni, Garth, Jens, Lars, and Sven, for example. You can find many lovely Norwegian, Swedish, and Danish girls' names too, including Arla, Beda, Birgitta, Blenda, Disa, Gressa, Gretchen, and Meri.

While many Scandinavians, particularly Norwegians, have common Biblical names, such as John, Peter, Ester, and Evelyn, it is fashionable today to give children names with a more Nordic flavor. Common names include Björn, Erik, Gunnar, Hans, Jens, Josef, Karl, Knut, Lars, Nils, Olaf, Rolf, and Sven. Popular for girls are Astrid, Britta, Dorotea, Else, Helga, Ingrid, Jonina, Karin, Katrina, Margareta, Rakel, and Signe.

SLAVIC

Slavic names include Polish, Slovak, and Czech or Bohemian names. At first glance, some names used in these countries may appear awkward to many Americans. But the Slavic practice of pronouncing words with the stress on the first syllable combined with the soft "sh" instead of "s," and "zh" in place of "z," makes these names quite melodic. Anezka becomes AH-nehzh-kah, and Anicka is pronounced AH-neesh-kah.

Many boys' names end in *-slav* or the Polish *-slaw*, which means "glory." In addition to Jaroslav ("glory of spring"), other glory names include Budislav ("future glory"), Ladislav ("glorious government"), Miroslav ("glorious peace"), Vaslav ("glorious wealth"), and Vladislav ("glorious ruler"). Some of the more popular Czech names are Bohdan ("God-given"), Bohumir ("peace of God"), and Radomil ("love of peace"), as well as Filip, Jakub, Jan, Jiri, Josef, Karel, Pavel, Tomas, and Vilem. Common names for girls are Anezka, Bela, Ludmila, Maria, Rusalka, Svetla, and Zofie. Many Slavic girls' names are created by simply adding -a to a boy's name, making Pavela from Pavel, for instance.

Although Polish names typically end in -slaw (masculine) or -slawa (feminine), these are usually replaced by shorter nicknames. The Polish name Hortensja, for example, is often shortened to a prettier Tesia (TE-shuh), and Giertruda frequently becomes just Truda.

SPANISH

Spanish names are often taken from the calendar of saints, and many "typical" names in Spain, as well as in Mexico and other Latin American countries, have religious connotations. For girls, Maria is so popular that additional names relating to some quality of Mary, the mother of Jesus, have been added to differentiate among the thousands of Maria Garcias or Maria Chavezes. Such names include Maria de los Dolores ("Mary of Sorrows"), often shortened to Lola, Lolita, or simply Dolores, and Maria de la Cruz ("Mary of the Cross"), among others. Widely popular forms of such Virgin Mary names include Carmen ("Mary of Scarlet"), Jesusa ("Mary of Jesus"), Luz and Lucita, from Maria de la Luz ("Mary of the Light"), and Suela, from Maria del Consuela ("Mary of Consolation"). The popular name Pilar, meaning "pillar," used for both boys and girls, also refers to Mary, who stands as the base, or pillar, of the Christian religion.

Occasionally you will see combinations of other names with Maria, a technique you may want to use to create your own Spanish name. Thus, Maria plus Flora gives you Mariflor. Other examples are Maria and Romona, which blend to create Marona, and Maria plus Linda, Marinda.

The most popular Spanish names for boys have as many pet forms (or nicknames) as English names do. Francisco has at least sixteen Spanish variations, some of the most common being Chica, Curro, Paco, Pancho, and Paquito. Some favorite names for boys throughout the Spanish-speaking world include Jaime, Jésus, José, Juan, Luis, Mañuel, Mario, Miguel, Pablo, Pauel, Pedro, and Rafael.

Choosing an Astrological, Magical, or Numerological Name

✷ ✷ ✷

People from cultures around the globe have believed for centuries that many names have magical powers, and that by bestowing a particular name you can instill positive traits in your baby. Such thinking may have given rise to Faith, Hope, and Charity—American names first used by the Puritans.

Astrological names are bestowed according to time of birth in the hope that they will be lucky and work in harmony with the stars. A child born under Leo might be given a name meaning "lion," the symbol of that sign of the zodiac, or one meaning "sun," the star that governs Leo.

Eastern astrologers believe a lucky horoscope balances the basic elements—earth, fire, air, water, metal, and wood—to allow the universal order to work smoothly throughout a person's life. In China, if the astrologer who reads the baby's horoscope on the third day of life finds too many wood influences, he may correct this "evil" by giving the baby a metal name (because metal conquers wood) or a name meaning "earth" (since earth produces, and controls, metal ores).

Western astrological earth names include Blair ("child of the fields"), Clay ("of the earth"), and Ertha or Eartha (both meaning "child of the earth"). A child with too many wood influences may also be given a fire name, such as Edan (meaning "fire"), because fire burns up wood.

Likewise, if a baby's horoscope contains too many metal influences, the baby may be given an "aquatic," or water, name (such as Rea, meaning "a stream") because water rusts and erodes metal. Some astrologers also believe metal names, with meanings like "iron" or "hammer," improve a baby's health and fate.

Other magical names include Japanese color names like Akako ("red") and material names like Tetsu ("iron"). The color red, for instance, believed to cure diseases and ensure good health, was once considered a potent protector. The material names probably date back to an ancient idea that demons and evil spirits were born in the Stone Age and hence feared metals, especially iron. It was believed that if a tiny baby girl were named Tetsu, the evil spirits would shun her for a child with a less frightful name.

Many magical and astrological names are included in this book. Not only are there magical names of all the types mentioned above, but there are also some delightful magical names used in incantations to summon or exorcise spirits, plus a few deity names from the Egyptian Book of the Dead, often considered the original source of magic. A fascinating group of magic names are those of the English Gypsies, who've long had a close kinship with fortune-telling and the supernatural.

In many cultures down through history, numbers have also been believed to have some ability to influence fate. In Japan, where round numbers were once thought to be good omens, children are still occasionally named Sen ("thousand"), Michi ("three thousand"), or Yachiyo ("eight thousand generations"). Number names, while not common in the U.S., do occur. A man in Stanford, California, was named 4E Chittenden, and another American's birth certificate read Willie 5/8 Smith. In the 1970s in North Dakota, however, a judge refused to let a man change his name to 1069, noting that if he allowed such a name, there would be no way to stop a musician from changing his name to a series of eighth notes or a banker from signing his name as a dollar sign.

Many other beliefs are embodied in numerology, begun by the Greek philosopher Pythagoras, whose fascination with ciphers led him to number the letters of the alphabet. The result was numerology. One person who used numerology successfully

THE TWELVE ZODIAC SIGNS

SIGN	SYMBOL	ELEMENT
Aries ♈ (March 21–April 20)	Ram	Fire
Taurus ♉ (April 21–May 20)	Bull	Earth
Gemini ♊ (May 21–June 20)	Twins	Air
Cancer ♋ (June 21–July 22)	Crab	Water
Leo ♌ (July 23–August 22)	Lion	Fire
Virgo ♍ (August 23–Sept. 23)	Virgin	Earth
Libra ♎ (Sept. 24–Oct. 23)	The Balance	Air
Scorpio ♏ (Oct. 24–Nov. 22)	Scorpion	Water
Sagittarius ♐ (Nov. 23–Dec. 22)	Archer	Fire
Capricorn ♑ (Dec. 23–Jan. 20)	Goat	Earth
Aquarius ♒ (Jan. 21–Feb. 19)	Water Bearer or Sage	Air
Pisces ♓ (Feb. 20–March 20)	Fish	Water

	BIRTHSTONE	FLOWER	COLOR	RULING PLANET
♈	Diamond	Daisy	Deep red	Mars
♉	Emerald	Lily-of-the-Valley	Deep yellow	Venus
♊	Pearl	Rose	Violet	Mercury
♋	Ruby	Water Lily	Light green	Moon
♌	Sardonyx	Gladiolus	Light orange	Sun
♍	Sapphire	Aster	Dark violet	Mercury
♎	Opal	Cosmos	Yellow	Venus
♏	Topaz	Mum	Red	Mars
♐	Turquoise	Narcissus	Light purple	Jupiter
♑	Garnet	Carnation	Deep blue	Saturn
♒	Amethyst	Violet	Light blue	Uranus
♓	Bloodstone	Daffodil	Dark purple	Neptune

was Elda Furry. She went unnoticed as Elda Furry. Taking her husband's name, she became Elda Hopper, and as such, gained some recognition as a commentator and columnist. However, it was not until a numerologist selected the name Hedda Hopper for her that she achieved the fame she sought.

There are no "numerologically good" first names because the complete name must be factored in. To do this, add the numbers of the letters in a name, including the middle and last names, according to this chart.

1	2	3	4	5	6	7	8	9
A	B	C	D	E	F	G	H	I
J	K	L	M	N	O	P	Q	R
S	T	U	V	W	X	Y	Z	

Select a name you've been thinking of for your baby. Including the middle and last names, find the numbers that correspond to the letters of the name and add the digits together to get the name's destiny number. You will probably come up with two digits—81, for example. In this case, add 8 plus 1 and you will get 9. If you have two digits that add up to another two digits—98, for example, which gives you 17—simply keep adding the two together until you get a number under 10, in this case 1 plus 7 will give you 8. Eleven is seldom reduced to 2 because 7 and 11 are considered master numbers, bestowing great intelligence and leadership abilities.

Generally, the qualities associated with each number are as follows: 1. creative; 2. friendly, a follower; 3. artistic; 4. home-loving, peaceful; 5. a traveler, seeker of truth; 6. a scholar, with a social conscience; 7. intelligent, a leader; 8. ambitious, organized; and 9. righteous, just, a conscientious objector.

Magic names can be fun to play around with. And who knows? By fiddling around with a name's numerological or astrological significance, you may be giving your child even more than an interesting name.

GIRLS' NAMES

A

ABA (ah-BAH) Ghanaian: "born on Thursday."

ABEBI (ah-bay-BEE) Yoruba, Nigeria: "we asked for her and she came to us." *Abeni* (Yoruban)

ABELIA (ah-bel-LEE-ah, or Anglicized ah-BEEL-yah) Hebrew: "breath." A feminine form of Abel, originally from France. *Abella* (French)

ABIDA (ah-BEE-dah) Arabic: "she who worships"; or Hebrew: "the one my father knows."

ABIGAIL Hebrew: "my father is joyous." *Abagil, Abbe, Abbey, Abbi, Abbie, Abbigale, Abbygail, Abbygale, Abigal, Abigall, Abigayle, Abigel, Abigil, Gael, Gail, Gaila, Gaile, Gale, Gayle* (English)

ABINA (ah-bee-NAH, or Anglicized, ah-BEE-nah) Akan, southern Ghana: "born on Benada (Thursday)." *Abana, Abena* (Akan)

ABIONA (ah-BEE-o-nah) Yoruba, Nigeria: "born during a journey." Also a boys' name in Africa.

ABIRA (ah-BIR-ah) Hebrew: "strong." *Adira* (Hebrew)

ABITAL (ah-BEE-tahl or ah-be-TAHL) Hebrew: "my father is dew." Popular in Israel for girls and boys. *Avital* (Hebrew)

ABRIAL (ah-bree-ALE) French: "secure, open, or protected." *Abeale, Abre, Abreal, Abri, Abriala, Abriale* (English)

ABRIANA (ay-bree-AHN-ah) Hebrew: "mother of a mighty nation" or "mother of the multitude." Italian feminine form of Abraham. *Abra, Abree, Abrianna, Abrianne, Abrielle, Abrienne, Briana, Brianna* (English)

ACACIA (ah-KAY-shuh) Greek: "the guileless one." Biblical, referring to the blossoming acacia tree, symbolizing immortality and resurrection. See also Casey. *Acaysha, Akaysha, Cacia, Casey, Casia, Casie, Kacey, Kasi, Kassie, Kassya, Kassy* (English)

ADA Old English: "happy"; or Latin: "of noble birth"; or Hebrew: "an ornament." *Adda, Addi, Addie, Adi, Aida* (English)

ADALIA (ah-DAHL-yuh) German: "noble"; or Hebrew: "God is my refuge." *Adal, Adala, Adalee, Adali, Adalie, Adalin, Adall, Adaly, Adalyn, Addal, Addala, Addaly* (English)

ADAMINA (a-dah-MEE-nah) Hebrew: "daughter of the red earth." Feminine form of Adam. Name for a girl born under the earth signs of Capricorn, Taurus,

or Virgo. *Adama* (English, Hebrew)

ADAMMA (ah-DAHM-mah) Ibo, Nigeria: "child of beauty."

ADARA (ah-DAHR-ah) Greek: "beauty"; Hebrew: "noble and exalted"; or Arabic: "virgin." Name for a girl born under the sign Virgo.

> **"Big names often stand on small legs."**
>
> —WISE OLD PROVERB

ADELLE Old German: "noble." *Adaline, Addi, Addie, Addy, Adela, Adele, Adelina, Adeline, Adella, Alina, Aline, Edeline* (English); *Ada, Adela, Adele, Adelka, Dela* (Czech); *Adele, Adelina, Adeline, Aline* (French); *Akela* (Hawaiian); *Adelita, Alita, Dela, Lela* (Spanish)

ADELMA German: "noble protector."

ADERES (ah-de-RAYS) Hebrew: "an outer garment" or "a cape." *Aderet* (English, Hebrew)

ADESINA (ah-DAY-see-nah, or Anglicized, ah-day-SEEN-ah) Yoruba, Nigeria: "the coming of this baby has opened the way (for more children)." Often used in Nigeria when the parents have waited for a child.

ADIA (ah-DEE-ah) Swahili: "gift" or "present," implying the child is a gift from God.

ADIEL (AD-ee-el or ah-dee-AIL) Hebrew: "ornament of God." The shorter forms like *Adi* and *Adie* simply mean "an ornament." *Ada, Addie, Adi, Adie, Adiella* (English, Hebrew)

ADINA (ah-DEEN-ah) Hebrew: "noble." Also used in Israel. *Adena, Adene* (Hebrew)

ADIRA (ah-DEER-ah) Hebrew: "strong and powerful."

ADITI (ah-dee-tee) Hindi: "free and unbounded." In Hindu lore, Aditi is the mother of the gods and is often asked to bestow blessings on children and cattle or to grant protection and forgiveness.

ADOETTE (ah-do-AY-tuh, or Anglicized, ad-oh-ETT) Native American: "big tree." Perhaps originally given to a child born beneath a tree or believed to be akin to a tree spirit.

ADRIANNE, ADRIENNE Latin: "dark one." Also commonly used in France. *Addie, Adri, Adriana, Adrie, Adriena* (English); *Adriane* (German); *Adriana* (Italian)

ADYA East Indian from *Teluga Adivaram:* "Sunday." Name for a girl born on Sunday.

AGATE Latin: "the agate stone." The magical agate stone was once believed to cure the bites of scorpions and snakes, soothe the mind, drive away polluted air, and stop thunder and lightning. The stone was also believed to make one independent, an eloquent writer and speaker, and a favorite of princes. *Aggie, Agi* (English)

AGATHA Greek: "good" or "kind." The variation Agata is used around the globe, not only here but in Bulgaria, Ireland, Italy, Latvia, Mexico, Poland, Portugal, Romania, Russia, Spain, Sweden and most countries in Central and South America. *Ag, Agata, Aggi, Aggie, Aggy, Agna, Agnessa, Agneta, Agnetta* (English); *Agathe* (French, German); *Agathi* (Greek); *Agi, Agota, Agotha* (Hungarian); *Aga, Agatka, Atka* (Polish); *Agueda* (Portuguese); *Agafia, Agasha, Ganya, Gasha, Gashka* (Russian)

AGNES Greek: "pure." First made popular by Saint Agnes, a third-century virgin martyr. From the twelfth to sixteenth centuries, Agnes was one of the most common names in England, and in the sixteenth century it was among the top three (the others being Elizabeth and Joan). Lately this name has gone out of favor: In one study of stereo-

Naming Customs...

✳ ✳ ✳

Some names that are very *familiar*—in that we've all heard them—are still rarely used. In a study of nearly 200,000 baby names in New York State over a 13-year period, for example, only three baby girls were named Agatha.

types, only 12 percent of those asked thought Agnes would be good-looking, although the name was characterized by 63 percent as "kind" and by 80 percent as "trustworthy." *Aggi, Aggie, Agna, Agneti, Anesse, Anice, Annice, Annis, Nesa, Nesi, Nessa, Nessi, Nessie, Nessy, Nesta, Neysa* (English); *Agnessa* (Bulgarian); *Agnesa, Agneska, Anezka, Anka* (Czech); *Agnies* (French); *Agni* (Greek); *Una* (Irish); *Agne, Agnella, Agnesca, Agnese, Agnesina, Agnola, Anete, Hagne* (Italian); *Agne, Agniya* (Lithuanian); *Agneta* (Norwegian, Swedish); *Aga, Agnieska, Jaga* (Polish); *Ines, Inez* (Portuguese); *Agnessa, Nessa, Nessia, Nyusha* (Russian); *Neza* (Slavic); *Ines,*

Inez, Necha, Necho, Nesho, Ynes, Ynez (Spanish); *Akanesi* (Tongan)

AH-KUM (ah-koom) Chinese: "good as gold."

AH-LAM (ah-lahm) Chinese: "like an orchid."

AHAVA (ah-HAH-vah) Hebrew: "beloved." *Ahavat, Ahuda, Ahuva, Ahuvah* (Hebrew)

AIDA Old English: "happy." Popularized in Italy by the Verdi opera of the same name. See Ada.

AIKO (ah-ee-koh) Japanese: "little love" or "beloved child."

AILEEN (ay-LEEN, eye-LEEN) Anglo-Irish: "light bearer." *Ailene, Ailey, Aili, Aleen, Alena, Alene, Eileen, Eleen, Elene, Ileana, Ileane, Ilena, Ilene, Leana, Lena* (English); *Aila, Aili* (Finnish); *Ailinn* (Portuguese)

AIMEE (AY-mee) French form of Amy, "loved one."

AINA (ah-EE-nah) Scandinavian: "always" or "until the end." Especially well known in Finland.

AISHA (ah-EE-shah) Arabic: "woman"; or Swahili: "life." A common Moslem name that varies slightly throughout the world; Ayasha was one of the prophet Muhammad's favorite wives. See Ayasha. *Aesha, Aiesha, Aishah, Aisia, Asha, Ashia,*

Ayasha, Ayeisha, Ayesha, Aysha, Ieesha, Ieeshia, Iesha, Ieshia, Myeisha, Myesha, Myeshia, Myisha, Yiesha (Arabic, English)

AIYANA (eye-YAH-nah) Native American: "eternal bloom."

AKAKO (ah-kah-ko) Japanese: "red." This was once a magical name, red being considered a charm to cure diseases, particularly blood ailments. In one ancient Japanese tale, a powerful tree spirit was conquered because men attacking it painted their faces red, wore red shirts, and tied a red cord about the tree's trunk.

AKANKE (ah-kahn-KAY) Yoruba, Nigeria: "to know her is to pet her."

AKELA (ah-KAY-lah) Hawaiian form of Adelle, "noble."

AKI Japanese: "born in autumn."

AKILAH (AH-kee-lah) Arabic: "intelligent" or "logical."

AKINA (ah-kee-nah, or Anglicized, ah-KEE-nah) Japanese: "intensely bright spring flower" or "bright leaves."

ALAKE (ah-lah-KAY) Yoruba, Nigeria: "one to be petted if she survives." Often bestowed on an unhealthy child.

ALALA (ah-LAL-ah) Greek: "Mars' sister" or "war goddess."

Name for a girl born under Aries or Scorpio, the signs ruled by the fiery planet Mars.

ALAMEA (ah-luh-MAY-uh) Hawaiian: "ripe" or "precious."

ALAMEDA (ah-la-MAY-dah, or Anglicized, al-ah-MEE-dah) Native American: "cottonwood grove"; or Spanish: "promenade."

ALANA (ah-LAH-nuh) Hawaiian: "an offering" or "light and buoyant."

ALANI (ah-LAH-nee) Hawaiian: "orange" or "orange tree." Refers in particular to the Oahu tree, with its oblong fragrant leaves, which are used for scenting cloth. Also a boys' name.

ALAQUA (ah-LAH-quah) Native American: "sweet gum tree."

> **"A good name keeps its lustre in the dark."**
>
> —OLD ENGLISH PROVERB

ALAUDA (ah-LAW-dah) Gaelic: "lark."

ALAULA (ah-lau-OO-lah) Hawaiian: "light of early dawn" or "sunset glow." Like most Hawaiian names, this one may be given to a child of either gender.

ALBERTA Old English: "noble and brilliant." A feminine form of Albert. *Albertina, Albertine, Alli, Allie, Berta, Berti, Bertie, Berty, Elberta, Elbertina, Elbertine, Elbi, Elbie, Elby* (English); *Alba, Berta* (Czech); *Albertina* (German, Italian); *Alverta* (Greek); *Albertine* (Latvian); *Albertyna, Alka, Berta* (Polish); *Berta, Bertunga* (Spanish)

ALBINA (al-BEE-nah) Latin *albinus:* "blond" or "white." Used today in many countries, including Italy, Russia, and Portugal, as well as the United States. *Alba, Albinia, Alvina, Alvinia* (English); *Alva, Bela, Bina* (Czech); *Alwine* (German); *Ala, Albinka* (Polish); *Alvina* (Russian)

ALEEZA Hebrew: "joy" or "joyful." *Aliza, Alizah, Alitza, Alitzah, Leeza* (English, Hebrew)

ALEKA (ah-LAY-kah) Modern Greek form of Alexandra, "helper and defender of mankind."

ALENA (ah-LAY-nah) Modern Russian form of Helen, "light" or "torch."

ALETA (ah-LAY-tah) Contemporary Spanish name meaning "little winged one." Derived from Latin. *Alida* (English)

ALETEA (ah-leh-TAY-uh) Modern Spanish name meaning "the truth."

ALEXANDRA Greek: "helper and defender of mankind." Once used primarily in Russia, now popular worldwide. *Alex, Alexa, Alexine, Alexis, Alli, Lexi, Lexie, Lexine, Lexy, Sanda, Sandi, Sandie, Sandra, Sandy, Saundra, Sondra, Zandra* (English); *Alekko, Aleksi, Aleksey, Sander* (Bulgarian); *Ales, Leska, Lexa* (Czech); *Alexandrie, Alexandrina, Alexandrine, Alexine, Alexius, Sandra, Sandrine* (French); *Alexis, Alexius* (German); *Aleka, Alexiou, Ritsa* (Greek); *Alexa, Elek, Eli, Lekszi* (Hungarian); *Alessandra, Alessia* (Italian); *Ala, Aleska, Alka, Ola, Olesia* (Polish); *Aleks, Aleksasha, Aleksey, Alesha, Alya, Lelya, Lesya, Oleska, Olesya, Sasa, Sasha, Shura, Shurka* (Russian); *Kina* (Scottish); *Alajandra, Alastrina, Alastriona, Alejandra, Alejandrina, Aleka, Alessanda, Alessandra, Alessandrina, Alessia, Alexa, Alexanderia, Alexandrina, Alexandrita, Alexena, Alexia, Alexina, Alexis, Ali, Alista, Alla, Alli, Anda, Drina, Elena, Lesy, Lexi, Sanda, Sandi, Sandra, Sandrina, Sasha, Sondra, Xandra, Zandra, Zondra* (Spanish)

ALEXIS Popular form of Alexandra in the United States and Germany. See Alexandra.

ALGOMA (ahl-GO-mah) Native American: "valley of flowers."

ALHENA (ahl-HEE-nuh) Arabic: "a ring." This name refers to a third-magnitude star in Pollux, part of the constellation of Gemini, the twins.

ALI Modern American form of Alice or Alison.

ALICE Greek *aletbia:* "truthful." *Aleta, Aletha, Ali, Alicea, Alicia, Alis, Alisa, Alisha, Alissa, Alithia, Allie, Ally, Allyce, Allys, Alyce, Alycia, Elisha, Ellie, Elsa, Elsie, Ilisha* (English); *Alisa* (Bulgarian); *Alica* (Czech); *Alix* (French); *Adelicia, Alexia, Alexie, Elise, Elschen, Else, Ilse* (German); *Alike, Aliz, Alizka, Lici* (Greek);

Alika (Hawaiian); *Alisz, Aliz, Alizka, Lici* (Hungarian); *Ailis* (Irish); *Alise* (Latvian); *Ala, Alisia* (Polish); *Elica, Eliza* (Romanian); *Alisa, Alya* (Russian); *Elza* (Slavic); *Alicia, Elsa, Licha* (Spanish); *Alicia, Elsa* (Swedish); *Alisi* (Tongan)

ALICIA Modern American form of Alice, also popular in Italy, Mexico, Spain, and Sweden. For other forms, see Alice. *Aleesha, Alisha, Alysha* (English)

ALIDA (ah-LEE-dah) Latin: "small, winged one"; or Spanish: "noble." *Aleda, Aleta, Alita, Dela, Elida, Elita, Leda, Leeta, Lela, Lita, Oleda, Oleta* (English); *Alette* (French); *Aletta* (Italian);

> **"***Must a name mean something?***"**
> *Alice asked doubtfully.*
>
> ———
>
> **"***Of course it must,***"**
> *Humpty Dumpty said. . . .*
> **"***My name means the shape I am . . .*
> *With a name like yours, you*
> *might be any shape,*
> *almost.***"**
>
> —LEWIS CARROLL, *ALICE IN WONDERLAND*

Adelina, Adelita, Aleta, Aletta,
Alidia, Alidita (Spanish)

ALIKE (ah-LEE-keh) Ibo,
Nigeria: from the longer name
Alikecopeleabola, "girl who
drives out beautiful women."
Bestowed because the child is
lovely. *Aleeka, Alika* (English)

ALILE (ah-LEE-leh) African:
"she weeps." Given by the Yao-
speaking people of Malawi to a
child born into unfortunate circumstances. *Aleela, Alila* (English)

ALIMA (ah-LEE-muh) Arabic:
"skilled in music and dancing."
Another meaning is "sea maiden,"
making this an appropriate name
for a girl born under one of the
water signs of Cancer, Scorpio, or
Pisces.

ALINA (ah-LEEN-ah) Slavic:
"bright" or "beautiful;" Celtic:
"fair"; or Old German: "little and
noble." Popular in Poland and
Russia. *Aleen, Aleena, Aleene,*
Alena, Alene (English); *Aline,*
Alya, Lina (Russian)

ALISA (ah-LEE-sah, or Anglicized, ah-LISS-ah) Modern Israeli
name meaning "a joy." See also
Aleeza. *Alissa, Alyssa* (English,
Israeli)

ALITA (ah-LEE-tah) A Spanish
form of Adelle, "noble."

ALKA (AHL-kah) Polish form of
Alexandra.

Important to Know...

✴ ✴ ✴

Does higher educa-
tion influence baby
names? Maybe.

In one such provoca-
tive *American Journal of
Sociology* study, the top
ten baby names that tend
to correspond most with
a mother's college educa-
tion were Emily (no. 1),
followed by Allison, Lau-
ren, Megan, Catherine,
Elizabeth, Sarah, Laura,
Erin, and Rachel. More
than 1.5% of college grad-
uates and postgraduates
called their daughters
Allison—a name almost
never chosen by women
who have dropped out of
high school.

ALKAS (AHL-kas) Native
American: "she is afraid."

ALLEEN (ah-LEEN) Dutch
name meaning "alone."

ALISON, ALLISON Irish
Gaelic: "small and truthful."

Currently one of the most popular names in this country among mothers with a college education. (See box, page 56). *Ali, Alie, Alli, Allie, Alyson, Lissi, Lissy* (English); *Allsun* (Irish)

ALMA (AHL-mah) Spanish and Italian name that literally means "soul" or "spirit," with a connotation of nourishment. In other words, the child feeds one's soul or lifts the spirit.

ALMIRA (ahl-MEE-ruh) Hindi: "clothes basket." The Hindus believe that God is manisfested in everything, and thus children in India were once often named after common household objects. Each time the name was pronounced, God's name was spoken, an act considered a step toward salvation. In Arabic this name means "fulfillment of the Word" or "truth without question."

ALNABA (ahl-NAH-bah) Navaho: "wars passed each other." In the Navaho tradition of naming girls after events of war, this name indicates two battles raged in opposite directions.

ALOHA (ah-LO-hah) This familiar Hawaiian name has connotations of love, affection, mercy, kindness, charity, greetings, and farewell.

ALOHI (ah-LO-hee) Hawaiian: "shining" or "brilliant." Also a boys' name.

ALONA (ah-LO-nah) Hebrew: "oak tree." The feminine form of Alon.

ALTSOBA (alt-SO-bah) Navaho: "all are at war."

ALUDRA (uh-LOO-druh) Greek and Arabic: "virgin." Name for a girl born under Virgo, the virgin.

ALUMIT (ah-loo-MEET) Hebrew: "girl" or "secret." Modern Israeli name. *Alma, Aluma, Alumice* (Hebrew, English)

ALVERTA Modern Greek form of Alberta, "noble and brilliant."

ALZUBRA (ahl-ZOO-bruh) Arabic: Refers to a tiny star of the fifth magnitude in the constellation Leo, the lion. Hence, a name for a child born under that sign.

AM (uhm) Vietnamese: "lunar" or "female principle." The latter refers to the Asian concept of the universe, which states that in the beginning two sources of energy existed—male and female—and from these the world was born.

AMA (AH-mah) Akan, south Ghana: "born on Saturday," from the word Memenda ("Saturday").

AMADIKA (ah-mah-DEE-kah) southern Rhodesia: "to be beloved." Popular among the Wataware people, this is a name a mother gives to herself if her life has been filled with problems;

the connotation is "once my husband loved me, but he doesn't anymore."

AMALIA (ah-mah-lee-ah, with the stress falling on one of the first three syllables, depending on the language) Currently used in Germany, Holland, Hungary, Poland, Romania, Spain, and the United States, this international name is a form of Amelia, "industrious" or "flatterer." See Amelia and Emily.

AMALIYA (ah-mah-LEE-yah) A Russian form of Amy, "beloved."

AMANDA Latin: "lovable" or "worthy of love." *Manda, Mandaline, Mandi, Mandie, Mandy* (English); *Amandine* (French); *Amata* (Spanish)

AMARA (ah-MAH-rah) Esperanto form of Mary, "bitter." Esperanto is an artificial international language devised by Polish oculist and philologist Ludwig Zamenhof (1859–1917). Esperanto, which is fairly easy for people who speak many different European languages to master and read, means literally, "one who is hoping." Zamenhof's hope was that the entire world would one day be united by a common language.

AMARIS "child of the moon"; or Hebrew: "God has promised." In astrology the moon is the ruler of the sign Cancer, the crab. Early

astrologers believed Cancer was the constellation through which souls passed from heaven into human bodies.

AMATA (ah-MAH-tah) Spanish form of Amy, "beloved."

AMAUI (ah-MOW-ee) Hawaiian: "thrush," referring to a gentle Hawaiian thrush which is a dusky olive-brown color.

AMAYA (ah-MAH-yah) Japanese: "night rain."

AMAYETA (ah-mah-YEH-tah) Miwok: "big manzanita berries."

AMBER Arabic: "jewel"; or Old French: "fierce one." Amber, a semiprecious jewel made of fossil resin and containing bits of plants, insects, and feathers, was used in ancient magical healing rites. Many people picture a girl named Amber to be warm, friendly, and confidently assertive. *Amberlea, Amberlee, Amberly, Ambur* (English)

AMBIKA (ahm-BEE-kah) Hindi: "the mother." One of the more than one thousand Hindu names for Shakti, the great Goddess Mother of the universe, goddess of power and destruction.

AMELIA Gothic *amala:* "industrious"; or Latin: "flatterer." *Amali, Amalia, Amalie, Amelina, Amelita, Ami, Amie, Amilia,*

Emelie, Emelina, Emeline,
Emelita, Emilia, Emilie, Emily,
Melia (English); *Amalia* (Czech);
Amalie, Emilie (French); *Amalia,*
Emilia, Ilma, Malcsi, Mali, Malika
(Hungarian); *Ama, Amelcia,*
Melcia (Polish); *Milica* (Slavic)

AMI Modern American spelling
of Amy, "beloved."

AMINA (ah-MEE-nah) Arabic:
"peace" or "security." The name of
the prophet Muhammad's
mother.

AMINEH (ah-MEE-ne) Arabic:
"faithful."

AMIRA (ah-MEE-ruh) Hebrew:
"speech" or "utterance."

AMISSA (ah-MEE-suh) Hebrew:
"friend" or "truth." *Amisa*

AMITA (ah-MEE-tuh) Hebrew:
"truth."

AMMA (ah-mah) Hindi: "mother
goddess."

AMOKE (ah-mo-KEH) Yoruba,
Nigeria: "to know her is to pet
her." Popular nickname in Nigeria.

AMY Latin: "beloved." Also a
short form of Amelia. *Aimy, Ame,*
Ami, Amie (English); *Aimeé,*
Amelie (French); *Amalia,*
Amadea (Italian); *Ema* (Roma-
nian); *Amaliya* (Russian); *Amada,*
Amata (Spanish); *Amata*
(Swedish)

AN (ahn) Vietnamese: "peace,"
"safety," or "security."

ANABA (ah-NAH-bah) Navaho:
"she returns from war." See Alnaba.

ANABELA (ah-nuh-BEL-ah)
Hawaiian form of Annabelle,
"graceful" or "beautiful."

ANAIS (ah-nah-EES) A pro-
vincial French form of Anne
("graceful") gaining use in the
United States. Made well-known
by writer Anaïs Nin. Also
associated in many people's
minds with Anaïs Anaïs perfume.

ANALA (ah-NAH-luh) Hindi:
"fire." Another name for the
Hindu god Agni, god of fire. Also
a boys' name.

ANANDA (ah-nahn-dah) Hindi:
"bliss." Often used in India as a
name component to create new
names.

ANASTASIA Greek: "of the
Resurrection." Very popular in
Russia (where it's pronounced
ah-nah-STAH-see-ah), this name
was introduced into Russia
through the Greek Orthodox
Church. Made famous by the
Grand Duchess Anastasia, a
daughter of Czar Nicholas who,
some say, escaped death when
the family was assassinated
during the Russian Revolution of
1918. *Anastace, Anastice,*
Anastyce, Anstice, Stacey, Staci,
Stacia, Stacie, Stacy (English);

Anastazia, Stasa, Staska
(Czech); *Anastasie* (French,
German); *Anya, Asya, Nastacia,
Nastasha, Nastashia, Nastasia,
Nastasya, Nastka, Nastusya,
Nessa, Stasya, Tasenka, Taska,
Tasya* (Latvian, Lithuanian,
Russian); *Tasia* (Spanish)

ANDA (AHN-dah) Spanish:
"going." A pretty name from
Mexico and Spain. The longer
variation Andeana means "a
walker" or "a goer."

ANDEE Short form of Andrea,
now popular as a given name.
Ande, Andi, Andie, Andy
(English)

ANDREA Latin: "womanly"; or
Greek: "a man's woman."
Feminine form of Andrew or
Andreas; still one of the more
popular girls' names in the United
States. *Andee, Andera, Andie,
Andra, Andrean, Andreana,
Andree, Andreea, Andreena,
Andri, Andria, Andriana,
Andrienne, Andrietta, Andrina,
Andrine, Andy, Dreena, Drena,
Drina, Rena, Rina* (English);
Andreé (French); *Aindrea* (Irish)

ANDULKA (AHN-dool-kah)
Czech and Slovak form of Ann,
"graceful." See Ann.

ANE (AH-neh) Hawaiian form
of Ann.

ANEKO (ah-NAY-koh) Japanese:
"older sister."

ANELA (ah-NEL-ah) Hawaiian:
"angel." Used by early Hawaiian
Christians to designate the few
pagan gods they still believed in.

ANEVAY (ah-neh-VAY) Native
American: "superior."

ANEZKA (ah-nehzh-kah) A
very popular form of Ann in
Czech-speaking countries. See
Ann.

ANGELA Greek: "angel" or "one
who brings good news." Nearly
every culture in the world has a
name that means "angel." See, for
example, the Cambodian name
Tevy and the Arabic Malak. *Angel,
Angele, Angelina, Angelle, Angi,
Angie, Angy, Anjele, Anjelina,
Anji, Anjie, Anjy* (English); *Andela*
(Czech); *Angele* (French);
Anakela (Hawaiian); *Erela*
(Hebrew); *Angyal, Angyalka*
(Hungarian); *Aingeal* (Irish);
Angelina, Anhelina, Gelya, Lina
(Russian); *Ange, Angele, Angeles,
Angelfina, Angelina, Angelines,
Angelita* (Spanish)

ANGELICA (an-JEL-ih-kuh)
Greek: "angelic." This pretty name
is popular in many countries,
including the United States and
Scotland. Made well known by
American actress Anjelica
Huston. For many more forms,
see Angela. *Anjelica* (English);
Angelique (French); *Angelika*
(German, Lithuanian); *Angelica,
Angeliki* (Greek); *Angelica*
(Spanish)

Did You Know . . .

✦ ✦ ✦

After Ronald Reagan was elected president, many little girls were named Reagan. Similarly, singer LaToya Jackson inspired a spate of little LaToyas. Yet despite such trends, only 10% of parents actually name their babies after the rich and famous.

ANGELIQUE (ahn-zheh-LEEK) A stylish French form of Angelica that has an exotic ring. See Angelica, above.

ANGENI (ahn-jeh-NEE) Native American: "spirit angel."

ANGIE Popular American form of Angela, often used as an independent name.

ANI Hawaiian: "beautiful."

ANICE (ah-NEES) A contemporary American form of Agnes. *Anis, Anisa, Anisha, Anissa, Annis, Annissa* (English)

ANIKA (ah-NEE-kah) Hausa, Africa: "sweetness of face." Also a Czech form of Ann.

ANILA (uh-nee-lah) Hindi: "the wind god," referring to the Hindu god with whom the forty-nine godlings of the wind are associated. The feminine form of Anil.

ANISHA (ah-NISH-uh) Sanskirt: "lord."

ANITA Spanish form of Ann, "graceful."

ANIWETA (ah-nee-WAY-tah) Ibo, Nigeria: "Ani (a spirit) brought it." This is typical of many Ibo short-sentence names, which often refer to the child's birth, future, or a hope of the parents. Also a boys' name.

ANJU (AHN-joo) Hindi: "an honor" or "shining."

ANN, ANNA, ANNE Hebrew: "graceful." A truly international name, used in Bulgaria, France, Germany, Italy, Mexico, Poland, Russia, Spain and most countries in Central and South America, as well as in the United States. *Ana, Anette, Anita, Anni, Annie, Anny, Hanna, Hannah, Nan, Nana, Nanci, Nancy, Nanna, Nina* (English); *Andula, Andulka, Anicka, Anuska* (Czech); *Annikki* (Finnish); *Annette* (French); *Anitte, Annchen, Anneli, Anni, Hanne, Nettchen* (German); *Nani, Noula* (Greek); *Ana, Ane* (Hawaiian);

Anci, Aniko, Annus, Annuska, Nina, Nusi (Hungarian); *Annetta, Annina* (Italian); *Anya, Anyuta, Asenka, Aska, Asya, Hanna* (Latvian); *Anikke, Annze, Ona, Onele* (Lithuanian); *Ania, Anka, Hania, Hanka* (Polish); *Anicuta* (Romanian); *Anninka, Annuska, Anya, Asenka, Asya, Nyura* (Russian); *Anica, Anita, Nana, Nita* (Spanish); *Ane* (Tongan); *Chana, Channa, Hana, Hannah* (Yiddish)

ANNABELLE Hebrew and Latin: "graceful and beautiful." *Anabel, Anabela, Anabella, Anabelle, Ani, Annabella, Anna-Belle, AnnaBelle, Anni, Bella, Belle* (English); *Annabla* (Irish); *Anbel, Anibal* (Spanish)

ANNA MARIA Hebrew: "graceful and bitter." *AnnaMarie, AnnMaria, Annmarie* (English)

ANONA (ah-NO-nah) Latin: "yearly crops." Name for a girl born under one of the earth signs of Capricorn, Taurus, or Virgo.

ANTHEA (ahn-THAY-ah) Greek: "lady of flowers."

ANTONETTA (ahn-to-NET-tah) Slavic and Swedish form of Antonia.

ANTONIA Latin: "inestimable" or "priceless." *Netta, Netti, Nettie, Nety, Toinetta, Toinette, Toni, Tonia, Toney, Tony* (English);

Antoinette, Antonie, Toinette, Toinon (French); *Tosia* (Polish); *Antonina, Tonya, Tosky, Tosya* (Russian); *Antonieta, Antonina, Antuca, Tona* (Spanish); *Antonetta* (Swedish)

ANYA Popular in Estonia, Latvia, Russia, and the Ukraine. See Ann.

ANZU (AHN-zoo) Japanese: "apricot," the emblem of women. In Western lore the apricot symbolizes timid love.

AOLANI (ow-LAH-nee) Hawaiian: "heavenly cloud."

APONI (ah-PO-nee) Native American: "butterfly." The Pima Indians believed that the Creator took the form of a butterfly and fluttered all over the world until he found the best place for man.

APRIL Latin: "open" or "born in April." Name for a girl born under the signs of Aries or Taurus. *Aprilette, Aprille, Averil, Averill, Averille, Averyl, Avril* (English); *Aprili* (Spanish)

AQUENE (ah-KAY-neh) Native American: "peace."

ARABELA Latin: "beautiful altar." Spanish form of Arabella.

ARELLA (ah-RAY-luh) Hebrew: "angel" or "messenger." *Arela* (English, Hebrew)

ARETE (ah-RAY-teh) Modern Greek form of Grace, "graceful" or "lovely."

ARETHA Greek: "best." *Areta, Aretta* (English); *Arette* (French); *Arethi* (Greek)

ARIANA (ahr-ee-AHN-ah) Welsh: "like silver." A melodic name from Wales that's sure to gain wider use in this country. *Ari, Ariane, Ariann, Arianne* (English)

ARIANNE (ar-ee-AHN) Greek: "the very holy" or "pleasing one." A French form of Ariadne gaining popularity in the United States. In Greek mythology, Ariadne—the daughter of King Minos—gave the hero Theseus a ball of string, which guided him out of the labyrinth after he'd slain the Minotaur. Hence, "Ariadne's thread" has come to mean "a reliable pathway out of a difficult situation." *Ariana* (English); *Ariane* (French)

ARIEL Hebrew: "lioness of God." *Ariela, Ariella* (English, Hebrew)

ARISTA (ah-REE-stuh) Latin: "harvest." Name for a girl born under the sign of Virgo, the virgin, maiden of the harvest.

ARIZA (ah-REE-zuh) Hebrew: "cedar panels." Refers to the beautiful, prized wood that lined the walls of King Solomon's

temple. A traditional Jewish name used in Israel as well as the United States. *Arza, Arzice, Arzit* (Hebrew)

ARNA (AHR-nah) Hebrew: "cedar tree." *Arnice, Arnit* (Hebrew)

ARNINA (ahr-NEE-nuh) Many meanings have been given for this traditional Hebrew name: "mountain," "singer," "to shine," and "messenger." *Arni, Arnice, Arnit* (Hebrew)

ARTHA (AHR-tah) Hindi: "wealth" or "worldly prosperity," a goal which practical as well as spiritual Hindus regard as one of the four ends of man.

ARUSHA (ahr-OO-shah) Sanskrit: "red." In Hindu mythology, this name refers to the reddish-brown horses of the "sun of fire," or the rising sun. *Arushi* (Hindi)

ASA (AH-sah) Japanese: "born in the morning."

ASABI (ah-sah-BEE) Yoruba, Nigeria: "one of select birth."

ASELA (ah-SEH-lah) Spanish: "the slim ash tree."

ASHA (AH-shah) Arabic: "woman"; or Swahili: "life." See Aisha.

ASHLEY Old English: "One from the ash-tree meadow." Popular in Britain and Australia as well as America. *Ashlee, Ashleigh, Ashlie* (English)

ASHLING Irish: "dream" or "vision." Popular in Ireland, where it's spelled *Aisling. Ash, Ashlin, Ashly* (English); *Aislinn* (Irish)

ASISA (ah-SEE-sah) Hebrew: "juicy" or "ripe." A spiritual name implying that the child is the fruit of God.

ASIZA (ah-SEE-zah) African: "forest spirit." The Dahomey believe the asiza are spirits who dwell in the forests and grant magical powers to men.

ASOKA (ah-sho-kah) Hindi: "non-sorrow flower." The non-sorrow flower allegedly blooms orange or scarlet when touched by the foot of a gentle maiden.

ASTA Old Norse: "divine strength"; or Greek *aster:* "like a star," referring to the aster flower. Very popular today in Norway. See Astrid.

ASTERA (as-TAIR-ah) Hebrew: "the aster flower." Popular Israeli flower name from the aster, which because of its star-shaped leaves has been called the star-flower. *Asta, Asteria, Asteriya* (Hebrew)

ASTRID Old Norse: "divine strength." One of the most popular names in Denmark. *Asta, Astrud, Astyr* (English)

ATARA (ah-TAH-ruh) Hebrew: "a crown." *Ataret* (Hebrew)

ATIDA (ah-TEE-duh) Hebrew: "the future." A traditional Jewish name used in Israel.

ATIRA (ah-TEE-rah) Hebrew: "a prayer."

LEGENDS & LORE

Throughout history in many cultures, a child's name has been thought to reflect his or her deepest or truest self and is, therefore, inseparably bound up with the soul. In the Upanishad, one of India's ancient books of wisdom, we are told, "The name is endless, and by it one gains the endless world."

AUD (owd) Norwegian: "deserted" or "empty." Because of a Norwegian preference for names with a distinctly Scandinavian sound, this was once one of the most popular names in Norway.

AUDEY Modern American form of Audrey.

AUDREY Old English: "noble strength." *Audey, Audi, Audie, Audree, Audri, Audrie, Audry* (English)

AULII (OW-lee) Hawaiian: "dainty."

AURIEL Latin: "golden one." *Oralia, Orelia, Oriel, Orielle* (English); *Aurelie* (French)

AUSTIN A form of Augustine ("belonging to Augustus") originally used for boys but now also used for girls.

AVANI (ah-VAHN-ee) Sanskrit: "the good earth." A popular Hindu name for girls.

AVERILL Old English: "born in April." Name for a girl born under the signs of Aries or Taurus. *Avril, Avrill, Averyl* (English)

AVI (AH-vee) Hebrew: "my Father" or "my God." A contemporary Jewish name from Israel. Also a boys' name.

AVIVA (ah-VEE-vah) Hebrew: "springtime," with the conno-

tation of youthfulness and freshness. *Avivah, Avivice, Avrit* (Hebrew)

AWANATA (ah-wah-NAH-tah) Miwok: "turtle." The turtle is prominent in some Indian myths. The Korusa, for example, believed that in the beginning there was only the Old Turtle swimming in a limitless ocean. He dove down, brought up a mouthful of dirt, and created the world.

AWENDELA (ah-wayn-DAY-lah) Native American: "early day." Name for a child born just before dawn.

AWENITA (ah-way-NEE-tah) Native American: "a fawn."

AYAKO (ah-yah-koh) Japanese: "colorful, ornamental fabric," referring specifically to damask.

AYAME (ah-yah-meh) Japanese: "iris." The iris is the Eastern emblem of the warrior and the Japanese flower of May. In astrology the iris is the "herb" of the moon, which governs the sign Cancer.

AYASHA (EYE-ish-ah or, Anglicized, ah-YAHSH-ah) Arabic: "life." One of the prophet Mohammad's favorite wives. See Aisha.

AYELET (ah-yeh-LAYT) Hebrew: "deer" or "gazelle."

AYITA (ah-YEE-tah) Native American: "the worker."

AYOKA (ah-YO-kah) Yoruba, Nigeria: "one who causes joy all round." Usually bestowed as a nickname.

AYONDELA (ah-yohn-DAY-lah) Umbundu, Africa: Proverb name meaning "a little tree bends and bends, as we all bend toward death." Many African names derive from proverbs that reveal some philosophy of life.

AZAMI (ah-zah-mee) Japanese: "thistle flower." In Eastern mythology, the thistle symbolizes defiance and surliness.

AZIZA (ah-ZEE-zah) Swahili: "precious."

AZIZE (uh-ZEEZ) Turkish: "dear," "precious," or "rare."

B

BABARA (BAH-buh-ruh) Hawaiian form of Barbara: "stranger."

BADRIA (bah-DREE-ah) Dari: "moonlike." Originally from Afghanistan.

BAILEY (BAY-lee) Old French: "public administrator" or "an office of justice," referring to a bailiff; or Old English: "from the berry meadow or forest." Orig-

inally a boys' name now used almost exclusively for girls. *Bailee, Bailie, Baily, Baylee, Bayley* (English)

BAKA (bah-kah) Hindi: "crane." The crane is a symbol of longevity.

BAKULA (bah-koo-lah) Hindi: "the bakula flower." According to Hindu myth, the bakula bursts into bloom when sprinkled with wine from the mouth of a beautiful girl.

BALALA (BAH-lah-lah) Mashona, southern Rhodesia: "You must eat much to grow." Often bestowed in Africa on an especially small baby.

BALANIKI (bah-lah-NEE-kee) Hawaiian form of Blanche, "white, fair-skinned one."

BARBARA Latin: "a stranger" or "foreigner." When the barbarians attacked Rome, Romans thought the barbarians' speech sounded like "barbarbarbarbar." Thus, Barbara came to be the name for anyone not like the Romans. (For the legend of St. Barbara, see box, page 67.) *Bab, Babb, Babette, Babica, Babita, Babs, Barba, Barbette, Barbi, Barbie, Barbra, Barby* (English); *Bara, Barbora, Barborka, Baruska* (Czech); *Barbe* (French); *Babette* (German); Voska (Greek); *Babara* (Hawaiian); *Bairbre* (Irish); *Varenka, Varka, Varvara, Varya,*

The Legend of St. Barbara

✷ ✷ ✷

Parents who choose the name Barbara for their baby are often unaware that this name is connected with a fabulous legend. Although no one knows exactly when St. Barbara was born, she was already being adored as a saint in the seventh century. The daughter of a wealthy, mean-tempered atheist, Barbara was shut up in a tower from a young age so she'd be "protected" from the world. Legends of her beauty spread, however, and through her father she received an offer of marriage. It was refused.

One day Barbara's father decided to go away on a long journey. But before he left, he had a bathhouse erected near his daughter's tower for her to use while he was gone. He specifically told the builders of the bathhouse to install two windows. But, unbeknownst to her father, Barbara had secretly become a Christian. And once he left on his journey, she had *three* windows installed to symbolize the Holy Trinity. When her father returned, he flew into a rage over this "betrayal" of his beliefs: How *dare* she become a Christian! He dragged her before the governor of the area, who had her brutally tortured. When she refused to give up her faith, she was beheaded. Barbara's father himself carried out the death sentence. But his wickedness did not go unpunished: on his way home, he was struck by lightning and burned to a cinder.

To this day, it is said that if people call on St. Barbara, they will be protected in thunderstorms and able to escape burning buildings unharmed. Barbara is also the patron saint of miners and artillerymen. In classical paintings, she's often depicted in a three-windowed tower, sometimes with cannons nearby.

Vava, Vavka (Russian); *Varina* (Slavic); *Barbo* (Swedish)

BARIKA (ba-REE-ka) Arabic: "to bloom" or "be successful."

BATINI (bah-TEE-nee) Swahili: "innermost thoughts."

BATYA (bah-TEE-uh) Hebrew: "daughter of God." A modern Jewish name originally from Israel. *Basia, Basya, Batia* (Hebrew)

BEATRICE Latin: "she makes others happy." *Bea, Bee, Trixi, Trixie, Trixy* (English); *Blaza, Blazena* (Czech); *Beatrix* (French, German, Italian); *Beatrise* (Latvian); *Beatriz* (Portuguese); *Beatriks, Beatrisa* (Russian); *Bea, Beata, Beate, Beatisa, Beatrisa, Beatriz, Bebe, Beitris, Ticha, Trisa* (Spanish)

BECCA (BEK-ah) Bobangi, Africa: "to forecast or predict"; or Ngombe, Africa: "borrow." A common name in Africa with a variety of meanings. Also a short form of Rebecca ("bound") gaining popularity as an independent name. See Rebecca.

BEHIRA (beh-HEE-rah) Hebrew: "light," "clear," or "brilliant."

BEL Hindi: "the sacred wood apple tree." It is said the branches of the sacred wood apple cannot be broken or used for firewood except by Brahmins.

BELA (BYEL-ah) Old French: "white, fair-skinned one." Widely used in Czech-speaking countries. *Blanche* (English)

BELICIA (bel-EE-see-ah, or Anglicized, beh-LISH-ah) Spanish form of Isabel, "dedicated to God." See Isabel.

BELINDA Old Spanish *bella linda*: "pretty." *Bel, Bella, Belle, Bellinda, Linda, Lindy* (English, Spanish)

BELISA (be-LEE-sah) Latin: "slender one." Popular Spanish name from a character in Lope de Vega's sixteenth-century comedy *The Sword of Madrid*.

BELLA Old English: "nobly bright" or "beautiful." A Hungarian form of Alberta. Also a short form of Belinda. *Bela, Belle*

BELLOMA Latin: "warlike" or "war goddess." Name for a girl born under the signs of Aries or Scorpio, which are ruled by the war planet Mars.

BENA (BAY-nah) Native American: "pheasant."

BENITA (beh-NEE-tah) Latin: "blessed." Spanish form of Benedicta, which is in turn a feminine form of Benedict. *Bena, Bennedett, Bennedette, Benni, Bennie, Binnie, Dixie* (English); *Benoite* (French); *Benicia* (Spanish)

BERNADETTE French: "as brave as a bear." A female form of Bernard, originally from France but now equally popular in the United States. St. Bernadette was a nineteenth-century saint who had many visions of the Virgin Mary near Lourdes in France. *Berna, Bernadine, Berneta, Bernetta, Bernette, Berni, Bernie, Bernita, Berny* (English); *Bernette, Nadette* (French); *Bernardina* (Italian, Portuguese, Spanish); *Bena, Bernarda, Dina, Ina* (Polish)

BETA Czech and Slovak form of Elizabeth, "dedicated to God."

BETH Once a nickname for Elizabeth ("dedicated to God"), but now used independently. See Elizabeth.

BETHANY Aramaic: "house of poverty." This popular modern American name actually comes from the name of a village near Jerusalem, where Jesus often visited Martha, Mary, and Lazarus.

BETI (BAY-tee) English Gypsy: "little" or "small."

BETULA (beh-TOO-luh) Hebrew: "girl" or "maiden."

BIAN (BEE-uhn) Vietnamese: "to be hidden" or "secretive."

BIANCA Popular Hungarian, Italian, and Spanish form of Blanche, "white, fair-skinned one."

LEGENDS & LORE

According to old Pennsylvania Dutch lore, an unbaptized baby who cries is crying for a name.

Made a familiar name in this country by socialite and former wife of Mick Jagger, Bianca Jagger. See Blanche.

BIBI (bee-bee) Arabic: "lady." A Swahili term of politeness.

BINA (BEE-nuh) Hebrew: "understanding" or "intelligence"; Bobangi, Lolo, and Ngala, Africa: "dance"; or Arapaho: "fruits." An international name that has developed independently in many widely different cultures. *Binah* (African); *Buna* (Israeli)

BINTI (BEEN-tee) Swahili: "daughter."

BIRGIT (beer-GEET) A popular Norwegian form of Bridget. One variation, *Bergitte,* is one of the most popular names in Denmark, whereas the form *Birgitta* is favored in Sweden. See Bridget.

BITKI (BIT-kee) Turkish: "plant."

BLAINE Irish Gaelic: "one who serves St. Blaan," referring to a seventh-century saint. Originally a boys' name now also used for girls. *Blain, Blane, Blayne* (English)

BLAIR Scottish Gaelic: "from the flat or level place." Hence, the connotation "child of the fields." Originally a Scottish last name, now used for both girls and boys. *Blaire* (English)

BLANCHE Old French: "white, fair-skinned one." *Blanch, Blanshe* (English); *Bela, Blanka* (Czech); *Bianca* (Hungarian, Italian, Spanish); *Branca* (Portuguese); *Blanca, Blanchi, Blanquita* (Spanish); *Blanka, Blenda* (Swedish)

BLOM Afrikaans, South Africa: "flower."

BLUM (bloom) Yiddish: "flower." *Bluma* (Yiddish)

BLY Native American: "high"; or Afrikaans: "happy." Among some Native Americans, this name was bestowed in the hopes the child would grow tall. Also a boys' name.

BO Chinese: "precious"; or Old Norse: "householder." Made well known as a name for girls by American actress Bo Derek, who starred in the film *10*. Also a pet form of Bonita.

BOBINA (bo-BEE-nah) Czech form of Roberta, "brilliantly famous." *Berta, Roba* (Czech)

BOHDANA (bo-DAH-nah) Slovak: "Given by God." Popular in the Ukraine as the feminine form of Bohdan. Bohdan Chmelnyckyj was a famed seventeenth-century Cossack leader. *Danya* (English, Russian)

BONA Hebrew: "a builder."

BONITA Spanish: "pretty." *Bo, Boni, Bonie, Nita* (Spanish)

BONNIE Middle English: "good." *Bonni, Bonny, Bunni, Bunnie, Bunny* (English)

BRADY Old English: "from a broad island" or "broad eye." A boys' name now also used for girls. *Bradi, Bradie, Braedy, Braydee* (English)

BRANDY Old English: literally "to burn wine." A girls' name coined from the strong, sweet liqueur. *Brandee, Brandi, Brandie* (English)

BRENNA (BREN-ah) Celtic: "strong; forceful"; or Irish Gaelic: "a raven."

BRIANNA (bree-AHN-nah) Irish Gaelic: "strong one." A trendy feminine form of Brian. Also a variant of Abriana. *Breanna, Breanne, Briana, Brianne,*

LEGENDS & LORE

Plant a flower and name it. If the one for whom it is named loves you, the flower will flourish.

Brina, Bryana, Bryanna, Bryanne (English)

BRICE Celtic: "strong and brave." Originally a boys' name now also used for girls. *Bryce* (English)

BRIDGET Irish Gaelic: "strength" or "protecting." Originally from Ireland, now popular worldwide. *Berget, Bergit, Brid, Bride, Bridgid, Bridie, Brietta, Brighid, Brigid, Brigit, Brita, Brydie* (English/ Irish); *Bergette, Brigide, Brigitta, Brigitte* (French); *Brigette, Brigitta* (German); *Berek* (Greek); *Brigada, Brigida* (Italian); *Brigita* (Latvian); *Birget, Birgitta, Gitta* (Norwegian); *Bryga, Brygida, Brygitka* (Polish); *Bridita, Brigida, Brigidita, Gidita* (Spanish); *Brigitta, Biddy* (Swedish)

BRITA This form of Brittany is especially popular in Norway.

BRITTANY Latin: "from Britain." *Brett, Brit, Britany, Britt, Britta, Brittni* (English); *Brita* (Norwegian)

BRONA Greek *berenike:* "coming before victory." Modern Czech name. *Berenice* (English)

BRONTE (BRON-tay or BRON-tee) Greek: "thunder." A sophisticated literary name generally associated with the Brontë sisters—Charlotte, Emily, and Anne, all novelists. Charlotte Brontë wrote *Jane Eyre,* and Emily wrote *Wuthering Heights.*

BROOKE Old English: "dweller by the brook." A masculine nature name now used more often for girls. Brought into public aware-ness as a girls' name by model-turned-actress Brooke Shields. *Brook, Brooks* (English)

BRYN (brin) Welsh: "from the hills." A favorite for boys in Wales, but used in this country for both boys and girls. *Brin, Brinn, Bryne, Brynn, Brynne* (English)

BUA (BOO-uh) Vietnamese: "hammer," "written charm," or "amulet." In Vietnam, such metal names are often thought to bring luck or good health.

BUNA (BOO-nah) Mende, Africa: "the buna tree," referring to an African tree with edible, scarlet fruit; or Bobangi, Lolo,

Soko, Ngala, and Ngombe, Africa: "a fighter."

C

CAI (kay) Vietnamese: "female."

CAITLIN (KATE-lin or, in Ireland, kath-LEEN) This trendy contemporary American name is actually an Irish form of Katherine, "pure." See Katherine.

CALANDRA (kah-LAHN-drah) Greek: "a beauty" or "a lark." *Cal, Calla, Callie, Kalandra, Kolandra, Landra* (English); *Calandré* (French); *Calandria* (Spanish)

CALIDA (kah-LEE-dah) Spanish: "warm" or "loving."

CALLIE (KAL-ee) A pet form of Calandra, "a beauty" or "a lark." *Cali, Calie, Calley, Calli, Cally, Kali, Kalie, Kalley, Kalli, Kallie, Kally* (English)

CAM (kam) Vietnamese: "sweetness, like an orange."

CAMERON Scottish Gaelic: "one with a wry or crooked nose." Originally a boys' name now gaining popularity for girls. See also Kameron. *Cam, Camerron, Cammi, Cammie*

CAMILA Latin: "a young attendant at a ceremony," referring to the beautiful ceremonial girl who helped in ancient pagan rites. Especially well known in Spanish cultures around the world. *Cam, Cami, Cammi, Camilla, Cammie, Cammy, Milli, Millie, Milly* (English); *Camila* (Czech); *Camille* (French); *Kamila, Kamilla* (Hungarian, Latvian); *Camilla* (Italian); *Kamilka, Milla* (Polish); *Cama, Camala, Camile, Camilla* (Spanish)

CAMILLA Modern American name meaning "born free." Also an Italian and Spanish form of Camilla or Camile.

CAMPBELL Scottish Gaelic: "a crooked mouth." Originally a Scottish clan name used for boys, now occasionally bestowed on girls. *Bell, Cam, Campy* (English)

CANADA Iroquois: "where the heavens touch the earth." Name of the country recently coined as a girls' name.

CANDI A Spanish pet form of Candida or an American pet form of Candice ("brightly white").

CANDICE Greek: "glowing white"; or Latin: "brightly white." Made well known by actress Candice Bergen. *Candace, Candee, Candi, Candie, Candy, Kandee, Kandi, Kandice, Kandie, Kandy* (English)

Poetic Vietnamese Names

✹ ✹ ✹

Vietnamese names for girls are frequently just one or two syllables long and contain beautiful hidden meanings. Here's a sampling of some of these lovely, short Asian names: *Am* ("lunar principle" or, more loosely translated, "child of the moon"); *An* ("peaceful" or "secure"); *Cam* ("sweetness, like an orange"); *Chau* ("a pearl," connoting preciousness); *Hoa* ("peace" or "flower"); *Kieu* ("beautiful" or "graceful"); *Lien* ("lotus"); *Mai-Ly* ("the plum-tree blossom"); and *Tao* ("apple").

CANDRA (KAHN-drah) Hindi: "moon." Name for a girl born under the sign of Cancer, ruled by the moon. In the tarot deck, Pisces corresponds to the card of the moon.

CANNA (KAHN-nah) Mende, Africa: "clear"; Congo, Africa: "purposeful"; or Swahili: "deny." A name with a variety of meanings used in many parts of Africa.

CAPRICE Italian: "fanciful one."

CARA Hausa, Africa: "to increase or complain"; Irish Gaelic: "friend"; Italian: "beloved"; Vietnamese: "diamond" or "precious jewel." A lovely name used in many cultures. *Carina, Carine, Carra, Kara, Karina, Karine, Karra* (English)

CAREY (KAIR-ee) A contemporary short form of Caroline ("little womanly one") now used as an independent name. *Cari, Carri, Carrie, Cary, Karey, Kari, Karri, Karrie, Kary* (English)

CARI Turkish: "flowing like water." Also a recently developed variant spelling of Carrie, a pet form of Caroline, "little womanly one."

CARINA (kah-REEN-ah or kah-RIN-ah) A contemporary variation of Katherine or Karin, "pure." *Cariana, Carin, Carina, Carine, Carinn, Carinna* (English)

CARISSA Latin: "dear one." *Caressa, Cari, Carice, Carie, Carisa, Carrie, Karessa, Karisa, Karise, Karisha, Karyssa* (English)

How Soon Will Your Baby Know Her Name?

✶ ✶ ✶

When shown a picture of themselves and asked, "Who is that?," 50% of fifteen-month-old babies will respond by giving their own names. By 22 months of age, 67% of babies can do so. An infant's ability to recognize the sound of their own name, of course, begins even earlier. As young as 6 months, many babies will perk up and pay extra-special attention when they hear their names spoken.

CARITA Latin *caritas:* "charity." Especially popular in Italy.

CARLA A favorite English and Hispanic form of Caroline, "little womanly one." See Caroline.

CARLOTA Spanish and Portuguese form of Charlotte. One of the most popular names in Portugal. *Carlotta*

CARLY A contemporary pet form of Caroline, "little womanly one." Made well known by singer Carly Simon. *Carli, Carlie, Karli, Karlie, Karly* (English)

CARMEL (kar-MEL) Hebrew: "garden." Name of a mountain in Israel, as well as a town in California. *Carma, Carmelle, Carmi, Carmie, Carmy* (English); *Carmela, Carmelina,*

Carmelita, Lita (Italian, Spanish)

CARMEN Spanish: "crimson"; or Latin: "a song." A shortened form of Maria del Carmen, another name for Mary, mother of Jesus. *Carma, Carmia, Carmina, Carmine, Carmita, Charmaine, Karma, Karmia, Karmina, Karmine, Karmita* (English); *Carmine* (Italian); *Carmena, Carmencita, Karmen, Mina* (Spanish)

CARNA Hebrew *karnis:* "horn." Often used today in Israel. *Carniela, Carniella, Carnis, Carnit, Karniela, Karniella, Karnis, Karnit* (Hebrew)

CAROL Latin: "strong and womanly"; or Old French: "a joyful song." The masculine form is Charles or Carl. *Carel, Carole,*

Caryl, Karel, Karol, Karole, Karyl
(English); *Carole* (French); *Kalola*
(Hawaiian); *Carola* (Spanish)

CAROLINE, CAROLYN
French, Latin: "little womanly
one." *Cari, Carla, Carleen,*
Carlene, Carli, Carlie, Carline,
Carly, Carol, Carole, Carri,
Carrie, Carroll, Cary, Caryl,
Charla, Charleen, Charlena,
Charlene, Charline, Kari, Karie,
Karla, Karleen, Karli, Karlie,
Karly, Karoline, Lina, Line,
Sharleen, Sharlene, Sharline
(English); *Karla, Karlinka,*
Karola, Karolina (Czech); *Lina*
(Finnish); *Charlotte* (French);
Charlotte, Karla, Karoline,
Lina, Linchen, Line, Lotchen
(German); *Karolina, Lina, Linka*
(Hungarian); *Carla, Carlotta*
(Italian); *Karlene* (Latvian);
Karolina, Karolinka, Ina, Inka
(Polish); *Carlota, Lola, Lolita,*
Tota (Spanish); *Carla, Carlera,*
Carlina, Carlita, Carolinda,
Karila, Karla, Karlita, Lotta
(Swedish)

CARON French form of Karen,
"pure."

CARRIE Popular contemporary
American form of Caroline. *Cari,*
Carri

CARTER Old English: "a cart
driver." Originally a boys' name
now also used for girls. *Karter*
(English)

CASEY Irish Gaelic: "brave and

vigilant." Another boys' name
that's now been adopted by girls.
Casi, Casie, Kaci, Kacie, Kasey
(English)

CASIAH (KASH-ah) Hausa,
Africa: "persuasive" or "grass,"
possibly referring to a kind of dry
grass that grows in Africa. *Casia,*
Cassia (English)

> **"When I like
> people immensely,
> I never tell their
> names to anyone.
> It is like
> surrendering a
> part of them."**
>
> —Oscar Wilde

CASINA (kah-SEEN-ah) Hausa,
Africa: "from Casina," a town in
Hausa.

CASSA (KAY-sah or KAH-sah)
Hausa, Africa: an African name
with many meanings, including
"bowlegged" or "child of the
earth." Also a name for a girl born
under one of the earth signs of
Capricorn, Taurus, or Virgo.

CASSANDRA Greek: "helper of men." Perhaps a feminine form of Alexander. *Cass, Cassie, Cassy, Kassandra, Sandi, Sandra*

CASSIDY Irish: "ingenious and clever" or "curly-haired." A traditional boys' name in Ireland, this is used more commonly for girls in the United States. *Cass, Cassi, Cassie, Kassidy* (English); *Caiside* (Irish)

CASSIE A pet form of Cassandra ("helper of men") frequently used as an independent name. *Cass, Cassi, Kass, Kassi, Kassie* (English)

CATHERINE Greek: "pure." One of the most popular names in the world. See Katherine for almost one hundred variations.

CAYLA A unique, artistic-sounding, recently developed form of Katherine, "pure." Also spelled *Kayla*.

CECILIA (seh-SIL-yah) Latin: "dim-sighted." Used not only in the United States, but also in the Czech Republic, Italy, Mexico, Portugal, the Republic of Slovakia, Romania, and Spain. The masculine form is Cecil. *Cecely, Cecyl, Cecyle, Cele, Celia, Celie, Cicely, Cicily, Cissi, Cissie, Cissy, Sissi, Sissie* (English); *Ceciliia, Sesiliia* (Bulgarian); *Cecilie, Cile, Cilka* (Czech); *Cecile, Cecily* (French); *Cacilia, Cecilie, Cilli, Cilly* (German); *Kikilia*

(Hawaiian); *Cili* (Hungarian); *Sheila* (Irish); *Cecylia, Cesia* (Polish); *Cecilla, Chela, Chila* (Spanish); *Celia* (Swedish)

CELESTE Latin: "heavenly." A sophisticated, strong-sounding name kept in the limelight most recently by actress Celeste Holm. *Celesta, Celestina, Celestine, Celia* (English); *Celestin, Celestyna, Tyna, Tynka* (Czech); *Celeste, Celestine, Celie* (French); *Celestina* (Italian, Portuguese, Spanish); *Cela, Celestyn, Celestyna, Celina, Celinka, Cesia, Inka, Selinka* (Russian)

CELINE (seh-LEEN, or in French, say-LEEN) A form of Selina, "heavenly" or "goddess of the moon." A sexy, exotic-sounding name used in France as well as the United States. See Selina.

CELLA (CHEL-ah) Italian form of Francesca, "free one" or "from France."

CERELLA (se-RAY-luh or se-REL-luh) Latin: "of the spring." Name for a girl born under one of the signs of Aries, Taurus, or Gemini. *Cerelia* (English)

CERISE French: "cherry." *Cherise* (French)

CHAN Cambodian: "a sweet-smelling tree."

CHANDA (CHAN-dah or SHAN-dah) Contemporary American

Umbundu Proverb Names

✱ ✱ ✱

Among the Umbundu-speaking peoples of Africa, babies are often given names that are shortened forms of popular proverbs. Some examples of these fascinating names are:

Cakusola (chah-koo-SO-luh): "If you loved, you followed the messenger," given to a child born shortly after the parents have been honored in some way.

Catava (chah-TAH-vah): from the saying *"Ca tava otulo; capatala olongembia,"* "It consented sleep; it protested pain." Loosely translated, this means "she wanted to sleep but was in too much pain to do so."

Cilehe (chee-LAY-heh): from *"Ci lehe no; oi kaile,"* "Just let it stink, let it be." Loosely translated, this saying means if something is bad, just leave it alone or you will make it worse. Another version of the same saying is "Let it stink, it is his own," meaning we all must handle our own problems.

Cinofila (chee-noh-FEE-lah): from the proverb *"Ocina o fila te nda o ci lia,"* "A thing you die for only if you eat it." The saying is used to describe the hunter who overcomes all obstacles to find meat.

Ciyeva (chee-YAY-vah): "You hear it, but you don't do it."

Cohila (cho-HEE-luh): from *"Ca uhila onene, kutima ku vala,"* "It is silent on the part of the young, at heart it hurts." In other words, the young are quiet about the things that bother them.

creation, possibly a short form of Chandra, "moon" or "moon god." *Chan, Chandah, Shan, Shanda, Shandah* (English)

CHANDELLE (shahn-DELL) Old French: "like a candle." A child who illuminates or brightens the world around her. *Chan, Chandell, Shan, Shandell, Shandelle* (English)

CHANDI (chahn-dee) Hindi: "angry" or "fierce," sometimes loosely translated as "the great goddess." One of the more than one thousand names for the Hindu goddess Shakti. See Shakti.

CHANDLER (CHAND-ler) Old English: "candlemaker." Originally an occupational name for someone who made candles and small wax figures for religious services. *Chandi, Chandie, Chandy* (English)

CHANDRA (CHAHN-druh) Hindi: "moon" or "moon god." See Candra.

CHANEL (shah-NEL) Old French: "dweller near the channel or canal." Possibly inspired as a first name for girls by legendary twentieth-century fashion designer Coco Chanel. *Chanelle, Channelle, Shanel, Shanell, Shanelle* (English)

CHANNA (chah-nuh) Hindi: "chickpea." According to traditional Hindu mythology, all herbs, plants, and trees were "fathered by heaven, mothered by earth, and rooted in the primeval ocean." *Chan, Shan, Shanna* (English)

CHANTAL (shahn-TAHL) French: "from the stony place." A spiritual name often bestowed by French parents to honor the much-admired St. Jean de Chantal, who helped found a new order of nuns. *Chantel, Chantele, Chantell, Chantelle, Shantal, Shantalle, Shantel, Shantell, Shantelle* (English)

CHARISSA (char-RIS-sah or kah-RIS-sah) Latin: "dear or artful"; or Greek: "grace." *Carissa, Karissa, Rissa* (English)

CHARLIE An energetic, carefree form of Charlotte. A name once given only to boys, it's become increasingly common for girls ever since Charlie perfume was first introduced. *Charley, Charly* (English)

CHARLOTTE French: "little womanly one." Like Caroline, this name is a feminine form of Charles. In France, boys formally named Charles are often nicknamed Charlot. *Carla, Carlene, Carli, Carlie, Carly, Charleen, Charlene, Charline, Charyl, Cheryl, Karla, Karli, Karlie, Karline, Karly, Lola, Loleta, Loletta, Lolita, Sharleen, Sharlene, Sharline, Sheree, Sheri, Sherisa, Sherissa, Sherri, Sherrie, Sherrill, Sherry* (English); *Karla,*

Karlicka (Czech); *Lolotte* (French); *Karla, Lottchen, Lotte, Lotti* (German); *Karlotta* (Greek); *Sarolta, Sari* (Hungarian); *Sarlote* (Latvian); *Lottie* (Polish); *Carlota* (Spanish, Portuguese); *Salote* (Tongan)

CHARMAINE (shar-MAIN) Latin: "a singer"; or Greek: "delightful, joyous." Currently enjoying a revival in popularity. *Charmain, Charmayne, Sharmain, Sharmaine, Sharmayne* (English)

> **"***In real life, unlike in Shakespeare, the sweetness of the rose depends upon the name it bears.***"**
>
> —HUBERT HUMPHREY

CHARRON (SHAR-ron) Contemporary American spelling of Sharon, "a princess" or "a plain" where roses bloomed.

CHASTITY Latin: "chaste" or "pure." A virtue name which gained some media attention after Cher and Sonny Bono named their daughter Chastity.

CHAU (chow) Vietnamese: "a pearl," connotating that the child is precious.

CHAVI (CHAH-vee) English Gypsy: "child" or "daughter." *Chavali* (English)

CHAYA (ki-YAH) Hebrew: "life" or "living." *Kaija* (Hebrew)

CHAZMIN (CHAZ-min) An exotic contemporary version of Jasmine, "the jasmine blossom." *Chaz* (English)

CHELSEA Old English: "ship's port." A name once used mostly in Australia that became familiar worldwide in the 1990s after Bill and Hillary Clinton moved to the White House with their daughter Chelsea. *Chelsey, Chelsi* (English)

CHENOA (chay-NO-ah) Native American: "white dove," with the connotation of peace in nature.

CHER French: "dear" or "beloved." From the French name Cherie.

CHEYENNE Dakota, Native American: "to speak strangely." A girl named after the Cheyenne Indians of the Western plains. *Cheyanne* (English)

CHIKA (chee-ka) Japanese: "near," possibly in the sense of near and dear. *Chikako* (Japanese)

CHILALI (chee-LAH-lee) Native American: "snowbird."

CHINA Contemporary American name borrowed from the name of the country. For many people, the name has an exotic and delicate sound. *Chyna, Chynna* (English)

CHLOE (KLOH-ee) Greek: "a young, green shoot" or "greenish-yellow." In Greek mythology, Chloe was the name given to the goddess of green grain. An ancient name that has recently come back into favor. *Cloe* (English)

CHO Japanese: "born at dawn"; may also mean "butterfly."

CHOLENA (cho-LAY-nah) Native American: "bird."

CHOOMIA (CHOO-mee-ah) English Gypsy: "a kiss."

CHRISTEL A German form of Christina.

CHRISTINA Greek *christianos:* "Christian." With all its variations, this is one of the most popular names in the world. *Chris, Chrissie, Chrissy, Christi, Christie, Christy, Chrystal, Cristina, Crystal, Kris, Krissi, Krissie, Krissy, Tina, Tinah* (English); *Crystina, Krista, Kristina, Kristinka, Tyna* (Czech); *Krista* (Estonian); *Kristia* (Finnish); *Christine, Crestienne* (French); *Christel, Christiane,* *Chrystel, Crista, Stina, Stine, Tine* (German); *Christina, Tina* (Greek); *Kriska* (Hungarian); *Cristin, Cristiona* (Irish); *Cristina* (Italian); *Krista, Kristine* (Latvian); *Krysia, Krysta, Krystka, Krystyna, Krystynka* (Polish); *Cristina* (Portuguese); *Khristina, Khristya, Tina* (Russian); *Kirsten, Kirstin, Kristin* (Scandinavian); *Cristiana, Cristy* (Spanish)

CHU-HUA (chuh-hwah) Chinese: "chrysanthemum." In China, the chrysanthemum is the flower of autumn and October. In Far Eastern astrology, it is the flower of Scorpio.

CHUMA (CHOO-mah) Mashona, southern Rhodesia: "bead."

CHUN Chinese: "spring."

CIAH (KEE-ah) Hausa, Africa: "difficult." *Kia* (English)

CIARA (see-AR-ah, or Irish KEER-ah) Irish Gaelic: "black one" or "black-haired." A traditional name in Ireland. *Keera, Kira* (English); *Ciar* (Irish)

CICELY (SIS-ah-lee) A trendy contemporary form of Cecilia ("dim-sighted"). Made well known by actress Cicely Tyson.

CILKA (CHEL-kuh) Czech form of Cecilia, from Latin meaning "dim-sighted."

Saintly Irish Names

✶ ✶ ✶

Many Irish saints' names from centuries ago no longer seem appropriate when naming a modern little girl. Names like Caoimseach, Craobhnait, Finneacht, and Suiabhseach are prime examples of holy names that are definitely "out." But here are versions of musical-sounding Irish saints' names that still seem contemporary.

Aideen: an ancient Irish name of uncertain origin, frequently bestowed in honor of St. Aideen from Moylurg.

Brigid, or Anglicized, *Brigit:* "strength." St. Brigid, the Patroness of Ireland, founded the famous convent at Kildare. She died on February 1, A.D. 525, and her feast day is February 1.

Ciara: "black" or "dark." The name of a seventh-century saint from Tipperary.

Enya: "kernel." This modern development of the older Irish name Eithne was popularized most recently by Enya, the Irish singer-composer. St. Eithne was the daughter of a king and one of the first Irish converts to Christianity.

CILLA Contemporary form of Priscilla, "one from primitive or ancient times."

CINDY A pet form of Cynthia ("moon") frequently used independently. *Cindi, Cyndi, Sindy, Syndi* (English)

CIPRIANA (see-pree-AH-nah) Greek: "from the Island of Cyprus." The Zuni Indians borrowed this name from Spanish, changing it to *Sipiana*.

CLAIRE Latin: "brilliant" or "illustrious." A modern form of the older name Clara, Claire is often used in the United States and in France. *Clair, Clairine, Clare, Clari, Clarice, Clarie, Clarina, Clarine, Clarissa, Clarisse, Clarita* (English); *Klara* (popular in many languages, including Bulgarian, Czech, Polish, Russian, and Swedish); *Clairette, Clarette* (French); *Clarissa, Klarissa* (German); *Kalea* (Hawaiian); *Klarika* (Hungarian, Slavic); *Chiara, Clarissa* (Italian); *Clareta, Clarisa, Clarita* (Spanish)

CLAUDIA Latin: "lame." This unusual meaning probably came from the name's association with the Roman emperor Claudius, who walked with a limp. The masculine form is Claude. *Claudeen, Claudette, Claudi, Claudie, Claudina, Claudine* (English); *Claude, Claudette, Claudine* (French); *Claudeta, Claudina, Claudita* (Spanish)

COCHETA (sho-CHAY-tah) Native American: "the unknown."

CODY Irish: "helper or assistant" or "child of the wealthy one." Originally a surname and a boys' name, now also used for girls. *Codey, Codi, Codie, Kodey, Kodi, Kodie, Kody* (English)

COFFEE (KOFF-ee) Hausa, Africa: "inspiring a feeling of fear." In English, of course, this name simply means "coffee" or "coffee-colored." *Cof, Coffi, Coffie* (Hausa)

COLANDA (koh-LAHN-dah) Contemporary American, possibly modeled after Yolanda, "the violet flower."

COLBY Old Anglo-Norse: "from the coal-black settlement" or "black-haired." This boys' name, now also used for girls, has a strong, yet friendly sound. *Colbee, Colbey, Colbi, Colbie, Kolbee, Kolbey, Kolbi, Kolbie, Kolby* (English)

"*A good name is better than a golden girdle.*"

—FRENCH PROVERB

COLEY (KOLL-ee) Hausa, Africa: "a peddler of small wares." In Africa, this is usually a boys' name, but in this country it's also used for girls. *Colee, Colie* (English, Hausa)

COLLEEN (kol-LEEN) Irish Gaelic: "a girl" or "a lassie." An Irish-sounding name that's popular in English-speaking countries, even though it's not actually used in Ireland. Made well known by Australian-born novelist Colleen McCullough, author of *The Thorn Birds*. *Colene, Coline, Collen, Collene, Colline* (English)

CONNIE Originally a nickname for Constance, but has become a given name in its own right. *Conni, Conny* (English)

CONSTANCE Latin: "firm" or "constant." *Con, Conni, Connie, Conny, Constancia, Constanta, Constantia* (English); *Constanz, Konstanze* (German); *Dina, Kosta, Kostatina, Tina* (Greek); *Kani* (Hawaiian); *Concettina, Constantia, Constanza* (Italian); *Konstantin, Kostenka, Kostya, Kostyusha, Kotik* (Russian); *Constancia, Constanza* (Spanish)

CORA Greek: "maiden." *Corella, Corene, Coretta, Corette, Corey, Cori, Corie, Corin, Corina, Corine, Corinn, Correen, Correne, Corri, Corrie, Corrina, Corrinna, Corry, Kora, Korey, Kori, Korrie, Korry* (English); *Corinne, Corrine* (French)

CORINNE (koh-RINN) This French version is currently the most popular form of Cora in this country. Can also be spelled *Korinne.*

CORNELIA Latin: "yellowish" or "cornell tree." Used around the globe—in Mexico, Portugal, Romania, and Spain. *Cornela, Cornella, Cornelle, Cornie, Neely, Nell, Nelli, Nellie, Nelly* (English); *Kornelia* (Czech); *Cornelie* (French); *Kornelia, Nele* (German); *Melia, Nelia* (Spanish); *Kornelis* (Swedish)

COSETTE (koh-SETT) French: "victorious army" or "victorious people." A feminine form of Nicholas from France. *Cozette* (English); *Cosetta* (Italian)

COURTNEY Old French: "one who lives at the court or on the farm." In a study at Guilford College in Greensboro, North Carolina, people stereotyped the name Courtney as extremely "strong," "smart," "upper class," "attractive," "overconfident," "strong-willed," "creative," and "a leader." Currently one of the most popular names in this country, given to newborns more often than Lisa or Mary.

CRYSTAL Latin: "clear as crystal." Popularized in many countries in the 1980s by Krystal Carrington, a character on the TV series *Dynasty. Chrys, Chrystal, Cristel, Cristol, Krys, Krystal, Krystol* (English)

CYBIL Variation of Sybil ("a prophetess") made well known most recently by model-turned-actress Cybil Sheppard. See Sybil.

CYNTHIA Greek: "moon." The astrological sign of Cancer is ruled by the moon. *Cindi, Cindie, Cindy, Cyndi, Cyndie, Cynth, Cynthie* (English); *Kynthia* (Greek); *Cintia* (Portuguese); *Cinta* (Spanish)

D

DACEY Irish Gaelic: "a Southerner." Once used only for boys, now also used for girls. *Dacee, Daci, Dacie, Dacy, Dasee, Dasey, Dasi, Dasie, Dasy, Daycee, Dayci, Daycie, Daycy* (English)

DAGAN (DAY-gun) Hebrew: "corn" or "ceremonial grain." *Daga, Daganya, Dagi, Degana, Degania* (English)

DAGMAR Old German: "glorious day," "famous thinker," or "glory of the Danes." Used world-wide; often found in such countries as the Czech Republic, Denmark, Germany, and Sweden. *Dagmara, Dasa* (Czech); *Dagi, Daggi, Dagmara* (Estonian); *Daga* (Polish)

DAGNY Old Norse: "new day." A feminine form of Dag, very popular in Norway. *Dagna, Dagne* (Danish, Norwegian, Swedish)

DAHLIA (DAHL-yah) Old Norse: "from the valley." A flower name derived from the last name of Swedish botanist Andrew Dahl. *Dalia, Daliah* (English)

DAI Japanese: "great one."

DAISY Old English: "the day's eye." *Daisee, Daisey, Daisi, Daisia, Daisie, Dasey, Dasi, Dasie, Dasy, Daysee, Daysie, Daysy* (English)

DAKOTA Native American: "a friend." Still used mostly for boys, but gaining popularity for girls. Actors Melanie Griffith and Don Johnson have a girl named Dakota.

DALE Old English: "from the dale or valley." Sometimes used as the first element in combination names like *Dale Lee* or *Dale Lynn*. *Dalena, Dalene, Dalenna, Dayle, Daylee, Daylin, Daylyn, Daylynn* (English); *Dael* (Dutch); *Daelyn, Dahl, Daly* (Scandinavian)

DALILA (dah-LEE-lah) Swahili: "gentle." *Dalia* (Swahili)

DALLAS Scottish Gaelic: "from the valley meadows." Originally referred to a place in Scotland, but through modern usage more often associated with the city in Texas. Still used mostly for boys, but also for girls. *Dallis* (English)

DALMA (DAHL-mah) Hausa, Africa: "lead metal" or "tin."

DALYA (DAHL-yah) Hebrew: "a tree branch" or "to draw water." A contemporary Jewish name also used in Israel. *Dalia, Dalice, Daliya, Dalit* (English, Hebrew)

DAMARA (dah-MAR-ah) Greek: "calf," with the connotation of gentleness. *Damaras, Damaress, Damaris, Damiris, Demaras, Demaris, Mara, Mari, Maris* (English)

DAMICA (dah-MEE-kah) French: "friendly." *Damey, Dami, Damice, Damie, Damika* (English)

DAMITA (dah-MEE-tah) Spanish: "little noble lady."

DANA (DAY-nah) Celtic: "from Denmark." In Celtic mythology, Dana was the mother of the gods. Originally a boys' name, most popular today for girls in the United States and Scandinavia. Also a Hebrew form of Daniel. *Daina, Dane, Danna, Dansy, Dayna* (English)

DANEAN (da-NEEN) Contemporary American coinage, possibly a combination of Dan ("judge") plus Jean ("God is gracious"). *Daneen, Danine* (English)

DANELL A recently developed form of Danielle, "God is my judge." *Dane, Dani* (English)

DANETTE Another contemporary American name created from Danielle. The feminine form of Daniel. *Daneen, Danella, Danett, Danetta, Dani, Danice, Danie, Danise, Danita* (English)

DANICA (DAN-i-kah) Slavic: "the morning star."

" *Everybody has a name anybody has a name and everybody anybody does what he does with his name feels what he feels about his name, likes or dislikes what he has to have with having his name, in short it is his name unless he changes his name unless he does what he likes what he likes with his name.* **"**

—GERTRUDE STEIN

DANIELLE (dan-YEL) Hebrew: "God is my judge." A popular variation—*Daniela*—is used in this country, the Czech Republic, Poland, and Spain. *Danela, Danell, Danella, Danelle, Dani, Daniela, Danila, Danilla, Danille, Danyel, Danyell, Danyelle* (English); *Danica, Danika* (Czech); *Dania* (Danish, Norwegian, Swedish); *Daniell* (French); *Dania, Danit, Danya* (Hebrew); *Danielka, Danka* (Polish); *Danikla, Danila, Danya* (Russian)

DANYA (DAHN-yah) Modern American name also popular in the Ukraine and Israel. See Danielle.

DAPHNE (DAF-nee) Greek: "laurel." A classical nature name drawn from Greek mythology. Daphne, daughter of the river god, was a nymph who longed to remain unmarried and free. When Apollo pursued and caught her, she called on her father for help and he turned her into a laurel tree. *Daffi, Daffie, Dafne, Dafnee, Daph, Daphe, Daphna, Daphnee* (English)

DARA Hebrew: "pearl of wisdom." *Darah, Darda, Daria, Darice, Darissa, Darra, Darya* (English)

DARBY Old English: "from the village with a deer park." Originally a boys' name now also used for girls. *Darbey, Darbi, Darbie, Derby* (English)

DARCIE Irish Gaelic: "black"; or Old French: "from the fortress." Contemporary American development of the boys' name Darcy, now used more often for girls. *Darcey, Darci, Darcy, Darsey, Darsi, Darsie, Darsey* (English)

DARDA Hebrew: "pearl of wisdom." Another meaning for this modern Hungarian name is "dart."

DARILYNN A contemporary American development of Darlene, "little darling one."

DARLA A popular modern form of Darlene, sometimes used as part of a combination name, such as Darla Ann or Darla Sue.

DARLENE Old English, French: "little darling one." *Dareen, Dari, Darilyn, Darilynn, Darla, Darleen, Darlin, Darline, Darlyn, Darlyne, Darrilyn* (English)

DARON (DAIR-on) Irish Gaelic: "little great one." Contemporary American development of the masculine name Darren. *Darin, Darine, Darinne, Darren, Daryn* (English)

DARRAH (DAHR-rah or DAIR-rah) Hausa, Africa: "big and fine" or "laughing"; Efik, Africa: "one who causes joy and rejoicing"; or Irish Gaelic: "black" or "dark oak." Traditionally a boys' name in Ireland but used as a girls' name in Africa and gaining popularity for girls in the United States. *Darah* (English); *Darragh* (Irish)

DARU (DAH-roo) Hindi: "divine daru," referring to a species of pine or cedar. An ancient Hindu sacrificial post was said to be carved from daru wood.

DARYL Old French: "little beloved one." Originally a boys' name, but brought into public awareness as a girls' name by actress Daryl Hannah. *Daril, Darrel, Darrell, Darryl* (English)

DARYN Greek: "gift." Contemporary form of the masculine Darin. *Darynn, Darynne* (English)

DASHA (DAH-shah) A popular Russian pet form of Dorothy, "gift of God." See Dorothy.

DAWN Middle English: "daybreak." *Dawna, Dawne, Dawnelle, Dawnette, Dawnita, Dawnyelle* (English)

"De-" names Many contemporary American names have been recently created using the prefix *"De-"* or *"Da."* Among the most common are: *Dalana, Dalane, Daleen, Dalice, Darisha,*

Time-of-Birth Names

✹ ✹ ✹

Many parents give their babies names that reveal when they were born. Baby girls born early in the morning are often called Dawn, Dawna, or Dawnette; similarly, girls born in spring are sometimes called April or May.

Time-of-birth names have also had a long, respected tradition in other countries. In Japan, for example, girl babies are called *Asa* ("born in the morning"), *Cho* ("born at dawn"), *Yoi* ("born in the evening"), and *Sayo* ("born at night"). Other Japanese time-of-birth names for girls include *Haru* ("born in spring"); *Natsu* ("born in summer"); *Aki* ("born in autumn"); and *Fuyu* ("born in winter"). The Arabic name *Laila* (also spelled *Leila* and *Layla*) is used in many cultures for a girl "born at night."

Dashawna, DeAngela, Dejana, Delena, Delinda, Deline, Delise, Delisha, Deneisha, Denisha, Deshawna

DEANDRA (dee-AN-druh) A contemporary American blend of Deanne plus Andrea or Sandra. *Dea, Deanna, Deanne, Dee, Deeandra, Deedee, Dian, Dianda, Diandra, Diandre* (English)

DEANNA Old English: "from the valley." Feminine form of Dean. *Dea, Deana, Deane, Deann, Deanne, Deena, Dena* (English)

DEBORAH Hebrew: "a bee." First became a favorite Christian name in the seventeenth century, when it was adopted by the Puritans. *Deb, Debi, Debbi, Debbie, Debby, Debora, Debra, Debralee* (English); *Devora* (Bulgarian, Greek, Russian); *Deboran* (German); *Kepola* (Hawaiian); *Debera, Debora, Devora, Devorah* (Spanish); *Dwora* (Yiddish)

DEDE (DEH-de) Ochi and Ga, Ghana: "first-born daughter."

DEDRA (DEE-drah) Contemporary American spelling of Deirdre, "one who rages" or "a wanderer."

DEEDEE Hebrew: "beloved." In Israel this name is also used for boys as a pet form of Jedidiah. *Didi* (Hebrew)

DEENA Modern short form of Deanna, "from the valley." *Dina* (English)

DEGULA (deh-GOO-lah) Hebrew: "excellent" or "famous."

DEIRDRE (DEER-dreh) Irish Gaelic: "one who rages" or "a wanderer." *Dedra, Deidra, Deidre, Deidrie, Dierdrie* (English)

DEKA (DEE-kah) Somali, East Africa, "one who pleases."

DELA (DAY-lah) A Spanish form of Adelle, "noble."

DELANEY (de-LAY-nee) Irish: "child of the challenger." *Delaina, Delaine, Delayna, Delayne, Laney, Layna* (English); *Delaine* (French)

DELIA Greek: "visible one." Another name for Artemis, the Greek goddess of the forest and moon. The name comes from the Isle of Delos, where Artemis was said to be born.

DELICIA (deh-LISH-ah) Latin: "delightful." Also used in Mexico and many countries in Central and South America. See Dilys. *Delesha, Delice, Delisa, Delise, Delisha, Delisiah, Delissa, Delycia, Delys, Delyse, Delysha, Delysia, Delyssa* (English); *Dee, Dela, Delia, Delise* (Spanish)

DELLA A pet form of Adelle ("noble") frequently used as an independent name. *Dela, Dell, Delle* (English); *Dela* (Hawaiian)

DELLE (dehl or DEH-luh) Hebrew: "a jar." Another name for the constellation Aquarius, the water bearer.

DELMA German: "noble protector." Originally a pet form of Adelma, now used as an independent name. *Delmi, Delmira, Delmy* (English). See Adelma.

DELTA Greek: "fourth one," referring to the fourth letter of the Greek alphabet.

DELU (DAY-loo) Hausa, Africa: "first girl born after three boys." Another name given in this situation is *Iggi*.

DEMA (DEM-ah) Mende, Africa: "forgetful one."

DEMI (deh-ME or DEH-me) French: "half." Also a short form of the older name Demetria, "belonging to Demeter," the Greek fertility god. Popularized by actress Demi Moore.

DEN Japanese: "asked for by her ancestors." Name for a very precious baby.

DENA (DAY-nah) Native American: "a dale" or "a valley"; or Hausa, Africa: "to cease," perhaps given to a child the parents intend to be the last. Also a pet form of Deanna.

DENISE Greek: "belonging to the God of wine." A feminine form of Denice. *Danice, Danise, Deneice, Denese, Denice, Deniece, Denisha, Denisse, Denize, Dennie, Dennise, Denny, Denyce, Denyse, Dinnie, Dinny* (English)

> **"** *Native Americans regard their names not as mere labels, but as essential parts of their personalities. A native person's name is as vital to his or her identity as the eyes or teeth.* **"**
>
> —WILMA MANKILLER, THE FIRST WOMAN TO BE ELECTED CHIEF OF THE CHEROKEE NATION

DENISHA Contemporary form of Denise, rapidly growing in popularity.

DERICA (DAIR-ih-kah) Old German: "the people's ruler." Contemporary feminine form of Derek. *Dereka, Dericka, Derika, Derrica, Derrika, Derry*

DERORA (deh-ROR-ah) Hebrew: "flowing brook," "freedom," or "bird," referring in particular to the swallow. Nature name used originally in Israel. *Deroit, Derorice* (Hebrew)

DERYA (DAIR-yah) Hawaiian: "ocean."

DESHAWNA Contemporary name combining De+Shawn, literally "from John." See "De-" names, page 87. *Deshana, Deshanna, Shana, Shanna, Shawna*

DESIREE (dez-ih-RAY) French: "the desired one." *Desarae, Desaree, Desiraye, Desiré, Dezarae, Dezaray, Dezirae, Deziree* (English); *Desi, Desideria, Desirita* (Spanish)

DESSA (DESS-ah) Mende, Africa: "flat or unexpressive"; or Hausa, Africa: "an herb." A pretty girls' name from Africa.

DESTINY Old French: "fate." *Destanee, Destine, Destinee, Destini, Destinie* (English); *Destina* (Spanish)

DEVA (DAY-vah) Hindi: "divine." Hindu name for the moon goddess. The same name is also used by the Mende-speaking people of Africa, where it means "life."

DEVAKI (day-vah-kee) Sanskrit: "black" or "divine." Hindu name for the goddess who was the mother of the powerful god Krishna.

DEVANEE (day-vah-nee) Sanskrit: "God-like, divine." A spiritual name from India.

DEVASHA (deh-VAH-sha) Hebrew: "sweet as honey." A contemporary Israeli name with a soft, feminine feel about it. *Devash* (Hebrew)

DEVI (DAY-vee) Sanskrit: "goddess." One of the many names for Shakti, the Hindu goddess of power and destruction. *Dayvi, Devee, Deyvi* (English)

DEVIKA (day-vee-kah) Sanskrit: "a little goddess." This pet form of Devi is often used independently.

DEVIN (DEV-in) Irish Gaelic: "a poet." A gender-free name growing in popularity. *Devan, Devlin, Devlyn, Devon, Devyn* (English)

DEVORA (day-VOR-ah) Russian form of Deborah, "a bee." See Deborah.

DEWI (Anglicized, DEW-ee) Malay: "goddess."

DEZBA (DEHZ-bah) Navaho: "going to war."

DIA (DEE-ah) Mende, Africa: "middle child." A similar Mende name, spelled *Diah*, means "a small rice-eating bird."

DIANA Latin: "goddess," referring to the Roman goddess of the moon and the hunt. Made familiar around the world by England's late Princess Diana of Wales. *Deana, Deanna, Dee, Di, Diahann, Dian, Dianna, Diane, Dianne, Dyan, Dyana, Dyane, Dyann, Dyanne* (English); *Kiana* (Hawaiian); *Diani* (Portuguese)

DIBBY Hausa, Africa: "a fortune-teller."

DICKLA (dee-KLAH) Hebrew: "a palm tree" or "date tree." Originally from Israel. *Dikla, Diklice, Diklit* (Hebrew)

Magic Names

✶ ✶ ✶

Throughout time, people have attributed magical powers to names. One of the most famous magical names—*Agla*—is said to be taken from the first letters of the Hebrew phrase *Ataw Gebor Leolam Adonai*, which means "Thou art mighty forever, Lord." Until the sixteenth century, the words were used as a charm by rabbis and some Christians to exorcise demons. The same magic name was also used in Germany, where it was thought to be derived from *Allmächtiger Gott, lösch' aus*, meaning, "Redeem, Almighty God." Another powerful magical name, used by occultists in hexagram rituals to banish and invoke spirits, is *Ararita*, taken from the first letters of the words in an incantation meaning, "One is His Beginning; One is His Individuality; His Permutation is One." Another magic name used to invoke spirits is *Belatha*, which means "Thou Essence, Air Swift-streaming, Elasticity!"

DILLA (DILL-ah) Hausa, Africa: "a jackal"; or Mende, Africa: "a python." In the latter case, this name refers to a mythical python-shaped creature believed to attack children at night; therefore, it may be bestowed by African parents as a magic name to ward off evil.

DILYN (DILL-in) Irish Gaelic: "faithful." A feminine form of Dillon or Dylan. *Dilan, Dilen, Dilinn, Dillan, Dillen, Dillyn* (English)

DILYS (de-LEES) Welsh: "perfect." *Dalice, Dalicia, Dalisha, Delicia, Delisha, Dilees, Dylice* (English)

Did You Know . . .

✶ ✶ ✶

The *"nick"* in *nickname* originally came from the Middle English *eken* or Old English *eacan*, meaning "to add to or increase." An *ekename* was an additional name, or an "also name." Eventually an *ekename* became a *nekename*, and the word *nickname* was born.

DINA Popular around the world as a nickname for many longer names, including the Greek Konstantina and the Russian Dinah. In some parts of Africa, this is given as a nickname to a boy who is always seeking a comfortable place to sit, the meaning being "he sat down wherever he went."

DINKA Dinka, Africa: "people," referring to a tribe of about a million people who have lived since long ago on the plains around the southern Nile.

DINNA (DIN-nah) Mende, Africa: "the broad-leafed dinna plant," which grows in African swamps; or Bini, Africa: "the one who has arrived."

DIONNE (dee-OWN or dee-ON) Greek: "god of wine." Made familiar in many countries by singer Dionne Warwick. A feminine form of Dennis. *Dion, Diona, Diondra, Dione, Dionna* (English)

DIOR (dee-OR) French: "golden." *Diora, Diore, Diorra, Diorre* (English)

DISA Old Norse: "active sprite," meaning a goddess; or Greek: "double." Contemporary American name also used in Denmark and Sweden.

DITA (DEE-tah) Czech form of Edith, meaning "rich gift." See Edith.

DIXIE French: "ten," referring to the ten-dollar bills issued in New Orleans which had *dix,* or "ten," boldly printed on each side. Nickname for the American South. *Dix, Dixee, Dixi, Dixy* (English)

DIZA Hebrew: "joy." *Ditza, Ditzah* (English)

DOBA (DOH-bah) Navaho: "there was no war." Navaho girls' names typically commemorate war or peace.

DODIE Hebrew: "beloved." Comes from the same source as the boys' name David. *Doda, Dodi* (English)

DOLA (DOH-lah) Mende, Africa: "a baby" or "a kind of bird."

DOLORES Spanish: "sorrow." A shortened form of the longer name Maria de los Dolores, "Mary of the Sorrows," referring to the seven tragic events in the life of Mary, mother of Jesus. *Delora, Delores, Deloris, Delorita, Lola, Lolita* (English); *Dolore, Kololeke* (Hawaiian); *Dela, Delores, Dolo, Dolorcitas, Doloritas, Lola, Lolita, Lora, Loras* (Spanish)

DOMINI Once a pet form of Dominique, "belonging to God" or a variation of Domina, "lady," now used as an independent name.

DOMINIQUE (dom-in-NEEK) Latin: "belonging to God." Originally a French form of Dominica, Dominique is now more popular in this country. *Dom, Dominee, Domini, Dominic, Dominica, Dominick, Dominik* (English); *Doma, Domek, Dominik, Dumin* (Czech); *Dominik* (German); *Dominik, Niki* (Polish); *Dominika, Domka, Mika, Nika* (Russian); *Chumina, Dominga* (Spanish)

DONA (DOH-nah) Hausa, Africa: "to drink deeply." *Donah, Donnah* (English)

DONI American creation from Donna, "lady," or Donalda, "ruler of the world." *Donie, Dony, Donni, Donnie, Donny* (English)

DONNA Latin: "lady," originally, "mistress of the house." *Dona, Donella, Donelle, Donetta, Donia, Donica, Doniella, Donnell, Donni, Donnie, Donny, Ladonna* (English); *Kona* (Hawaiian)

DOORIYA (DOO-ree-yuh) Irish: "the deep." Romantic English Gypsy name referring to the sea. *Dooya* (English)

DORA Short form of Dorothy, "God's gift," as well as other names like Theodora and Isadora. Used independently as a name after the publication of *David Copperfield* by Charles Dickens, who used it for one of his characters. *Dorah, Doralin, Doralyn, Doralynne, Doreen,*

Gift Names

✶ ✶ ✶

The idea of a child being a gift from God is embedded in dozens of names throughout the world. Among the many spiritual "gift names," we find the Nigerian *Aniweta* ("the spirit Ani brought it"), the Ukrainian *Bohdana* ("given by God"), the English *Dorothy* and its many variations, including the Russian *Dasha* ("God's gift") and the German *Dorlisa*, the English *Edith*, with its many forms including the Czech *Dita* and the Hungarian *Duci* ("rich gift"), and the Swahili *Zawadi* ("gift").

Dorelia, Dorena, Dorette, Dori, Dorrie, Dorry (English)

DORIAN Greek: "child of the sea." Name for a girl born under one of the zodiac water signs of Cancer, Pisces, or Scorpio.

DORIS Greek: "bountiful" or "one from the ocean." *Dori, Doria, Dorice, Dorise, Dorita, Dorri, Dorrie, Dorris, Dory* (English); *Dorisa, Kolika* (Hawaiian)

DORIT (do-REET) Hebrew: "a generation." Brought to this country from Israel. *Dorice*

DOROTHY Greek: "God's gift." Popular in many forms world-wide. *Dode, Dodi, Dodie, Dody, Doll, Dolley, Dolli, Dollie, Dolly, Dora, Dori, Dorolice, Dorothea,* *Dorothia, Dorthy, Dory, Dosi, Dot, Dotti, Dottie, Dotty* (English); *Dora, Dorka, Dorota* (Czech); *Doralice, Dorette, Dorolice, Dorothee* (French); *Dorchen, Dore, Dorle, Dorlisa, Thea* (German); *Theadora* (Greek); *Dorotea, Koleka, Kolokea* (Hawaiian); *Dorte* (Norwegeian); *Dorka, Dorosia, Dorota* (Polish); *Dol, Dorotthea* (Romanian); *Dasha, Dorka, Doroteya, Dosya* (Russian); *Dora, Dori, Dorinda, Doro, Dorotea, Doroteyo, Theadora* (Spanish); *Lolotea* (Zuni Indian)

DORY French: "golden-haired one." Originally a boys' name, now used for both genders. *Dori, Dorri, Dorrie, Dorry* (English)

DOSHI (DOH-shee) Hausa, Africa: "direct and determined," from the word *dochie*, meaning "a direct route." In Africa, the *dochie* is also a type of girls' dance.

DOSYA (DOHS-yah) Popular Russian pet form of Dorothy, "God's gift."

DREW Greek: "strong"; Old Welsh: "wise"; or Old German: "a vision." Also a short form of Andrew. Made widely known as a girls' name by actress Drew Barrymore. *Dru, Drue* (English)

DRINA (DREE-nah) A Spanish pet form of Alexandra, "helper and defender of mankind." *Dreena* (English)

DRISA (dree-SAH) Hindi: "daughter of the sun." In the zodiac, the sun governs the sign of Leo. Also, modern short form of Drisana. *Dreesa, Dreesha, Drisanna, Drisha, Risa, Risha* (English)

DUCI (DOO-tsee) A modern Hungarian form of Edith, "valuable gift."

DURAH (DUR-ah) Hausa, Africa: "well-fed" or "stuffed." A happy, healthy baby. *Dura, Durrah* (English, Hausa)

DURVA (dure-vah) Hindi: "durva grass." A Hindu name referring to a holy grass used in ceremonial worship.

DUSCHA (DOO-shah) Russian: "soul." An endearment used in the same way one might use the terms "honey" or "sweetheart."

DUSTY Old German: "a fighter." Originally a short form of the boys' name Dustin, now also used for girls. *Dustee, Dusti, Dustin, Dustyn* (English)

DYAN A contemporary form of Diana, "goddess of the moon and the hunt." Associated in many people's minds with actress Dyan Cannon. *Dyann, Dyanna, Dyanne* (English)

DYANI (di-YAH-nee) Native American: "a deer."

E

EARTHA Old English: "child of the earth." Nature name, possibly for a child born under one of the earth signs of Capricorn, Taurus, or Virgo. *Erna, Ertha, Herta, Hertha* (English)

EBA (EBB-ah) Africa. Mende: "I certainly disagree"; Bonbangi: "crocodile"; Bini: "the gray parrot's red tail feather"; Congo: "palm tree" or "palm oil"; or Ngala: "understanding." A common African name with many origins and meanings.

EBBIE (EBB-ee) Bini, Africa: "darkness." *Ebby* (Bini)

EBONY Popular contemporary name meaning "blackness," referring to black ebony wood. *Ebbony, Ebonee, Eboney, Eboni, Ebonie* (English)

EDA (ED-uh) Bini, Africa: "gray-haired" or "rainwater." Also spelled *Edda.*

EDDA Old Norse: "poetry" or "composer (or singer) of songs"; or Old German: "one who strives." Variation of Hedda.

EDENA (e-DEN-ah) Hawaiian development of Edna.

EDITH Old English: "valuable gift." *Dita, Eda, Ede, Edie, Editha, Edithe, Ediva, Edyth, Edythe, Eyde* (English); *Dita, Ditka, Edita* (Czech); *Editha* (German); *Edi, Ekika* (Hawaiian); *Duci, Edit* (Hungarian); *Edetta, Edita* (Italian); *Edite* (Latvian); *Eda, Edda, Edka, Edyta, Ita* (Polish)

EDIYA (ee-DIE-ah) Hebrew: "ornament of God." A spiritual name from Israel. *Edia, Ediah, Edya, Edyah* (English, Hebrew)

EDNA Hebrew: "rejuvenation." *Edena* (Hawaiian)

EGA (AY-guh) Yoruba, Nigeria: "palm bird," from the proverb, "He who does not understand the cry of the palm bird complains of the noise it makes."

EILEEN A form of Aileen, "light-bearer." See Aileen.

EIRENE (eye-REH-neh) Old Norse: "peace."

EKIKA (eh-KEE-kah) Hawaiian form of Edith, "valuable gift."

ELA Polish form of Elvira, "white" or "blond." Also a short form of the Polish Melania, "dark in appearance" or simply "black" or "dark."

ELAMA (el-AH-mah) Hebrew: "Jehovah's people." A traditional Jewish name from Israel.

ELEANOR Form of Helen, "light" or "torch." See Helen.

ELECTRA (e-LEK-tra) Greek: "shining" or "brilliant." In Greek mythology, Electra was one of the seven sisters who were transformed into the constellation of the Pleiades in the night sky. Only six stars are visible. The seventh—Electra—is said to have left her place so she wouldn't have to witness the ruin of Troy, which her son had founded. *Elektra* (English)

ELENA (EL-len-ah or eh-LAY-nah) A sophisticated-sounding form of the internationally popular Helen, "light" or "torch." Elena is the form preferred in many

LEGENDS & LORE

Christians in nineteenth-century Germany would light candles, naming each one for a saint. The name of the candle that burned the longest would then be bestowed on the child.

European countries, including Bulgaria, the Czech Republic, Italy, and Spain. See Helen.

ELENI (eh-LEH-nee) Contemporary Greek version of Helen, "light" or "torch." See Helen.

ELESE (eh-LESS-eh) Old German: "noble." A Hawaiian form of the almost-never-used Elsie.

ELI (ELL-ee) Norwegian form of Ellen, "light."

ELIANA (el-lee-AH-nah) Hebrew: "Jehovah has answered (our prayers)." A traditional Jewish name from Israel. *Eliane, Elianna, Liana, Lianne* (English)

ELIDI (eh-LEE-dee) Greek: "gift of the sun." Name for a child born under Leo, which is ruled by the sun, or under the other two fire signs, Aries and Sagittarius.

ELIORA (ell-ee-OR-ah) Hebrew: "the Lord is my light." A contemporary Israeli name. *Eleora* (Hebrew)

ELISE (ah-LEES) A trendy pet form of Elizabeth, "dedicated to God." The French pronunciation of this name is ay-LEES. *Elyse* (English)

ELISKA (EL-lis-kah or EL-izh-kah, with the *s* pronounced like the *z* in *azure*) Czech development of either Alice, "truthful," or Elsie, "noble."

ELIZABETH Hebrew: "dedicated to God." Because this name is associated with Elizabeth, mother of John the Baptist, it's one of the most popular names in the world. *Bess, Bessi, Bessie, Bessy, Beth, Betsey, Betsi, Betsy, Bett, Betta, Bette, Betty, Buffy, Ellie, Elsa, Else, Elsi, Elsie, Elisa, Elissa, Eliza, Elyse, Elyssa, Libbi, Libbie, Libby, Lisa, Lisbet, Lisbeth, Liz, Lizabeth, Lizbeth, Lizzi, Lizzie, Lizzy* (English); *Elisveta* (Bulgarian); *Alzbeta, Beta, Betka, Betuska, Eliska* (Czech); *Betti, Elisabet, Elsbet, Elts, Etti, Etty, Liisa, Liisi* (Estonian); *Lisa, Lise* (Danish); *Lusa* (Finnish); *Babette, Elisa, Elisabeth, Elise, Lisette, Lizette*

(French); *Betti, Bettina, Elis, Elisabet, Elsbeth, Elschen, Else, Ilse, Lieschen, Liese, Liesel, Lisa, Lise, Lisette* (German); *Elisavet* (Greek); *Elikapeka* (Hawaiian); *Boski, Bozsi, Erzsebet, Liszka, Liza, Zizi* (Hungarian); *Eilis* (Irish); *Betta, Bettina, Elisa, Elisabetta, Lisettina* (Italian); *Elizabete, Lisbete* (Latvian); *Elzbieta* (Lithuanian); *Ela, Eliza, Elka, Elzbieta, Elsbietka, Elzunia, Liza* (Polish); *Isabel, Izabel* (Portuguese); *Elisabeta* (Romanian); *Betti, Elsavetta, Lisenka, Lizanka, Lizka, Yelisabeta, Yelizaveta* (Russian); *Elspeth* (Scottish); *Belicia, Belita, Bella, Chabica, Chavelle, Chela, Elisa, Isa, Isabel, Isabelita, Isabella, Issa, Iza, Izabel, Izabela, Izabella, Liseta, Sabela, Ysabel, Yza, Yzabel, Yzabela* (Spanish)

ELLAMA (ehl-lah-mah or ee-lah-mah) Hindi: "mother goddess," referring to the Hindu goddess worshiped as the guardian of south India. *Elamma* (English, Hindi)

ELLEN An English form of Helen, "light" or "torch." See also Helen and Elena. *Elea, Elin, Elyn, Ellan, Ellin, Ellon* (English)

ELLI Estonian form of Helen, "light" or "torch."

ELMA (EL-muh or el-MUH) Turkish: "apple."

ELSA Popular Spanish and Swedish form of Alice, "truthful." See Alice.

ELSE (AIL-seh) Old German: "noble." A favorite in Denmark.

ELVIRA Spanish: "elflike"; or Latin: "white" or "blond." Used around the world—in Hungary, Latvia, Russia, Spain, and Sweden, as well as this country. The name, never a great favorite, has gone totally out of style in the United States since its association with TV horror show hostess Elvira. *Elvire* (German); *Ela, Wirke, Wira* (Polish)

ELZA (EL-zah) Hebrew: "God is my joy." Popular in Israel. In Russia, this name is occasionally used as a form of the Old German Elsa, "noble."

EMA Hawaiian form of Amy, "beloved," or of Emma, "universal."

EMILY Gothic: "industrious"; or Latin: "flatter." See also Amelia. *Amalea, Amalie, Ameldy, Amelia, Amella, Em, Ema, Emera, Emi, Emie, Emilie, Emlyn, Emlynn, Emlynne, Emma, Emmi, Emmie, Emmy* (English); *Emiliia* (Bulgarian); *Ema, Emilie, Emilka, Milka* (Czech); *Emilie* (French); *Amalie, Amilia, Amilie, Amma, Emmi* (German); *Emalia, Emele* (Hawaiian); *Eimile* (Irish); *Emilia* (Italian); *Aimil* (Scottish); *Ema, Emilia, Emilita, Mema, Neneca, Nuela* (Spanish)

EMMA Old German: "strong" or "all-embracing." Also a form of Emily. *Em, Emmi, Emmie, Emmy* (English)

EMUNA (eh-MOO-nuh) Hebrew: "faithful." *Emunah* (Hebrew)

ENA (EN-nah, or Anglicized, EE-nah) Efik, Africa: "adorned" or "beaded," referring to a long white bead worn in Africa as an ornament.

ENID (EE-nid) Old Welsh: "soul" or "life." A heroine in Arthurian legend, Enid was the spotlessly pure wife of Geriant, a knight of the Round Table.

ENOLA (ay-NO-lah) Native American: The common inter-pretation that this name is simply "alone" spelled backward seems unsatisfactory because of the Native American tradition of bestowing names that are deeply and personally meaningful. No other explanation, however, could be found.

ENYA (EN-yah) Irish Gaelic: "a kernel" or "seed." A modern form of the old Irish name *Eithne.* Saint Eithne was the daughter of a king and an early Irish convert to Christianity. Made known worldwide by Irish singer and composer Enya. *Ena, Etha, Ethenia, Ethna, Etna, Etney* (Irish)

ERELA (eh-REL-lah) Hebrew: "angel" or "messenger." The Israeli equivalent of Angela.

ERICA, ERIKA Old Norse: "eternal ruler" or "always powerful." The spelling Erika is used not only in English-speaking countries, but also in the Czech Republic, France, Germany, Hungary, Latvia, and Sweden. The same name, also spelled with a K, is used by the Efik-speaking people of Africa and means "proceeding on." *Ericka, Errika, Rickee, Ricki, Rickie, Ricky, Rikki, Rikky* (English); *Elika* (Hawaiian)

ERIN Irish Gaelic: "from Ireland"; or Old Norse: "peace." Popular Irish-sounding name now used extensively in this country. *Eri, Erina, Erinn, Erinna, Eryn* (English)

ESHE (EH-shuh) Swahili: "life."

ESI (eh-SEE, or Anglicized, ES-ee) Fante, Ghana: "born on Sunday."

ESMEE (EZ-may) French: "beloved," from the French verb meaning "to love." A name brought from France, where it's still used today.

ESTA Persian: "star." Contem-porary development of the older Biblical name Esther.

ESTELLA Latin: "child of the stars." *Estelle, Stella, Stelle*

(English); *Estelle* (French); *Estrella, Estrelletta, Estrellita* (Spanish)

ESTHER Persian: "star," specifically the planet Venus. *Essa, Essi, Essie, Essy, Ester, Esta, Etti, Ettie, Etty, Hester, Hesther, Hetty* (English); *Hester* (Dutch); *Eister, Eistir* (Irish); *Ester* (Italian); *Ester, Estercita* (Spanish)

ETENIA (ay-TAY-nee-ah) Native American: "the wealthy."

EVA (AY-vah or EE-vah) Hebrew: "life-giving." A truly international name used not only in this country but in Austria, Bulgaria, Denmark, Germany, Greece, Hungary, Italy, Mexico, Norway, Portugal, Romania, Russia, Spain, and Sweden. *Eba, Ebba, Eve, Evelin, Evelina, Evelyn, Evlyn* (English); *Evicka, Evka, Evuska* (Czech); *Eeva* (Finnish); *Evaine* (French); *Evchen, Evi* (German); *Evathia* (Greek); *Ewalina* (Hawaiian); *Evi, Evike, Vica* (Hungarian); *Ewa, Ina, Lina* (Polish); *Yeva, Yevka* (Russian); *Evetta, Evia, Eviana, Evie, Evin, Evita* (Spanish); *Chava* (Yiddish)

EVANGELIA (eh-vahn-GEE-lee-ah) Contemporary Greek form of Angela, "angel" or "one who brings good news." *Evangela, Evangelina, Evangeline, Lia, Litsa* (English)

EVETTA (ee-VET-tah) Congo, Africa: "a dog hunt." *Evette* (English)

EYOTA (eh-YO-tah) Native American: "the greatest." Also used for boys.

EZRELA (ehz-RAY-luh) Hebrew: "God is my help" or "God is my strength." Also used in Israel. *Esraela, Ezraella* (English, Hebrew)

F

FAITH Old English: "ever faithful, always true." A virtue name introduced by the Puritans and once again growing in popularity. *Fe* (Spanish)

FALDA Icelandic: "folded wings."

FANYA (FAHN-yah) Russian form of Frances, "free one" or "from France." See Frances.

FARA (FAIR-ah or FAR-ah) Hausa, Africa: "joyful; a cause for rejoicing"; Efik, Africa: "to leave off or desist" (perhaps given in Africa to a child the parents intend to be their last). Also a variation of Farrah, "pleasant, lovely one." *Farra* (Efik, Hausa)

FARIH (FAIR-ih) Hausa, Africa: "bright, white light" or "the beginning," referring to a child who's first-born. In Arabic, this complex name for girls means "confederate," "playful," "one who runs well," or "perplexed." *Fari, Farry* (Hausa)

FARRAH Middle English: "pleasant, lovely one"; or Arabic: "happy." Made well known in this country by actress Farrah Fawcett. *Fara, Farah, Farra* (English)

> **"A good name is more precious than rubies."**
>
> —WISE OLD PROVERB

FATIMA (FAH-tee-mah) Arabic: literally, "one who weans an infant" or "one who abstains (from the forbidden)"; however, the name is so associated with Fatima, the favorite daughter of Muhammad, that it has come to mean simply "daughter of the Prophet." Popular throughout the Moslem world. (Fatima is believed to have lived from A.D. 670 to 632 and was married to Ali.) *Fatimah, Fatma* (Arabic)

FAWN Old French: "a young deer." *Fauna, Fawna, Fawnah, Fawniah* (English)

FAYE Middle English: "faith"; or French: "a fairy." Often used as a middle name. *Fay* (English)

FAYINA (figh-EE-nah) Russian and Ukrainian form of Frances or Francesca, "free one" or "from France." See Frances.

FAYOLA (fah-YO-lah) Yoruba, Nigeria: "good luck" or "walks with honor."

FELDA Old German: "from the field."

FELICIA Latin: "happy" or "lucky." A feminine form of Felix, also used in Italy, Poland (where it's pronounced FEL-shuh), and Spanish-speaking countries. *Falicia, Falisha, Felice, Felicity, Felisha, Lisha, Phelicia, Philicia* (English); *Felice, Felicie, Felicite, Felise, Filicie* (French); *Fela, Felicia, Felka* (Polish); *Falicia, Feliz* (Spanish)

FELICITY A popular British version of Felicia.

FEMI (FEH-mee) Yoruba, Nigeria: "love me."

FIALA (fee-AH-lah) Czech: "the violet."

FLAIR Latin: literally, "to give off a sense of smell" or "to be fragrant." The contemporary meaning is "one with a discriminating sense or natural ability"— a child with class.

FLANN An Irish form of Florence, "flourishing." Also a nickname for Flannery.

FLANNERY Irish Gaelic: "red-haired." A strong Irish-sounding name with literary overtones due to its association with American novelist and short-story writer Flannery O'Connor. *Flan, Flann* (English)

FLO Native American: "like an arrow." Used for both girls and boys. Also short for Flora and Florence.

FLORA Latin: "flower." A truly international name used not only in the United States but also in Bulgaria, Germany, Norway, Russia, Sweden, and many other countries. *Flo, Flore, Floressa, Flori, Floria, Floriana, Florianne, Florida, Florie, Florri, Florrie, Flory, Florry* (English);

Kveta, Kvetka (Czech); *Fleure, Flore* (French); *Fiora* (Italian); *Flora, Lora, Lorka* (Russian); *Fiora, Flor, Flores, Floridita, Florinda, Florita* (Spanish)

FLORENCE Latin: "flourishing" or "from Florence." *Flo, Florance, Florine, Florri, Florrie, Floss, Flossie, Flossy* (English); *Florentia* (German); *Flann* (Irish); *Fiorenza* (Italian); *Florencia, Florentina* (Spanish)

FOLA (FAW-lah) Yoruba, Nigeria: "honorable one."

FONTANNE (fawn-TAN) French: "a fountain." *Fontaine, Fontana, Fontann, Fontanna, Fontayne* (English)

Important to Know ...

✳ ✳ ✳

When looking for a name that's a bit different, you may want to avoid *overly* unusual spellings of traditional names (such as Behty for Betty, Phran for Fran, or Bil for Bill). In one *Journal of Social Psychology* study, unusually spelled names were seen as belonging to people who were less successful, less popular, less warm, and less cheerful than people who spelled their names more conventionally. Many forms of communication today (such as job applications, E-mail, and phone directory business ads) require no face-to-face contact. So how a name *looks* on a page may be as important as how it sounds.

FRANCES Latin: "free one" or "from France." *Fan, Fani, Fanni, Fannie, Fanny, Fran, Franci, Francie, Frankey, Frankie, Franni, Frannie, Franny* (English); *Franca, Francka* (Czech); *Françoise* (French); *Franz, Franze, Franziska* (German); *Fotina* (Greek); *Ferike, Franci* (Hungarian); *Cella, Francesca* (Italian); *Fraka, Franciszka, Frania* (Polish); *Francise* (Romanian); *Fedora* (Russian); *Chica, Francisca, Paca, Pancha, Panchita, Paquita* (Spanish)

FRANCESCA (fran-CHESS-kah) A trendy Italian form of Frances, "free one" or "from France." See Frances.

FRANCI (FRAN-see) Contemporary American and Hungarian form of Frances, "free one" or "from France." *Fran, Francie, Fransi* (English)

FREDERICA Old German: "peaceful ruler." *Freda, Fredda, Freddi, Freddie, Freddy, Fredericka, Frederika, Fredi, Fredie, Fredrica, Fredrika, Frida* (English); *Fedriska* (Czech); *Frederique* (French); *Frida, Fritze, Frizinn* (German); *Frici, Frida* (Hungarian); *Frederika* (Norwegian); *Fryda, Fryderyka* (Polish); *Frida* (Spanish)

FREYA (FRAY-ah, or Anglicized, FREE-yah) Old Norse: "a noble lady." In Norse mythology, Freya was Odin's wife and goddess of fertility, beauty, and love. She loved spring flowers and music, and was particularly fond of elves. *Freja, Freyja, Froja* (Scandinavian)

FRIEDA (FREE-dah) Old German: "peaceful one." *Freda, Frida* (English)

FRITZI Once a nickname for Frederica, now used independently. *Fritz, Fritzie* (English)

FUYUKO (foo-YOO-koh) Japanese: "winter-born child." Variation: *Fuyu*, "born in winter." Time-of-birth names like this are popular in many cultures (see box, page 87).

G

GABI (gah-bee, or Anglicized, GAB-ee) Arabic: "misunderstood, obscure, or concealed." Also a pet form of Gabriela. *Gabie* (Arabic)

GABRIELA, GABRIELLE Hebrew: "God's heroine" or "God is my strength." A feminine form of Gabriel also used in France. *Gabi, Gabie, Gabriella, Gaby, Gavriella, Gavrielle* (English); *Gaby, Gigi* (French); *Gavi, Gavriela, Gavriella, Gavrielle, Gavrilla* (Hebrew)

GADA (GAH-dah) Hebrew: "happy" or "lucky"; or Aramaic: "luck." A plant name in Hebrew. Also used in Israel.

GAFNA (GAHF-nah) Hebrew: "vine."

GAIL Hebrew: "my father is joyous." Short form of Abigail. *Gael, Gale, Gayel, Gayelle, Gayle, Gayleen, Gaylin, Gayline, Gaylyn, Gaylynn* (English)

GALA (GAH-lah, or Anglicized, GAY-lah) Old Norse: "single"; or Middle Dutch: "wealthy."

GALI (gah-LEE) Hebrew: "a hill," "a mound," "a spring," or "a fountain." Also used in Israel. *Gal, Galice, Galit* (Hebrew)

GALINA (gah-LEE-nah) Russian development of Helen, "light," or "torch." Originally from Greek, this name came into Russia through the Eastern Orthodox Church. See Helen.

GALYA (GAHL-yah) Hebrew: "God has redeemed." Also a boys' name in Israel. In Russia, this is a pet form of Galina.

GANESA (guh-NAY-shah) Hindi: "god of good luck and wisdom." In the Hindu religion, Ganesa is depicted as a rotund, pink god with an elephant's head and a snake tied about his potbelly.

GANIT (gah-NEET) Hebrew: "garden." Originally from Israel. *Gana, Ganice* (Hebrew)

GARI Teutonic: "spear" or "spear maiden." A feminine form of Gary.

GAURI (GAU-ree) Hindi: "yellow" or "fair." One of the many names for the Hindu goddess Shakti. Refers either to the yellow harvest or the yellowish gauri buffalo, both associated with the goddess. *Gari, Gouri* (Hindi)

GAVRILLA (gahv-REE-luh) A contemporary form of Gabriela which originally came to this country from Israel. See Gabriela for other forms.

GAYLE Old French: "joyful." Also a short form of Abigail ("my father is joyous"). *Gail, Gale, Gayel* (English)

GAZIT (ga-ZEET) Hebrew: "hewn stone." Originally from Israel.

GEELA (GEE-lah) Hebrew: "joy."

GELYA (GEL-yah) Russian form of Angela, "angel," or "one who brings good news."

GEMINI Greek: "twin." Name for a girl born under the sign of Gemini, ruled by Mercury and symbolized by the twins.

Gemina, Geminine, Mini (English)

GEN (jen) Japanese: "the origin," "source," or "spring."

GENEEN Contemporary form of Jeanine, "God is gracious." See Jean. *Ganeen, Ganine, Genine, Janeen, Janine, Jeneen* (English)

GENEVA Old French: "the juniper tree" or "from the mouth of the river," referring to the Swiss city Geneva. *Gena, Geneve, Genevia, Genna, Janeva, Janevra* (English)

GENEVIEVE Origin unclear, but said to be either Celtic or German, with the possible meanings "race" (referring to the human race) or "woman." Could also be linked to Jennifer, from Old German: "white phantom" or "white wave." *Gena, Genavieve, Geneva, Geneveeve, Genivieve, Genni, Gennie, Genny, Genovera, Genoveva, Gina, Janeva, Jenevieve, Jenni, Jennie, Jenny* (English)

GEORGIA Latin: "farmer." A feminine form of George. *Georgena, Georgene, Georgetta, Georgette, Georgi, Georgiana, Georgie, Georgina, Georgine, Georgy* (English); *Jirca, Jirina, Jirka* (Czech); *Georgette, Georgienne, Gigi* (French); *Georgina, Georgine* (German); *Gyorci, Gyorgyi* (Hungarian); *Gerda* (Latvian); *Georgina, Gina*

(Russian); *Georgina, Georginita, Gina, Jorgina* (Spanish)

GERALDINE Old German: "spear brave" or "spear strong." The feminine form of Gerald. *Geraldina, Geri, Gerri, Gerrie, Gerry, Jeri, Jerri, Jerry* (English); *Gerhardine* (German); *Giralda* (Italian); *Geraldina, Gerarda* (Spanish)

GERDA (GAIR-dah) Old Norse: "protection" or "enclosure." Also a Latvian form of Georgia and an Estonian form of Gertrude.

GERI Popular familiar form of Geraldine, often blended with other names, such as Anne, Erika, or Lynn to create new names. Examples: *Geralyn, GeriAnn, Geriann, Gerianna, Gerianne, Gericka, Gerika, Gerilyn, Gerilynn* (English)

GERMAINE Latin: "the German," which in turn comes from Celtic for "the shouter." Originally a French name, now used in many parts of the world. *Germain, Germana, Germane, Germayne, Jermain, Jermaine, Jermane, Jermayn, Jermayne* (English)

GESINA (gay-SEEN-ah) Hausa, Africa: "rice, wheat, or ears of corn." An African name signifying fertility and abundance.

GESSICA Italian form of Jessica, "wealthy." *Gesica*

What If Your Baby Grows Up Hating Her Name?

✶ ✶ ✶

When naming your baby, one fear may be that your child will grow up hating the name you chose. Relax. Psychological studies consistently show that happy, well-adjusted people who like themselves also tend to like their names, no matter what they are, even if it takes a while.

Gertrude, for example, is commonly disliked by many children. One writer named Ann Bayer confessed in *Seventeen* magazine that as a little girl she absolutely abhorred her middle name Gertrude: "When I confided it to anyone, the reaction was always the same: a screech of horror followed by giggles followed by a sympathetic glance and then a final

snort of amusement." But as this woman grew up and came to fully appreciate her own uniqueness, she also grew to like her middle name. She writes, "I can't say that I'm crazy about its original German meaning—"spear maiden"—but the name has a certain headstrongness, a kind of I'm-Gertrude-wanna-make-something-of-it quality that appeals to me. Whenever I write a story I always name the heroine Gertrude. It has become my hallmark, a code word for the part of me that's most unique."

It's generally best not to inflict a humorous name on a child. Calling twins Pete and Repeat might be amusing at first, but the joke soon grows stale. Likewise, rhyming names such as Mary Perry or Ronson Johnson may make a child the butt of jokes at school. Still, even an odd name won't necessarily cause a child to want to change it. Until his death in the 1950s, a Wisconsin man named Oofty Goofty Bowman (after a circus clown) insisted he always liked his name and never tried to conceal it by using initials.

Many children (especially teenage girls) go through a stage when they dislike their name, no matter what it is. Girls named Tia and Krishna want more ordinary names, while those called Sara and Emily wish their names were more exotic. Though parents sometimes worry when their daughter suddenly wants to change her name, psychologists say this may actually be a sign of healthy growth: The adolescent is developing a strong, unique personal identity and part of this evolving independence may involve considering a whole new name.

Once they get through their insecure teenage years most kids settle down and come to love the names they once detested. But for those who don't, it's fairly easy in most states to change one's name by simply going to court. About 50,000 Americans change their names each year. Why some people choose the new names they do, however, often remains a mystery. A clerk in the New York State Supreme Court tells of a Mr. Murphy who had grown weary of his name, which he found "too Irish and too common." So he petitioned the court to change his name—to Kelly!

GEVA (GAY-vah) Hebrew: "hill." Modern Israeli name; also a place-name in the Bible.

GIANNA (jee-AH-nah) Short form of Gioranna ("God is gracious"), popular in Italy. See Jane. *Gian, Giann, Giannetta, Giannina* (Italian)

GIBBY (GIB-ee, or Anglicized, JIB-ee) Hausa, Africa: "gap-toothed." In some parts of Africa, many women have a gap between their front teeth, which is called *sakaya yallah,* or "opening of God," and is understood as a sign of wisdom.

GIGI A cute, playful French nickname for Gabrielle, used in this country as an independent name. Also, name given as a French nickname for Georgia.

GILADA (gee-LAH-dah) Hebrew: "my joy is eternal" or "my hill is a witness." *Giladah* (Hebrew)

GILDA Old English: "covered with gold." Popularized world-wide in the 1980s by American actress and comedienne Gilda Radner. *Gilde, Gildie, Gildy* (English); *Gildi, Gildita* (Spanish)

GILLIAN (JILL-ee-an, some-times pronounced GILL-ee-an) Latin: "youthful and downy-haired." A form of Juliana. One of the most popular names in the Middle Ages, now making a comeback. *Gilian, Gill, Gillan,*

Gilli, Gillianne, Gillie, Gilly, Gillyanne, Jill, Jillian, Jilliann, Jillianne, Jillyan, Lian (English)

GILLY (GILL-ee) Mende, Africa: "stiff, rigid, and erect" or "quiet; silent."

GINA Japanese: "silvery." Also a short form of many longer Western names, including Regina ("queen"), Eugenia ("well-born" or "noble"), and Virginia ("maid-enly"). *Geena* (English)

GINGER Latin: "the ginger spice" or "the ginger flower." See Virginia.

GINNY Another short form of Virginia, "maidenly."

GIRISA (gee-REE-shah) Hindi: "mountain lord." One of the many Hindu names for the god Siva. Also used in India as a boys' name.

GISA (GEE-suh) Hebrew: "hewn stone"; or Teutonic: "gift." *Gissa, Giza, Gizza* (English, Hebrew)

GISELLE (jeh-SEL, or for a more French pronunciation, zhee-SEL) Old German: "a pledge" or "a hostage." *Gisela, Gisele, Gisella* (English); *Giza, Gizela* (Czech); *Gisele, Gisella* (French); *Gizi, Gizike, Gizus* (Hungarian); *Gisela* (Italian, Spanish); *Gizela* (Latvian)

GITA (GEE-tah) Yiddish: "good." Also a Slavic form of Margaret, "a pearl." See Margaret.

GITANA (gee-TAH-nah) Spanish: "gypsy."

GITTA Short form of the Norwegian Birgitta, "strength" or "protecting." See Bridget. *Gitte* (Norwegian)

GIZI (GEE-zee) Hungarian form of Giselle, "a pledge" or "a hostage." See Giselle.

GLADI (GLAH-dee) Hawaiian form of the flower name Gladys, "gladiolus."

GLADYS Latin: "a small sword" or "the gladiolus blossom." Because of its close association with the word "gladness," this name has a happy sound. *Glad, Gladis, Gleda* (English); *Gladi* (Hawaiian)

GLEDA (GLAY-dah) Icelandic: "make happy or glad."

GLENDA Welsh: "fair" or "holy and good."

GLENNA Irish Gaelic: "one who lives in the glen or valley." The feminine form of Glenn. *Glen, Glena, Gleneen, Glenesha, Glenice, Glenine, Glenisha, Glenn, Glenne, Glenneen, Glenni, Glennie, Glennine* (English)

Trait Names

✳ ✳ ✳

Some parents believe (perhaps subconsciously) that they can instill certain positive traits in a child by giving their baby a name like Grace, Hope, Prudence. The Puritans, of course, carried this practice to extremes by calling their babies such names as *Fear-Not, Search-the-Scriptures,* and *File Fornication.* This practice of giving a baby a name with "magical" powers was carried to an all-time high (or low, depending on your viewpoint) by a Rhode Island couple in the 1700s. The name they bestowed on their tiny son? *Through-Much-Tribulation-We-Enter-Into-The-Kingdom-Of-Heaven Clapp.* Reportedly, whenever the boy told anyone his full name, the person invariably replied, "Amen."

GLENNETTE (glen-NET) A trendy contemporary development from Glenna, "one who lives in the glen or valley." *Glen, Glenn, Glenette* (English)

GLORIA Latin: "glory." *Gloree, Glori, Gloriana, Gloriane, Glorianne, Glorie, Glorria, Glory* (English)

GLYNNIS Welsh: "holy, fair one." *Glenice, Glenis, Glenise, Glennice, Glennis, Glennys, Glenwys, Glenys, Glenyse, Glinnis, Glynis* (English)

GOLDA Old English: "golden-haired." Made a familiar name worldwide by twentieth-century Israeli Prime Minister Golda Meir. *Goldi, Goldia, Goldie, Goldina, Goldy* (English)

GOZY (GO-zee) Swahili: "skin."

GRACE Latin: "graceful" or "lovely." A virtue name regaining some popularity. *Grazielle* (French); *Gratia* (German); *Arete* (Greek); *Kaleki* (Hawaiian); *Gracia* (Hungarian); *Grazia, Graziella, Graziosa* (Italian); *Graca* (Portuguese); *Engracia, Gracia, Graciana, Graciela* (Spanish)

GREER Latin: "watchful." Once a nickname for Gregoria, now used independently. Brought into prominence as a girls' name by twentieth-century actress Greer Garson.

GRESSA (GRAY-sah) Norwegian: "grass." Nature name.

GRETA German and Austrian form of Margaret, "a pearl." Still associated internationally with legendary film star Greta Garbo. See Margaret. *Gretal, Gretchen, Grete, Gretel, Grethal, Grethel, Gretta, Grette, Gryta* (English, German)

GRETCHEN Another form of Margaret, "a pearl."

GUADALUPE (gwah-dah-LOO-pay) Spanish: "valley of the world." A very popular Hispanic name referring to the Virgin Mary. *Guada, Guadaloupa, Guadaloupe, Guadalupana, Guadalupi, Guadelupe, Guadolupa, Guadolupe, Lupe, Lupeta, Lupina, Lupita* (Spanish)

GUINEVERE Old Welsh: "white wave" or "white phantom." The extremely popular Jennifer was originally a variation of this name of King Arthur's queen. *Gaynor, Guener, Guenever, Guenievre, Guinever, Gweniver* (English)

GUNDA (GOON-dah) Old Norse: "warrior" or "battle maiden." Though seldom used in this country, this name is popular in Norway.

GURIT (goo-REET) Hebrew: "young animal," referring in

particular to the lion cub. In astrology the lion is symbol of the sign Leo. *Gurice* (Hebrew)

GWEN A short form of Gwendolyn used frequently nowadays as an independent name.

GWENDOLYN Old Welsh: "fair-browed" or "blessed ring." This romantic-sounding name was the original source of the name Wendy. *Gwen, Gwena, Gwenda, Gwendeth, Gwendi, Gwendolen, Gwendolin, Gwendoline, Gwendolyne, Gwendolynn, Gwenna, Gwinn, Gwyneth, Gwynn, Gwynne, Wenda, Wendie, Wendoline, Wendy* (English)

GYPSY Old English: "a gypsy" or "a wanderer." *Gipsy* (English); *Gitana* (Spanish)

H

HABIBAH (hah-BEE-bah) Arabic: "beloved." The feminine form of Habib. *Haviva* (Hebrew)

HADIYA (hah-DEE-yah) Swahili: "gift."

HAGIA (hah-GEE-uh) Hebrew: "joyful" or "festive." *Hagice, Hagit* (Hebrew)

HALEY (HAY-lee or HAL-ee) Irish Gaelic: "scientific" or "ingenious." *Hali, Halie, Halli, Hallie, Hally, Hayley, Haylie* (English)

HALONA (hah-LO-nah) Native American: "happy fortune."

HAMA Japanese: "shore." A variation is *Hamako* ("shore child").

HANA Japanese: "flower" or "blossom"; Arapaho: "sky" or "black cloud." Also a Czech and Polish form of Hannah, "graceful." *Hanae, Hanako* (Japanese)

HANIA (hah-NEE-uh) Hebrew: "resting place." Similar to the Israeli names Hanice and Hanit, which mean "spear." *Haniya, Haniyah* (English, Hebrew)

HANNA (HAHN-nah) Hausa, Africa: "prevented" or "forbidden"; or Arabic: "congratulations" or "to your health!" Also a short form of the Hebrew name Hannah.

HANNAH Hebrew: "graceful." A Hebrew form of Ann, this traditional Biblical name has dozens of variations throughout the world. See also Ann. *Hana, Hanna* (English); *Hana, Hanicka, Hanka* (Czech); *Hanni* (Finnish); *Hanna, Hanne, Hannele, Hanni* (German); *Anci, Aniko, Anna, Annuska, Nina, Ninacska, Nusi* (Hungarian); *Ona* (Lithuanian); *Hana, Hania, Hanka* (Polish)

African Order-of-Birth Names

✱ ✱ ✱

Order-of-birth names are common in many countries. In Africa, such names can become quite specific, as some of the following indicate:

Alaba: Yoruba, Nigeria: "second child born after twins."

Bojo: Bari, southern Sudan: "despiser of her twin," for a first-born female twin

Do: Ewe, Ghana: "first child after twins."

Dofi: Ewe, Ghana: "second child after twins."

Doto: Zaramo, Tanzania: "second of twins."

Kako: Bari, southern Sudan: "girl born after one daughter has died."

Kehinde: Yoruba, Nigeria: "second-born of twins"

Poni: Bari, southern Sudan: "second-born daughter."

Jwan: Bari, southern Sudan: "third-born daughter."

Pita: Bari, southern Sudan: "fourth-born daughter."

Sukoji: Bari, southern Sudan: "first-born daughter following a son."

Twia: Fante, Ghana: "born after twins."

HARA (HAHR-ah) Hindi: "seizer." Feminine form of the Hindu name Hari, one of the 1,008 names for the god Siva, the destroyer in the Hindu triad of gods.

HARMONY Latin: "harmonious one." In mythology, Harmonia was Aphrodite's daughter. *Harmonee, Harmoni, Harmonia, Harmonie* (English)

HARPER Old English: "harp player." A boys' name now also used for girls. First made widely known as a girls' name by *To Kill a Mockingbird* author Harper Lee.

HARRIET Old German: "ruler of the house or home." *Harriette, Harriott, Henrietta, Henriette, Hetti, Hettie, Hetty* (English); *Jindraska* (Czech); *Henriette* (French); *Henriete* (Latvian); *Henia, Henka, Henrieta* (Polish); *Enrieta* (Romanian); *Enriqueta, Enriquita, Kika, Kiki, Queta* (Spanish); *Arriet* (Swedish)

HARUKO (hah-roo-koh) Japanese: "born-in-spring child" or "tranquil." A time-of-birth name (see box, page 87). Variation: *Hayu,* "born in spring."

HASANA (hah-SAH-nah) Hausa, Africa: "first-born female twin." Among the Hausa people of Nigeria, this name is always given to a first-born female twin. The second born twin, if a girl, is called *Huseina,* and if a boy, *Husseini.*

HASIKA (hah-SEE-kah) Sanskrit: "laughter." A happy Hindu name from India.

HASINA (hah-SEE-nah) Swahili: "good"; or Hebrew: "strong."

HATEYA (hah-TEH-yah) Miwok *hate:* literally "to press with the foot." The connotation is "bear making tracks in the dust."

HAYA (hah-yah) Japanese: "nimble" or "quick."

HEATHER Middle English: "flowering heath," referring to the heather flower or shrub. The purple heather is considered symbolic of admiration and beauty in solitude, and the white blossom is said to protect one against danger. Popular contemporary flower name.

HEDDA Old German: "strife in battle." *Heda, Heddi, Hedi, Heddie, Heddy, Hedy* (English); *Hedvick, Hedvika* (Czech); *Hede* (German); *Eda* (Polish, Spanish)

HEDIA (hay-DEE-ah) Hebrew: "the voice (or echo) of God." *Hedya* (Hebrew)

HEDY Greek: "sweet" or "pleasant." Also a variation of Hedda. *Edilia* (Spanish)

HEIDI Old German: "noble and cheerful." Once a nickname for the German *Adelheid,* Heidi has become an independent name and is now often listed among the top one hundred most popular girls' names in the United States. *Heide, Heidie* (English)

HELEN Greek: "light" or "torch." This name became popular worldwide due to the fame of Helena, the subject of many legends and mother of Emperor Constantine. It was said that Helena discovered the true cross of Jesus and was the daughter of the British king known in the nursery rhyme as "Old King Cole." *Elaine, Elana, Elane, Elayne, Eleanor, Eleanora, Eleanore, Elena, Eleni, Elenora, Elenore, Elle, Ellen, Elli, Ellie, Elly, Ellyn, Ellynn, Elnora, Lana, Lena, Lenore, Leona, Leonora, Leonore, Leora, Liana, Liora, Nell, Nelli, Nellie, Nelly, Nora, Norah* (English); *Elena* (Bulgarian); *Alena, Elena, Elenka, Hela, Helena, Helenka, Heluska, Jelena, Lenka* (Czech); *Hele, Leena, Lenni* (Estonian); *Helli, Laina* (Finnish); *Elaine* (French); *Elli, Lena, Lene, Leni* (German); *Eleni, Elenitsa, Nitsa* (Greek); *Elenoa, Elenola, Elia, Elianora, Helena* (Hawaiian); *Ila, Ileana, Ilka, Ilona, Ilonka, Iluska, Lenci* (Hungarian); *Eleanora, Leonora* (Italian); *Ale, Aliute* (Lithuanian); *Eleonora* (Polish); *Elena, Elenuta* (Romanian); *Alena, Alenka, Elena, Halina, Lena, Lenka, Lili, Liolya, Nelya, Olena, Olenka, Yelena* (Russian); *Elaina, Elena, Elenita, Elenor, Eleonor, Eleonora, Ileanna, Ilena, Iliana, Lenora, Leonor, Leonora, Leni, Leontina* (Spanish); *Elen, Elin, Ellin* (Welsh)

HELGA Old German: "pious" or "religious." A favorite in Norway and Germany.

HELKI Miwok *hele:* "to touch." The more colorful connotation is "jacksnipe digging into the ground with its bill." The jacksnipe is said to come out of hiding only in winter. Also, a short form of Wilhelmina, "unwavering protector."

HENKA Polish form of Harriet, "ruler of the house or home." See Harriet for other variations.

HERMINA Czech form of Hermine, from the Greek, "child of the earth." Name for girls born under the earth signs of Capricorn, Taurus, and Virgo. *Herma, Mina* (English)

HERTHA Form of Eartha, "child of the earth." Hertha was the Teutonic goddess of fertility and peace.

HETA Hopi: "race after a rabbit hunt." This nickname is a corruption of the word *yeta,* the traditional race to the village after a rabbit hunt. Used by the rabbit clan of the Hopis.

HILDA German: "battle maiden." This is a source of many German names, including *Hildegarde* ("battle wind" or "battle fortess"), *Hildemar* ("battle celebrated"), and *Hildreth* ("battle counselor"). *Hilde, Hildi, Hildie, Hildy, Hylda* (English)

HILLARY Latin: "cheerful" or "happy." Once a boys' name, this name was popular for girls even before Hillary Clinton became First Lady. *Hilary* (English); *Hilaire* (French); *Hilaria, Ilaria* (Spanish)

HINDA (HIN-dah) Yiddish: "a deer." Hinda was one of Muhammad's wives.

HIRA (HIGH-rah or hee-RAH) Hausa: "chatty"; or Arabic: "a young palm shoot."

HIROKO (here-oh-koh) Japanese: "generous or magnanimous child."

HISA (hee-sah) Japanese: "long-lasting," with the connotation of longevity. *Hisae, Hisako, Hisayo* (Japanese)

HITI (HEE-tee) Banti Eskimo: "hyena." Such totemic names, symbolizing a person's close identification with an animal, have been common in many cultures.

HOA (hwah) Vietnamese: "flower" or "peace."

HOKU (HO-koo) Hawaiian: "star." Like most traditional Hawaiian names, this is used for both boys and girls.

HOLA (HO-lah) Hopi *mahola:* "seed-filled club," referring to the club used by dancers in Hopi religious ceremonies.

HOLLY Old English: "holy" or "holly tree." Traditionally, the holly is symbolic of foresight and defense and is the Eastern United States' flower of December. Often

"*Hilary, a happy-sounding name for a girl or boy, is one of 'the doubles' and so can be confusing. On seeing a reference to a Hilary in the news or as the signature to a letter to the Editor, one wonders about the sex of the person in question. But, either way, it is natural to visualize a sanguine and serene character.*"

—IVOR BROWN, *A CHARM OF NAMES*

Miwok Indian Seed Names

✦ ✦ ✦

Among the most expressive of all names in the world are those of the Miwok Indians of central California. Often the meanings of these names are incredibly complex and refer to an incident that occurred at the time of the baby's birth or at some time during the mother's or father's life. Since seeds were a principal source of food and material for making jewelry in Miwok tribes, Miwok names frequently mention seeds and, in doing so, reveal much about Indian life. Here are some of these seed names and their elaborate hidden meanings.

Helkimu: "hitting bushes with seed beater."

Howotmila: "running hand down the branch of a shrub to find seeds for beads" (from *howotu,* "beads").

Huatama: "mashing seeds in a mortar."

Kanatu: "making mashed seeds into a hard lump."

bestowed on a girl born during the Christmas season. *Holli, Hollie, Holley* (English)

HONG Vietnamese: "pink."

HOPE Old English: "a hope or expectation." A virtue name first popular with the Puritans, who often created combination names like Hope-Still and Hope-on-High. *Hopi, Hopie* (English); *Esperance* (French); *Esperanza* (Spanish)

HOSANA (hoh-ZAN-ah) Latin: "praise the Lord." *Osanna* (English)

HOSHI (ho-shee) Japanese: "star." A traditional Japanese name. *Hoshie, Hoshiko, Hoshiyo* (Japanese)

HUA (hwa) Chinese: "flower."

HUATA (hoo-AH-tah) Miwok: "carrying seeds in a burden basket."

HULDA Old German: "gracious" or "beloved"; or Hebrew: "weasel." Name of a Biblical prophetess. *Hildie, Huldi, Huldy* (English, German)

HUMITA (hoo-MEE-tah) Hopi: "shelled corn."

HUNTER Middle English: "a hunter." A strong-sounding name for girls, originally given only to boys.

HUSO (HOO-so) Ovimbundu, Africa: "the feigned sadness of a bride." The name is probably bestowed in Africa because the newborn baby's expression is thought to resemble that of a bride.

HUYANA (hoo-YAH-nah) Miwok: "rain falling."

I

IANTHA (ee-AHN-thah) Greek: "violet-colored flower."

IBBY (IB-bee) Bini, Africa: "like charcoal"; or Hausa, Africa: "the kola nut."

IDA (AY-dah) Old German: "industrious one"; or Old English: "happy and prosperous." A name used worldwide, not only here but in France, Germany, Hungary, Italy, Portugal, Russia, and many other countries. *Idaleene, Idalene, Idalia, Idalina, Idaline, Idella, Idelle* (English); *Iduska* (Czech); *Ide* (French); *Idette* (German); *Aida, Idalia* (Italian); *Itka* (Polish); *Ita* (Yiddish)

IKU (ee-koo) Japanese: "nourishing."

ILANA (ee-LAH-nah) Hebrew: "a tree." Especially popular in Israel. *Elana, Elanit, Ilanit* (English, Hebrew)

ILENE Variation of Eileen, which in turn is a form of Helen. *Ileen, Ileena, Ileene, Ilena* (English); *Ileana, Leana* (Spanish)

ILIA (eye-LEE-ah or ILL-ee-ah) Latin: "from Ilium (or Troy)." In Roman mythology, Ilia was the mother of Romulus and Remus. The same name was also used by Native Americans, but the Indian meaning has been lost.

ILIANA (ee-lee-AHN-ah) A pretty, Spanish form of Helen, "light" or "torch." *Liana* (English, Spanish)

ILISHA A contemporary American development of Alicia, originally from Alice, "truthful." *Alisha, Elisha, Ilise, Ilissa, Ilysha, Lisha* (English)

ILKA Slavic: "flattering" or "ambitious." Used in many Slavic countries. Also a form of Helen.

ILONA (EE-loh-nuh) Hungarian: "beauty." Also a Hungarian form of Helen, "light" or "torch." *Ili, Ilonka, Lonci*

ILSE (ILL-suh) German pet form of Elisabeth. *Ilsa*

IMA (EE-mah or EYE-mah) Japanese: "now." *Imako* (Japanese)

IMALA (EE-mah-lah) Native American: "disciplinarian."

IMAN (ih-MAHN) Arabic: "believer." Popularized by Iman, the exotic-looking international model.

IMMA (EEM-mah or EYE-mah) Akkadian: "one who pours water from a jug." Name for the constellation Aquarius, the water bearer.

INA (EYE-nah or EE-nah) Africa. Hausa: "a stutterer"; Efik: "a rendezvous or encampment"; Poto: "a dancer"; or Ngombe: "to sow or plant." A girls' name from Africa with a multitude of meanings. Also a short form of many names ending in *"-ina"*, such as Clementina, Edwina, and Wilhelmina.

INDIA Sanskrit: "river," or more specifically "from the region of the sacred river Indus." Country name now used for girls, possibly inspired by character India Wilkes in *Gone With the Wind. Inda, Indee* (English)

Naming Customs . . .

✳ ✳ ✳

Among Laplanders, whenever a child fell ill, his or her baptismal name was changed to outwit the disease. At every new illness, the child was rebaptized.

INDIGO Greek: "one from India," or "dark blue," referring to the lovely dark indigo blue once closely associated with India.

INDIRA (in-DEER-ah) Hindi: "splendid one," referring to Indra, the Hindu god of heaven and thunderstorms. Made known worldwide by Indian prime minister Indira Gandhi. *Indra, Indria* (Hindi)

INES (ee-NAYS, or Anglicized, eye-NEZ) Spanish form of Agnes, "pure." *Inesita, Inessa, Inez, Ynes, Ynesita, Ynez* (Spanish)

INESSA (ee-NES-sah) A Russian development of Ines.

INGRID Old Norse: "Ing's ride" or "hero's daughter." In Norse mythology, Ing (the god of the harvest, fertility, peace, and prosperity) took an annual ride on his golden boar, whose tusks tore up the earth so men and women could plant seeds. This is one of the most fashionable names in Norway and is used throughout Scandinavia. *Inga, Inge, Ingeberg, Ingeborg, Inger, Ingmar* (Scandinavian)

INOA (ee-NO-ah) Hawaiian: "name" or "name chant."

IRENE Greek: "peace." Eirene, the original version of this name, was the goddess of peace in Greek mythology. *Eirena, Eirene, Erena, Erene, Ireen, Iren, Irena, Iriana, Irin, Irina, Irine, Rene* (English); *Irenka, Irka* (Czech); *Eirene, Eirini, Ereni, Nitsa, Rena* (Greek); *Iren, Irenke* (Hungarian); *Eireen* (Irish); *Ira, Irisha, Irka, Irusya* (Latvian); *Irini* (Romanian); *Arina, Arinka, Ira, Irena, Irina, Irisha, Iryna, Jereni, Orina, Orya, Oryna, Rina, Yarina, Yaryna* (Russian); *Irenea* (Spanish); *Ailine* (Tongan)

IRISA (ee-REE-sah, often Anglicized, eye-REE-sah or eye-RIS-uh) Greek: "the iris flower." Originally a Russian form of the name Iris. In Western astrology the iris is the "herb" of the moon, which governs the sign of Cancer. In Japan the iris is the emblem of the warrior and the flower of May. A similar name is also found in Greek mythology, where Iris is the goddess of the rainbow and a messenger of the gods. *Iris, Irisha, Irissa, Risa, Risha, Rissa* (English)

IRMA Old German: "universal or whole." A German pet form of many names beginning with *Irm-*, such as *Irmine* or *Irmgard*. *Erma* (English, German)

ISA (EE-sah) This short form of Isabel is a favorite in Germany.

ISABEL Old Spanish: "dedicated to God." Stylish Spanish form of Elizabeth. Spelled *Izabella*, this name is used and recognized in many countries, including the Czech Republic, Hungary, Poland, and Russia. *Bella, Belle, Isa, Isabella, Isabelle, Issi, Issie, Issy* (English); *Belle, Isabeau* (French); *Isa* (German); *Bella, Izabel* (Hungarian); *Iza, Izabel* (Polish); *Bela, Bella, Izabela, Izabele* (Russian); *Iseabal, Isobel* (Scottish); *Belia, Belica, Belicia, Belita, Chabela, Chabi, Chava, Elisa, Isabelita, Liseta, Ysabel* (Spanish)

ISHANA (ish-AHN-ah) Sanskrit: "desirable." A pretty Hindu name from India. *Ishani* (Hindi)

ISHI (ee-shee) Japanese: "stone." *Ishie, Ishiko, Ishiyo* (Japanese)

ISTAS (EE-stahs) Native American: "snow."

ITALIA (ee-TAL-ya) Latin: "one from Italy."

ITUHA (ee-TOO-hah) Native American: "the strong, sturdy oak."

IUANA (ew-AH-nah) Native American: "blowing backward as the wind blows over the waters of a bubbling stream."

IVA (IH-vah, or anglicized, EYE-vah) Africa. Bini: "to promise" or "a proverb given as a hint in conversation," or Swahili: "ripened."

IVANA (ee-VAH-nah) Slavic form of Jane, "God is gracious," made widely known by socialite Ivana Trump. *Ivania, Ivanna, Ivannia, Ivanya, Vana* (English); *Ivanka* (Czech); *Ivanna* (Russian)

IVRIA (eev-REE-uh) Hebrew *ivri:* "from the other side (of the Euphrates River)" or "from Abraham's land." Ivri was the term originally used for the Jewish people in the Bible. *Ivriah, Ivrit* (Hebrew)

IVY Old English: "ivy vine." In classical Greek and Roman mythology, the ivy was considered sacred. *Iva, Ivie, Ivi* (English)

IZA (EE-sah) Modern Polish form of Louise, "famous warrior-maiden."

IZARA (ih-ZAR-ah) Hausa, Africa: "section of a tree."

IZUSA (ee-ZOO-sa) Native American: "white stone."

J

JACINTA (ha-SEEN-ta, or Anglicized, jah-SIN-tuh) Spanish: "hyacinth." *Jacinna, Jacinth, Jacyth* (Spanish)

JACLYN Contemporary form of Jacqueline, popularized by actress Jaclyn Smith.

JACQUELINE Hebrew: "the supplanter." A feminine form of Jacob. *Jacaline, Jacalyn, Jackalin, Jackalyn, Jacki, Jackie, Jacolyn, Jacquelyn, Jacqueta, Jacquetta, Jaclyn, Jaclynn, Jaculyn, Jaqueline* (English); *Jaquelina* (Spanish)

JADE Spanish: "the jade stone." In Burma and Tibet jade is considered a supernatural charm. When worn, the stone is said to strengthen weak hearts and divert lightning. When tossed into water, it causes mist, rain, and snow. And if poison is poured into a cup made of jade, legend has it the cup will crack. *Jayde* (English)

JAEL (ya-AIL) Hebrew: "wild she-goat" or "mountain goat." Originally from Israel where it's used for both girls and boys. Also a name for a child born under the sign of Capricorn, symbolized by the goat.

JAFIT (ya-FEET) Hebrew: "beautiful" or "lovely." *Jaffa, Jaffice* (Hebrew)

JALA (JAHL-ah) Africa. Mende: "large, fresh-water fish," or "lion," or "the small-leafed wild indigo"; Hausa: "glory to God;" and Arabic: "bright, polished, splendid." A common name in Africa with a multitude of meanings.

JAMIE, JAIME Hebrew: "the supplanter." A feminine form of James. *Jaimi, Jaimie, Jaimy, Jamee, Jamey, Jami, Jayme, Jaymee, Jaymi, Jaymie* (English)

JAMIE LEE Hebrew, English: "the supplanter" + "who lives in the meadow." A compound name like Mary Ann or Sue Ellen that has become recently popular, possibly due to its association with actress Jamie Lee Curtis. *Jamielee* (English)

JAMIELEE Hebrew, English: "the supplanter" + "who lives in the meadow." Contemporary name created from Jamie + Lee. *Jaimelee* (English)

JAMILA (jah-MEE-lah) Arabic: "beautiful." A favorite Moslem name. The Prophet Mohammad taught that ugly names should be changed; hence he renamed a girl

called Asiyah (or "rebel") Jamila. *Jameela, Jameelah, Jamilah, Jamillah, Jamillia* (English, Arabic)

JANAE (ja-NAY or zha-NAY) Exotic contemporary form of Jane ("God is gracious"), patterned to sound like Renée. *Janay* (English)

JANE Hebrew: "God is gracious." This feminine form of John has literally hundreds of variations throughout the world. *Jan, Jana, Janae, Janean, Janeen, Janel, Janela, Janella, Janelle, Janessa, Janet, Janeta, Janetta, Janette, Janey, Janice, Janie, Janina, Janine, Janis, Janna, Jannelle, Jany, Jayne, Jaynell, Jayney, Jayni, Jaynie, Jean, Jeanette, Jeani, Jeanie, Jeanne, Jeanette, Jeanine, Jenni, Jennie, Jenny, Jess, Jessi, Jessie, Jessy, Jinni, Jinnie, Jinny, Joan, Joana, Joanna, Joanne, Joeann, Johanna, Joni, Jonie, Jony* (English); *Ohanna* (Armenian); *Jone, Yoana* (Basque); *Joana* (Brazilian); *Jana, Janica, Janka, Jenka, Johanka, Johanna* (Czech); *Jensine, Johanna* (Danish); *Janne* (Finnish); *Johanna, Jutta* (German); *Ioanna* (Greek); *Janka, Zsanett* (Hungarian); *Sheena, Shena, Sinéad* (Irish); *Gian, Giann, Gianna, Giannetta, Giannina, Giovanna* (Italian); *Zanna* (Latvian); *Jama, Janina, Jasia, Joanka, Joanna, Joasta, Zannz* (Polish); *Jenica* (Romanian);

Ioanna, Ivanna (Russian); *Seonaid* (Scottish); *Iva, Ivana, Ivanka* (Slavic); *Juana, Juanita, Nita* (Spanish); *Seini* (Tongan)

> **❝ '*It's giving girls names like that,' said Buggins, 'that nine times out of ten makes 'em go wrong. It unsettles 'em. If ever I was to have a girl, if ever I was to have a dozen girls, I'd call 'em all Jane.'* ❞**
>
> —H. G. WELLS, REFERRING TO THE NAME EUPHEMIA

JANESSA A contemporary blend of Jane ("God is gracious") + Vanessa ("butterflies"). This newly created name is bestowed not so much for its underlying meaning, but simply because the parents like it. *Janess, Jannessa, Janissa* (English)

JANNA (JAHN-nah) Arabic: "harvest," "plucked fruits," or "a small plant."

JARDENA (yar-DEH-nah) Hebrew: "to flow downward." A feminine form of Jordan from Israel.

JARITA (ja-REE-ta) Arabic: "an earthen water jug." In Hindu legend, Jarita was a mother bird who risked her own life to save her four sons in a burning forest and, as a result, became human.

JASMINE Persian: "the jasmine blossom." The jasmine is considered symbolic of amiability and sweetness. *Jasmin, Jasmina, Jazmin, Jessamine, Jessamyn, Jessi, Jessie, Jessy* (English); *Yasiman, Yasmine* (Hindu); *Jazmin, Jazmina, Yasmin, Yasmina* (Spanish)

JAYLENE (jay-LEEN) Contemporary American invention, probably from Jay ("a jay bird" or "chatterer") plus the feminine ending *-ene*. *Jaylee, Jaylen, Jaylin, Jayline, Jaylyn, Jaylynn* (English)

JAYNE (jay-neh or jane) Sanskrit: "victorious." Also a variant spelling of Jane. *Jaya, Jayna* (Sanskrit)

JEAN French: "God is gracious." A Scottish form of Jane or Joan now used in many parts of the world. See Jane. *Jeane, Jeanette,*

Jeanie, Jeanine, Jeanette, Jean-nette, Jennica, Jennine (English); *Janne* (Finnish); *Jeanne* (French); *Kini* (Hawaiian); *Janka, Johanna* (German, Hungarian); *Giovanna, Giovanni* (Italian); *Jana* (Latvian); *Janina, Janka, Janeska, Jasia, Jena, Nina* (Polish); *Ivana* (Slavic)

JELENA (yay-LAY-nah or juh-LAY-nuh) Russian form of Helen, "light" or "torch." See Helen.

JEMINA (jay-MEE-nuh) Hebrew: "right-handed." *Jem, Jemi, Jemma, Jemmi, Jemmie, Jemmy* (English)

JENA (jay-nah) Sanskrit: "patience." A popular name in India.

JENESSA (jeh-NES-sah) Contemporary American creation from Jen, or Jennifer ("white phantom" or "white wave") plus the popular feminine ending *-essa.*

JENICA (zhye-NEE-kah, or Anglicized, jeh-NEE-kah) Contemporary Romanian form of Jane.

JENA, JENNA (JEN-ah) Mende, Africa: "a small bird." Also a contemporary variation of Jennifer, often used to create new names. Examples are: *Jennabel, Jennalee, Jennalyn, Jennanne, Jennarae*

JENNIFER Old Welsh: "white phantom" or "white wave." One of the most popular names in the United States. *Genn, Gennifer, Genny, Ginnifer, Ginny, Jen, Jenifer, Jeniffer, Jenn, Jenni, Jennie, Jenny, Jeny* (English)

JESSICA Hebrew: "wealthy." *Jessalyn, Jessi, Jessica, Jessie, Jesslyn* (English); *Janka* (Hungarian); *Gessica* (Italian)

JESSIE Once a pet form of Jessica, now used as an independent name. In Scotland this is a pet form of Janet. *Jess, Jessey, Jessi, Jessy* (English)

JETTA (JET-tah) Congo, Africa: "encircled" or "surrounded." A child surrounded by love. *Jette* (Congo)

JILLIAN Latin: "innocent, downy-haired one." *Gilli, Gillian, Gillie, Jill, Jilliana, Jillie* (English)

JIN Japanese: "super-excellent." This unusual name is seldom bestowed in Japan, possibly because it was once believed that a child who receives too demanding a name will never live up to it.

JINA (JEE-nah) Swahili: "name."

JOANA A form of Jane, "God is gracious." This form is especially popular in Brazil. See Jane. *Joan, Joanie, Joann, Joanna, Joanne, Johanna, Johannah, Joeanna, Joeanne* (English)

JOBY Hebrew: "afflicted" or "persecuted." Originally a nickname for Jobina, but now used more often as an independent name. *Jobi, Jobie* (English)

JODI Hebrew: "praised." A cheerful pet form of Judith that has now gained status as an independent name. *Jodie, Jody* (English)

JOELLA (joh-EL-ah or, for a more French pronunciation, zhoh-EL-lah) Hebrew: "the Lord is willing." The feminine form of Joel. Also popular in Israel. *Joela, Joelle, Joellen, Joellyn* (English); *Joelle* (French)

JOLA (JOE-lah) Mende, Africa: "very tall."

JOLAN (YO-lawn or jo-LAN) Greek: "violet blossom." Hungarian form of Yolanda. See Yolanda for other forms.

JOLINE Hebrew: "she will increase." As a contemporary feminine form of Joseph, this name has become more frequently used than the older Josephine. *Joleen, Jolene* (English)

JONINA (yo-NEE-na or jo-NEE-na) Hebrew: "dove," referring to the dove of peace. *Jona, Jonati, Jonit, Yona, Yonit, Yonita* (English, Hebrew)

JORA (JOR-ah) Hebrew: "autumn rain." Name for a girl born under the autumnal water sign, Scorpio. *Joran* (English, Hebrew)

JORDAN Hebrew: "to flow downward," referring to the Jordan River where John the Baptist baptized Christ. Formerly a boys' name, now becoming a favorite for girls. *Jordann, Jordanne, Jordyn* (English); *Jordane* (French); *Jardena* (Hebrew); *Jordana* (Spanish)

JORDANE (zhor-DANE) This French form of Jordan is also gaining popularity in the United States.

JOYITA (hoh-YEE-tah, or Anglicized, joy-EE-tah) Spanish: "an inexpensive but beautiful jewel." *Joy, Joya* (English, Spanish)

JUANITA (wah-NEE-tah) Spanish form of Jane, "God is gracious." See Jane. *Wanika, Wanita* (Hawaiian); *Juana, Nita* (Spanish)

JUDITH Hebrew: "of Judah" or "praised one." *Jodi, Jodie, Jody, Judi, Judie, Judy* (English); *Judita* (Bulgarian); *Jitka* (Czech); *Judithe* (French); *Ioudith* (Greek); *Jodi* (Hebrew); *Juci, Jucika, Judit, Jutka* (Hungarian); *Giulia* (Italian); *Judite* (Latvian, Portuguese); *Judita* (Lithuanian); *Judit* (Norwegian, Swedish); *Yudif, Yudita* (Russian)

JULIA Latin: "youthful." A truly international name, Julia is familiar not only in this country but also in most of Central America, Mexico, Norway, Poland, Portugal, Spain, and Sweden. See Gillian. *Gillie, Juli, Juliana, Julianna, Julie, Juliet, Julietta, Julina, Juline, Julissa* (English); *Jula, Julca, Juliana, Juliska, Julka* (Czech); *Juliane, Juliette* (French); *Juli, Julianna, Julinka, Juliska* (Hungarian); *Sile* (Irish); *Jula, Julcia* (Polish); *Iulia* (Romanian); *Yulinka, Yuliya, Yulka, Yulya* (Russian); *Sileas* (Scottish); *Jula, Juliana, Yula* (Serbian); *Juliaca, Juliana, Julieta, Julita* (Spanish)

JULIE Form of Julia used in many countries, including France and Germany as well as the United States.

JUN (joon) Chinese: "truth"; or Japanese: "obedient."

JUNE Latin: "born in June." A time-of-birth name, once quite fashionable much as April currently is.

JUNELLA A contemporary combination of June + Ellen, with the meaning "born in June." Name for a girl born under the sign of Gemini, the twins, or Cancer, the crab.

JUSTINE Latin: "just or upright." A French feminine form of Justin, this is a contemporary form of the older name Justina. St. Justina, a Christian of Antioch, was martyred on September 26 in the year A.D. 304. It is said that although she was "shockingly tortured," her faith never wavered. *Justeen, Justina, Justyne* (English); *Jestine, Jestina* (Welsh)

K

KACHINA (kah-CHEE-nah) Native American: "sacred dancer."

KADY (KAY-dee) Contemporary form of Katy ("pure") or as a variation of Cady ("battle"). *Kadee, Kadi, Kadia, Kadiane, Kadianne, Kadie, Kadienne* (English)

KAGAMI (kah-gah-mee) Japanese: "mirror," in the sense of clear and pure reflections.

KAI (kigh) Hawaiian: "sea" or "seawater."

KAIKO (kah-ee-koh) Japanese: "forgiveness child." The shorter form of this name—*Kai*—means simply "forgiveness."

KAILA (kigh-EE-lah) Hebrew: "crowned with laurel." Originally from Israel.

KAITLIN (KAYT-lin) Stylish variation of Caitlin, an Irish form

of Catherine, meaning "pure."
Kaiti, Kaitlan, Kaitleen, Kaitlen,
Kaitlin, Kaitlinn, Kaitlyn,
Kaitlynn, Kaity, Katelyn, Katlin
(English)

KALA (KAH-lah) Hindi: "black"
or "time." One of the 1,008 names
for the Hindu god Siva. Also a
Hawaiian form of Sara, "princess"
or "one who laughs."

KALAMA (kah-LAH-mah)
Hawaiian: "the flaming torch."
The name of the wife of
Kamehameha III, who ruled
Hawaii from 1837 to 1847.

KALANI (kah-LAH-nee)
Hawaiian: "chieftain from the
sky," implying a child is highborn
or noble and spiritual. *Lani*
(Hawaiian)

KALANIT (ka-la-NEET)
Hebrew: "the brightly colored
kalanit blossom," referring to a
flower common in the
countryside of Israel.

KALEA (kah-LEH-ah) Hawaiian
form of Claire, "brilliant" or
"illustrious."

KALEKI (kuh-LEH-kee)
Hawaiian form of Grace,
"graceful" or "lovely."

KALENA (kah-LEH-nah)
Hawaiian form of Karen, "pure."

KALERE (kah-LAY-rah) African:
"small woman." First used in the

Niger Delta, this name predicts
the baby will grow to be short in
height.

KALI (ka-LEE or KAH-lee) Hindi:
"black goddess" or "time, the
destroyer." One of the many
names for the Hindu mother
goddess Shakti. As a girls' name in
India, Kali is often equated with
its gentler meaning: "bud," or
"unblossomed maiden."

KALIFA (kah-LEE-fah) Somali:
"chaste, holy one."

KALILA (kah-LEE-lah) Arabic:
"girlfriend" or "sweetheart." A
term of endearment in Arabic
countries. *Kaleela, Kalilah,*
Kalilla, Kaylee, Kaylil (English)

KALINA (kah-LEE-nah)
Hawaiian form of Karen, "pure."
Kaleena, Leena, Lina (English)

KALINDA (kah-leen-dah, or
Anglicized, ka-LIN-dah) Hindi:
"the sun." Hindu nature name
borrowed from the mythical
Kalinda Mountains, from which
the sacred river Jumna, or Jamna,
flows. *Kaleenda* (Hindi)

KALINDI (ka-leen-dee, or
Anglicized, kah-LIN-dee) Hindi:
"the Jumna River," one of the
seven sacred rivers in India.
While in ancient times nature
names were considered lowly
in India, today many Hindu
girls are named after rivers and
flowers.

Should Your Children's Names Complement Each Other?

★ ★ ★

There are no rules about naming brothers and sisters. If you want to choose a trendy name like Brianna for a girl and then, several years later, give her baby brother a Biblical name like Joshua, it's perfectly okay. If, however, you'd like all your children's names to "go together" so they sound related, here are several ways to find a good match.

◆ Consider choosing all your children's names from the same background. The Biblical names Jacob, Rachel, and Sara all sound related, as do Caitlin, Rory, and Sean (all Irish). Ariana, Jose, and Tamika don't sound at all related. On the other hand, naming your children different names may give family meals a wonderful feeling of diversity, like a United Nations meeting.

◆ Rather than choosing names with the same initial letter, consider going with similar endings. Names like Caryn, Dustin, and Kevin sound alike — yet also quite different.

◆ Avoid rhyming names like Lacey, Stacy, and Tracey. Although it may sound cute at first, over the years you'll get tired of hearing people ask, "You mean like Donald Duck's nephews Huey, Dewey, and Louie?"

◆ Another intriguing technique is to give children distinctly different first names along with middle names that match. The parents of twin girls who were born healthy after a rare utero surgery felt their prayers had been answered, and called their daughters Sarah Faith and Jessica Hope. By doing so, they've given their twins a chance to be seen as individuals in school, yet they've also given them a beautiful "hidden" connection, rather like a family secret.

KALISKA (kah-LEE-skah) Miwok: "coyote chasing deer." According to one Miwok legend, the coyote created the world and all the animals and then held a conference on how he should build man. Each animal wanted man to be like him. The lion wanted him to have a loud roar, the bear wanted him to be silent and strong, and the beaver insisted he have a flat tail. But the coyote said he could think of something better than any one of these qualities, and that night while everyone slept, he stole the best ideas he had heard that day and created humans.

KALLI (KAH-lee, or Anglicized, KAY-lee) Greek: "lark." Once a nickname for Calandra, now used as an independent name. Another possible Greek meaning is: "beautiful blossom." *Cal, Calli, Callie, Kal, Kalle, Kallie, Kally* (English)

KALOLA (KAH-loh-luh, or Anglicized, kah-LOH-lah) Hawaiian for Carol, "strong and womanly."

KALUWA (kah-LOO-wah) Usenga, Africa: "the forgotten one." The Usengas believe that spirits who can never be reincarnated because their names have been forgotten are wandering the earth, working evil. To appease these demons, children are sometimes given this name.

KALYCA (kah-LEE-kah) Greek: "rosebud." *Kali, Kalica, Kalie, Kalika, Kaly* (English)

KAMA (KAH-mah) Hawaiian form of Thelma: "the nursling"; also Hindi: "love." According to mythology, the Hindu god Kama rides a parrot and shoots flower-tipped love arrows from a sugar-cane bow with a bowstring of bees.

KAMALI (KAH-mah-lee or kah-MAH-lee) Mashona, southern Rhodesia: "spirit." Kamali is a spirit believed to protect new-born babies when there is an illness in the village.

KAMARIA (kah-mah-REE-ah) Swahili: "like the moon."

KAMATA (kah-MAH-tah) Miwok: "throwing gambling bones on the ground in a hand game." This name reveals an unusual pastime among Miwok women.

KAMEA (kah-MAY-ah) Hawaiian: "the one," implying "my one and only." *Kameo* (Hawaiian)

KAMEKE (kah-MAY-ke) Umbundu, Africa *omeke:* "a blind person." Name given in Africa to a baby with small, squinty eyes.

KAMEKO (kah-may-koh) Japanese: "tortoise child," indicating a hope for longevity. A varation is *Kameyo,* "generations of the tortoise."

KAMERON Scottish Gaelic: "one with a wry or crooked nose." A spelling variation of the Scottish clan name Cameron, originally used for boys but now becoming popular for girls. *Kamren, Kamrin, Kamron, Kamryn* (English)

KAMI (kah-mee) Japanese: "lord." *Kamiko* (Japanese)

KAMMILE (kah-MEEL) Arabic: "perfect one." Also a contempory American spelling of Camille, "a young attendant at a ceremony." *Kameel, Kamil, Kamila, Kamilla, Kamillah* (Arabic)

KANA (kah-nah) Japanese: "a character in the alphabet."

KANANI (kuh-NAH-nee) Hawaiian: "the beauty." *Ani, Nani* (Hawaiian)

KANDACE Contemporary American variation of Candice, "glowing white" or "brightly white." *Kandee, Kandi, Kandice, Kandis, Kandiss, Kandy* (English)

KANE (KAH-nee) Japanese *kaneru:* "the doubly accomplished." *Kaneru* literally means "to do two things at once." In Japanese, the same sound is also used for a character which means "bronze."

KANENE (kah-NAY-ne) Umbundu, Africa: "a little thing in the eye is big." Popular proverb name. For more on proverb names, see page 77.

KANI (KAH-nee) Hawaiian: "sound." Also a Hawaiian form of Connie, "firm, constant."

KANIKA (kah-NEE-kah) Mwera, Kenya: "black cloth."

KANOA (kah-NO-ah) Polynesian: "the free one." Originally from Hawaii.

KANYA (KAHN-ya) Hindi: "virgin." Hindu name for a child born under the astrological sign of Virgo. Kanya is also another name for the goddess Shakti.

KAPUA (kah-POO-ah) Hawaiian: "blossom."

KAPUKI (kah-POO-kee) Bari, southern Sudan: "first-born daughter." Popular among the Bari living on the banks of the Upper Nile.

KARA A short form of Katherine ("pure"). Also see Cara.

KAREN Greek *katharos:* "pure." Originally a form of Katherine. Common in Russia as well as the United States. *Caren, Carin, Caron, Caryn, Kari, Karon, Karyn* (English); *Kaarina* (Finnish); *Kalena, Kalina* (Hawaiian); *Karina* (Latvian); *Karina, Karine, Karyna* (Russian); *Karin* (Swedish)

KARI Contemporary form of Caroline, "little womanly one." *Karee, Karey, Karie, Karrie, Karry, Kary* (English)

KARIDA (kah-REE-dah) Arabic: "untouched or virginal."

> **"There is everything in a name. A rose by any other name would smell as sweet, but would not cost half as much during the winter months."**
>
> —GEORGE ADE, AMERICAN AUTHOR AND DRAMATIST

KARIMA (kah-REE-mah) Arabic: "generous, friendly, precious, and distinguished," often interpreted as simply "generous." The feminine form of Kareem. *Kareema, Karimah* (English)

KARINA (kah-REE-nah) Contemporary diminutive of Katherine, "pure." *Kareen,*

Kareena, Karinah, Karine, Karinna, Karinne (English)

KARISSA Latin: "dear one." Variation of the older name Carissa. Some creative parents may also have created this name by combining the popular prefix *Ka-* with the well-known Melissa. *Karessa, Karisa, Karise, Karisha, Karyssa* (English)

KARLA Czech, English and German development of Charlotte. Interestingly, the same name was borne by an Australian Aborigine man and meant "fire." The Aboriginal tribe with whom this man lived had such a taboo against speaking a dead person's name that when Karla died, his name was extinguished from the language and a new word for fire was introduced. See Charlotte.

KARMA Hindi: "action." Karma embodies the Hindu principle that all one's actions morally affect this or a future life. Hence this name can also be interpreted as "fate" or "destiny."

KARMEL Hebrew: "vineyard," "garden," or "farm." Originally from Israel. *Carmel, Carmeli, Carmi, Carmia, Carmiel, Karmeli, Karmi, Karmia, Karmiel* (English)

KARMEN A Spanish variation of Carmen, "crimson" or "a song." See Carmen.

KAROL Contemporary variation of Carol, "strong and womanly." See Carol.

KAROLINA (kar-oh-LEEN-ah) Hungarian and Russian development of Caroline, "little womanly one." See Caroline.

KASA (KAH-shah) Hopi *patsip-qasa:* "fur-robe dress," a type of lizard with a tough hide. From the Hopi Indian earth cult. *Kahsha, Kasha* (English)

KASEY Stylish contemporary spelling of Casey, "brave and vigilant." *Kacey, Kaci, Kacie, Kacy, Kasi, Kasie, Kaycee, Kayci, Kaycie* (English)

KASI (KAH-shee) Hindi: "from the holy city." A popular name among the Hindus of Madras, Kasi is the colloquial name for Banaras, one of the seven holy Hindu cities. The city was once the capital for the Kasi tribe.

KASINDA (kah-SEEN-dah, or Anglicized, ka-SIN-dah) Umbundu, Africa *osinda:* "the earth that blocks the passage behind a burrowing animal." Used by the Ovimbundu of Africa for a child born into a family that already has twins.

KASSANDRA Greek: "helper of men." A variant spelling of Cassandra. *Kasaundra, Kasondra, Kass, Kassi, Kassie, Kassondra, Kassy, Sandra, Saundra, Sondra* (English)

KASSIA Modern Polish form of Katherine, "pure." See Katherine.

KASSIDY Stylish contemporary spelling of Cassidy, "ingenious and clever" or "curly-haired." See Cassidy.

KATA (ka-tah) Japanese: "worthy one."

KATE Popular pet form of Katherine now used as an independent name. See Katherine for nearly one hundred other forms of this globally popular

Important to Know . . .

✱ ✱ ✱

If you have a girl, how much she likes her name may depend on her age. One study found that in elementary school, girls tend to like short names like Chris or Kate. But during adolescence, they shift their preferences toward longer, "trendier" names like Nicolette, Sigourney, and Alexandra.

name. *Kati, Katie, Katy* (English); *Keti* (Tongan)

KATEKE (ka-TAY-ke) Umbundu, Africa: from the Ovimbundu proverb "Kateke tueya tua lia palonga; kaliye kalo peya oku lila povinlindo," meaning "The days we came, we ate out of dishes; now it comes to eating out of wooden bowls." Loosely translated: "We have stayed too long and worn out our welcome."

KATELYN Fashionable contemporary spelling of Caitlin, an Irish form of Catherine ("pure"). Now found on many "top 100" lists.

KATHERINE, KATHRYN Greek *katharos:* "pure." With its many variations, this has been one of the most popular names in the world since the fourteenth century. *Caitlon, Caitrin, Cari, Cass, Cassi, Cassie, Cassy, Casy, Catarina, Caterina, Catharina, Cathe, Catheline, Catherine, Cathi, Cathie, Cathleen, Cathy, Cayla, Kara, Kate, Katee, Kathi, Kathie, Kathleen, Kathryn, Kathy, Kati, Katie, Katy, Kay, Kayce, Kayla, Kit, Kitti, Kittie, Kitty* (English); *Kata, Katarina, Katerina, Katica, Katka, Katuska* (Czech); *Katharina, Kati, Rina* (Estonian); *Kaisa, Katri, Katrina* (Finnish); *Catant, Catherine, Trinette* (French); *Katchen, Katharina, Kathe, Katrina, Trina, Trinchen, Trine*

(German); *Kata, Katalin, Kati, Katica, Katika, Kato, Katoka, Katus* (Hungarian); *Katrin* (Icelandic); *Caitlin, Caitria* (Irish); *Caterina, Cathe* (Italian); *Kofryna* (Lithuanian); *Karena, Karin, Katla* (Norwegian); *Kasia, Kasienka, Kasin, Kaska, Kassia* (Polish); *Catarina* (Portuguese); *Ekaterina, Katenka, Katerinka, Katinka, Katka, Katryna, Katya, Ketya, Kisa, Kiska, Kitti, Kotinka* (Russian); *Catalina* (Spanish); *Katsa, Kolina* (Swedish); *Catrin* (Welsh)

KATHLEE A contemporary blend of Katherine ("pure") + Lee ("poetic child" or "one who lives in the pasture meadow").

KATHLEEN A popular variation of Katherine, "pure." *Cathleen* (English). See Katherine.

KATHY Originally a nickname for Katherine ("pure"), but now used as a given name. For many variations on this favorite old name, see Katherine.

KATIE Fashionable short form of Katherine ("pure") now frequently used as an independent name. *Kate, Katee, Kati, Katy* (English)

KATSU (KAH-tsoo) Japanese: "victorious." Variation: *Katsuko*, "victorious child."

KATURA (KAH-too-rah) Babudja, southern Rhodesia, *ku*

tura: "I feel better now," referring to the words a mother may speak after giving birth. Literally, the name means "to take a load from one's mind."

KATYA (KAHT-ya) Russian pet form of Katherine, "pure."

KAULA (KOW-luh) Hawaiian: "a prophet."

KAULANA (kah-oo-LAH-nah, or Anglicized, kow-LAH-nuh) Hawaiian: "famous one."

KAVERI (kah-VAIR-ee) Hindi: "the sacred Kaveri River." The seven sacred rivers play an important role in Hindu ceremonies, and it is believed that bathing in these rivers, particularly in the Ganges, washes away one's most evil sins. In ancient times a man of high caste was forbidden to marry a girl with a nature name because her name indicated she was inferior. Today, however, many girls are given such names.

KAVINDRA (ka-VEEN-drah) Hindi: "mighty poet." Often used in India as a name element to create other names.

KAWENA (kuh-WEH-nuh) Hawaiian: "the glow" or "glowing," referring to the glow of a fire, the sunrise, or the sunset. A favorite in Hawaii.

KAY Scandinavian, English: "one who keeps the keys." Also a pet form of many names beginning with *K*, particularly Katherine, "pure." *Kaye, Kayla, Kaylee, Kaylin* (English)

KAYA (KAH-yah) Hopi *kakahoya:* "my elder little sister," implying that while the baby is small she is still wise; or Japanese: "a rush" or "a yew."

KAYLA A currently trendy American form of Kay or Katherine, "pure."

KAYLEE A modern creation, probably a blend of Kay + Lee. *Kailee, Kailey, Kayley, Kayly* (English)

KAYLYN Another contemporary creation, blending Kay ("pure") + Lynn ("waterfall" or "pool below a waterfall"). Therefore, the pretty connotation is one of pure, splashing water. *Kailin, Kaylin, Kaylynn* (English)

KAZUKO (kah-zoo-koh) Japanese: "first child" or "obedient child." Variation: *Kazu,* "first" or "obedient."

KEAHI (keh-AH-hee) Hawaiian: "the fire."

KEALA (keh-AH-luh) Hawaiian: "the fragrance."

KEELIN (KEE-lin) Irish Gaelic: "slender-fair." The name of an Irish saint. *Caolinn* (Irish)

KEELY Irish Gaelic: "beautiful."

KEI (kay or keh-ee) Japanese: "rapture" or "reverence." A favorite in Japan, where a common variation is *Keiko*, "joyous child" or "child of rapture."

KEIKI (ke-EE-kee or KAY-kee) Hawaiian: "child."

KEISHA (KEE-shah or KAY-shah) Fashionable American name, the origin of which is unclear. May be a version of the African Keshia ("favorite one"). See Lakeisha.

KEKONA (keh-KO-nuh) Hawaiian: "second-born child."

KELDA Old Norse: "fountain" or "spring." Used in Scandinavia as well as this country. *Keli, Kelie, Kelli, Kellie, Kelley, Kelly*

KELILA (keh-LEE-lah) Hebrew: "crown" or "laurel," a symbol of victory and beauty. A favorite in Israel. *Kaile, Kayle, Kelilah, Kelula, Kyla, Kyle* (Yiddish)

KELLEN A recently developed and currently trendy variation of Kelly or Ellen, bestowed on both girls and boys.

KELLY Irish Gaelic: "warrior." Originally a boys' name, now commonly used for girls. Also a pet form of Kelda. *Keli, Kelia, Kellen, Kelley, Kelli, Kellia, Kellie, Kellina, Kelisa* (English)

KELSEY Old English: "victory ship" or "from Ceal's Island (the high island in the marsh)"; or Irish Gaelic: "warrior." Also used for boys. *Kelci, Kelcie, Kelsi, Kelsie, Kelsy* (English)

KENDA Modern American creation, "child of clear, cool water." Also a name for a girl born under one of the water signs of Cancer, Scorpio, or Pisces. *Kendi, Kendie, Kendy, Kennda, Kenndi, Kenndie, Kenndy* (English)

KENDALL Old English: "from the bright or clear-river valley." Originally a boys' name now more popular for girls. *Kendal, Kendahl, Kendyl, Kyndal* (English)

KENDRA Old English: "knowledgeable." Rapidly gaining popularity, possibly because it sounds strong yet slightly exotic.

KENISHA (keh-NEE-shah) A contemporary blend of Ken + Aisha and literally means "a beautiful life."

KERANI (ke-RAH-nee) Sanskrit: "sacred bells." Popular among the Todas of India. *Kera, Keri, Kerie, Kery, Rani* (English)

KERRY Irish Gaelic: "dark one." Originally a place-name for a county in Ireland. Once a boys' name, now more common for girls. *Keree, Keri, Kerie, Kerrey, Kerri, Kerrie* (English)

KERRY-ANN Irish Gaelic,
Hebrew: "dark, graceful one."
Popular since the 1960s. *Kerri-Ann, Kerrianne, Kerryann, Kerry-Anne* (English)

KESAVA (ke-SAH-vah) Hindi:
"having much (or fine) hair."
Another name for the Hindu
god Vishnu, also known as
Krishna.

KESHIA (keh-SHE-ah) Africa:
"favorite one." Popular contemporary American name. Made
famous by child actress Keshia
Knight Pulliam, who played Rudy
on *The Cosby Show.*

KESI (KE-see) Swahili: "a child
born when her father is in
trouble."

KESSIE Fanti or Ashanti,
Ghana: "chubby one." Bestowed
in Africa on a child who is
chubby at birth.

KETZIA (ket-ZEE-ah) Hebrew:
"cinnamonlike bark." Hence, the
name has the connotation of
fragrance. *Ketzi, Kezi, Kezia*
(English)

KEZIA (ke-ZIGH-ah) Hebrew:
"cassia," for the cassia tree.
Biblical name, one of Job's
daughters. *Kesia, Kesiah, Keziah,
Kissie, Kizzie, Kizzy* (English)

KHRISTINA A Russian form of
Christina, "Christian," now also
used in this country. See Christina.

KIA (KEE-ah) Either a short form
of the Irish Kiana ("ancient" or
"one from the past") or a contemporary invention with no
special meaning. Names beginning with the prefix *Ki-* have
recently become quite trendy in
the United States. Other new
"Ki-" names recently invented by
creative American parents
include: *Kiandra, Kiandrea,
Kianni, Kilana, Kilauna,
Kilaundra, Kiona, Kiondra*

KIANA (kee-AHN-ah) Irish
Gaelic: "ancient" or "one from the
past." An Irish-sounding name
growing in popularity in United
States. The feminine form of
Kian. This is also a Hawaiian
variation of Diana, "goddess." *Kia,
Kiann, Kianna, Kianne*
(English)

KIARA (kee-AR-ah) A
contemporary feminine form of
Kiaran, name of a seventh-
century Irish saint, often
confused with Kiera. *Kiarra*
(English)

KICHI (kee-chee) Japanese: "the fortunate one." *Kichiko, Kichiyo* (Japanese)

KIELE (kee-EL-eh) Hawaiian: "gardenia" or "fragrant blossom."

KIERA (KEER-ah) Irish Gaelic: "little black one." Popular in Ireland and growing in popularity in the United States. The masculine form, Kieran, is now also used for girls. *Keara, Keira, Kieran, Kierra* (English)

KIKI (KEE-kee) Spanish nickname for Enriqueta, the English equivalent of which is Harriet, "ruler of the house or home." Also a short form of many names beginning with *Ki-*.

KIKILIA (kee-kee-LEE-uh) Hawaiian form of Cecilia, "dim-sighted." See Cecilia.

KIKU (kee-koo) Japanese: "chrysanthemum." A favorite in Japan, this name refers to the Japanese flower of September. In the East the mum is a symbol of longevity; in Western astrology it's the flower of Scorpio.

KIKUNO (kee-KOO-noh) Japanese: "chrysanthemum field."

KILEY (KIGH-lee) Irish Gaelic: "beautiful" or "graceful." A last name now used as a first name for girls. *Kiely, Kyley* (English)

KILLIAN Irish Gaelic: "small and fierce" or "a warrior." Originally used for boys, this Irish saint's name is now also given to girls. *Kilian* (English)

KIM Old English: "ruler" or "chief." Also a nickname for Kimberly.

KIMAMA (ki-MAH-mah) Shoshone: "butterfly." According to one Native American legend, the Creator took the form of a butterfly and flew all over the world, looking for the best place to create humans.

KIMBERLY Old English: "from the royal-fortress meadow" or "from the brilliant one's meadow." *Kim, Kimberlee, Kimberli, Kimberlie, Kimmi, Kimmie, Kym* (English)

KIMI Japanese: "peerless" or "sovereign." *Kimie, Kimiko, Kimiyo* (Japanese)

KINA (KEE-nah) A nickname used in Scotland, short for Alickina, a Scottish form of Alexandra, "helper and defender of mankind." See Alexandra for nearly one hundred other forms of this internationally popular name.

KINI (KEE-nee) Hawaiian form of Jean, "God is gracious." Also a boys' name, meaning "king."

KINUKO (kee-NOO-koh) Japanese: "silk-cloth child." *Kinu* (Japanese)

KIOKO (kee-oh-koh) Japanese: "happy child."

KIONA (kee-OH-nah) Native American: "brown hills."

KIRA (CURE-ah or KEE-rah) Old Persian: "the sun"; or Latin: "light." A feminine form of Cyrus. The variations Kiran and Kirina are also used by Hindus in India. *Kiran, Kiri, Kiriana, Kirina, Kirini, Kirla, Kirra, Kyra* (English)

KIRBY Middle English: "from the church village." Originally a place-name and a surname, now used for both girls and boys.

KIRIMA (ki-ri-ma) Banti, Eskimo: "a hill."

KIRSI (KEER-see) Dravidian, India: "the flowering amaranth." Popular among the Todas of India.

KIRSTEN A Scandinavian form of Christina, "Christian." Popular in Scandinavia (particularly in Sweden and Norway) as well as the United States. See also Christina. *Keirstan, Kersten, Kerstine, Kirsteen, Kirstien, Kirstin, Kirstine, Kirston, Kirstyn* (English)

KIRSTY Scottish pet form of Christine, especially popular in England and Wales. *Kersty, Kirsti, Kirstie, Kyrsty* (English)

KISA (KEE-sa) Russian: "kitty" or "pussycat." A favorite nickname in Russia.

KISHI (kee-shee) Japanese: "beach." Connotes longevity.

KISKA (KEE-ska) Favorite Russian form of Katherine, "pure." See Katherine.

KISMET Contemporary American name meaning "fate" or "destiny."

KISSA (kiss-SAY, or Anglicized, KISS-ah) Luganda, Uganda: "born after twins."

KISTNA (KIST-nah) Hindi: "the sacred Kistna River." Also a short form of Krishna, "delightful."

KITA (kee-tah) Japanese: "north"; or Spanish: "a kitten."

KIWA (kee-wah) Japanese: "born on a border."

KLARIKA (KLAH-ree-kah) Hungarian and Slavic form of Claire, "brilliant" or "illustrious." See Claire.

KLARISSA (klah-REES-ah) German form of Claire gaining popularity in the United States. See Claire.

KLESA (KLAY-sa) Hindi: "pain." The negative meaning is purposely designed to ward evil spirits away from the child.

KODI (KOH-dee) Irish: "helper or assistant" or "child of the wealthy one." Also spelled Cody. *Kodey, Kodie, Kody* (English)

KOEMI (koh-ay-mee) Japanese: "a small smile."

KOKO (ko-ko) Japanese: "stork." The stork is a Japanese symbol of longevity.

KOLENYA (ko-LAYN-ya) Miwok *kole:* "to cough." The unusual meaning is "fish coughing." According to a Karok Indian legend, the fish was the first living thing created. In the zodiac, the fishes are the symbol of Pisces.

KOLIKA (koh-LEEK-ah) Hawaiian form of Doris, "bountiful" or "from the ocean."

KOLINA (ko-LEE-na) Pretty Swedish form of Katherine, "pure." See Katherine.

KONA (KO-na) Hindi: "angular." Kona is another name for Saturn, the black god in the Hindu religion. At one time, the name was given to a baby in the hope of appeasing this god. Also a Hawaiian form of Donna ("lady")

and an occult name for a girl born under the sign of Capricorn, which is ruled by the planet Saturn.

KONANE (ko-NAH-neh) Hawaiian: "bright as moonlight."

KORI Contemporary American name derived from Cora ("maiden"). *Cori, Corie, Corrie, Corry, Cory, Korie, Korri, Korrie, Korry, Kory* (English)

KORIN Contemporary spelling of Corrine, which is in turn a French form of Cora, "maiden." *Koreen, Korina, Korine, Korrina, Korrine* (English)

KOSTYA (KO-stya) Popular Russian form of Constance, "firm" or "constant." See Constance.

KOTO (koh-toh) Japanese: "harp." *Kotoko* (Japanese)

KRISHNA Hindi: "delightful." Once used primarily in India, now fashionable in this country. Krishna is a Hindu incarnation of Vishnu, the god protecting all creation. It is believed that when some great evil has occurred, Vishnu comes down to earth in human form as either Krishna or another incarnation, Rama. See Devaki. *Kistna, Kistnah, Krisha, Krishnah, Krisya, Krisyah* (English)

KRISTA Form of Christina, "Christian," originally used in

Eastern Europe but now popular in many countries, including the U.S. See Christina.

KRISTIN A Scandinavian form of Christina, "Christian," also a favorite in the United States. *Kristan, Kristen* (English)

KRYSTA An exotic-looking Polish form of Christina.

KRYSTAL Currently fashionable spelling of Crystal, "as clear as crystal." *Kristal, Kristel, Kristell, Krystel* (English)

KUAI HUA (kwigh hwa) Chinese: "mallow blossom." In China the mallow is the flower of September and symbolic of the power of magic against evil spirits. The English equivalent is Melba.

KULYA (KOOL-ya) Miwok: "sugar-pine nuts burned black." The name may indicate that at birth there was so much excitement, the pine nuts on the coals were ignored and thus burned.

KUMI (koo-mee) Japanese: "braid." A popular Japanese variation is *Kumiko* ("braid child").

KUMUDA (kuh-MOO-da) Sanskrit: "lotus." This flower is revered by both Hindus and Buddhists. The Hindus associate it with the birth of Brahma, and

many Hindu deities often sit enthroned upon its petals. In contrast, Buddhists believe in a heaven where souls lie enveloped in lotus buds upon the Sacred Lake of Lotuses until they are admitted to paradise on judgment day.

KUNI (koo-nee, or Anglicized, KOO-nee) Japanese: "country-born." A popular Japanese variation is *Kuniko* ("country-born child").

KURI (koo-ree) Japanese: "chestnut." The chestnut tree occasionally appears in Asian legends, including one story of a mythical tree so large its branches shaded several provinces, and so magical it could not be cut down.

KUSA (KOO-sa) Hindi: "the sacred kusa grass." Also called *darbha,* this sacred grass has long leaves tapering to needle points and is said to have come from the hair of the god Vishnu in his incarnation as a turtle. A ring of kusa worn during sacred rites is said to protect against evil and purify one of all sin. An annual kusa festival is held on the eighth day of the moon during the month of Bhadrapada (August–September), at which time an offering of the grass is believed to obtain immortality for ten of one's ancestors.

KWANITA (kwah-NEE-tah) Zuni form of the Spanish Juanita,

"God is gracious." The English equivalent is Jane.

KYLA A Yiddish form of Kelila ("crown" or "laurel"). Also a feminine form of Kyle ("good-looking" or "one who lives near the chapel").

KYOKO (kee-OH-koh) Japanese: "a mirror."

KYRA (KIGH-rah or KEE-rah) An exotic spelling of Kira, "light" or "the sun." See Kira.

L

LACEY Favorite contemporary American form of Larissa, "cheerful one." *Lacee, Lacie, Lacy* (English)

LADONNA Contemporary blend of the prefix *La-* + Donna ("lady"). (See box on *"La-"* names, page 141.)

LAHELA (lah-HAY-lah) Hawaiian development of Rachel, "an ewe." See Rachel.

LAILA (LAY-lah) A form of Leila, "born at night." See Leila.

LAKA (LAH-kah) Hawaiian: "attract" or "tame." Name of the Hawaiian goddess of the hula.

LAKEISHA (lah-KAY-shah or lah-KEE-shah) Contemporary American name, the origin of which is unclear. May be a combination of the prefix *La-* ("that one") + Aisha, the Arabic name meaning "life." Other spellings include *Lakaysha, Lakeesha, Lakesha, Lakeshia, Lakeysha,* and *Lakisha*. (See box, facing page, for other recently invented *"La-"* names.)

LAKYA (LAHK-yah) Hindi *laksmanavaram:* "born on Thursday."

LALA Slavic: "tulip."

LALITA (lah-LEE-tah) Hindi: "charming." One of the more than one thousand names for the Hindu goddess Shakti. See Shakti.

LANA (LAH-nah) Hawaiian: "bouyant" or "to float." Also a popular form of Helen.

LANI (LAH-nee) Hawaiian: "sky" or "heavenly." (For more about Hawaiian sky names, see the box on page 143.)

LARA (LAH-rah) Latin: "shining and famous"; Greek: "cheerful one." Also a popular pet name in Russia for Larissa. See Larissa.

LARAINE (lah-RAYN) French: "from Lorraine," a region in France. Modern form of the older and now less used Lorraine.

Newly Coined "La-" Names

✶ ✶ ✶

Many names recently invented by American parents use the *"La-"* prefix, followed by a more familiar name. There's a kind of theatrical "star" quality to these names, almost as if the name itself were saying "presenting the one and only... Brenda, Cara, Keisha, etc." Examples of newly coined *"La-"* names include: *Labrenda, Lacara, Lachonda, Lacinda, Ladaisha, Ladasha, Ladawn, Ladonna, Ladonya, Lakaiya, Lakeisha, Lakendra, Lakenya, Lalisa, Lamesha, Lamisha, Laneesha, Laneisha, Lanesha, Lanessa, Lanetta, Lanette, Lanita, Lanora, Larine, Larita, Lasandra, Lashanda, Lashanna, Lashannon, Lashanta, Lashante, Lashawna, Lashawnda, Lashona, Lashonda, Lashondra, Lashonna, Latanya, Latara, Latasha, Latisha, Latona, Latonya, Latrice, Latrisha, Lavette, Lavonna, Lavonne, Lawanda.*

Lorain, Loraine, Lorayna, Lorayne, Lorrane, Lorrayne, Raina, Rayna

LARI Once a nickname for Laura, "crowned with laurel," or Lara, "shining and famous," but used today as an independent name. In astrology, the laurel is the plant of the sun, which governs the sign Leo. See Laura.

LARISSA (lah-REE-sah) Russian name from the Greek for "cheerful one." *Lara, Larochka* (Russian)

LATASHA (lah-TAH-shah) Contemporary creation from the prefix *La* + Natasha ("born on Christmas"). See Lakeisha and box above for other *"La-"* names. *Latacia, Latashia, Latosnia, Letasha, Tasha* (English)

LATISHA (lah-TEE-shah) Latin: "gladness." Contemporary development of the older and seldom used Letitia. *Laytisha, Leda, Leta, Letice, Leticia, Letisha, Letitia, Letti, Lettie, Letty, Tish, Tisha* (English); *Leetice* (French); *Leticia* (Hungarian, Portuguese, Spanish); *Letizia* (Italian); *Letycia* (Polish)

LATONYA Contemporary combination of the prefix La + *Tonya,* in which case the meaning is "that inestimable, priceless one." Another of the many intriguing *La-* names that have sprung up recently around the world. *Latonia, Tonia, Tonya* (English)

LATOYA Spanish: "victorious." Comes originally from Victoria and made popular by singer LaToya Jackson. An alternate explanation is that this is a short form of Latonya ("inestimable" or "priceless").

LAURA Latin *laures:* "crowned with laurel." Has been in the top fifty most popular names for over one hundred years. The feminine form of Lawrence. *Lari, Larilia, Laureen, Laurel, Laurella, Lauren, Laurena, Laurene, Lauretta, Laurette, Lauri, Laurice, Laurie, Lauriette, Laurine, Lora, Loree, Loreen, Loren, Lorena, Lorene, Loretta, Lorette, Lori, Lorinda, Lorita, Lorna, Lorri, Lorrie, Lorry* (English); *Lora* (Bulgarian); *Laure, Laurette* (French); *Lola* (Hawaiian); *Lorenza* (Italian); *Laurka* (Polish); *Laurinda* (Portuguese); *Lavra* (Russian); *Laureana* (Spanish)

LAUREN A fashionable modern form of Laura. Made well known by actress Lauren Bacall and model Lauren Hutton. *Laurin, Lauryn, Lorin, Lorrin, Loryn, Lorynn, Lorynne* (English)

LAVERNE Old French: "from the grove of alder trees." *Lavern, Laverna, La Verne, LaVerne* (English)

LAVINIA (lah-VEEN-yah) Latin: "purified" or "a lady from Latium." *Lavin, Lavina, Lavine* (English)

LAYLA (LAH-ee-lah, or Anglicized, LAY-lah) Arabic: "born at night." Popular Swahili name. See Leila.

LEA Hebrew: "weary." Used in France, Hungary, and Sweden as well as this country. *Leah, Lee, Leigh, Lia, Liah* (English); *Lia* (French, Italian, Portuguese); *Leah* (Yiddish)

LEANDRA Latin: "like a lioness." Name for a girl born under the sign of Leo. *Leodora, Leoine, Leoline, Leona, Leonanie, Leonelle, Leonette, Leonice, Leonissa* (English)

LEANNA A spelling variation of Liana, "the liana vine."

LECIA (LEE-sha) Short form of such names as Alicia, Felicia, and Leticia, now used independently. *Leesha, Lisha* (English)

LEDAH (LEE-dah) Hebrew: "birth"; also a form of Letitia,

Hawaiian Sky Names

✳ ✳ ✳

Many traditional Hawaiian names speak of the sky. These names frequently have a spiritual, heavenly connotation. Among them:

Ahulani (ah-hoo-LAH-nee): "heavenly shrine."

Alohilani (ah-loh-hee-LAH-nee): "bright sky."

Hokulani (hoh-koo-LAH-nee): "star in the sky."

Iwalani (ee-wah-LAH-nee): "heavenly seabird."

Kakaulani (kah-cow-LAH-nee): "placed in the sky."

Leilani (lay-LAH-nee): "heavenly child."

Malulani (mah-loo-LAH-nee): "under heaven's protection."

Okalani (oh-kah-LAH-nee): "of the heavens."

Pililani (pil-ee-LAH-nee): "close to heaven."

"gladness." *Leda, Lida, Lidah* (English)

LEE Chinese: "plum"; Old English: "one who lives in the pasture meadow"; or Irish Gaelic: "poetic child." Also a form of Lea, "weary."

LEEBA Hebrew: "heart." Originally from Israel.

LEENA Estonian form of Helen, "light" or "torch." *Elli, Hele, Lenni* (Estonian)

LEEZA Short form of Aleeza, "joyful." *Leesa* (English)

LEHUA (le-HOO-ah) Hawaiian: "sacred to the gods." Also the name of a native flower in Hawaii.

LEILA (LAY-lah) Arabic: "born at night." Leila is the heroine in the ancient Persian legend *Leila and Majnun. Laila, Layla, Leilia, Lela, Lila* (English)

LEILANI (lay-LAH-nee) Hawaiian: "heavenly child." (See box, page 143.)

LELA (LAY-lah) Popular Spanish form of Adelle, "noble." See Adelle.

LENA (LAY-nah, or Anglicized, LEE-nah) Hebrew: "dwelling" or "lodging"; or Latin: "alluring one." Popular in Israel. Also a nickname for the German Magdalene and the Russian Galina. *Lenah, Lina, Linah* (English); *Liene* (Latvian)

LENKA (LEN-kah) Czech form of Helen, "light" or "torch." See Helen.

LEONIE (lay-OH-nee or LAY-oh-nee) French: "lioness." A child born under the astrological sign of Leo. The feminine form of Leon. *Leola, Leona, Leone, Leonia, Leonice, Leonie, Leontyne, Liona, Lona, Loni* (English); *Liona* (Hawaiian)

LEOTIE (leh-oh-TEE, or Anglicized, lay-O-tee) Native American: "prairie flower."

LESKA (LESH-kah or LES-kah) A Czech pet form of Alexandra, "helper and defender of mankind." See Alexandra.

LESLIE Scots Gaelic: "one who lives in the gray fortress." Originally a Scottish place-name and a boys' name, now used almost exclusively for girls. *Lesley, Lesli, Lesly, Lezli, Lezlie, Lezly* (English)

LESYA (LESH-yah) A favorite Russian pet form of Alexandra, "helper and defender of mankind."

LETA (LAY-tah, or Anglicized, LEE-tah) Swahili: "bring." In Africa this name may be combined with a second name to mean "bring happiness" or "bring luck." In the United States, this is also a short form of Letitia ("gladness") and Latonia ("sacred to Latona"), a name identified with the Greek goddess Leto, mother of the moon and sun.

LEVANA Latin: "the rising sun." Appropriate name for a baby born under the sign of Leo, ruled by the sun.

LEVANI (le-VAH-nee) Fijian: "anointed with oil."

LEVIA (le-VEE-uh or LE-vee-ah) Hebrew: "to join." The feminine form of Levi.

LEXA Popular Czech nickname for Alexandra, "helper and defender of mankind."

LEXIE Used today as an independent name, once a nickname for Alexandra, "helper and defender of mankind." *Lecksi, Leksi, Leksie, Lexi, Lexia* (English)

Chinese Flower Names

★ ★ ★

It enhances status in China for a girl to have a beautiful name. As a result, many girls are named after flowers. The name *Fang* in Chinese doesn't refer to a sharp tooth, as it would in English, but to a beautiful fragrance. The combination name *Fang-Hua* carries the meaning, "sweet-smelling flower." Other Chinese flower names for girls include: *Ah-Lam* ("resembling an orchid"); *Chu-Hua* ("chrysanthemum blossom"); *Lien* ("lotus"); *Lien-Hua* ("lotus blossom"); *Li-Hua* ("pear blossom"); *Mei-Lien* ("beautiful lotus"); *Mu-Lan* ("magnolia flower"); and *Mu-Tan* ("tree peony flower").

LEYA (LAY-yah, or Anglicized, LEE-yah) Spanish: "loyalty to the law." Also used by the Tamil of south India to designate the constellation and astrological sign Leo.

LI (lee) Chinese: "plum blossom" or "plum tree."

LI-HUA (lee hwah) Chinese: "pear blossom." In China the pear blossom is the flower of August and a symbol of longevity.

LIA Contemporary name used in France, Greece, Italy, Portugal, the United States, and other countries, either from the Greek ("one who brings good news") or from the Hebrew Leah ("weary"). See Lea.

LIAN Chinese: "the graceful willow." Also a pet form of Gillian.

LIANA French *liane:* "the liana vine," referring to a brilliantly blossomed tropical climbing plant. *Lean, Leana, Leane, Leanna, Liane, Lianna, Lianne* (English); *Oliana* (Hawaiian)

LIBBY Contemporary American pet form of Elizabeth, "dedicated to God."

LIDA (LEE-dah) Popular nickname in Russia. See Lidia.

LIDIA Greek: "from Lydia," an ancient country in Asia Minor, or "happy." Lidia is used around the globe. *Lydia, Lydie* (English); *Lidka* (Czech); *Lydie* (French);

Lidi (Hungarian); *Lida, Lidka* (Polish); *Lida, Lidiya, Lidka, Lidochka* (Russian)

LIEN (lay-en or lee-en) Chinese: "lotus." The buds, blossoms, and seeds of the eight-petal lotus are all visible simultaneously, and hence in China the flower is considered a symbol of the past, present, and future. The lotus also symbolizes purity, and a familiar proverb in China is: "The lotus springs from the mud." Also used in Vietnam. See Kumuda for Buddhist beliefs regarding the flower.

LIEN-HUA (lay-en hwah or lee-en hwah) Chinese: "lotus flower." In China the lotus is the flower of summer and July. See Lien.

LIENE (Anglicized lee-AY-nuh, or lee-EN) Latvian form of Lena, "dwelling" or "alluring one." *Liayna* (English)

Miwok Indian Chicken-Hawk Names

✱ ✱ ✱

The chicken hawk appears in many Miwok Indian names, which are always quite expressive. Among these fascinatingly detailed nature names:

Noksu: "smell of a chicken hawk's nest."

Putepu: "chicken hawk walking back and forth on a limb."

Tiwolu: "chicken hawk turning its eggs with its bill while they are hatching."

Tiloisi: "chicken hawk tearing a gopher snake with its talons."

Yutkiye: "chicken hawk lifting ground squirrel from the ground."

Yutticiso: from *yutuk:* "stick on"; means "lice thick on a chicken hawk." (Yuck!)

LIESEL, LIESL (LEES-ul or LEE-zul) Austrian and German short form of Elizabeth, "dedicated to God." Sometimes also listed as a German form of Lillian. Made well known by the oldest of the von Trapp children in *The Sound of Music.*

LIL A short form of many names beginning with *"Lil-,"* including Lillian, "the lily flower."

LILA (LEE-luh, or Anglicized, LIGH-luh) Hindi: "the free, playful will of God"; Persian: "lilac"; or a Polish nickname for Leopoldine, "bold defender of the people." Also a pet form of Lillian. A global name with many meanings.

LILIA (lee-LEE-uh, or Anglicized, LIL-ee-uh) Hawaiian: "the lily flower." A pretty Hawaiian variation is *Lileana* (lee-lee-AH-nuh). See Lillian.

LILIANA Form of Lillian ("the lily flower"), now becoming more popular than the name from which it was derived. *Liana, Lil, Lili, Lilie, Lilli, Lillie, Lily, Lilly* (English)

LILIHA (lee-LEE-hah) Hawaiian: "disgust." The name of a woman governor of the Hawaiian isle of Oahu during the 1820s.

LILITH Arabic: "of the night." In Eastern mythology, Lilith was Adam's first wife. She was created separately from Adam and was the first feminist, challenging Adam's authority as head of the household. When Adam refused to compromise, Lilith left him, and God then created Eve from Adam's rib so there would never be any question of Adam's (or man's) superiority. Lilith is said to have become a demon.

LILKA (LIL-kuh) Polish form of Louise, "famous warrior-maiden." See Louise.

LILLIAN Latin *lilium:* "the lily flower." *Lil, Lila, Lili, Lilia, Lilian, Liliana, Liliane, Lilla, Lilli, Lillie, Lilly, Lily* (English); *Lilli* (Estonian); *Lilya* (Finnish); *Lieschen, Liesel, Lili, Lilian, Lilli, Lily* (German); *Lileana, Lilia* (Hawaiian); *Boske, Bozsi, Lilike* (Hungarian); *Lilana* (Latvian); *Leka, Lelya, Lena, Lenka, Lili, Olena, Olenka* (Russian); *Liljana* (Serbian); *Lilia, Liliana, Lilias, Liliosa* (Spanish)

LILUYE (lee-LOO-ye) Miwok: "chicken hawk singing when soaring."

LIN Chinese: "beautiful jade." Also a spelling variation of the English Lynn. A favorite middle name.

LINA (LEE-nah) Popular Russian pet form of many names. See Adelle, Angela, and Caroline.

LINDA Spanish: "pretty one." *Lindi, Lindie, Lindy, Lynda*

(English); *Lindi, Lindia, Lindita* (Spanish)

LINDSEY Old English: "from the isle of the serpents" or "from the linden-tree island." Traditionally a boys' name, but now used almost exclusively for girls. *Linda, Lindsay, Lindsie, Linsey, Linsi, Linsie, Linsy, Lyndsay, Lyndsey, Lyndsy* (English)

LINETTE Old French: "a linnet bird." This nature name comes originally from a Latin word meaning "flax," the seeds on which the linnet bird feeds. *Lanettte, Linet, Linetta, Linette, Linnet, Lynette, Lynnet, Lynnette* (English)

LING Chinese: "delicate and dainty."

LINNEA (li-NAY-ah) Old Norse: "lime tree." Also the name of a small Scandinavian mountain flower. *Linea, Linna, Linnae, Linnaea, Lynea, Lynnea* (English)

LIOLYA (lee-OHL-yah) A Russian form of Helen, "light" or "torch."

LIONA (lee-OH-nah) Hawaiian development of Leona, "lioness."

LIORA (LIE-or-ah or lee-OR-ah) Hebrew: "I have light." A contemporary name from Israel. Also an American variation of Helen, "light" or "torch." *Leora, Leorah, Leorit, Liorit* (Hebrew)

LIRIT (li-REET) Hebrew: "poetic," "lyrical," or "musical." Contemporary Israeli name.

LIRON (lee-ROHN) Hebrew: "my song." Another contemporary name from Israel.

LISA Contemporary form of Elizabeth, "dedicated to God," which became quite popular in all English-speaking countries in the 1980s. Also a Scandinavian favorite. See Elizabeth.

LISETA (lee-SAY-tah) Contemporary Spanish form of Elizabeth. See Elizabeth for dozens of variations.

LISETTE (li-SET) French pet form of Elizabeth, "dedicated to God"; German form of Elizabeth; or a French form of Louise, "famous warrior maiden." *Lizette* (English, French)

LISHA (LEE-shah) Pretty, short form of many names. See Lecia.

LISSA Once a nickname for Melissa ("honey" or "a bee") or Millicent ("honest" or "diligent"), but now used as an independent name. The melissa plant is a Western symbol of sympathy and love and an Arabic emblem of rejuvenation.

LISSILMA (li-SEEL-mah) Native American: "be thou there."

LITONYA (li-TOHN-yah) Miwok *litanu:* "to dart down." Connotatively, the name means "hummingbird darting down after having flown straight up." In the occult world the hummingbird is considered a love charm to enchant members of the opposite sex.

LITSA (LEET-sah) Modern Greek form of Evangelia, which is a form of Angela, "angel" or "one who brings good news." See Angela and Evangelia.

LIV A short form of Olivia ("olive tree" or "olive branch") made well known around the globe by actress Liv Ullmann.

LIVANA (lee-VAH-nah) Hebrew: "white" or "the moon." In astrology the moon governs the sign of Cancer. *Leva, Levana, Liva* (English)

LIVANGA (lee-VAHN-gah) Umbundu, Africa: From the Ovimbundu proverb *"Livanga oku soka ku livange oku lia,"* "Be first to think, but don't be first to eat." The proverb warns of the danger of being poisoned by rotten meat if one does not think first and check it for spoilage.

LIVIA (LIV-ee-ah) Hebrew: "crown." Also a short form of Olivia. *Levia* (Israeli)

LIVIYA (li-VEE-yah) Hebrew: "lioness." The variations Livia and Levia also mean "crown." *Levia, Leviya, Livia* (Hebrew)

LIVONA (li-VO-nah) Hebrew: "spice" or "incense." *Levona* (Hebrew)

LIZA (LIE-zah) Form of Elizabeth ("dedicated to God") used in English-speaking countries as well as Russia. See Elizabeth. *Lyza* (English)

LIZANNE (li-ZAHN) Exotic French-sounding form of Elizabeth recently invented by American parents. *Lizana, Lizina* (English)

LIZBETH A short, trendy form of Elizabeth, "dedicated to God." *Lisabet, Lisabeth, Lisabette, Lisbet, Lizabeth, Lizabette, Lizbett, Lizbeth, Lyzbeth* (English)

LIZETT Yet another contemporary American creation originally from Elizabeth, "dedicated to God." *Lizet, Lizette, Lyzet, Lyzett, Lyzette* (English)

LOIS A form of Louise, "famous warrior-maiden."

LOKELANI (loh-keh-LAH-nee) Hawaiian: "heavenly rose." A Hawaiian sky-flower name.

LOLA Popular contemporary American form of Dolores and

Charlotte. Also a Hawaiian development of Laura, "crowned with laurel."

LOLITA Spanish pet form of the name Maria de los Dolores ("Mary of the Sorrows") for the mother of Christ. See Dolores.

LOLOTEA (loh-loh-TAY-ah) Zuni development (through the Spanish name Dorotea) of Dorothy, "God's gift."

> **"**Giving a name, indeed, is a poetic art; all poetry, when it comes to that, is but a giving of names.**"**
>
> —British essayist Thomas Carlyle

LOMASI (loh-MAH-see) Native American: "pretty flower."

LONI (LAH-nee) A short form of Leona ("lioness") made familiar by American actress Loni Anderson.

LORA An older spelling of Laura, "crowned with laurel," now making a comeback.

LORENA Also a form of Laura. *Laurena, Laurin, Loren* (English)

LORETTA (lo-RET-ah or lo-RAY-tah) Spanish: "pure." Also a form of Laura, "crowned with laurel." *Laret, Larette, Lauret, Laureta, Lauretta, Loret, Loreta, Lorette* (English)

LORI Popular pet form of Laura, now commonly used as an independent name. *Lauri, Laurie, Loriann, Lorianne* (English)

LORNA Originally a Scottish place-name, made famous by R. D. Blackmore's nineteenth-century romantic novel *Lorna Doone. Lornna* (English)

LOTA (LOH-tah) Hindi: "portable drinking cup." One ancient Hindu practice was to name a child after an inanimate object. See Almira for an explanation of the custom.

LOTTA (LOHT-tah) A Swedish form of Caroline, "little womanly one."

LOUISE Old German: "famous warrior maiden." *Eloise, Lois, Lou, Louisa, Louisetta, Lu* (English); *Aloyse, Lisette* (French); *Aloisa, Luise* (German); *Eloisia* (Greek); *Eloisa* (Italian, Swedish); *Lovisa* (Norwegian); *Iza, Lodoiska, Ludka, Ludwika, Luisa* (Polish); *Louisa* (Romanian); *Lutza, Luyiza* (Russian);

Aloisa, Aluisa, Eloisa, Eloise, Luisa, Luisina, Luiza, Lula, Lulita (Spanish)

LUANA (loo-AHN-ah) Hebrew, Old German: "graceful battle maiden," a blend of Louise ("famous warrior maiden") + Anna (graceful). Also Hawaiian: "joyous" or "happy." *Louann, Louanna, Louanne, Luane, Luann, Luanna, Luanne* (English)

LUCIA (loo-SEE-ah) Form of Lucy ("light") used in many countries. Especially popular among early Christians naming their girls after Saint Lucia, who was martyred in the fourth century.

LUCITA (loo-SEE-tah) Spanish name shortened from Maria de la Luz, "Mary of the Light," referring to the mother of Jesus. *Lusita* (Zuni)

LUCY Latin *lucia:* "light," implying the child brings light. The feminine form of Lucius or Luke. *Lou, Lu, Luce, Lucette, Luci, Luciana, Luciane, Lucida, Lucie, Lucile, Lucille* (English); *Lucine* (Bulgarian); *Lucia, Lucie* (Czech); *Lucienne* (French); *Luzi, Luzie* (German); *Luke* (Hawaiian); *Luca, Lucia* (Hungarian); *Lucia* (Italian); *Lucija* (Latvian); *Lucya* (Polish); *Luzija* (Russian); *Luci, Lucika, Lucka* (Slavic); *Luciana, Lucila* (Spanish)

LUISA (loo-EE-sah) Spanish and Polish form of Louise, "famous warrior maiden." *Luisana, Luisanna, Luise, Luisetta, Luiza, Lujza, Lula, Lulita* (Spanish)

LULANI (loo-LAH-nee) Hawaiian: "the highest point in heaven." A lofty Hawaiian name for girls and boys.

LULU Native American: "rabbit"; or Anglo-Saxon: "soothing influence."

LUNA Spanish: "moon" or "satellite." Popular among the Zuni Indians. In astrology the moon rules the sign of Cancer, whereas the tarot card of the moon corresponds to Pisces.

LUSA Finnish form of Elizabeth, "dedicated to God."

LUSELA (loo-SAY-lah) Miwok: "bear swinging its foot when licking it." Of all animals, the bear is probably the most popular in Miwok names.

LUYU (LOO-yoo) Miwok *luyani:* literally, "to shake the head," with the connotation "dove shaking its head sideways."

LUZ (loose) Spanish: "light." This popular Spanish name is a shortened form of Maria de la Luz, "Mary of the Light."

LYDIA Greek: "from Lydia," an ancient country in Asia Minor, or "happy." See Lidia.

LYNDA Variant spelling of Linda, "pretty one."

LYNDSAY Variation of Lindsey, "from the isle of the serpents" or "from the linden-tree island." See Lindsey.

LYNN Old English: "waterfall" or "pool below a waterfall." *Lin, Linell, Linelle, Linn, Linne, Lyn, Lyndel, Lyndell, Lyndelle, Lynelle, Lynette, Lynna, Lynne, Lynnelle* (English); *Lina* (Spanish)

M

MAB Irish Gaelic: "joyous"; or Welsh: "baby." In English, Irish, and Welsh myths, Mab was queen of the fairies. *Mave, Mavis* (English); *Maeve* (Irish); *Mavis* (French)

MACHI (mah-chee) Japanese: "ten thousand." A round number considered a good omen. Hence, the connotation is "fortunate." The longer name *Machiko* means "fortunate child" or "child who learns truth."

MACKENZIE Irish Gaelic: "child of the wise leader." *Mac, Mack, MacKenzie, McKenzie, Kenzie* (English)

MADDIE Fashionable contemporary American form of Madeline or Madison. *Maddi, Maddy* (English)

MADELINE Greek: "from Magdala (high tower)," the Palestinian city with a high tower on the Sea of Galilee where Mary Magdalene once lived. *Lena, Lenna, Lina, Linn, Lynn, Lynne, Mada, Madaleine, Madalena, Madaliene, Madaline, Madalyn, Madalyne, Maddi, Maddie, Madelaine, Madelena, Madelina, Madge, Madlen, Madlin, Madlyn, Mady, Magda, Magdalena, Mala, Malena, Marla, Marleen, Marlena, Marlina, Marline* (English); *Magda, Magdelena* (Czech); *Madeleine* (French); *Marlene* (German); *Lena, Lene, Magda, Magdelina, Magia, Marlene* (Polish); *Madelina, Magda, Magdalina, Mahda* (Russian); *Lena, Madia, Madena, Madina, Magaly, Magda, Magola* (Spanish)

MADISON English: "the son of Mad, or Matthew (gift from Jehovah)." Originally a surname, now popular as a first name for girls. *Maddi, Maddie, Maddy* (English)

MAEKO (my-ee-koh) Japanese: "truthful child."

MAEMI (mah-ay-mee) Japanese: "smile of truth."

MAEVE (MAYV) Irish form of Mab, "joyous." Name of a legendary Irish queen.

Important to Know ...

✷ ✷ ✷

If you give your girl a trendy "masculine" name like Blair, Madison, or Payton, in the hopes she'll be respected in the boardroom, make sure you keep *using* the name as your daughter grows up. A study in *The Journal of Social Psychology* found that college women who had masculine names and used them (as opposed, say, to going by a middle name) were less anxious, less neurotic, and more culturally sophisticated. They also scored higher on leadership potential.

MAGARA (MAH-gah-rah) Mashona, southern Rhodesia *ku gara:* "to sit" or "to stay." Often given by southern Rhodesians to a baby who cries so much her parents don't know what to do. The name refers to the long hours the parents sit and cuddle the infant.

MAGDA (MAHG-dah) A world-wide form of Madeline, "from Magdala." This truly international name is used not only in English- and Spanish-speaking countries, but also in the Czech Republic, Poland, and Russia.

MAGENA (mah-GEH-nah) Native American: "the coming moon." *Gena* (English)

MAGGIE A short form of Margaret ("a pearl") with an old-

fashioned flair. Now used as an independent name. *Maggi, Maggy* (English)

MAHALA (mah-HAIL-ah) Native American: "woman"; or Hebrew: "tenderness." *Mahalah, Mahalia, Mahela, Mahelia, Mahila, Mahilia* (English)

MAHESA (mah-HEH-shah) Hindi: "great lord." One of the 1,008 names for the Hindu god Siva, also used for boys. *Maheesa, Maheesha, Mahisa, Mahisha* (English)

MAHINA (mah-HEE-nah) Hawaiian: "moon." See Luna for astrological significance.

MAHIRA (mah-HEE-rah) Hebrew: "quick" or "energetic." *Mehira* (Hebrew)

MAHOGANY Contemporary American creation with the connotative meaning "the color of mahogany wood."

MAI (may or migh) Japanese: "brightness"; French: "the month of May"; Navajo: "coyote"; or Vietnamese: "blossom." A name that has developed independently in many cultures.

MAIRE (ma-REE or MAU-ree) Irish form of Mary, "bitter." Gaining some popularity among American parents seeking Irish-sounding names.

MAITA (mah-EE-tah) Spanish form of Martha, "lady of the house" or "mistress."

MAJA (MAH-jah) Arabic: "splendid." Short form of the longer *Majidah*.

MAKADISA (mah-kah-DEE-sah) Baduma, Africa: "she was always selfish." Bestowed as a nickname by the Baduma people in Africa.

MAKANA (mah-KAH-nah) Hawaiian: "gift or present."

MAKANI (mah-KAHN-ee) Hawaiian: "the wind."

MAKARA (mah-KAHR-ah) Hindi: "born during the lunar month of Capricorn." *Kara* (English)

MALAK (MAH-lak) Arabic: "angel." Very popular in Arabic countries.

MALIA (mah-LEE-ah) Hawaiian form of Mary, "bitter." Also a Zuni name derived from the Spanish Maria. See Mary.

MALILA (muh-LEE-lah) Miwok: "salmon going fast up a rippling stream."

MALINA See Madeline. This name, from the Tabascan language, is also a favorite among Mexican Indians.

MALKA Hebrew: "a queen."

MALLORY Old French: "one who wears plate mail"; or Old German: "an army counselor." Also used for boys. *Mal, Mallorey, Mallori, Mallorie, Malori, Malorie, Malory* (English)

MANA (MAH-nah) Hawaiian: "supernatural power."

MANABA (mah-NAH-bah) Navaho: "war returned with her coming." See Doba.

MANDA Pet form of Amanda, now occasionally used as an independent name. Also a Spanish form of Armanda ("harmony" or "battle maiden") and one of the Hindi names for Saturn, god of the occult. *Armanda, Mandi, Mandie, Mandy* (English)

MANDARA (mahn-DAH-rah) Hindi: "the mythical mandara tree." It is said that in the shade of the mandara tree in the Hindu paradise, all worldly cares are forgotten. According to ancient tree-worship beliefs, plants were not only conscious but able to feel pain. Each tree was believed to contain a tree spirit who had to be given flowers and sweetmeats. In return, the tree could be consulted as an oracle and had the power to grant children fame and wealth. Before a tree was cut, the cutter prayed to the tree deity so that the god would find another tree and not be angry with him.

MANDISA (mahn-DEE-sah) Xhosa, South Africa: "sweet."

MANDY Originally a nickname for Amanda, "worthy of love," now used as an independent name. See also Manda. *Mandi, Mandie* (English)

MANGENA (mahn-GAY-nuh) Hebrew: "song" or "melody." *Mangina* (Hebrew)

MANI (MAH-nee) From the prayer *om mani padme hum,* the first and greatest of all charms among Tibetan Buddhists. Though the meaning of these sacred words is unknown, repeating them is believed to thwart evil and impart all wisdom and knowledge.

MANON (French mah-NOHN, or Anglicized, MAN-un) A French pet form of Mary, now used independently. Though unusual in this country, this is a favorite in France.

MANSI Hopi: "plucked flower." *Mancey, Manci, Mancie, Mancy, Mansey, Mansie, Mansy* (English)

MANYA (MAHN-yah) A popular Russian nickname. See Mary.

MARA A favorite around the world. Used in Hungary, Russia, Serbia, and other countries as a form of Mary ("bitter"), and in the Czech Republic as a short form of Tamara, "palm tree." See Mary.

MARALYN (MARE-ah-lin) A variation of Marilyn ("bitter and graceful" or "bitter waterfall"). See Marilyn. *Mara-Lyn, MaraLyn,* (English)

MARCI Once a nickname for Marcia ("martial or warlike one"), used today as an independent name. *Marcie, Marcy, Marsi, Marsie, Marsy* (English)

MARCIA Latin: "martial or warlike one," referring to the Roman god Mars. The feminine form of Marcus. See Marci above. *Marcelia, Marcella, Marci, Marcille, Marcy, Marquita, Marsha* (English)

MARGANIT (mahr-gah-NEET) Hebrew: "the marganit flower,"

referring to a flower with red, blue, and golden blossoms that's native to Israel.

MARGARET Latin: "a pearl." Popular in many forms world-wide. *Daisy, Greta, Gretta, Madge, Mag, Maggi, Maggie, Maggy, Marga, Marge, Margery, Marget, Margie, Margo, Margret, Marguerite, Margy, Marjorie, Marjory, Meg, Megan, Meggi, Meggie, Meggy, Meghan, Peg, Peggi, Peggie, Peggy, Rita* (English); *Margarid* (Armenian); *Greta* (Austrian); *Marketa* (Bulgarian); *Gita, Gitka, Gituska, Margareta, Margita, Marka, Marketa* (Czech); *Marga, Margarete, Mari, Meeri, Reet* (Estonian); *Marjatta* (Finnish); *Margot, Marguerite* (French); *Greta, Grete, Gretel, Gretchen, Margareta, Margarete, Margit, Margot, Margret* (German); *Margareta, Margaritis, Margaro* (Greek); *Penina* (Hebrew); *Gitta, Manci, Margit, Margita, Margo* (Hungarian); *Margarita* (Italian, Lithuanian); *Grieta, Margrieta* (Latvian); *Margreta, Margrete* (Norwegian, Swedish); *Gita, Margisia, Margita, Rita* (Polish); *Margarida* (Portuguese); *Gita, Perla* (Slavic); *Marga, Margara, Margarita, Marguarita, Marguita, Rita, Tita* (Spanish); *Makelesi* (Tongan); *Marged, Meaghan, Meg, Megan, Meghan, Mared* (Welsh); *Gita* (Yiddish)

MARGAUX Contemporary American creation, said to have come from Margaux champagne, but may also be an exotic spelling of Margo.

MARGO Hungarian form of Margaret ("a pearl") now common in the United States.

MARI (mah-ree) Japanese: "ball." A favorite Japanese name. The variation *Mariko* means "ball child." Also a contemporary American spelling of Mary.

MARIA The popularity of the Virgin Mary's name among Spanish-speaking peoples makes this the most common Spanish name in the world. See Mary. Among many Spanish variations: *Carmen, Dolores, Jesusa, Lucita, Luz*

MARIAH (mah-RIGH-ah) Form of Moriah, "God is my teacher."

MARIANA A blend of Mary ("bitter") + Anna ("graceful"), also sometimes considered simply a variation of Mary. *Marianna* (English); *Marien* (Dutch); *Maryam* (Greek); *Mariane* (French)

MARIE A popular form of Mary ("bitter") used around the world. In France, as in the United States, Marie is often used as the first element in compound names, such as *Marie-Ange* (Marie + Angela), *Marie-Josée*, and *Marie-Claire*.

MARIKO (mah-ree-koh) Japanese: "circle child." *Mari* (Japanese)

MARILEE A blend of Mary ("bitter") + Lee ("one who lives in the pasture meadow" or "poetic child"). *Marilea, MariLee, Marylea, Marylee, Merrilee* (English)

MARILYN A blend of Mary ("bitter") + Ellen ("light") or Lynn ("waterfall"). First popularized in the 1920s by musical star Marilyn Miller (born Mary Ellen Reynolds) and later by Marilyn Monroe (born Norma Jean Mortenson). *Maralin, Maralyn, Maralyne, Maralynn, Marillin, Marillyn, Marilynn, Marilynne, Marlyn, Marolyn, Marrilyn, Marylin, Marylyn, Merilyn, Merilynn* (English)

MARINI (mah-REE-nee) Swahili: "fresh, healthy, and pretty."

MARISHA (mah-REE-sha) Popular pet form of Mary, "bitter," originally from Russia. See Mary. *Mareesha, Reesha, Risha* (English)

MARISSA Latin: "of the sea." *Mareesa, Maris, Marisa, Marrisa, Marysa, Maryssa, Meris, Merisa, Merissa, Morissa, Risa, Rissa* (English); *Maryse* (Dutch); *Maritza* (German); *Marita* (Spanish)

MARITZA (mah-REET-zah) Arabic: "blessed."

MARLA A short form of Marlene "from Magdala (high tower)" now used as an independent name. See Marlene and Madeline.

MARLENE (mahr-LAY-ne, or Anglicized, mar-LEEN) German form of Madeline "from Magdala (high tower)," popularized in the United States by actress Marlene Dietrich. *Layna, Lena, Leyna, Marla, Marlaina, Marlaine, Marlane, Marlea, Marleah, Marlee, Marleen, Marlena, Marley, Marlie, Marline, Marlyn* (English)

MARLISA (mar-LEE-sah) A contemporary American blend of Mary ("bitter") + Lisa (short form of Elizabeth, "dedicated to God"). *Lissa, Lyssa, Marlis, Marlise, Marlissa, Marlyse, Marlyssa, Marlysse* (English)

MARNI Hebrew: "to rejoice." Pet form of Marnina, now used in this country as an independent name. *Marnie, Marny* (English)

MARSHA A form of Marcia, "martial or warlike one."

MARTA An internationally popular form of Martha, used not only in this country but also in Bulgaria, the Czech Republic, Hungary, Italy, Lithuania, Norway, Poland, Romania, Russia, most of the Spanish-speaking world, Sweden, and the Ukraine. See Martha.

MARTHA Aramaic: "lady of the house" or "mistress." See also Marta. *Mart, Marta, Marti, Martie, Marty, Matti, Mattie, Matty, Pat, Patti, Patty* (English); *Marticka* (Czech); *Marthe* (French, German); *Martus, Martuska* (Hungarian); *Marcia, Masia* (Polish); *Moireach* (Scottish); *Maita, Martina* (Spanish)

MARTINA Czech form of Marcia ("warlike") or Spanish form of Martha ("lady of the house"). Made well known by Czech-born tennis player Martina Navratilova. The feminine form of Martin. *Marta, Martie, Marty, Tina* (English): *Martine* (French)

MARTIZA (mahr-TEE-zah) Arabic: "blessed one."

MARU (mah-roo) Japanese: "round."

MARY Hebrew: "bitter." One of the world's most popular names, Mary commemorates the mother of Jesus Christ and was once considered too sacred to be given to a child. But from the twelfth century on, the name became increasingly popular around the globe. *Mame, Mamie, Mara, Marabel, Marella, Maren, Mari, Maria, Mariam, Marian, Mariana, Marianna, Marice, Maridel, Marie, Mariel, Marietta, Mariette, Marilee, Marilin, Marilyn, Marion, Marita, Marla, Marlo, Marya, Maryann,* *Maryanna, Maryanne, Marylin, Marylinn, Marylyn, Maura, Maure, Maureen, Maurene, May, Meri, Meriel, Merrill, Meryl, Millie, Mimi, Minette, Minni, Minnie, Minny, Miriam, Mitzi, Molli, Molly, Muriel, Muriell, Polli, Pollie, Polly* (English); *Maryam* (Arabic); *Marca, Marenka, Marienka, Mariska, Maruska* (Czech); *Marye* (Estonian); *Maija, Maijii, Maikki, Marja* (Finnish); *Manette, Manon, Marie, Maryse* (French); *Marika, Maroula, Roula* (Greek); *Mara, Marcsa, Mari, Maria, Marika, Mariska* (Hungarian); *Maire, Maura, Maureen, Moira, Moire, Moya, Muire* (Irish); *Mare* (Latvian); *Marija* (Lithuanian); *Macia, Manka, Maryla, Maryna* (Polish); *Maricara* (Romanian); *Manka, Manya, Maria, Marinka, Marisha, Mariya, Maruska, Marya, Masha, Mashenka, Mashka, Mura* (Russian); *Mairi, Moira, Moire, Muire* (Scottish); *Mari, Maria, Mariquita, Marita, Maruca, Maruja* (Spanish); *Mirjam* (Norwegian, Swedish); *Mele* (Tongan); *Miriam* (Yiddish); *Meli* (Zuni)

MARYA (MAHR-yah) Arabic: "brightly white" or "pure."

MARYAM Arabic form of Mary, "bitter," referring specifically to the mother of Jesus.

MASAGO (mah-sah-go) Japanese: "sand," referring to the

sand's eternal quality and expressing a hope for the child's long life.

MASHA (MAH-shah) Classic Russian form of Mary, "bitter."

> **"I have a passion for the name of 'Mary,' For once it was a magic sound to me. And still it half calls up the realms of fairy . . ."**
>
> —GEORGE GORDON, LORD BYRON

MASIKA (mah-SEE-kah) Swahili: "born during the rainy season."

MATANA (mah-TAH-nah) Hebrew: "gift." Contemporary Israeli name referring to the baby as a gift from God. (See box, page 94.)

MATILDA Old German: "battle maiden." This name is used in Central America, Estonia, Italy, Latvia, Lithuania, Mexico, Norway, Romania, Russia, Spain, and Sweden, as well as the United States. In most parts of the world, Tilda and Tilli are favorite pet forms. *Mat, Mathilda, Matti, Mattie, Matty, Maud, Maude, Tilda, Tildy, Tillie, Tilly* (English); *Matylda, Tylda* (Czech); *Mahaut, Matilde* (French); *Maddy, Malkin, Mathilde, Matty, Patty* (German); *Matelda* (Italian); *Macia, Mala, Tila* (Polish); *Mati, Matilde, Tilda, Tilde* (Spanish)

MATRIKA (mah-TREE-kah) Hindi: "mother." One of the many names for the Hindu goddess Shakti. See Shakti.

MATSU (maht-soo) Japanese: "pine." In Asia, the pine is a symbol of stability and firm old age, as well as the plant of January. *Matsuko* (Japanese)

MAUREEN Irish Gaelic: "little Mary" or "little bitter one"; or Old French: "dark-skinned." *Maura, Maurene, Maurine, Moira, Mora, Moreen* (English); *Morena* (Spanish)

MAUSI (MAW-see or MAU-see) Native American: "plucking flowers."

MAY Latin: "great"; or Arabic: "discerning." A time-of-birth name. *Mae, Maia, Maya, Maye* (English)

MAYA (MY-yah) Sanskrit: "God's creative power" or "illusion, fantasy." In the Hindu religion,

God's powers include the ability to act through women and men to create life. According to sacred Hindu writings, "God resides in the heart of all beings, and by His maya moves them from within as if they were turned by a machine." Some parents also bestow this name as a contemporary form of May ("great"). Famous namesake: poet Maya Angelou.

MAYLA Contemporary American creation, possibly a phonetic spelling of Mela, "religious gathering," "black," or "dark."

MAYOREE (may-YOHR-ee) Thai: "beautiful."

MAYSA (MAY-sah) Arabic: "one who walks proudly."

MEDA (MAY-duh) Native American: "prophet," "priestess," or "edible root."

MEEDA (MEE-dah) Irish Gaelic: "my thirst," implying a child is like a refreshing drink of water. In Ireland, this name is spelled *Mide. Mida* (English); *Mide* (Irish)

MEENA (MEE-nah) Sanskrit: "precious stone" or "a fish." *Mina* (Hindi)

MEGA (MEH-gah) Spanish: "gentle, mild, and peaceful."

MEGAN, MEGHAN (MAY-gun or MEH-gun) Greek: "great and mighty." Also a Welsh form of Margaret, "a pearl." *Meagan, Meaghen, Meg, Megen, Meghann* (English)

MEI (may) Chinese–Hawaiian: "beautiful." Many Chinese–Hawaiian names use this as an element. Examples: *Mei-Hua* ("beautiful flower"); *Mei-lien* ("beautiful lotus"); *Mei-Xing* ("beautiful star"); and *Mei-Zhen* ("beautiful pearl"). An alternative origin is the Latin *maia*, "great one," in which case the English equivalent is May.

MEIKO (may-ee-koh) Japanese: "a bud."

MEIRA (meh-EE-rah, or Anglicized, MEE-rah) Hebrew *m'eeraw:* "light." Popularized in Israel by Israeli prime minister Golda Meir, who changed her name from Golda Meyerson following the Israeli custom of choosing a Hebrew name. *Meera, Mira* (English)

MEL A Portuguese form of Melissa, "honey."

MELA (MAY-lah) Hindi: "religious gathering." Also a Polish form of Melanie, "black" or "dark." *Mayla* (English)

MELANIE Greek: "black" or "dark." Melanie is probably derived from Melanesia, the name of a region northeast of Australia, where the people are predominantly dark-skinned. Melanesia literally means "black islands." This name is used not only in the English-speaking world, but also in the Czech Republic, France, and Germany. Another Czech, French, German, Italian, and Polish form of the name is *Melania*. *Mel, Melani, Melany, Melenia, Melli, Mellie, Melly, Meloni, Melonie, Melony* (English); *Ela, Mela, Melka* (Polish); *Melana, Melaniya, Melanka, Melanya, Melashka, Melasya, Milya* (Russian); *Melena* (Slavic)

MELANTHA Greek: "black flower." The name probably comes from the deep-purple lily that once grew along Mediterranean shores.

MELBA Latin *malva:* "the mallow flower"; or Greek *malako:* "soft" or "slender." In China the mallow is considered a magic charm against evil; it's also the flower of September and of the astrological sign Virgo. *Malva, Melva* (English)

MELCIA (MELT-shuh, or Anglicized, MEL-shuh) Polish form of Amelia, "industrious" or "flatterer." See Amelia.

MELI (MEH-lee) Zuni form of Mary, "bitter." Also a Greek form of Melissa, "honey" or "a bee."

LEGENDS & LORE

If you want a person to love you, write his or her name three times on a piece of paper and wear it in your left shoe.

MELIA (meh-LEE-ah or MEEL-ya) Spanish form of Cornelia, "yellowish" or "cornell tree." See Cornelia. Also a short form of Amelia ("industrious" or "flatterer").

MELINDA Originally a form of Melissa, but used as an independent name since the 1800s, and gaining popularity.

MELISSA Greek: "honey" or "a bee." *Lindi, Lissa, Lynda, Malina, Malinda, Malinde, Mallie, Mally, Malina, Mel, Melina, Melinda, Melli, Mellie, Melly, Melynda* (English); *Meli* (Greek); *Mel* (Portuguese)

MELKA (MEL-kah) Polish form of Melanie, "black" or "dark." See Melanie.

MELODY Greek: "music" or "song." *Melodi, Melodie* (English)

"Sexy" Names:
Drawbacks in the Corporate World?

★ ★ ★

Far in the future, your baby girl will one day grow up. And when she does, her name may be perceived as "sexy" or "unsexy." If she has a sexy name, she may have more dates as a young woman, but she may also have more trouble scaling the corporate ladder. Such were the findings of a study done by Deborah Linville at Rensselaer Polytechnic Institute (a popular training ground for Fortune 500 company managers).

Linville asked seniors and grad students at RPI to rate 250 women's names on a scale from 1 (nonsexy) to 7 (sexy). She then asked students in another group to play boss and decide—on the basis of their first names only—which women they'd hire and promote. Male students promoted women with "unsexy" names like Edna and Elvira much faster and more readily than they did those with names that were considered sexy, such as Cheryl and Michelle. Linville's conclusion: When choosing women for jobs, men are prejudiced by the sexiness of the women's first names.

Names considered sexiest? You have to remember that such names will change over the years. But in this study the sexy names were Adrienne, Alicia, Andrea, Candace, Christine (ranked number one), Dawn, Gail, Heather, Holly, Jacqueline, Jennifer, Julia, Kathy, Maria, Marilyn, Melanie, Renée, Susan, Tamara, and Tina. Names with the least sex appeal (and hence likeliest to make it to that corner office) were Alma, Cornelia, Doris, Edna, Elvira, Esther, Ethel, Florence, Magdalena, Myrtle, Rosalind, Silvana, and Zelda.

MELOSA (meh-LO-sah) Spanish: "honeylike, sweet, or gentle."

MENORA (me-NOR-uh) Hebrew: "a candelabrum." Modern Israeli name. *Menorah* (Hebrew)

MERAH (mare-raah) Malay: "red-haired."

MERCEDES (mer-SAY-dees) Middle English: "mercy, compassion." Spanish name from the longer Santa Maria de las Mercedes ("Our Lady of Mercies"), referring to Mary, mother of Jesus.

MEREDITH Old Welsh: "a guardian from the sea." *Meri, Merideth, Merri, Merrie, Merry* (English)

MERI Finnish: "the sea." In Hebrew the same name means "rebellious," implying bitterness, and may come from Mary or Miriam.

MERIWA (me-RI-wah) Banti Eskimo: "thorn." This may have been used originally as a magic name to ward off evil spirits, to trick them into believing the child was unloved because she had a name with a prickly meaning.

MERYEM (MAY-re-em) Turkish development of Miriam ("rebellious" or "bitter") or Mary ("bitter").

MERYL One of the hundreds of variations of Mary, "bitter."

Popularized most recently by actress Meryl Streep. *Maryl, Merryl, Merle* (English)

MESHA (MAY-shah) Hindi: "ram." Hindu name for a child born under the sign of Aries, the ram.

MIA (MEE-ah) Modern American and Israeli name from Michaela, "Who is like God?" Also a pet form of Maria. Made well known by actress Mia Farrow.

MICHELE, MICHELLE Hebrew *Mikhael:* "Who is like God?" Much more popular today in the English-speaking world than the older form Michaela. The feminine form of Michael. *Mia, Michal, Michel, Micki, Mickie, Micky* (English); *Michaelle* (Italian)

MICHI (mee-chee) Japanese: "the righteous way." In Japanese, another character associated with this sound means "three thousand," expressing the hope that the family will extend for many generations. *Michiko* (Japanese)

MIDORI (mee-doh-ree) Japanese: "green." At one time Japanese color names referred to human qualities; Midori implies a hope that the child will be illustrious.

MIEKO (mee-eh-koh) Japanese: "child of prosperity."

MIGINA (mee-GEE-nah) Omaha Indian: "moon returning." Indicates the child was born during the new moon. In astrology the moon governs the sign of Cancer; the tarot card of the moon corresponds to Pisces.

MIKA (MEE-kah) Native American: "the knowing raccoon"; or Japanese *mikazuki:* "the moon of the third night (of the old lunar month)," or "new moon." In Russia this is a pet form of Dominika, "belonging to the Lord" or "born on Sunday." A short, easy-to-pronounce name that has developed in many cultures.

MIKI (mee-kee) Japanese: "stem." Possibly refers to the family tree. *Mikie, Mikiyo* (Japanese)

MIKKA (mee-kah) Japanese: "three days."

MILA (MEE-lah) Slavic: "loved by the people." A popular Czech name. The longer version is Ludmila.

MILADA (mi-LAH-dah) Czech *mi lada:* "my love." *Lada* refers to a goddess of youth, fertility, and love.

MILANA (mee-LAHN-ah) Italian: "from Milan, Italy." *Mila, Milan, Milanna* (English)

MILENA (MI-le-nah or mi-LAY-nuh) Slavic form of Melanie, "black" or "dark."

MILI (MEE-lee or MIL-ee) Hebrew: "who is like me." Contemporary Israeli name. Also a short form of Millicent or Millie.

MILICA (MI-lits-uh, or Anglicized, mi-LEE-kah) Originally from the ancient Gothic *amal,* "hard work," this name means "industrious." Slavic form of Amelia.

MILLIANI (mee-lee-AHN-ee) Hawaiian: "a gentle caress."

MILLICENT Old German: "industrious." *Lissa, Mel, Melli, Mellicent, Mellie, Mellisent, Melly, Mili, Milli, Millie, Millisent, Milly* (English)

MIMI French form of Helmine, "unwavering protector." Also a short form of Miriam, "bitter" or "rebellious."

MIN (min) Chinese: "sensitive" or "quick."

MINA (MEE-nah) A truly global name used by many cultures around the world. A Czech pet form of Hermina, "child of the earth"; English, German, and Polish short form of Helmine, "unwavering protector"; and a Hindu astrological name for a child born under Pisces, symbolized by the fishes.

MINAL (mee-NAHL) Native American: "fruit."

MINDA Hindi: "knowledge" or "wisdom."

MINDY Originally a nickname for Minna ("unwavering protector"), now used as an independent name. *Mindi, Mindie* (English)

MINEKO (mee-neh-ko) Japanese: "peak." Loosely translated, means "mountain child."

MINERVA Old Latin: "the mindful one." Name of the Roman goddess of wisdom. *Min, Minni, Minnie, Minny* (English); *Minette* (French)

MINNA German form of Helmine, "unwavering protector."

MINOWA (mi-NO-wah) Native American: "moving voice."

MINYA (MIN-yah) Osage: "older sister."

MIO (MEE-oh) Japanese: "triple cord." *Mioko* (Japanese)

MIRA (MEER-ah) Latin: "wonderful"; or Modern Israeli: "exalted." Also a short form or variation of many names, including Mirabel, Miranda, and Myra.

MIRABEL Spanish: "beautiful one." *Bella, Belle, Mira, Mirabella, Mirabelle* (English, Spanish)

MIRANDA Latin: "extraordinary one" or "worth admiring." *Maranda, Meranda, Mina, Mira,*

Mirinda, Mironda, Mirranda, Myranda, Randa, Randee, Randi, Randie, Randy (English)

MIRELLA (mi-RELL-ah) Hebrew: "God spoke," implying the child is the product of God's word. *Mireil, Mirela, Mirelle, Miriella, Mirilla, Myrella, Myrilla* (English)

MIRI (MEE-ree) English Gypsy: "mine." Also a Hebrew form of Miriam.

MIRIAM Hebrew: "rebellious" or "bitter." The original Hebrew form of Mary. *Mimi, Minni, Minnie, Mitzi* (English); *Mirjam* (Finnish); *Miri* (Hebrew); *Meliame* (Tongan)

MISTY Old English: "shrouded in mist." *Misti, Mistie, Mystee, Mysti* (English)

MITUNA (mi-TOO-nah) Miwok *mituye:* "to roll up." The connotation is "wrapping a salmon with willow stems and leaves after catching it."

MITZI Popular contemporary form of Miriam, "rebellious" or "bitter."

MIWA (mee-wah) Japanese: "the farseeing." The Japanese variation *Miwako* means "farseeing child."

MIYA (mee-yah) Japanese: "temple" or "Shinto."

MIYO (mee-yo) Japanese: "beautiful generations," often varied to *Miyoko,* "beautiful generations child."

MIYUKI (mee-yoo-kee) Japanese: "deep snow," connoting the peaceful silence following a heavy snowfall. *Yuki* (Japanese)

MOANI (moh-AHN-nee) Hawaiian: "fragrance."

MODESTY Latin: "modest one." Virtue name first used by Christians during the Roman Empire. *Modesta, Modestee, Modestene, Modestina* (English)

MOIRA (MOY-rah) Scottish form of Mary, "bitter." *Moirah, Moire, Moya, Moyra, Moyrah* (English)

MOLLY A perky, Irish-sounding form of Mary that isn't really Irish. Often associated with the song "Sweet Molly Malone." *Molli, Mollie*

MONA Greek: "just"; Italian: "my lady"; or Miwok: "gathering jimson-weed seed." The sound of this name has appealed to people across many cultures.

MONET (moh-NAY) French: "descendent of the protector." An artistic-sounding contemporary name borrowed from French impressionistic painter Claude Monet.

MONICA Latin: "wise adviser" or "nun"; or Greek: "alone." *Mona* (English); *Monique* (French); *Monika* (German); *Monca* (Irish)

MONIQUE (moh-NEEK) An exotic French form of Monica. *Mique* (French)

MORA Spanish: "little blueberry."

MORELA (moh-RAY-lah, or Anglicized, moh-REL-ah) Polish: "apricot." *Morella* (English)

MORENA (moh-RAY-nah) Spanish form of Maureen, "little Mary" or "little bitter one." See Maureen.

MORGAN Old Welsh: "seashore." In Arthurian legend, Morgan Le Fay was King Arthur's sister. *Morganne, Morgen, Morgenne* (English)

MORI (moh-ree) Japanese: "forest." A Japanese nature name. The variation *Moriko* means "forest child," whereas *Moriyo* means "forest generation."

MORIAH (moh-RYE-ah) Hebrew: "God is my teacher." *Moria, Morice, Moriel, Morit* (Hebrew)

MORRIN (MOR-rin) Irish Gaelic: "long-haired one." An English version of the ancient Irish name Muireann. *Morain, Morayne, Moriann, Morianne,*

Morin, Morri, Morrie, Morry, Murinn, Murrian (English); *Muireann, Muirinn, Murainin* (Irish)

MOYA A variation of Moira ("bitter"), the Scottish form of Mary. Popular in Great Britain.

MOZELLE (mo-ZE-le, or Anglicized, mo-ZEL) Hebrew: "taken from the water." Feminine form of Moses. *Moselle* (English)

MU-LAN (moo-lahn) Chinese: "magnolia blossom." In China the magnolia is the flower of May and a symbol of sweetness.

MU-TAN (moo-tahn) Chinese: "tree peony blossom." In China the peony, called the king of flowers, is the flower of March and spring and a symbol of love and affection.

MULYA (MOOL-yah) Miwok: "knocking acorns off a tree with a long stick," from *mule*, "to beat or hit." Acorns and fish were the chief foods of many Native Americans, and a number of stories are told about acorns. According to one Indian legend, all the creatures loved the first-born man except the she-frog, who envied his beautiful legs. Determined to get rid of the man, the frog spit poison into the man's water, and he died. The first-born man had promised he would give the Indians their most valued possession, and from his ashes sprang the first oak, covered with acorns as large as apples.

MUNA (MOO-nah or moo-NAH) Arabic: "desire" or "wish." Or Hopi: "freshet," given to a child born during the season the streams rise; From the Hopi cloud cult.

MUNIRAH (moo-NEE-rah) Arabic: "shedding light or illumination." *Muneera, Munira* (English)

MURA (moor-ah) Japanese: "village." The name may refer to the fact that a child or her parents came to the city from a village.

MURIAL Greek: "bitter" (a form of Mary); or Irish: "shining sea." *Marial, Meriel, Muriel, Muriell, Murielle* (English); *Muireall* (Scottish)

MURPHY Irish or Scottish Gaelic: "sea warrior." A common last name in Ireland, now popular in this country as a first name for girls and boys. *Murph, Murphie* (English)

MYA (MY-ah) Burmese: "emerald."

MYISHA (my-EE-shah) A form of the Arabic Aisha ("woman" or "life.") *Myeisha, Myesha, Myeshia*

MYRA (MY-rah) Latin: "sweet-smelling oil." A literary name invented by a seventeenth-century poet who used the name in his love poems. The feminine form of Myron.

MYRNA Gaelic: "gentle, beloved." *Merna, Mirna, Moina, Morna, Muirna, Murnia, Moyna* (English)

MYSTIQUE (miss-TEEK) French: "washed in an air of mystery." An exotic contemporary invention. *Mistique* (English)

NABILA (nay-BEE-lah) Arabic: "nobly born." *Nabeela, Nabiha, Nabilah* (Arabic)

NADDA (nah-DAH) Arabic: "generous" or "dewy." Popular in Arabic countries. *Nada, Naddah* (Arabic)

NADIA (NAHD-yah) Slavic: "hope." Used especially in Russia. Made well known by Romanian gymnast Nadia Comaneci. *Nadeen, Nadine* (English); *Nadine* (French); *Nadina* (Latvian); *Nata* (Polish); *Dusya, Nada, Nadenka, Nadina, Nadiya, Nadka, Nadya* (Russian)

NADIRA (nah-DEE-rah) Arabic: "precious" or "rare." *Nadirah*

NAGIDA (nah-GEE-dah) Hebrew: "wealthy" or "ruler."

NAIDA (nah-EE-dah or NAY-dah) Latin: "a river or water nymph." Name for a girl born under one of the water signs of Cancer, Pisces, or Scorpio.

NAILA (NAH-ee-lah) Arabic: "one who succeeds." *Nailah* (Arabic)

NAJILA (nah-JEE-lah) Arabic: "bright eyes." *Naja, Najah, Najilah* (Arabic)

NAKIA (nah-KEE-ah) Arabic: "pure." *Nakiah* (Arabic)

NALANI (nah-LAH-nee) Hawaiian: "the heavens."

NAMIKO (nah-mee-koh) Japanese: "wave child." *Nami* (Japanese)

NANA (NAH-nah) Hawaiian: "spring." Also a form of Anna, "graceful."

NANCY A variation of Anna, "graceful." *Nanci, Nancie* (English); *Nanice* (Tongan)

NANI Hawaiian: "beautiful." Also a contemporary Greek form of Ann, "graceful."

NARA Japanese: "oak"; or Old English: "nearest one." Also a Native American place-name. In Japan the oak is a symbol of steadfastness and stability.

According to one prehistoric myth, man sprang from the oak, thus making it the most sacred of trees.

NARESHA (nah-RESH-ah) Sanskrit: "king" or "lord." The feminine form of Naresh.

NARIKO (nah-ree-koh) Japanese: "thunder child," "humble child," or "child who climbs high." *Nari* (Japanese)

NASHAWNA Contemporary blend of the prefix *Na-* + Shawna. Many similar *"Na-"* names have recently been created. Others include: *Nakeesha, Nakeisha, Nakisha, Nareesha, Narisha, Natisha, Natonya, Natosha, Natoya* (English)

NASHOTA (nah-SHO-tah) Native American: "twin." Appropriate name for a girl born under the sign of Gemini, the twins.

NASNAN Athabascan, Carrier Indian: "surrounded by a song."

NASTACIA Latvian, Lithuanian, and Russian short form of Anastasia, "of the Resurrection." *Nastasha, Nastashia, Nastasya* (Russian)

NASYA (NAH-see-ah, or Anglicized, NAHS-yuh) Hebrew: "miracle of God." Contemporary name from Israel. *Nasia* (Hebrew)

NATA Native American: "speaker or creator"; Hindi: "rope dancer." Also a Polish form of Nadia, "hope," and a Polish and Russian form of Natalie.

NATALIA (nah-TAHL-yah) Form of Natalie, "born on Christmas."

NATALIE Latin: "born on Christmas." Familiar in the Czech Republic, France, and Germany, as well as this country. *Nat, Natala, Natalina, Nati, Natie, Natti, Nattie, Natty, Nataline, Nathalia, Nathalie, Netti, Nettie, Netty, Noel, Noelle, Novella* (English); *Natalia, Natasa* (Czech); *Natalle, Nathalie, Noelle,* (French); *Natalia* (German, Portuguese); *Nacia, Nata, Natalia, Natka* (Polish); *Nata, Natalka, Natalya, Natasha, Talya, Tasha, Tashka, Taska, Tasya, Tata, Tuska, Tusya* (Russian); *Neda* (Slavic); *Natacha, Nati, Talia* (Spanish)

NATANE (nah-TAH-neh) Arapaho: "daughter."

NATANIA (nah-TAHN-ya) Hebrew: "a gift of God." The feminine form of Nathan. *Natanya, Nathane, Nathania, Natonya* (English)

NATASHA Russian form of Natalie, "born on Christmas." See Natalie.

NATESA (nah-TAY-shah, or Anglicized, nah-TE-sah) Hindi: "dance lord." One of the 1,008

names for the Hindu god Siva.
Siva is usually pictured with
either one or five faces, four
arms, and a third eye which
appeared in order to save the
world from darkness when his
wife playfully covered his two
eyes with her hands. The third
eye can allegedly turn men to
ashes.

NAVIT (nah-VEET) Hebrew:
"beautiful" or "pleasant." *Nava,
Navice* (Hebrew)

NECI (NE-see, or Hungarian, NE-
tsi) Latin: "intense and fiery,"
referring to one who lives
intensely. A traditional Hungarian
name.

NEDA (NEH-dah) Old English:
"prosperous guardian." The
feminine form of Edward. Also a
Slavic form of Natalie, "born on
Christmas."

NEDIVA (neh-DEE-vah)
Hebrew: "noble and generous."

NEELA (NEE-lah) Mende,
Africa: "a cicada" or "pitch dark."

NEELY Contemporary
American feminine form of Neal,
"a champion." See Neila.

NEEMA (NEE-mah or neh-EH-
mah) Swahili: "born during a
prosperous time."

NEILA (NEE-lah) Irish Gaelic: "a
champion." The feminine form of

Neil. *Nea, Neala, Neali, Nealie,
Nealy, Neela, Neeli, Neelie, Neely,
Neili, Neily, Nia* (English)

NEKA (NAY-kah) Native
American: "the wild goose." This
may have been bestowed by a
proud father who, following a
tribal tradition, named his
daughter for a feat he had
accomplished, in this case the
shooting of many wild geese.

NELDA (NEL-dah) Irish Gaelic:
"a champion" or "a cloud." In
Ireland, this is a feminine form of
Niall, or Neal.

NELIA (nay-LEE-ah) Spanish
form of Cornelia, "yellowish" or
"cornell tree." See Cornelia.

NELKA (NEL-kah) Latin: "rock."
Contemporary Polish form of
Petronella, an older feminine
form of Peter. *Ela, Nela, Petra*
(Polish); *Peitra, Petra, Petrona,
Petronila, Tona* (Spanish)

NELLY A pet form of Helen
("light" or "torch"). *Nel, Nelli,
Nellie* (English)

NEMY (NEE-mee) Mende,
Africa: "sweet."

NENA (NEH-nah) Mende, Africa:
"very young" or "a black-seeded
plant with hard fruit."

NENAH, NENEH Trendy
contemporary American spellings
of Nina, "girl."

NENET (neh-NET) Egyptian: "the goddess Nenet." In Egyptian mythology, the goddess Nenet personifies the inert, motionless character of the primeval waters in which the Creator is said to have lived.

NEPA (NEH-pah) Arabic: "walking backward." This is another name for the constellation Scorpio, the scorpion. Alchemists believed that iron could be turned into gold only when the sun was in Scorpio.

NERISSA Greek: "daughter of the sea." Name for a girl born under one of the water signs of Cancer, Pisces, or Scorpio. *Nerice, Nerine, Nerisse, Rissa* (English)

NESSA Russian pet form of Anastasia, "of the Resurrection." See Anastasia.

NETIA (NEHT-ee-uh) Hebrew: "plant" or "shrub." Used in Israel as well as the United States. *Neta, Netta* (English, Hebrew)

NETIS (NAY-tis) Native American: "trusted friend."

NETTA (NET-tah) Mende, Africa: "a door." *Neata, Neta* (Mende)

NEVADA Spanish: "white as snow." From the state of the same name. *Neva* (English)

NEZA (NEH-zhuh) A Slavic form of Agnes, "pure." See Agnes.

NIA (NEE-ah) A pet form of Neila ("a champion") growing in popularity as a given name.

NIABI (nee-AH-bee) Native American: "a fawn."

NICHELLE (ni-SHEL, rhymes with Michelle) A French form of Nicole ("victorious army" or "victorious people"), gaining popularity in this country. *Nichele* (French)

NICOLE, NICHOLE (ni-KOHL) Greek: "victorious army" or "victorious people." The feminine form of Nicholas. *Colette, Collete, Cosette, Nichol, Nicholle, Nicki, Nickie, Nicol, Nicola, Nicoleen, Nicolete, Nicoli, Nicoline, Nicolle, Nikki, Nikolette, Nikolia* (English); *Nichele, Nichelle, Nicolette* (French); *Niki* (Greek)

NIDA (NEE-dah) Omaha Indian: "the Nida creature," referring to a mythical being or animal which, according to Omaha legend, crept elf-like in and out of the earth. Also an Indian name referring to the bones of extinct mammals, such as the mastodon.

NIDA (NEE-dah) Arabic: "call."

NIKA Russian pet form of Dominique, "belonging to God."

LEGENDS & LORE

When lighting a fire, give it the name of someone you love. If the fire goes out, your love is unrequited. If it burns, your love is returned.

NIKI Modern Greek form of Nicole, "victorious army" or "victorious people."

NILI (NEE-lee) Hebrew: an abbreviation for the words "the glory (or eternity) of Israel will not lie or repent," from I Samuel 15:29. During World War I, a pro-British/anti-Turkish underground organization in Palestine was named Nili. Current Israeli name for both girls and boys.

NILLA (NIL-lah) Mende, Africa: "glorious." *Nola* (Mende)

NIMA (NEE-mah) Hebrew: "thread"; or Arabic: "a blessing." *Nimah, Nimat* (Arabic)

NINA Native American: "mighty"; or Spanish: "girl." Also a familiar form of Ann. *Nena,*

Nenah, Neneh, Ninetta, Ninette, Ninnetta, Ninnette (English)

NINITA (nee-NEE-tah) Spanish: "little girl." Popular among the Zuni Indians.

NIPA (NEE-pah) Todas, India: "stream."

NIREL (ni-RAYL) Hebrew: "God's light" or "planted field." Comes to us from Israel.

NIRVELI (neer-VAY-li) Todas, India: "water" or "water child."

NISHA (NEE-sha) Trendy contemporary name ending now also used independently. In India, this name comes from Sanskrit and means "night." *Neesha, Neisha, Nesha, Neshia, Nishi* (English)

NISHI (nee-shee) Japanese: "west." A Japanese proverb goes, "From the east the root, from the west the fruit."

NISSA Hausa, Africa: "a remembered loved one"; or Scandinavian: "friendly elf" or "friendly brownie"; or Hebrew: "to test." *Nisa* (Hebrew); *Nisse* (Scandinavian)

NITA (NEE-tah) Choctaw: "bear." Also a pet Spanish form of Anita or Ann, "graceful."

NITARA (ni-TAH-rah) Sanskrit: "deeply rooted."

NITSA Popular modern Greek form of Helen, "light" or "torch." See Helen.

NITUNA (nee-TOO-nah) Native American: "my daughter."

NIZANA (nee-ZAH-nah) Hebrew: "bud." Hebrew flower name. *Nitza, Nitzana, Zana* (Hebrew)

NOELLE (no-EL) Form of Natalie, "born on Christmas." *Noel, Noele, Noeleen, Noeline, Noell* (English); *Nowlle* (French

NOGA (NO-gah) Hebrew: "shining" or "morning light." Also a boys' name in Israel.

NOLA Irish Gaelic: "white shoulders"; or Latin: "bell," referring to an Italian town associated with the invention of church bells. This is also a form of the African name Nilla, "glorious." *Nolana, Noleen, Nolena, Nuala* (English)

NOLCHA (NOHL-chah) Native American: "the sun."

NONA Hausa, Africa: "breast milk"; or Latin: "nine," implying "ninth-born child." A possible numerological name.

NORA A pet form of Helen, "light" or "torch." See Helen for many other forms of this name used around the world.

NORI (nor-ee) Japanese: "precept" or "doctrine." *Norie, Noriko* (Japanese)

NORMA Latin: "model or pattern." Sometimes considered a feminine form of Norman.

NOURA (NO-rah) Arabic: "light," indicating a hope that the child's presence will bring illumination.

NOVA Hopi: "chasing (a butterfly)." From the Hopi badger cult. Also Latin: "young or new."

NUDAHR (noo-DAHR) Arabic: "gold." A precious child. Popular in Arabic countries.

NUMA (NOO-mah) Hausa, Africa: "ripened." Also an Arabic form of the Biblical Naomi, "beautiful and pleasant."

NUNA (NOO-nah) Native American: "land."

NURIA (noo-REE-ah) Hebrew: "fire of the Lord." Currently used in Israel as well as the United States. *Nuri, Nuriel* (Hebrew)

NURIT (noo-REET) Hebrew: "little yellow flower." The plant from which this name comes blooms annually in Israel. *Nurice, Nurita* (Hebrew)

NUSI (NOO-shi) Hungarian form of Hannah, "graceful." See Hannah.

Six Hidden Messages a Name Can Send

★ ★ ★

When naming your baby, what *unconscious* meaning is your baby's name sending to the world?

- *"I come from a distinguished old family."* If you have distinguished family ties, you may want a name that's been in your family for generations. Many wealthy Americans from Joseph Kennedy to John D. Rockefeller have done this when naming their sons. If this is a message you want to convey, use Roman numerals after your baby's name—not "Jr." (see page 19). The name should truly sound distinguished: John J. Montgomery III.

- *"I'm unique and creative."* If you feel your child will be a true "pioneer" in some way choose names a bit more offbeat. Many actors have changed their names

for this very reason. Christiana Judd became Wynnona, Susan Weaver opted for Sigourney, Caryn Johnson became the one and only Whoopi Goldberg. When Demi Moore and Bruce Willis named their daughters Rumer Glenn and Scout Larue, this is one message they sent.

- *"I'm reliable and predictable."* If you hope your child will be successful in business (a great investment banker, stockbroker, or CEO), stick with the tried-and-traditional. You might even consider a first and middle name that could be shortened to impressive-sounding initials (James Paul, for example, can be called J. P., and Jacqueline Blaine can become J.B. in the boardroom). It's true, though, that successful executives have all sorts of names.

◆ *"I'm proud of my heritage."* A name that's obviously from a specific culture—such as Caitlin if you're Irish, Karim if you're Arabic, Manuel if you're Hispanic, or Zen if you're Japanese—will say your baby has deep roots in a proud tradition. Saintly and Biblical names like Luke, Mark, Matthew, Rachel, and Sara convey this message, as do names that are traditionally Hindu, Jewish, or Moslem. Many African-Americans have chosen baby names like Keshia, Latoya, and Yanci (Hausa for "freedom") to celebrate their identity.

◆ *"I'm culturally sophisticated."* Decades ago, experts were appalled when Americans gave their babies names like Jared O'Hara or Tanaka Jones. After all, didn't everyone "know" that O'Hara was an Irish last name and "deserved" an Irish first name? Times have changed. Many Americans now view mixing first and last names from vastly different cultures as sophisticated—telling the world, "I respect many ways of life." When actress Melissa Gilbert gave her baby boy the Sioux name Dakota, author Marianne Williamson named her little girl India Emmeline, and newscaster Paula Zahn called her son Jared Branden, they were sending this message.

◆ *"I'm someone to take seriously."* Recently, some parents are giving boys strongly "macho" names like Conan, Flint, Spike, and Wolf. Strong-sounding girls' names include formerly masculine names like Gordon, Kenneth, and Tyler. Long gone are the overly sweet names for girls like Candy, Honey, Sugar, and Taffy. Naming your daughter Dallas, Jordan, or Tyson, you're also saying "Don't dismiss my opinions. I deserve your *respect."*

NUWA (noo-WAH) Chinese: "mother goddess."

NYOKO (nee-YOH-koh) Japanese: "treasured child" or "gem."

NYSSA Greek: "the beginning." Also a contemporary spelling of Nissa, "friendly elf" or "friendly brownie." See Nissa. *Nysa* (English)

OBA (oh-BAH) Yoruba, Nigeria: "ancient river goddess."

OBELIA (oh-BEEL-ya) Bini, Africa: loosely translated, "off the beaten path." Refers to a track cut through the bush with a machete and not meant to be used as a path. Hence, the implication: a child who goes her own way. *Belia, Belya* (English)

OCTAVIA Latin: "eighth-born child." *Octaviana, Tavia, Tavie* (English); *Octavie* (French); *Ottavia* (Italian)

ODELIA Hebrew: "I will praise God"; Old English: "from the wood hill"; or Old Anglo-French: "wealthy." *Delia, Odella, Odelyn* (English); *Odetta, Odette, Odile, Odilia* (French); *Oda, Odila, Odile* (German)

ODERA (oh-DAY-ruh) Hebrew: "plow."

ODETTA French form of Odelia, "wealthy." *Oddetta, Odette* (English)

ODINA (oh-DEEN-ah) Algonquian: "mountain."

OGIN (oh-GEEN) Native American: "the wild rose."

OHARA (oh-hah-rah) Japanese: "small field." Originally a Japanese surname. Spelled *O'Hara*, this is also an Irish name meaning "child of the bitter or sharp one."

OKALANI (oh-kah-LAH-nee) Hawaiian: "of the heavens" or "from Heaven." (See box, page 143.)

OKI (oh-kee) Japanese: "in the middle of the ocean." Possibly given originally to a child born at sea.

OLA (OO-lah) Old Norse: "ancestral relic." Comes from Scandinavia. The feminine form of Olaf.

OLATHE (o-LAH-tha) Native American: "beautiful."

OLENA (oh-LEN-ah or ol-YEN-ah) Russian form of Helen, "light" or "torch." See Helen.

OLESIA (oh-LE-shuh) Polish form of Alexandra, "helper and defender of mankind." See Alexandra.

OLGA Old Norse *helga:* "holy one." First popularized by Saint Olga, who spread Christianity in Russia during the tenth century. Still one of the most popular names in Russia today, Olga is now used around the world. *Elga, Helga, Olia, Olva* (English); *Olina, Olunka, Oluska* (Czech); *Olli, Olly* (Estonian); *Ola, Olenka* (Polish); *Lelya, Lesya, Olenka, Olesya, Olka, Olya, Olyusha* (Russian)

OLIANA (oh-lee-AH-nuh) Hawaiian: "oleander." Refers to an evergreen with white or red blossoms.

OLINDA Latin: "sweet-smelling." *Olynda* (English)

OLISA (o-LEE-sah) Ibo, Africa: "God." In Africa, this name is often used as part of a longer name. *Belu Olisa,* for example, implies that nothing is possible without God's help or approval.

OLIVIA Latin: "olive tree" or "olive branch." *Olive, Ollie, Olva, Liv, Livia, Livrie, Nola, Nollie* (English); *Oliwia* (Hawaiian)

OLYMPIA Greek: "from Olympus" or "heavenly." *Olympe* (French); *Olympie* (German); *Olimpia* (Italian, Spanish)

OMA (OH-mah) Bini, Africa: "a large tree"; Arabic: "commander." In Arabic cultures, the feminine form of Omar.

Letting Your Baby Choose Her Own Name

✳ ✳ ✳

American parents who are having trouble settling on a name might consider some customs from other cultures. Among the Kaffirs of India, the moment after the baby is born, it is placed at the mother's breast while another woman rapidly recites names until the baby begins to feed. The name spoken at the precise moment the baby takes its first suck of milk is the baby's name for life. A variation in other cultures is to recite names rapidly until the baby sneezes or smiles.

OMUSA (oh-MOO-sah) Miwok: "to miss with arrows," referring to a time the child's father tried to shoot a deer and missed.

ONA (OH-nah) Bini, Africa: "a pattern" or "this one." Also a Lithuanian form of Hannah, "graceful." See Hannah.

ONATAH (oh-NAH-tah) Iroquois: "corn spirit and daughter of the earth." According to Iroquois legend, the corn spirit was captured by the spirit of evil while looking for dew. She was imprisoned underground until the sun guided her back to her lost fields. She never again looked for dew.

ONAWA (oh-NAH-wah) Native American: "wide-awake one." For a child who never sleeps and keeps her parents awake or for a baby who is brightly alert.

ONI (OH-nee) Yoruba, Nigeria: "child born on holy ground"; or Beni, Nigeria, "desired."

ONIDA (oh-NEE-dah) Native American: "the looked-for one."

OPRAH Of uncertain meaning. May come from Hebrew: "a fawn" or "a runaway." The popularity of actress and talk-show hostess Oprah Winfrey dominates the image of this name, which originally came from the older and rarely used Biblical name Orpah. *Ophra, Ophrah, Opra* (English)

ORAH Hebrew: "light." *Ora, Oralee, Orit, Orlice, Orly* (Hebrew)

ORELLA Latin: "an announcement from God." *Orela, Orell* (English)

ORENDA Iroquois: "magic powers." This name refers to the power inherent in all things, from rocks to man. According to Iroquois belief, this force can affect and control others; therefore, owning an object or animal with great strength is said to increase one's inner potential. The Huron Indians call this same force Oki; the Sioux named it Wakanda.

ORI (OR-ee) Bini, Africa: "a corncake," referring to an African cake usually wrapped in a large leaf. *Orie, Orrie* (Bini)

ORIANA (or-ee-AN-nah) Celtic: "golden"; or Latin: "dawning." *Oralia, Orelda, Orelle, Orlann, Orlene* (English)

ORIEL (or-ee-EL) Latin: "golden one." A variation of Auriel. *Oralia, Orielle* (English)

ORINDA (oh-RIN-dah) Hebrew: "pine tree"; or Irish: "light-skinned."

ORINO (o-ree-no) Japanese: "weaver's field." *Ori* (Japanese)

ORIOLE Latin: "golden one." Nature name from a species of bird often flecked with yellow or golden-orange.

ORLENDA Russian *orlitza:* "female eagle." This name was first used by English Gypsies.

ORNICE Hebrew: "fir" or "cedar tree." *Orna, Ornit* (Hebrew)

OSA (OH-sah) Bini, Africa: "god-like," referring to the Creator of the universe. Other meanings for this Bini name are "beautiful" and "friend." *Ossa* (Bini)

OSANNA (oh-ZAHN-ah) Latin: "Praise the Lord." A variation of Hosanna.

OSEN (oh-sen) Japanese: "thousand." This unusual name was originally bestowed because of a belief in the magical power of round numbers.

OSHANA (oh-SHAH-nah) Contemporary invention from the prefix *"O-"* + Shawna ("God is gracious"). *Oshanda, Oshanna, Oshawna* (English)

OSTEN (AH-sten) German: "from the East." A German place-name now used for girls.

OVA (OH-vah) Hausa, Africa: "born in January"; or Bini, Africa: "sunshine."

OYA (OH-yah) Miwok: "to name," the connotation being

"naming or speaking of the kuiatawila bird (jacksnipe)."

P

PADMA (PAHD-mah) Hindi: "lotus." The national flower of Hindu India, the padma opens by day and closes at night. In Hindu belief, the god Brahma sprang from a mystical lotus, which grew from the navel of the god Vishnu.

PAGE, PAIGE Greek: "child"; or Old English: "a young attendant." Currently trendy. *Paget, Pagett* (English)

PAKA (PAH-kah) Swahili: "pussycat."

PAKUNA (pah-KOO-nah) Miwok: "deer bounding while running downhill."

PALILA (pah-LEE-luh) Hawaiian: "bird."

PALOMA (pah-LOH-mah) Spanish: "dove." A symbol for peace. Made well known recently by daughter of Pablo Picasso, designer Paloma Picasso.

PAMELA Greek: "all-honey." Created in the sixteenth century by poet Sir Philip Sidney, who also created the name Stella. *Pam,*

Pamelina, Pamella, Pammi, Pammie, Pammy (English)

PANDITA (pahn-DEE-tah) Hindi: "scholar."

PANYA (PAHN-yah) Swahili: "mouse," referring to a tiny baby. Also a favorite Russian form of Stephanie, "crowned one."

PAPINA (pah-PEE-nuh) Miwok: "a vine growing on an oak tree."

PARI (pah-REE) Persian: "a fairy eagle."

PASHA Greek *pelagos:* "from the sea." Popular in Russia. *Palasha, Pashka, Pelageya* (Russian)

PATI (PAT-ee) Miwok: literally "to break by twisting," but connotes "twisting willows for carrying fish." In astrology, the fishes are the symbol of Pisces.

PATIA (pah-TEE-uh) Spanish Gypsy: "leaf." The name connotes the freshness of spring.

PATIENCE Latin: "one who endures with courage." A virtue name similar to Chastity, Prudence, and Serenity.

PATRICIA Latin: "noble." An ancient name (recorded as early as the sixth century), which has now been replaced in popularity with its shorter forms like Trisha and Trish. The feminine form of

Patrick. *Pat, Patrice, Patsy, Patti, Patty, Tricia, Trish, Trisha* (English)

PAULA Latin: "little." A family name in many countries, including Hungary, Latvia, Poland and the Spanish-speaking world, as well as the United States. *Pauletta, Paulette, Pauli, Paulie, Paulina, Pauline, Paulita, Pauly, Polli, Pollie, Polly* (English); *Paulina* (Bulgarian); *Pavla, Pavlina* (Czech); *Paolina* (Italian); *Pawlina, Pola, Polcia* (Polish); *Pavla, Pavlina, Pavlinka* (Russian); *Paulita* (Spanish)

PAUSHA (POH-shah) Hindi: "born during the Hindu lunar month of Pausha," which corresponds to the astrological sign of Capricorn.

PAVLA (PAHV-lah) Czech and Russian form of Paula, "little."

PAYTON Old English: "one from the fighter's estate." Also a pet form of Patrick. Originally a boys' name now also used for girls. *Peyton* (English)

PAZ (pahz) Spanish: "peace."

PAZI (PAH-zee) Ponca Indian: "yellow bird."

PAZIA (pah-ZEE-ah) Hebrew: "golden." Comes to this country from Israel. *Paz, Paza, Pazice, Pazit* (Hebrew)

PEDZI Babudja *ku pedza,*
southern Rhodesia: "to finish."
The name literally means
"finisher," and is bestowed on the
last child a mother and father
plan to have.

PEGGY Originally a pet form of
Margaret ("a pearl") used as an
independent name since the
1800s. *Peg, Peggi, Peggie, Peggy*
(English)

PEKE (PE-ke) Old German:
"shining" or "glorious." A form of
Bertha used in Hawaii, this name
originally refered to an ancient
German fertility goddess.

PELIPA (peh-LEE-pah) Greek:
"lover of horses." A Zuni form of
Philippe. See Philippa.

PEMBA (PEHM-bah) Bambara,
Africa: "the force of present
existence." According to Bambara
belief, Pemba works with Faro
(the force of the future), making
the world go around, moving the
stars, and directing the affairs of
mankind.

PENDA (PEN-dah) Swahili:
"admired" or "loved."

PENELOPE (pe-NEL-oh-pee)
Greek: "weaver." A multicultural
name, used in France, Italy,
Norway, Portugal, Spain, Sweden,
and other countries, as well as
the United States. *Pen, Penina,
Penine, Penni, Penny* (English);
Pinelopi, Pipitsa, Popi (Greek);

Pela, Pelcia, Penelopa, Lopa
(Polish)

PENI Athabascan, Carrier
Indian: "his mind." Once used by
a Carrier Indian prophet who is
said to have communicated with
the spirit world during cataleptic
fits and could allegedly hear what
people were thinking.

PENINA (pay-NEE-nah)
Hebrew: "coral"; or a Hebrew
form of Margaret, "a pearl."
Peninah, Peninit (Hebrew)

PENNY Originally a pet form of
Penelope ("weaver"), but long
used as an independent name.
Penney, Pennie (English)

PEONY Greek: "giving praise."
A flower name. *Peonie* (English)

PEPITA (pay-PEE-tah) Spanish
form of Josephine, "addition" or
"increase," implying the child will
be fruitful. Became quite popular
in Spanish countries after 1621,
when the Pope named March 19
a festival day for Saint Joseph.

PEPPER Latin: "the pepper
plant" or "spicy as pepper." Spicy
girls' names such as this have
replaced the sweet names that
were so popular in the past, such
as Cooky, Candy, and Taffy.

PERI Greek: "mountain
dweller"; Hebrew: "fruit"; or
Persian: "fairy." Used in many
countries.

PERLA (PER-lah) Slavic form of Margaret, "a pearl."

PERRY Latin: "traveler, stranger, or pilgrim." Originally a boys' name now also used for girls. *Perri, Perriann, Perrie, Perrin* (English)

PHILIPPA Greek: "lover of horses." The feminine form of Philip. *Phil, Philipa, Philippe, Philli, Phillie, Pippa, Pippy* (English); *Fiipote, Philippine* (French); *Filippa, Filippina,* *Pippa* (Italian); *Filipa, Filpina, Ina, Inka* (Polish); *Pelipa* (Zuni)

PHYLLIS Greek: "a leafy branch." In mythology, this was the name of princess who was turned into an almond tree. *Philis, Phillis, Philliss, Phillys, Phylis, Phylliss* (English); *Filide* (Italian); *Filis* (Spanish)

PIA Greek: "pious." Used in Spanish cultures as a feminine form of Pio.

Miwok Farewell-to-Spring-Seed Names

✳ ✳ ✳

The Miwok Indians, who speak a language known as Moquelumnan, frequently create names that reflect their partnership with nature, and mean even more than they first appear to. Among Miwok farewell-to-spring-seed names (which refer to a plant used by the Miwok), for example, we have:

Loiyetu: "farewell-to-spring in bloom."

Malkuyu: "farewell-to-spring flowers drying."

Memtba: from *memttu:* "to taste," and means "tasting farewell-to-spring seed after it has been mashed with the pestle but while still in the mortar."

Muliya: from *mule,* "to beat or hit," with the connotation, "hitting farewell-to-spring seed with a stick as the seed hangs on the bush."

PILAR (pee-LAHR) Spanish: "pillar" or "fountain base." A favorite in most of the Spanish-speaking world, this name refers to the Virgin Mary, pillar of the Christian religion.

PILISI (pi-LEE-see) Greek: "a green branch." A Hawaiian form of Phyllis. *Pilis* (Hawaiian)

PINDA (PIN-dah) Mende, Africa: "a good jumper."

PING Chinese: "duckweed"; or Vietnamese: "peaceful."

PINGA (PEEN-gah) Hindi: "dark" or "tawny." One of the more than one thousand names for the Hindu goddess Shakti. See Shakti.

PIPER Old English: "pipe player," referring especially to a strolling minstrel.

PIPPA Pet form of Philippa ("lover of horses"), increasingly used as a given name, especially in Britain.

PITA (PEE-tah) Bari, southern Sudan: "fourth-born daughter."

PLACIDA (plah-SEE-dah) Latin: "tranquil; calm." Popular in Spanish cultures as a feminine form of Placido. *Placidia* (Spanish)

POLLY Originally a pet form of Mary ("bitter") or Paula ("little"), now used as an independent name. *Polley, Polli, Pollie* (English); *Poli* (Tongan)

POLLYAM (poh-lee-YAHM) Hindi: "the goddess of the plague." Among the Hindus of Madras this is a popular name for both sexes and is bestowed to appease the plague spirit and to keep her from striking.

PONI (PO-nee) Bari, southern Sudan: "second-born child."

POPPY Latin: "the poppy flower." The poppy is the flower of August in the West and the Chinese flower of December. In Asian astrology the poppy is the herb of the moon, which governs the sign Cancer.

POSALA (poh-SAH-lah) Miwok: "to burst," with the connotation of "pounding farewell-to-spring seed."

PRIMA (PREE-mah) Latin: "first-born child" or simply "first."

PRISCA A Spanish form of Priscilla ("one from primitive or ancient times").

PRISCILLA (pris-SILL-ah) Latin: "one from primitive or ancient times." A name with an old-fashioned ring kept in the limelight in the twentieth century by actress Priscilla Presley. *Cilla, Precilla, Prescilla, Pricilla, Pris, Priscila, Priss, Prissila, Prissy,*

Sila (English); *Prisca, Priscella, Priscila, Prisilla, Prissy* (Spanish)

PRIYA (PREE-yah) Hindi: "sweet-natured" or "lovable." Popular in India. *Priyal, Priyam, Priyanka, Priyata, Pryasha, Pryati* (Hindi)

PRU A short form of Prudence ("intelligent, foresightful one") now used as an independent name. *Prudie, Prudy, Prue, Pruedi* (English)

PUA (POO-ah) Hawaiian: "flower."

PUALANI (poo-ah-LAH-nee) Hawaiian: "heavenly flower." Probably refers to the wild ginger blossom or the bird-of-paradise in bloom. *Puni* (Hawaiian)

PURA (PURE-ah) Latin: "pure." Used in Spanish cultures as a reference to the Virgin Mary, purest of all women.

QIANRU (CHYAN-roo) Chinese: "pretty smile."

QUANIKA (kwah-NEE-kah) Contemporary blend of the prefix *"Qua-"* + Nika ("belonging to God"). *Nika, Niki, Nikka,* *Nikki, Quanikka, Quanikki, Quanique* (English)

QUANISHA (kwa-NEE-sha) Contemporary American blend of *"Qua-"* + Aisha ("woman" or "life"). *Neisha, Nisha, Quaneisha* (English)

QUEISHA (KAY-shah) A variation of the popular Keisha, which in turn may come from the African Keshia ("favorite one"). *Quesha* (English)

QUERIDA (keh-REE-dah) Spanish: "beloved."

QUESTA French: "one who searches."

QUETA (KAY-tah) Short form of the Spanish name Enriqueta, which in turn is a form of Henrietta, "ruler of the household."

QUIANA, QUIANNA Exotic contemporary invention from the prefix *Qui-* + Anna ("graceful"). See also Kiana.

QUINETTE Latin: "fifth-born." *Quin, Quinci, Quincie, Quincy, Quinetta, Quintessa, Quintina, Tess, Tessa, Tessi, Tessie, Tina* (English)

QUINTESSA Latin: "essence." Gaining some attention, possibly because it sounds a bit like Contessa and hence has a regal flair. *Quentessa, Quentice, Quinta, Quintice* (English)

QUIRINA (ke-REE-nah) Latin: "warlike one," referring to the Roman god Mars. In Spanish cultures, this is a feminine form of the boys' name Quirino.

R

RABI (rah-BEE) Arabic: "breeze." Has the connotation of a pleasant, fragrant scent. *Rabiah* (Arabic)

RACHEL Hebrew: "an ewe." In the Bible, Rachel was Leah's sister and a rival for their husband Jacob's affection. *Rachele, Rachelle, Rae* (English); *Rahil* (Bulgarian); *Rachelle* (French); *Rahel* (German); *Lahela, Rahela* (Hawaiian); *Rakel* (Norwegian, Swedish); *Raquel* (Portuguese, Spanish); *Rakhil, Rakhila, Rashel* (Russian); *Lesieli* (Tongan); *Rachel, Ruchel* (Yiddish)

RADELLE (rah-DEL) Old English: "counselor to the elves." *Della, Delle, Radella* (English)

RADINKA (rah-DEEN-kah) Slavic: "energetic" or "active."

RADMILLA (rahd-MEEL-lah) Slavic: "worker for the people."

RAFA Arabic: "happy or prosperous one."

RAI (ray, or in Japanese, rah-ee) Japanese: "next." Variation: *Raiko* ("next child").

RAIDAH (rah-EE-dah) Arabic: "leader."

RAINA (RAY-nah) A short form of Regina ("queen"). *Rayna* (English); *Reina* (Spanish)

RAINIE Another short form of Regina, gaining use as an independent name. May also be a contemporary development from the Native American name *Raini*, "the Creator." Actress Andie MacDowell has a daughter named Rainie.

RAISA (rah-EE-sah) Yiddish: "rose." Made well known worldwide by Raisa Gorbachev. *Raissa, Raiza* (English); *Raizel* (Yiddish)

RAIZEL (RAY-zel) Yiddish: "rose flower." *Rayzil, Razil* (Yiddish)

RAJA (RAH-jah) Arabic: "the anticipated one" or "hoped for."

RAKEL A favorite in Sweden, form of Rachel, "an ewe."

RAMA, RAMAH (RAM-ah) Sanskrit: "pleasing," referring to the most revered Hindu deity; Hausa, Africa: "restoration" or "thin"; and Hebrew: "lofty, exalted one." A name used in many cultures.

RAMLA (RAHM-lah) Swahili: "fortune-teller."

RAMONA (rah-MO-nah)
Spanish: "mighty protector" or
"wise protector."

RANA (RAH-nah) Arabic: "eye-
catching" or "beautiful to gaze
upon." A favorite in Arabic
cultures. *Raniyah, Ranya*
(Arabic)

RANANA (rah-NAHN-ah)
Hebrew: "fresh." A traditional
Jewish name.

RANDA (RAHN-dah) Arabic:
"the sweet-smelling randa tree,"
referring to a tree that grows in
the desert.

RANDI Old English: "shield-
wolf." Popular today as a modern
feminine form of Randolph. The
name possibly refers to a war
shield that made its owner
invincible. *Randie, Randy*
(English)

RANE (RAH-neh) Latin: "queen"
or "pure." Popular in Norway. In
Iceland this name is used for
boys. See Regina.

RANI (RAH-nee) Hindi: "queen."

RANIELLE (ran-YEL) A contemporary American creation, possibly
modeled after Danielle ("God is
my judge"). *Rani, Raniel, Raniell,
Ranyel, Ranyelle* (English)

RANITA (rah-NEE-tah) Hebrew:
"song" or "joy." Originally from
Israel. *Ranice, Ranit* (Hebrew)

RAQUEL (rah-KELL) A Spanish
form of Rachel, "an ewe."
Associated in many parts of the
world with actress Raquel Welch.
See Rachel.

RASHA Arabic: "a young
gazelle."

RASHIDA (rah-SHEE-dah)
Swahili: "righteous"; or Sanskrit:
"one who follows the right
course." *Rasheeda, Rashi*
(Swahili)

RASIA (RAH-see-ah) Greek:
"rose."

RATRI (rah-TREE) Hindi:
"night." One of the many names
for the revered Hindu goddess
Shakti.

RAWNIE (RAW-nee) English
Gypsy: "lady."

RAYNA (RAY-nah) Scandinavian:
"mighty"; or Yiddish: "clean; pure."
Also a short form of Regina
("queen"). *Raynell, Raynette,
Reyna, Reyne* (English)

RAZILEE (rah-zi-LEE) Hebrew:
"my secret." *Razili* (Hebrew)

REA Greek: "poppy." Contemporary flower name. Can also be
translated as "a stream."

REBECCA Hebrew: "bound." In
the Bible, Rebekah was Isaac's
wife. *Becca, Becki, Beckie, Becky,
Bekka, Bekki, Bekkie, Rena,*

Rebeka (English); *Reveka* (Bulgarian, Greek); *Rebeka* (Czech, Hungarian, Polish); *Rebeca* (Portuguese, Spanish); *Reveca* (Romanian); *Revekka* (Russian); *Becky, Rebekah, Rifka* (Yiddish)

REENA (REE-nah) Hausa, Africa: "dyed with indigo" or "embroidered." Also another spelling of Rina.

REGAN Popular contemporary form of Regina ("queen"), brought into the mainstream as a girls' name while Ronald Reagan was president. *Reagan, Reaganne, Regin* (English)

REGINA Latin: "queen." *Gina, Raina, Raini, Rainie, Rayna, Regan, Regi, Regie, Reggi, Reggie, Reggy, Regine, Reyna, Rina* (English); *Reine, Reinette* (French); *Gina, Regina* (German); *Reina* (Italian, Spanish); *Rane* (Norwegian); *Ina, Renia* (Polish)

REIKO (rah-ee-ko, or Anglicized, RAY-koh) Japanese: "pretty child" or "next child." *Rei* (Japanese)

REN Japanese: "water lily" or "lotus." The lotus is the Buddhist symbol both of purity, because the flower grows from muddy water and remains untainted, and of perfection, because its fruit is ripe when the flower blooms, which embodies the oneness of Buddhist teaching and knowl-edge. The Buddhist paradise contains a pond filled with ambrosia and multicolored lotus blossoms, and the flower is said to have sprung from the graves of devout Buddhists.

RENA (RAY-nah) Hausa, Africa: "despised, disregarded, or refused." Bestowed in Africa to make evil spirits think the child is unwanted and hence not worth bothering with. Also a contemporary Greek form of Irene, "peace." See Irene. *Renah, Renna* (Hausa)

RENEE (re-NAY) Currently fashionable French form of Renata, "reborn." *René* (French)

RENIA (REN-yah) Polish form of Regina, "queen." For other forms, see Regina.

RESEDA (reh-SEE-duh) Latin: "the fragrant mignonette blossom."

RESHA (RESH-ah) Hausa, Africa: "a branch."

RESI (REH-see) A German pet form of Theresa, "reaper." See Theresa.

REVA (RAY-vah, or Anglicized, REE-vah) Hindi: "the sacred Narmada River." One of the seven sacred Hindu rivers in India.

REZ Hungarian: "copper." For a girl with copper-colored hair.

RHEA Latin: "the poppy flower"; or Greek: "a flowing stream." In ancient Egypt, Rhea was also another name for Nut, the goddess with a serpent's head and human body who personified the primeval waters in which the Creator first lived.

RHODA Greek: "rose." A contemporary flower name.

RHONDA Welsh: literally "noisy one," referring to a rushing river in the Rhondda Valley of Wales. *Rhona, Rhonette, Rhonnie, Ron, Ronda, Ronni, Ronnie* (English)

RIA Spanish: "the mouth of a river." Spanish nature name.

RIANA (ree-AHN-ah) Welsh: "nymph, goddess, or witch." Contemporary American version of Rhiannon, a legendary horse goddess in Welsh mythology who dressed in shimmering gold and rode a pale horse. *Rhiana, Rhianna, Rhianne, Rian, Riane, Rianne* (English)

RICHELLE (ri-SHELL) Contemporary American creation, possibly an alternative spelling of Rachel ("an ewe") or a feminine form of Richard. Growing in popularity because of its similarity to the more familiar Michelle. *Richi, Rikki, Shelley, Shelly* (English)

RIDA (REE-dah) Arabic: "favor." The name implies the child is in God's favor. Also a boys' name.

RIHANA (ree-HAH-nah) Arabic: "sweet basil." This name is frequently used by Moslems in the Middle East.

RIMA (REE-mah) Arabic: "a white antelope"; or Spanish: "rhyme, poetry." Poetic name of a young woman who could communicate with the birds and animals in the novel *Green Mansions.*

RIMONA (ri-MOH-nah) Hebrew: "pomegranate." Popular in Israel.

RIN Japanese: "park." Originally a place-name now given to girls.

RINA (REE-nah) Pet form of Katrina, Marina, Regina, Sabrina and other names ending in *"-ina."* Now used independently. *Reena* (English)

RIONA (ree-OH-nah) Latin: "a queen." A contemporary American form of the traditional Irish name *Rioghnach.*

RISA Latin: "laughter." Gaining popularity in the United States.

RISHA (REE-shah) Hindi: "born during the solar month of Vrishabha." On the Hindu calendar, Vrishabha corresponds to the sign of Taurus, the bull. Also a short form of Irisa, "the iris flower."

RITA A popular form of Margarita or Margaret, "a pearl."

Also a Hindu name meaning "correct or proper," referring to the concept of the underlying natural and moral order present in the universe.

RITSA (REET-sah) A contemporary Greek form of Alexandra, "helper and defender of mankind." See Alexandra.

RIVA (REE-vah) French: "shore" or "riverbank." *Ree, Reeva, Reva, Rivi, Rivy* (English)

ROBERTA Old English: "one who shines with fame." The feminine form of Robert. Popular in the mid-twentieth century, but now often replaced with its shorter pet forms, particularly Robin and Robyn. *Bobbet, Bobbette, Bobbi, Bobbie, Bobby, Robbi, Robbie, Robbin, Robby, Robena, Robin, Robina, Robinette, Robonia, Robyn, Robynn, Robynne* (English); *Berta, Bobina, Roba* (Czech); *Robine* (French); *Berta, Erta* (Polish); *Berta, Bertha, Bertunga, Ruperta* (Spanish)

ROBIN A gender-free name now used three times as often for girls as for boys. Although Robin is still more common, the spelling *Robyn* is gaining momentum. See Roberta, above, for other variations.

ROCHELLE (roh-SHELL) French: "from the small rock." *Rochele, Rochella, Roshele,*

Roshelle, Shelley, Shelly (English); *Rochella* (Italian)

ROHANA (roh-HAH-nah) Hindi: "sandalwood."

ROLANDA Old German: "from the famous land." A feminine form of Roland. *Roll, Rolli, Rollie, Rolly* (English); *Rolande* (French); *Orlanda* (Italian)

RONLI (ron-LEE) Hebrew: "joy is mine." *Rona, Roni, Ronia, Ronice, Ronit* (English, Hebrew)

RONNIE A short form of Veronica ("forerunner of victory") or Rhonda ("noisy one"), now used independently. *Roni, Ronni, Ronny* (English)

ROSA (ROH-za) A favorite Spanish form of Rose. See Rose.

ROSALEEN Irish diminutive of Rose, meaning "little rose." Dark Rosaleen is a symbolic name for Ireland.

ROSALIND, ROSALYN (ROZ-ah-lin) Spanish: "pretty rose"; or Irish: "little rose." *Ros, Rosaleen, Rosalinda, Rosaline, Rosalynd, Rosilyn, Rosina, Roslyn, Roslyne, Roslynn, Roz, Rozlyn* (English); *Rosalinde* (German)

ROSE Greek: "a rose." The rose is the flower of Gemini and a symbol of romantic love. *Rhoda, Rosalia, Rosalie, Rosella, Roselle,*

Rosetta, Rosette, Rosi, Rosie, Rozy, Zita (English); *Ruza, Ruzena, Ruzenka* (Czech); *Ruusu* (Finnish); *Roza, Rozalia, Rozsa, Rozsi, Ruzsa* (Hungarian); *Rois, Roisin* (Irish); *Rosa, Rosetta* (Italian); *Roze, Rozele, Rozyte* (Lithuanian); *Rozene* (Native American); *Roza, Rozalia* (Polish); *Ruza, Ruzha* (Russian); *Chalina, Chara, Charo, Rosa, Rosalba, Rosalia, Rosalin, Rosalina, Rosalinda, Rosana, Rosaura, Rosita, Shaba, Zita* (Spanish); *Losa, Lose* (Tongan)

ROSELANI (roh-se-LAH-nee) English, Hawaiian "rose" + *lani:* "heavenly rose." Refers to a small red rose that grows on the Hawaiian Islands.

ROSEMARY Latin *rosa-marine:* "dew of the sea," is the accurate meaning, though it's commonly and mistakenly viewed as a combination of Rose + Mary. A child named after the fragrant rosemary herb. *Romy, Rosemaree, Rosemaria, Rosemarie, Rosmarie, Rozmary* (English)

ROWAN (ROH-an) Celtic: "clad in white"; or Old English: "famous friend." Contemporary version of the older and now seldom used Rowena. *Roanna, Roanne* (English)

ROXANNE Persian: "the dawn." Name of Alexander the Great's wife and the heroine in

the classic *Cyrano de Bergerac. Roxana, Roxann, Roxanna, Roxi, Roxianne, Roxie, Roxine* (English); *Roxane* (Greek)

ROYCE Old English: "the king's child." Formerly a boys' name, but used for girls since the 1980s.

ROZ A short form of Rosalind or Rosalyn ("pretty rose" or "little rose"). *Ros, Rozi, Rozzi, Rozzie, Rozzy* (English)

ROZENE (ro-ZAY-nuh) Native American form of Rose, "a rose flower."

RUANA (roo-AH-nah) Hindi: "the ruana instrument," referring to a musical instrument used in India which resembles a viol. See Almira for an explanation of inanimate-object names.

RUBY Latin: "red," referring to the jewel. *Rubey, Rubi, Rubie, Rubye* (English)

RUCHI (ROO-chee) Hindi: "a love growing into a wish to please and shine before the beloved."

RUDI (ROO-dee) Old German: "famous wolf." The feminine form of Rudolph. *Rudie, Rudy* (English)

RUDRA (ROO-drah) Hindi: "rudraksha-plant child." Among the Hindus, the berries of the sacred rudraksha plant are used for making rosaries. The god Siva, as he contemplates the destruction of the world, is said to shed rudraksha-seed tears. The seeds nearly always have several "faces," and it is believed that anyone finding a one-faced seed will have his or her every wish and a life of wealth, luxury, and power.

"*A name is all.*"

—ANCIENT ROMAN PROVERB

RUFEN (roo-FEN) Chinese: "pleasant fragrance."

RURI (roo-ree) Japanese: "emerald." Naming children after precious stones dates back to an ancient belief that gems protect one from evil spirits. In the West, the emerald is the birthstone of May and of the astrological sign of Taurus, the bull.

RUSALKA (roo-sahl-kah) Czech: "wood nymph." A favorite in the Czech Republic.

RUTH Hebrew: "companion" or "compassionate and beautiful." In the Bible, Ruth was Naomi's devoted daughter-in-law who stayed with Naomi even after both their husbands had died. Eventually, Ruth remarried and gave birth to the grandfather of David. *Ruthann, Ruthanne, Ruthie, Ruthina, Ruthine* (English); *Ruthven* (Scottish)

RYBA (REE-bah) Czech: "fish." In astrology, fish is the symbol of Pisces.

S

SABINA Latin: "woman from the Sabine country." Used today in Bulgaria, the Czech Republic, Finland, Italy, Poland, Russia, the Ukraine, and Spanish-speaking countries, as well as Canada and the United States. *Sabia, Sabin* (English); *Bina* (Czech); *Sabine* (Finnish, German, Latvian); *Sabcia, Sabinka, Sabka* (Polish); *Savina, Savya* (Russian)

SABIRA (sah-BEE-rah) Arabic: "patient."

SABIYA (sah-BEE-ya) Arabic: "morning" or "the eastern wind." *Saba, Sabaya, Sabiyah* (Arabic)

SABLE Middle English: "black" or "sleek." *Sabel, Sabella, Sabelle* (English)

SABRA (SAH-brah, or Anglicized, SAY-brah) Hebrew: "thorny cactus." Refers to a prickly but edible fruit native to coastal plains of Israel. The name for a native-born Israeli. *Sabrina* (English, Hebrew)

SABRINA (sah-BREE-nah) Latin: "boundary line," referring to the

Severn River in England. *Brina, Sabreen, Sabreena, Sabrinna, Sabryna* (English)

SACHI (sah-chee) Japanese: "blissful or fortunate." The Japanese variation *Sachiko* means "blissful or fortunate child."

SADA (sah-dah) Japanese: "the chaste."

SADE (shar-DAY) Yoruba, Africa: "honored with a crown." Popularized by the West Indian singer Sade.

SADIRA Persian: "the lotus tree." For the significance of the lotus in Hindu and Buddhist beliefs, see Kumuda and Ren.

SADZI (sahd-ZEE, or Anglicized, SAHD-zee) Athabascan, Carrier Indian: "sun heart," referring to a clock.

SAGARA (sah-GAH-rah) Hindi: "ocean."

SAGE Latin: "knowing and wise" or "healthy and whole." Formerly a boys' name now also used for girls. *Saige* (English)

SAKARI (sah-KAH-ree) Todas, India: "sweet one."

SAKI (sah-kee) Japanese: "cape."

SAKUNA (sah-KOO-nah) East Indian: "bird."

SAKURA (sah-koo-rah) Japanese: "cherry blossom." In Japan the cherry blossom is the national flower, the flower of March, and a symbol of wealth and prosperity. In China it is the flower of April and a symbol of a good education.

SALA (SAH-lah) Hindi: "the sacred sala tree." The sala is said to contain a spirit who, if worshiped, brings rainfall; it is also believed that Buddha died under the sala's branches. One beam of this tree is said to bring blessings and peace to a home.

SALENA (sah-lay-nah) Hindi: "the moon." A beautiful name from India. In the zodiac, the sign of Cancer is ruled by the moon.

SALLY Originally a pet form of Sarah, "princess" or "one who laughs." *Sal, Salley, Salli, Sallie* (English)

SALOME (SAH-loh-may) Hebrew: "peace." In the New Testament of the Bible, Salome was the daughter of Herodias. *Sal, Saloma* (English); *Salama* (Arabic); *Salome* (French)

SAMANTHA Aramaic: "one who listens." Also a feminine form of Samuel. *Sam, Sami, Sammi, Sammie, Sammy* (English)

SAMARA (sah-MAH-rah) Hebrew: "a guardian" or "guarded by God."

Miwok Indian Bear Names

✴ ✴ ✴

Of all the animals, the bear is the most frequently mentioned in Miwok Indian names. Such names often refer to an event that occurred in the mother's or father's life. Among the many colorful "bear names" are:

Etumu: "to sun oneself," and means "bear warming itself in the sunlight."

Etumuye: "to climb a hill," meaning "bear climbing a hill."

Hausu: from *hausus*, meaning "bear yawning as it awakes."

Heltu: "bear barely touching people as it reaches for them."

Kutcuyak: from *kuici*, "good" and means "bear with good hair."

Lupetu: from *lile*, "up," or in this case "up over" or "on top of," and means "bear going over a man hiding between rocks."

Moemu: from *mo'ani*, "to meet," and *moeye*, "to join," and means "bears sitting down to look at each other."

SAMEH (SAM-eh) Arabic: "forgiver." Common among Moslem Arabs, this name refers to one of the ninety-nine qualities of God listed in the Koran. Strictly orthodox Moslems believe a name should come from the Koran or Muhammad's immediate family.

SAMI (sah-MEE, or Anglicized, SAM-ee) Arabic: "exalted or praised." Also a short form of Samantha, "one who listens."

SAMINA (sah-mee-nah) Hindi: "happy." *Sameena, Sameenah* (English)

SANDRA A short form of Alexandra, "helper and defender of mankind." *Sanda, Sandi, Sandie, Sandy, Saundra, Sondra, Zandra* (English)

SANURA (sah-NOO-rah) Swahili: "like a kitten."

SANUYE (sah-NOO-ye) Miwok: "red cloud coming with sundown."

SANYA (SAHN-yah) Sanskrit: "born on Saturday," from the word *Sanivaram,* meaning "Saturday."

SAPATA (sah-PAH-tah) Miwok: "bear dancing with forefeet around a tree" or "bear hugging tree." From the Miwok word *sapatu,* "to hug."

SARA, SARAH Hebrew: "princess" or "one who laughs." As Abraham's wife and Isaac's mother, Sara is an important figure in the Bible. The form Sara is popular around the globe, from the United States and Canada to Bulgaria, France, Germany, Hungary, Italy, Mexico, Norway, Portugal, Romania, Russia, Spain, and Sweden. *Sadella, Sadie, Sadye, Saida, Sally, Sareen, Sarene, Saretta, Sari, Sarina, Sarine, Sarinia, Satette, Zara, Zarah, Zaria* (English); *Sarotte, Zaidee* (French); *Kala* (Hawaiian); *Sari, Sarika, Sarolta, Sasa* (Hungarian); *Sala, Salcia* (Polish); *Sarka, Sarra* (Russian); *Chara, Charita, Sarita* (Spanish); *Sela* (Tongan)

SARIL (shuh-ril) Turkish: "the sound of running water."

SARINA (sah-REE-na) Contemporary pet form of Sara, "princess" or "one who laughs."

SARITA (sah-REE-tah) Hindi: "flowing," as a river flows. A nature name from India. Also a Spanish form of Sara.

SAROLTA (shaw-ROHL-tah) Hungarian form of Charlotte, "little womanly one." Also a Hungarian form of Sara, "princess" or "one who laughs."

SASA (sah-sah) Japanese: "assistant." Also a Hungarian form of Sara.

SASHA Favorite Russian form of Alexandra, "helper and defender of mankind." See Alexandra.

SATINKA (sah-TEEN-kah) Native American: "magic dancer."

SAURA (SOW-rah) Hindi: "sun worshipers." Refers to a Hindu sect devoted exclusively to the worship of the sun. The astrological sign Leo is ruled by the sun.

SAVANNAH Old Spanish: "from an open plain." Formerly a place-name made familiar as a girls' name by the film *Savannah Smiles. Savana, Savanna, Savanah* (English)

SAWA (sah-wah) Japanese: "marsh"; or Miwok: "rock," implying "rock on the edge of a river." Some Native Americans believed that many spirits dwelled in rocks, an idea perhaps suggested by the many tools made from rock or the fire sparked from flint.

SEANA (SHAWN-ah) A feminine form of Sean, which in turn is an Irish form of John, "God is gracious." *Seanna, Shana, Shanna, Shawna, Siana* (English)

SEDA (SAY-dah) Armenian: "echo through the woods." *Sayda* (English)

SEDNA (SED-nah) Eskimo: "the goddess of food." According to Eskimo legend, Sedna lives in the sea. If her taboos are violated, she causes a storm to keep seals, polar bears, and whales from leaving their homes.

SEKI (seh-kee) Japanese: "great." The old Japanese belief that a child with too ambitious a name will never live up to it is what makes Seki so unusual. Seki can also mean "stone" or "barrier," in the sense of a city or toll gate.

SELIMA (se-LEE-mah) Hebrew: "peace."

SELINA (seh-LEE-nah) Greek: "sprig of parsley" or "goddess of the moon"; or Latin: "heavenly." In astrology the moon rules the sign of Cancer, the crab. Associated most recently with Grammy-Award winning singer Selina

Quintanilla. *Cela, Celene, Celie, Celina, Celinda, Celine, Cellina, Sela, Selena, Selene, Selia, Selie, Selinda, Seline, Sena* (English); *Celine* (French)

SELINKA Popular Russian form of Celeste, "heavenly."

SELMA Arabic: "secure"; also a shortened form of Anselma, from Old Norse meaning "divinely protected."

SEMA Greek: "a sign from the heavens."

SEN Japanese: "wood fairy." Refers to an ancient Japanese hermit believed to live in the mountains and said to possess magical powers. The sen, or sennin hermit, usually pictured as a wrinkled old man with a flowing white beard, is said to have lived for thousands of years; hence, the name expresses a hope for longevity. Also used for boys.

SERENA (seh-RAY-nah) Latin: "peaceful, calm." *Reena, Rina, Saryna, Sereena, Serene, Serina, Seryna* (English)

SERENITY Latin: "peaceful; calm." A virtue name.

SHADA (SHAH-dah) Native American: "pelican."

SHAHAR (shah-HAHR) Arabic: "the moon." In astrology the moon governs the sign of Cancer.

SHAHLA (SHAH-luh) Dari: "beautiful eyes." Originally from Afghanistan.

SHAIMA (shah-EE-mah) Arabic: "one with a mole or beauty spot." Originally from Afghanistan.

SHAINA (SHAY-nah) Yiddish: "beautiful."

SHAKA Contemporary American name meaning "warrior." Many recently created names are combinations of the prefix *"Sha-"* followed by a familiar syllable or combination of syllables. Other recently invented "Sha-" names include: *Shadira, Shadonna, Shakayta, Shakeen, Shakeena, Shakeet, Shakira, Shalaine, Shalana, Shalaya, Shalayla, Shalee, Shaleen, Shaleena, Shalena, Shalisa, Shalise, Shalita, Shaliza, Shalynn, Shamaine, Shamara, Shamari, Shameka, Shamika, Shanay, Shanee, Shanel, Shanell, Shanelle, Shanessa, Shanetta, Shanette, Shania, Shanice, Shanika, Shanique, Shanita, Shaqueta, Sharana, Shareen, Shareena, Sharell, Sharelle, Sharene, Sharice, Sharina, Sharisa, Sharise, Sharissa, Sharona, Sharonda, Sharonna, Shateen, Shatina, Shatonna, Shatonya, Shatoya, Shavette, Shavon, Shavona, Shavonna, Shavonne*

SHAKTI (SHAHK-tee) Hindi: "energy." One of the major Hindu goddesses, Shakti embodies both virginal innocence and blood-thirsty destruction. As the eternal virgin, she is sometimes represented as a young girl of about fifteen. The Shakti of illicit love, in contrast, is associated with incest and adultery. Mythologist Joseph Campbell described Shakti-Maya as "the great Goddess Mother of the universe, who is the ultimate life and substance of us all, and whose womb, wherein we dwell, is both unbounded space, out there, and the inner-most, deepest ground of gently streaming peace, in here. . . ."

SHAMMARA (SHAH-mah-rah, or Anglicized, shah-MAR-ah) Arabic: "he girded his loins."

SHANA (SHAY-nah or, less commonly, SHAH-nah) A feminine form of Shawn (Sean), "God is gracious." Also a short form of Shannon. *Shanna, Shannah* (English)

SHANI (SHAH-nee) Swahili: "marvelous."

SHANICE (shah-NEES) Contemporary creation combining the popular prefix *"Sha-"* with Janice, a form of Jane ("God is gracious"). A new feminine form of John.

SHANNA Fashionable contemporary American form of Shannon.

SHANNON Irish Gaelic: "small, old, wise one." Once a boys' name now bestowed almost exclusively on girls. *Shan, Shani, Shanon, Shannah, Shannan, Shannen, Shauna, Shawna, Shawni* (English)

SHANTA (shahn-tuh) Hindi: "spiritual, serene, and peaceful." A variation from India is *Shanti*, "peaceful and calm."

SHANTEL (shan-TELL) A contemporary variation of Chantal ("from the stony place"). See Chantal.

SHAPPA (SHAH-pah) Native American: "red thunder." Given by Native Americans to a child born during a violent storm.

SHARADA (shah-RAH-dah) Sanskrit: "mature, ripe." In Hindu mythology, this name alludes to Durga, the "inaccessible" incarnation of the great mother goddess. *Sharda* (Hindi)

SHARAI (shah-RIGH) Hebrew: "a princess" or "a plain." This is the original Hebrew name from which the English Sharon is derived.

SHARIFA (shah-REE-fah) Arabic: "noble." *Shareefa, Sharifah* (Arabic)

SHARISSA Contemporary American creation, possibly a combination of Sharon ("a princess") plus Melissa ("honey" or "a bee"). Hence, the pretty connotation is "honey-sweet princess." See Shaka for other contemporary "Sha-" names. *Shari, Sharice, Sharie, Sharine, Sheri, Sherice, Sherie, Sherissa, Rissa* (English)

SHARLENE Variation of Charlotte, "little womanly one." A contemporary feminine form of Charles. *Charleen, Charlene, Charline, Sharla, Sharlane, Sharlaine, Sharleen, Sharlie, Sharline, Sharlyn* (English)

SHARMA Gaining popularity in the United States and appears to be an American creation from Sharon ("a princess") plus Mary ("bitter"). *Sharmine* (English)

SHARON Hebrew: "a princess" or "a plain," referring to the Biblical plain where roses bloomed. *Shari, Sharry, Sheri, Sherisa, Sherissa, Sherry, Sherryn, Shery* (English)

SHAVON, SHAVONNE (shah-VAWN) English phonetic spellings of the trendy Irish name Siobhan ("God is gracious"). See Siobhan.

SHAWNA A contemporary American form of Sean, which in turn is an Irish form of John, "God is gracious." Also a variation of Shannon, "small, old, wise one." *Sean, Shana, Shanna, Shauna,*

Shawn, Shawnee, Shawni, Shawnie (English)

SHAWNELL (shaw-NEL) A modern American creation, blending Shawn (a form of John) with the feminine suffix *-ell*. *Shaunel, Shaunell, Shaunelle, Shawna, Shawnel, Shawnella, Shawnelle* (English)

SHEA (shay) Irish: "majestic or learned." Originally an Irish last name, now used for girls and boys. *Shaela, Shaila, Shailyn, Shay, Shayana, Shayda, Shayla, Shaylee, Shayleen, Shaylene, Shaylyn, Sheala, Shealyn* (English); *Shay* (Irish)

SHEENA An Irish form of Jane, "God is gracious." *Sheenah, Sheina, Shena, Shina, Shiona* (English); *Sine* (Irish)

SHEILA Irish variation of Cecilia, "dim-sighted." *Seila, Selia, Shayla, Shaylah, Sheela, Sheelagh, Sheelah, Sheilah, Shela, Shelagh, Shelia, Shiela* (English); *Sile* (Irish)

SHELBY Old English: "from the village where the willows grew." Originally a place-name in Yorkshire, England, now occasionally also used for girls and boys. *Shebi, Shel, Shelbie, Shellie, Shelly* (English)

SHELLEY Old English: "from the wood on the slope." An English surname. Also a short form of Shirley and names that end in *-elle*, such as Michelle and Richelle. *Shelli, Shelly* (English)

SHERISSA (sher-ISS-uh) A contemporary form of either Sharon ("a princess" or "a plain") or Charlotte ("little womanly one). *Sharisa, Sharissa, Sher, Sheri, Sherisa* (English)

SHERRY A respelling of the French Chérie ("cherished"). Also a short form of Charlotte, Sharon, Shirley, and other names beginning with *"Sher-"* or *"Shar-."* *Sharee, Shari, Sharie, Sheree, Sherey, Sheri, Sherie, Sherilyn, Sherina, Sherita, Sherree, Sherrey, Sherri, Sherrita* (English)

SHERYL Variation of Cheryl, which is in turn a form of Charlotte ("little, womanly one"). *Sharell, Sheralin, Sheralyn, Sherileen, Sherill, Sherilyn, Sherlynn, Sherrill, Sherryl, Sheryll* (English)

SHIKA (shee-kah) Japanese: "deer." Implies docility and gentleness rather than grace and beauty.

SHINA (shee-nah) Japanese: "goods," in the sense of possessions. Can also mean "virtue."

SHINO (shee-no) Japanese: "slender bamboo," a symbol of fidelity.

SHIRI (SHEE-ree) Hebrew: "my song." *Shira, Shirah* (English, Hebrew)

SHIRLEY Old English: "from the bright clearing." *Shir, Shirl, Shirlee, Shirlene, Shirli, Shirlie, Shirline, Shirlyn, Shirlynn* (English)

SHIZU (shee-zoo) Japanese: "quiet" or "clear." Popular in Japan. *Shizue, Shizuko, Shizuyo, Suizuka* (Japanese)

SHOUSHAN (shoo-SHAHN) Armenian development of Susan, "lily."

SHUMANA (SHOO-mah-nah) Hopi: "rattlesnake girl." Originally used by the Hopis of the rattlesnake cult. *Chuma, Chumana, Shuma* (English)

SHURA (SHOO-rah) Contemporary Russian form of Alexandra, "helper and defender of mankind." See Alexandra.

SIDRA Latin: "related to a constellation" or "related to the stars." Name for a child born under any astrological sign.

SIERRA (see-AIR-ah) Irish: "black"; or Spanish: "sawtoothed," referring to the jagged profile of the rugged Sierra Mountains. *Serra* (English)

SIGNY (SIG-nee or SEEG-nee) Old Norse: "newly victorious"; or Latin: "a singer." Popular today in Norway. *Signe, Signi* (Danish, Norwegian, Swedish)

SIGRID (SIG-rid or SEEG-rid) Old Norse: "beautiful, victorious counselor" or "beautiful victory." A favorite Scandinavian name now used in many parts of the world. *Siri* (Danish, Norwegian, Swedish)

SIHU (SEE-hoo) Native American: "a flower" or "a bush."

SIKO (SEE-ko) Mashona, southern Rhodesia: "crier." Given in Africa to a baby girl who cries a lot the first day.

SILA (SILL-ah) Contemporary American form of Priscilla ("one from primitive or ancient times").

SILVIA A common spelling of Sylvia, "one who lives in the forest."

SIMONE (see-MOHN) Hebrew: "one who hears" or "the obedient one." The feminine form of Simon. Originally from France, but now commonly used in many countries. *Simona, Simonia, Simonne* (English); *Simona, Simonette* (French)

SINEAD (shi-NAYD) Trendy Irish form of Jane, "God is gracious." Made well known by rock singer Sinead O'Connor. *Seonaid* (Scottish)

French-Sounding Girls' Names

✳ ✳ ✳

If you're thinking of giving your baby girl a "French-sounding" name like Renée or Collette, you're not alone. In one survey of 193,142 baby names in New York, 11 of the top 50 names for girls originated in France. This is possibly because French names seem cultured, stylish, and sexy. Favorites in France also popular with Americans include Adrienne, Caroline, Catherine, Jacqueline, Michelle, Monique, Simone, and Celeste. None of the top 50 boys' names in the survey were French.

SIOBHAN (sh'-VAWN) Irish form of Jane ("God is gracious"). A traditional Irish name growing in popularity in the United States. *Charvon, Chavon, Chavonn, Chavonne, Chevon, Chevonne, Chivon, Shavon, Shavone, Shavonne, Shervan, Shevon, Shevonne, Shivohn* (English); *Siobahn, Siobhian* (Irish)

SIPETA (see-PAY-tah) Miwok: from *sipe*, "to pull out." The connotation is "pulling white sucker fish from under a flat rock."

SISIKA (si-SEE-kah) Native American: "swallow" or "thrush."

SISSY Originally a nickname for "sister" and made well known as a first name by actress Sissy Spacek.

SITA (SEE-tah) Hindi: "furrow"; or Spanish *zita:* "rose." In the Hindu religion, this is the name of the earth goddess who presides over agriculture and fruits and who is the wife of the god Rama. The Spanish form of the name comes from the Zuni Indians.

SITI (SEE-tee) Swahili: "lady."

SIVA (SHEE-vah) Hindi: "the god Siva." This Hindu name refers to the god Siva, the destroyer. *Sheeva, Shiva* (English)

SLOANE (slohn) Irish Gaelic: "a warrior." Originally a boys' name, now also used for girls.

SOFIA, SOPHIA Greek: "wisdom." The spelling Sofia is used in many countries around the world, including Canada, England,

Italy, Mexico, Russia, and Spain, as well as the United States. *Sophie, Sophy, Sunya* (English); *Zofia, Zofie, Zofka* (Czech); *Sofi, Sophoon* (Greek); *Sonja* (Norwegian); *Zocha, Zofia, Zosha, Zosia* (Polish); *Sofka, Sofya, Sonia, Sonya* (Russian); *Sonya* (Scandinavian); *Chofa, Chofi, Fifi, Sofi, Soficita* (Spanish); *Sofi* (Swedish); *Sofya* (Turkish); *Zofia* (Ukrainian)

SOLANA (so-LAH-nah) Spanish: "sunshine."

SOMA (SO-mah) Hindi: "moon." Hindu name given to a child born on *Somavara,* Monday, in the solar month Karka, under the sign of Cancer, which is ruled by the moon.

SONYA (SOHN-yah) Popular Russian and Scandinavian form of Sofia, "wisdom." *Sondya, Sonja* (English)

SORA (SO-rah) Native American: "a warbling songbird."

SORCHA (SOR-kah) Irish Gaelic: "clear or bright." An ancient Irish name still a great favorite in Ireland. *Sorcka, Sorka* (English)

SORRELL (soh-RELL) Old French: "Reddish-brown,"

How Classy Is Cackle?

★ ★ ★

While trying to find the perfect name for your baby, you may hear that some names (such as Ryan and Samantha) are "upper class," whereas others (like Rocky and Scarlett) are downscale. Has this theory been over-rated? Apparently so. When a reporter recently pulled together a list of first names that had appeared in the society columns of the prestigious *Philadelphia Inquirer,* he found this list of presumably highbrow first names borne by Philadelphia's upper crust: *Barkie, Bunky, Bunty, Cackle, Caughie, Choppy, Diny, Dodo, Dudy, Elfie, Floss, Frolic, Gee, Happy, Kinnie, Marby, Metsie, Minky, Peppi, Perky, Phippy, Pixie, Pooh, Sibby, Siggie, Taddi, Tenny, Trophy, Weezie, Wiggie, Winky, Wistie,* and *Woosie.*

referring to the color of sorrel, the wild herb. *Sorelle* (French)

SOSO (SOH-soh) Miwok: "tree squirrel biting a tiny hole in a pine nut."

STACY, STACEY Contemporary American creation from either Anastasia ("of the Resurrection") or Eustacia ("peaceful" or "fruitful"). *Staci, Stacia, Stacie* (English); *Stasa, Staska* (Czech); *Stasya, Tasenka, Taska, Tasya* (Latvian, Lithuanian, Russian); *Tasia* (Spanish)

STELLA Latin: "a star." Created in the sixteenth century by poet Sir Philip Sidney, who also created the name Pamela.

✳**STEPHANIE** Greek *stephanos:* "crowned." The feminine form of Stephen. *Stef, Stefa, Steffi, Steffie, Stepania, Stepanie, Stepha, Stephana, Stevena, Stevi, Stevie, Stevy, Teena* (English); *Stefania, Stefka* (Czech); *Stefanie, Trinnette* (French); *Stefani, Stefanie, Steffi, Stephanine* (German); *Stamatios* (Greek); *Stefa, Stefania, Stefcia, Stefka* (Polish); *Panya, Stefania, Stepa, Stepanida, Stepanyda, Stesha, Steshka* (Russian)

STEVIE A pet form of Stephanie, "crowned," used for both girls and boys. *Stevi, Stevy* (English)

STINA (STEE-na) German short form of Christel, or Christina, "Christian."

STOCKARD Possibly from Middle English: "dweller near a tree stump" or "dweller near a footbridge." Contemporary American name brought into vogue by actress Stockard Channing.

SUDHA (SOO-dah) Hindi: "nectar" or "juice," with a connotation of sweetness and beauty. In India, Sudha is frequently combined with other name elements to produce such names as *Sudha Sar* ("a shower of nectar), *Sudha Sindhu* ("ocean of nectar"), and *Sudhamukhi* ("nectar-faced," the name of a heavenly nymph).

SUE ELLEN Combination of Sue ("lily") + Ellen ("light" or "torch"). *Suellen, Sue Ellin, Suellin* (English)

SUELA (SWAY-lah) Spanish short form of Consuela, "consolation." *Chela, Suelita* (Spanish)

SUGI (soo-gee) Japanese: "cedar." A giant sugi or a group of such trees is often associated with a Shinto shrine, and hence the tree has become almost symbolic of the shaded mystery of such sanctuaries. In Japan the cedar is also an emblem of moral rectitude.

SUKE (SOO-ke) Hawaiian development of Susan, "lily." See Susan.

SUKI (soo-kee) Japanese: "beloved"; or Miwok: "chicken hawk with a long tail." Also an eighteenth-century form of Susan, often spelled *Sukey.*

SULA (SOO-lah) Icelandic: "the gannett," referring to a large seabird. Also a short form of Ursula, "little she-bear."

SULETU (soo-LEH-too) Miwok *sulete:* literally "to fly around." The jaybird appears in Native American creation legends as a mischief-maker who was doomed to become a lesser creature on earth. In most myths the poor jay's tragic flaw is false pride.

SUMI (soo-mee) Japanese: "the clear" or "the refined." *Sumiko* (Japanese)

SUMMER Middle English: "born in summer."

SUNI (SOO-nee) Zuni: "a Zuni Indian."

SUNKI (SHOON-kee, or Anglicized, SOON-kee) Hopi: "overtake." The name may refer to a proud feat in the father's life, such as the chasing and overtaking of wild game or an enemy. Used by members of the Hopi horn cult.

SURATA (soo-RAH-tah) Hindi: "blessed joy." The name refers to a mystical experience achieved through lovemaking.

SURI (SOO-ree) Todas, India: "knife." A nickname from the Todas for a child with a sharp nose. Once a name is used among the Todas, it cannot be bestowed again for four generations, and if by chance two people have the same name, one of them picks another.

SURYA (SOOR-yah) Hindi: "the sun god." In Hindu mythology, the sun god Surya is pictured with a dwarfish, burnished-copper body and red eyes. A Hindu name for a child born under the sign of Leo, which is ruled by the sun.

SUSAN Hebrew *shoshannah:* "lily" or "graceful lily." With all its forms, this name is one of the most popular in the world. A contemporary Israeli meaning is "rose." *Sue, Suka, Sukee, Sukey, Suki, Sukie, Suky, Susanna, Susannah, Susanne, Susetta, Susette, Susi, Susie, Susy, Suzanna, Suzannah, Suzanne, Suze, Suzetta, Suzette, Suzi, Suzie, Suzy* (English); *Shoushan* (Armenian); *Suzana* (Bulgarian); *Suzan, Zuza, Zuzana, Zuzanka, Zuzka* (Czech); *Susanne, Susetta, Suzanne, Suzette* (French); *Susanne, Suse* (German); *Kukana, Suke, Suse* (Hawaiian); *Sonel* (Hebrew); *Zsa Zsa* (Hungarian); *Sosanna* (Irish);

Susanna (Italian); *Zuska, Zuza, Zuzanna, Zuzia* (Polish); *Xuxu* (Portuguese); *Suzana* (Romanian); *Susanka* (Russian); *Siusan* (Scottish); *Chana, Sudi, Susana* (Spanish)

SUTKI (SHOOT-kee, or Anglicized, SOOT-kee) Hopi: "a broken coil of potter's clay." Used originally by Hopis in the cloud cult, this name may refer either to an event in the father's or mother's life, or the first thing one of the parents saw after their baby was born.

SUZAMNI (soo-ZAHM-nee) An Athabascan-speaking Carrier Indian name of French origin, this is a combination of Susan ("lily") plus Annie ("graceful").

SUZU (soo-zoo) Japanese: "little bell." A favorite in Japan, this name refers to the suzu, a tiny metal bell often placed in a silk charm bag and attached to a girl's undergarment so that a pretty tinkling is heard whenever she moves. Originally it was thought the sound would frighten demons; more recently it was believed the amulet would keep the child from falling. Japanese variations: *Suzue* ("branch of little bells"); *Suzuki* ("bell tree"); *Suzuko* ("bell child.")

SYBIL Greek: "a prophetess." In Greek and Roman mythology, sibyls were priestesses who could see the future and give

wise counsel. In their caves, sibyls would inscribe the names and fates of individuals on leaves gathered from the woods, and arrange the leaves in order. Should a wind rush through an opening of the door, it was believed the leaves would scatter and the oracle would be lost forever. *Cybil, Sib, Sibbie, Sibby, Sibelle, Sibilla, Sibyl, Sibylle, Sybilla, Sybille* (English); *Sibylla* (Dutch); *Cybele, Sibylle* (French); *Sibeal* (Irish)

SYDNEY Old French: "from the city of St. Denis, France." The feminine form of Sidney. *Sy, Syd, Sydny* (English)

SYLVIA Latin: "one who lives in the forest." Rhea Silvia was a nature goddess said to be the mother of Romulus and Remus, the brothers who founded Rome. *Silva, Silvana, Silvia, Sylva, Sylvana, Zilvia* (English); *Silvie* (French); *Silivia* (Hawaiian); *Silvia* (Italian); *Silvana, Silveria, Silvia, Silvina* (Spanish)

T

TABIA (tah-BEE-ah) Swahili: "talents."

TABITHA Greek: "gazelle." *Tab, Tabatha, Tabbi, Tabbie, Tabbitha, Tabby* (English)

TACI (TAH-shee) Zuni: "wash-tub." Probably originally bestowed because a washtub was the first object the mother or father saw after the baby was born.

TACY (TAY-see) Latin: "be silent." Originally an old Puritan name admonishing a child to be seen and not heard. Contemporary form of the older name Tacita. *Tace, Tacey* (English)

TADITA (tah-DEE-tah) Omaha Indian *tohito:* "to the wind!" or more loosely, "a runner." The name refers to the running of pipe bearers in a Hedewachie ceremony. *Tadeeta, Tadeta* (English)

TAIMA (tah-EE-mah) Native American: "crash of thunder." Used in various Indian cultures for a girl or boy born during a thunderstorm.

TAIPA (tah-EE-pah) Miwok: "to spread wings." The more elaborate connotation is "valley quail spreading its wings as it alights."

TAJA (TAH-jah) Hindi: "a crown." *Tajah, Talajara, Tejah, Tejal* (Hindi)

TAKA (tah-kah) Japanese: "tall," "honorable," or "a falcon."

TAKALA (TAH-kah-lah) Hopi: "corn tassel." From the cloud cult.

TAKARA (tah-kah-rah) Japanese: "treasure" or "precious object."

TAKENYA (tah-KEHN-yah) Miwok: "falcon swooping and knocking down its prey with its wings."

TAKI (tah-kee) Japanese: "a plunging waterfall."

TAKUHI (tak-koo-HEE) Armenian: "queen." *Takoohi* (Armenian)

TALA (TAH-lah) Native American: "wolf." The name implies intelligence and good luck.

TALASI (TAH-lah-shee, or Anglicized, tah-LAH-see) Hopi: "corn tassel flower." Used by Hopis in the cloud cult.

TALIA (tah-LEE-uh or TAL-ya) Hebrew: "heaven's dew." The variations *Talor* and *Talora* mean "dew of the morning." Also a Spanish form of Natalie, "born on Christmas." *Tal, Talya* (Hebrew)

TALISHA (tah-LISH-ah) Contemporary American creation. Seems to be a combination of the prefix *"Ta-"* + the popular ending *"-isha"* (from Aisha, "woman" or "life"). *Talisa, Talissa* (English)

TALULA (tah-LOO-lah) Choctaw: "leaping water." First made well known in the early twentieth century by actress Tallulah Bankhead. *Talli, Tallie, Tallulah, Tally* (English)

TAMA (TAH-mah) Native American: "thunderbolt"; Japanese: "jewel."

TAMAKI (tah-mah-kee, or Anglicized, tah-MAH-kee) Japanese: "armlet" or "bracelet." *Tamako, Tamayo* (Japanese)

TAMARA Hebrew: "a palm tree." Popular not only in this country but also the Czech Republic, Latvia, Russia, most Spanish-speaking countries, and the Ukraine. *Tamar, Tamarra, Tamer, Tami, Tamie, Tammara, Tammera, Tammi, Tammie, Tammy, Tamor, Tamour, Tamra, Tamyra* (English); *Mara* (Czech); *Tama, Tamarka, Tomochka* (Russian)

> **❝*Proper names are poetry in the raw.*❞**
>
> —W. H. AUDEN

TAMEKO (tah-may-koh, or Anglicized, TAH-may-koh) Japanese: "child of advantage or goodness." *Tame* (Japanese)

TAMIKA (tah-mee-kah, or Anglicized, tah-MEE-kah) Japa-

nese: "people child." Popular contemporary American name. *Tami, Tamike, Tamiko, Tamiyo* (Japanese)

TAMMY A pet form of Tamara ("a palm tree"), also used independently. *Tam, Tami, Tamie, Tammie* (English)

TANAKA (tah-nah-kah, or Anglicized, TAH-nah-kah) Japanese: "dweller in or near a rice swamp."

TANI (tah-nee) Japanese: "valley." A variation is *Taniko*, "valley child."

TANISHA Hausa, Africa: "born on Monday." Popular contemporary American name. *Taneisha, Tanesha, Taneshea, Taneshia, Tanicha, Taniesha, Tenecia, Teneisha, Tenesha, Teniesha, Tenisha* (English)

TANSY Hopi: "the tansy flower." Originally used by Hopis belonging to the tansy-mustard clan.

TANYA Popular Russian form of Tatiana, "a fairy queen." *Tania, Tanka, Tata, Tuska, Tusya* (Russian)

TAO Vietnamese: "apple"; or Chinese: "peach." The peach is one of the three sacred Buddhist fruits and a symbol of longevity and immortality. A similar name is *Tao Hua*, "peach blossom." Called the tree of the fairy fruit, the peach tree of the gods grew in the mythical gardens of the Royal Lady of the West. The tree was said to have bloomed only once in three thousand years, and exactly three thousand years later yielded the Fruits of Immortality. It is said these peaches were eaten by the Eight Taoist Immortals. In Taoist philosophy, Tao literally means "the way," referring to the unnameable source of all reality and the eternal order of the universe.

TARA Irish Gaelic: "rocky pinnacle." Also the name of the ancient capital of Ireland. In India, the same name refers to a Buddhist savior goddess. *Tarra, Tera, Terra* (English)

TARYN (TAIR-in or, less frequently, TAH-rin) Fashionable contemporary name, probably originally from Tara, "rocky pinnacle." *Taran, Tarin, Tarina, Tarryn, Taryna, Tarynn, Terin, Terinn* (English)

TASARLA (tah-SAHR-lah) English Gypsy: "morning" or "evening," referring to a time when the sun is low on the horizon.

TASHA Popular Russian form of Natasha, which in turn is a form of Natalie, "born on Christmas."

TASIDA (tah-SEE-dah) Sarcee Indian: "a rider." The literal

meaning is "on-top-(of a horse)-he-sits." Also used for boys.

TASSOS (TAH-sohs) Contemporary Greek form of Theresa, "reaper." See Theresa.

TASYA (TAHS-yah) A diminutive of Anastasia ("of the Resurrection") used in Russia and Spain as well as the United States. See Anastasia.

TATE Pet form of Tatum ("to be cheerful") now also used as a given name.

TATUM Middle English: "to be cheerful." Made well known by actress Tatum O'Neal. *Tate* (English)

TAURA (TAW-ra) Latin: "like a bull." Name for a child born under the sign of Taurus, the bull.

TAWIA (tah-WEE-ah) Fanti or Ashanti, Africa: "born after twins." Also a Polish form of Octavia, "eighth-born child."

TAWNIE (TAW-nee) English Gypsy: "little one." The feminine form of Tawno. *Tawni, Tawny* (English)

TAYLOR Middle English: "a tailor." Once a surname and boys' name, now increasingly popular for girls. Its newfound trendiness may spring from the fact that several female characters on soap operas such as *All My Children,*

As the World Turns, and *Melrose Place* have been given this name. *Tailor, Tayler* (English)

TAZU (tah-zoo) Japanese: "rice-field stork." The stork is a Japanese symbol of longevity.

TEAGAN, TEGAN (TAY-gun, rhymes with Megan) Welsh: "beautiful and fair." Modern development of the older name Tegwen. *Taegen, Taygan, Teegan, Tegan, Tegin, Tiegan, Tigan* (English)

TEMIRA (teh-MEE-rah) Hebrew: "tall." Expresses the hope a child will grow tall. *Timora* (Hebrew)

TEMPEST French: "stormy" or "tempestuous one." *Tempestt* (English)

TERA (teh-rah) Japanese: "calm arrow," implying an arrow that flies straight and true. When pronounced TAIR-ah, also a form of Teresa ("reaper") or a variation of Terra.

TEREZA Portuguese form of Theresa, "reaper." A favorite in Brazil. See Theresa.

TERRA (TAIR-ah) Latin: "earth." Name for a girl born under one of the earth signs of Capricorn, Taurus, or Virgo. *Tera* (English)

TERRI Pet form of Teresa ("reaper") used for girls and boys.

Teri, Teriana, Teriane, Teriann, Terrie, Terry (English)

TESIA (TE-shuh or TAY-shuh) Polish form of Theophila, "loved by God," or Hortense, "gardener." *Taisha, Taysha, Tesha, Teysha* (English)

TESS Contemporary American form of Tessa ("fourth child") or Theresa ("reaper"). *Tessa, Tessi, Tessia, Tessie* (English)

TETSU (tet-soo) Japanese: "iron." The name stems from an ancient belief that demons and evil spirits were born during the Stone Age and therefore dreaded the influence of metals. Iron has been considered especially potent and magical in many cultures. Among the Kachin people of Upper Burma, for example, iron knives are brandished over a mother and her newborn, and old rags are burned in the hopes that the iron and the stench will drive demons away. In another part of Burma, on the Irrawaddy River, iron pyrites are believed to frighten alligators.

TEVY (TEH-vee) Cambodian: "an angel."

THELMA Greek: "the nursling." *Kama* (Hawaiian)

THEMA (TAY-mah) Akan, Ghana: "queen." *Tayma* (English)

THERESA, TERESA Greek: "reaper." This name gained great popularity worldwide in the 1600s when parents began naming their babies after Saint Theresa of Avila in Castile, a mystic and nun who performed many miracles. *Tera, Terese, Teressa, Teri, Terie, Terri, Terrie, Terry, Tery, Tess, Tessa, Tessi, Tessie, Tessy, Trace, Tracey, Traci, Tracie, Tracy, Zita* (English); *Tereza* (Brazilian, Bulgarian, Portuguese); *Terezia, Terezie, Terezka, Reza, Rezka* (Czech); *Tereson, Therese* (French); *Resel, Resi, Therese, Theresia, Tresa, Trescha* (German); *Tassos* (Greek); *Rezi, Riza, Rizus, Teca, Tercsa, Terez, Tereza, Terezia, Terike, Teruska, Treszka* (Hungarian); *Teresina, Tersa* (Italian); *Terese* (Norwegian); *Renia, Terenia, Tereska, Tesa, Tesia* (Polish); *Terezilya, Zilya* (Russian); *Techa, Tere, Teresita, Tete* (Spanish)

THORDIS (THOR-des) Old Norse: "dedicated to Thor," the Norse god of thunder. A favorite in Norway. *Thora, Tora* (Scandinavian)

Naming Your Adopted Baby

★ ★ ★

Most of the time a distinctively different name will only make your child feel more special. But if you adopt a baby who's already quite special—say, you're white and you've adopted a Chinese baby, or you're black and your baby's from Guatemala—you may want to think twice about choosing a name that's too unusual. Instead, you can play up the family connection—especially if the baby's brothers and sisters have such traditional names as Dave, Joe, and Mary—and choose a name that won't make her or him stand out even more. You can always break any "rule," of course, and this case is no exception. For example, I once heard about a family who had adopted 27 children from all over the world: Each child had a distinctively ethnic name, and yet they all felt like one big, united family. In fact, their diversity helped define their family character.

THURSDAY Old Norse: "born on Thor's day," referring to the Norse thunder god (see box, page 381).

TIA (TEE-ah) Spanish: "aunt." Also a short form of Tiana ("fairy queen") and Tiara ("crowned" or "a royal headdress").

TIANA (tee-AHN-ah) Slavic: "fairy queen." Contemporary American form of the Russian name Tatiana. *Tia, Tiane, Tianna, Tianne* (English)

TIARA (tee-AR-ah or tee-AIR-ah) Latin: "crowned" or "a royal headdress." *Teara, Tia, Tiarra* (English)

TIFFANY Greek *theophaneia:* "appearance or manifestation of God." Originally a form of Theophania, now fashionable as a given name. Because of the close connection with the jewelry store Tiffany, the name has some connotations of wealth and class. *Tiff, Tiffani, Tiffanie, Tiffy* (English)

TILDA Estonian variation of Matilda, "battle maiden."

TIMMI Originally a nickname for Timothea, "honoring God," Timmi is gaining use as a gender-free name. *Timi, Timie, Timmie* (English)

TINA Short form of many names ending in *-tine* or *-tina* through-out the world, including the English Christina, the Greek Constantina, the Polish Khristina, and the Russian Valentina.

TIPONYA (ti-POHN-yah) Miwok *tipe:* literally "to poke," with the connotative meaning "great horned owl sticking her head under her body and poking an egg that is hatching." The owl appears frequently in Indian myths. According to a Kiowa legend, when the medicine man dies he becomes an owl, and when the owl dies he turns into a cricket. The eastern Cherokee say the cry of the screech owl portends illness or death; the Penobscot people say that if a man mocks a screech owl, the bird will burn him up; and the Pawnee see the owl as a protector from night evils.

TIRTHA (TEER-tuh) Hindi: "ford."

TIRZA (TEER-zah) Hebrew: "cypress tree" or "desirable."

TISA (TEE-sah) Swahili: "ninth-born."

TISHA (TISH-ah) Originally a short form of Patricia ("noble") or Latisha ("gladness") now used independently. *Tish* (English)

TIVONA (tee-VOH-nah) Hebrew: "lover of nature." Used today in Israel.

TIWA (TEE-wah) Zuni: "onions." Bestowed because the first object the father or mother saw after the baby was born was an onion.

TOBIT (toh-BEET) Hebrew: "good." Originally from Israel, where it's used for both girls and boys. *Tova, Tovah* (Hebrew)

TOBY Hebrew: "God is good." The feminine form of Tobias. *Tobi, Tobie* (English)

TOKI (toh-kee) Japanese: "time of opportunity."

TOKIWA (toh-kee-wah, or Anglicized, toh-KEE-wah) Japanese: "eternally constant." The name implies constancy as everlasting as the rocks.

TOLIKNA (toh-LEEK-nah) Miwok: "coyote's long ears flapping." In many Native American legends, the coyote created the world (see Kaliska). One story says the adventurous beast once went to the edge of the world and sat on the hole where the sun comes up; he then rode the sun across the sky.

TOMIKO (toh-mee-koh) Japanese: "happy child" or "child of fortune." *Tomi, Tomie* (Japanese)

TOMO Japanese: "knowledge" or "intelligence."

TONI Pet form of Antonia ("priceless"). The feminine version of Tony. *Tonie* (English)

TONYA (TOHN-yah) Russian pet form of Antonia, "inestimable" or "priceless."

Japanese Animal Names

✳ ✳ ✳

People in nearly all cultures name their children after animals. In our country, we have the common *Lionel* ("young lion"), for example, whereas the Scandinavians use *Björn* ("bear"). The Japanese also have such totemic names, which were once bestowed with the hope the child might develop an admirable trait of that animal. Examples of such Japanese names include: *Chidori* ("sanderling," a small bird); *Kuma* ("bear"); *Taka* ("hawk"); *Tatsu* ("dragon"); and *Washi* ("eagle").

Day-of-the-Week Names

✦ ✦ ✦

Americans have been known to name their children after the day on which they were born—especially if that day happens to be Tuesday. Actress Tuesday Weld was probably responsible for bringing this day-of-the-week name into vogue, even though her real name was Susan Kerr Weld.

In other countries (especially in Africa), naming a girl after her birth day is even more fashionable. Ghanaian day-of-the-week names for girls are:

Akosua: "born on Sunday"

Ajua: "born on Monday"

Abmaba: "born on Tuesday"

Ekua: "born on Wednesday"

Aba: "born on Thursday"

Epua: "born on Friday"

Ama: "born on Saturday"

Among the day-of-the-week names used by the Ga-speaking people of Africa are:

Kwashi: "born on Sunday"

Kudio: "born on Monday"

Kwabina: "born on Tuesday"

Kwaku: "born on Wednesday"

Kwau: "born on Thursday"

Koffi: "born on Friday:

Kwamin: "born on Saturday"

TORA Japanese: "tiger."

TORI Japanese: "bird." (See box, page 211.)

TOSHI (toh-shee) Japanese: "year." *Toshie, Toshiko, Toshiyo* (Japanese)

TOSIA (TOH-shuh) Polish nickname for Antonia, "inestimable" or "priceless."

TOSKI (TOSH-kee) Hopi: "a squashbug." Originally used by people in the cloud cult.

TOSYA (TOHS-yah) Popular Russian nickname for Antonia, "inestimable" or "priceless." See Antonia.

TOTSI (TOHT-see) Hopi: "moccasins." Used by the horn cult.

TOYA Short form of Latoya ("victorious"), popularized by singer Latoya Jackson.

TRACY Latin: "courageous"; or Irish Gaelic: "one who battles." Also a short form of Theresa, "reaper." *Tracey, Traci, Tracie, Trasey* (English)

TRAVA (TRAH-vah) Czech: "grass," implying the freshness of spring.

TRELLA Spanish: "little star." A short form of Estrella, "star," used not only in the United States, but also in Mexico and Spain.

TRESA (TRAY-sah or TRES-ah) German form of Theresa, "reaper." See Theresa.

TRINA (TREE-nah) Hindi: "piercing," referring to the sacred kusa grass; also a German form of Katherine. See Kusa and Katherine.

TRINETTE French form of Katherine, "pure." See Katherine.

TRISHA Hindi: "thirst," one of the 350 Hindu classifications of love. Also a diminutive of Patricia, "noble."

> **"What is a good pedigree? A good name."**
>
> —AN ANCIENT JEWISH SAYING

TRUDA Old German: "battle maiden" or "spear strength." A Polish form of Gertrude. *Trude, Trudey, Trudi, Trudie, Trudy* (English)

TUESDAY Middle English: "born on Tuesday."

TULA (TOO-lah) Hindi: "born under the astrological sign of Libra."

TULSI (TOOL-see) Hindi: "the sacred tulasi plant," referring to an Indian form of basil. The plant is said to resemble the hair of the goddess Vrinda. Because her spirit enters the plant each night, one is forbidden to pick the tulasi leaves after dark.

TUSA (TOO-sah) Zuni: "prairie dog."

TUWA (TOO-wah) Hopi: "earth."

TWYLA Middle English: "woven with a double thread." Made well known by choreographer Twyla Tharp. *Twila* (English)

TYANA (tie-AHN-ah or tee-AH-nah) A soft-sounding, modern American creation. Probably a variation of Tiana, "fairy queen," but may be a blend of Tyrone ("sovereign one" or "from Owen's land") + Ana ("graceful"). Many recently coined American names appear to be combinations of the mother's and father's first names. *Teana, Teanna, Tiana, Tyanna, Tyanne* (English)

TYNA (TEE-nah) A nickname for many Czech names, including Kristyna ("Christian") and Celestyna ("heavenly"). Also contemporary American spelling of Tina.

TYRA (TEER-ah or TIGH-rah) Scandinavian: "warrior," referring to Tyr, the Scandinavian god of battle.

TYSON Middle English: "the child of Ty." Ty is a form of Dionysus, the Greek god of wine. A strong-sounding name now used for both girls and boys.

U

ULA (OO-lah) Irish: "jewel of the sea"; Basque: "the Virgin Mary"; Hausa, Africa: "cat"; Old Norse: "wealthy"; or Soko, Africa: "laughing." Also a Spanish pet form of Eulalia, "well-spoken." A short, simple name that has developed independently in many cultures.

ULANI (oo-LAH-nee) Hawaiian: "cheerful."

ULIMA (oo-LEE-mah) Arabic: "learned and wise." *Uleema, Ulimah* (English, Arabic)

ULTIMA Latin: "aloof and distant" or "the farthest point," implying a child is the ultimate, or the best.

UMA (OO-mah) Sanskrit: "mother" or "splendid and tranquil," with connotations of light and beauty. One of the more than one thousand names for the Hindu goddess Shakti. Made well-known in this country by actress Uma Thurman. See Shakti.

UMAY (oo-MAY) Turkish: "hopeful."

UMEKO (oo-mee-ko) Japanese: "plum-blossom child." In Japan the plum blossom is a symbol of perseverance and patience and the emblem of the samurai. *Ume, Umeyo* (Japanese)

UNA (OO-nah) Old Irish: "lamb" or "hunger." In Irish myth, Una was the daughter of a legendary king and mother of a great warrior. One of the most popular girls' names in Ireland. An alternative origin is Hopi: "remember." The coyote is implied in the name because he is said to remember food that he has buried.

UNIQUE Latin: "the only one" or "one of a kind."

UNITY Latin: "oneness" or "in harmony." A contemporary American coinage. In modern usage, this has become a virtue name, much like Faith, Hope, or Charity.

URIT (yoor-EET) Hebrew: "bright." Originally from Israel. *Urice* (Hebrew)

URSULA Latin: "little she-bear." Currently fashionable name used in Bulgaria, many countries in Central and South America, Estonia, Germany, Mexico, and Russia, as well as the United States. *Orsa, Orsel, Orsola, Ursa, Urse, Ursel, Ursie, Ursley, Ursola, Ursuline, Ursy* (English); *Vorsila* (Czech); *Sula, Ulli, Urmi* (Estonian); *Ursule* (French); *Ulla, Ursel* (German); *Urzula* (Latvian); *Ursule* (Romanian); *Ursulina* (Spanish)

USHA (OO-shah) Hindi: "sunrise."

USHI (oo-shee) Chinese: "the ox." In ancient Chinese astrology,

Polynesian Nature Names

✳ ✳ ✳

Many Tongan names for girls speak of the beauties and romance of the South Sea islands. Among the loveliest and most melodic of these nature names are *Kakala* (a fragrant garland of flowers); *Lealiki* (the song of the waves on the shore); *Maili* (a gentle summer breeze); *Pua* (a blossoming tree); *Vailea* (the talking water); and *Vana* (a sea urchin).

not only the months but also the hours, days, and years are named after signs of the zodiac. There is a year, a month, a day, and even an hour of the ox.

UTAKO (oo-tah-koh) Japanese: "poem child." *Uta* (Japanese)

UTINA (oo-TEE-nah) Native American: "(woman of) my country."

V

VALDA Old Norse: "ruler" or "governor." Popular in Scandinavia.

VALERIE Old French: "strong one." *Val, Valaree, Valaria, Valerey, Valeria, Valery, Valerye, Valli, Vallie, Vally, Valry* (English); *Wala, Waleria* (Polish); *Lera, Lerka, Valka, Valya* (Russian); *Valeriana* (Spanish)

VALMA Contemporary Finnish form of Wilhelmina, "unwavering protector." See Wilhelmina.

VANA (VAHN-nah) Congo, Africa: "surrendered" or "spent."

VANDA (VAHN-dah) Congo: or Mende, Africa: "braid or plaint"; "falling lightly (like rain)." This is also a Slavic form of Wanda, "wandering one."

VANESSA Greek: "butterflies." Some say this name was invented by author Jonathan Swift and only later came to be associated with a butterfly. *Ness, Nessa, Nessi, Nessie, Nessy, Van, Vana, Vania, Vanna, Vanni, Vannie, Vanny, Vanya* (English)

VANNA Contemporary form of Vanessa ("butterflies"). Also short form of Ivanna, a Russian version of Jane ("god is gracious"). Made well known by TV game-show hostess Vanna White.

VANYA (VAHN-yah) Russian form of Jane, "God is gracious." Also an American form of Vanessa.

VARDIS (vahr-DEES) Hebrew: "rose." Contemporary Jewish name originally from Israel. *Varda, Vardia, Vardice, Vardina, Vardit* (Hebrew)

VARINA (vah-REEN-ah) A Slavic form of Barbara, "a stranger" or "a foreigner." See Barbara.

VEDA Sanskrit: "sacred understanding." Refers to the sacred Hindu writings that are believed to have existed before the beginning of time.

VENDA (VEN-dah) Mende, Africa: "filled."

VERA Latin: "true"; or Russian *vjera:* "faithful." A favorite in Russia, also used in other countries, including the Czech Republic, Hungary, Latvia, and Mexico. *Vere, Verena, Verene, Verina, Verine, Verla* (English); *Verka, Viera* (Czech); *Wera, Wiera, Wiercia, Wierka* (Polish); *Verasha, Verinka, Verka, Verusya* (Russian); *Wera* (Swedish)

VERONICA Greek: "forerunner of victory"; or Latin: "true image," possibly referring to the shroud of Christ. *Berenice, Bernice, Nika, Roni, Ronnie, Ronny, Veronika* (English); *Verona, Veronika, Veronka* (Czech); *Verenice, Verone, Veronique* (French); *Veronike* (German); *Berenike* (Greek)

VIANA (vee-AH-nah) An intriguing contemporary American creation, possibly based on the names Vivian ("alive") and Ana ("graceful"). *Vianna, Vianne, Vionne* (English)

VICKIE Originally a short form of Victoria ("victory") now also used as an independent name. *Vicki, Vicky, Viki, Vikie, Vikki, Viky* (English)

VICTORIA Latin: "victory." Became fashionable during Queen Victoria's reign in England and has been popular ever since. *Vicki, Vickie, Vicky, Viki, Vikie, Viky* (English); *Viktoria* (Bulgarian, Norwegian, Swedish); *Viktoria, Viktorie, Viktorka* (Czech); *Victoire* (French); *Nike* (Greek); *Vittoria* (Italian); *Vitoria*

(Portuguese); *Tora, Vika, Viktoria* (Russian); *Vika, Viki* (Serbian); *Victoriana, Victorina, Vitoria* (Spanish)

VIDA (VID-ah) Hebrew: "beloved." A feminine short form of the Hebrew Dawid, or David. The longer form is Davida.

> **"***It occurs to me that Vienna would make a pleasant name for a girl who likes dancing to tunes of the Blue Danube suavity. It would suit a waltzing girl better than Australia's Matilda.***"**
>
> —IVOR BROWN, *A CHARM OF NAMES*

VIENNA (vee-EN-ah) Latin: "from Vienna," in Austria. A city name similar to Savannah or Houston, given more frequently nowadays to girls.

VIRGINIA Latin: "maidenly."
*Ginger, Ginney, Ginni, Ginnie,
Ginny, Jinny, Vergie, Virgy*
(English); *Virginie* (French);
Vegenia, Wilikinia (Hawaiian);
Gina, Ginata, Ginia (Spanish)

VIRIDA Spanish: "green,"
connoting the freshness of
spring.

VISOLELA (vee-so-LAY-lah)
Umbundu, Africa: from the
Umbundu proverb, "Longings are
of waterfalls, but these you pick
over are of the drying trays." The
saying means, it is easy to use
your judgment about the ordinary things of life, such as maize
to be sorted in drying trays, but
there are also desires of the heart
that are as uncontrollable as
waterfalls.

VIVIAN Latin: "alive." *Viv,
Viviana, Vivianne, Vivie, Vivien,
Vivienne, Vivyan* (English);
Vivienne (French); *Viviana*
(Hawaiian, Italian)

WAKANDA (wah-KAHN-dah)
Sioux: "inner magical power." See
Orenda for a fuller explanation.
Kanda, Kenda, Wekenda (Sioux)

WALLACE Old English:
"from Wales." A last name now

occasionally used for girls as well
as for boys.

WANDA Old German: "wan-
dering one." This name is also
used by the Congolese people in
Africa, where it means "net" or
"spiderweb." *Wandi, Wandie,
Wandis, Wenda, Wendeline,
Wendi, Wendie, Wendy* (English);
Vanda (Czech, Portuguese,
Russian); *Wandzia* (Polish);
Vanda (Slavic); *Wanja*
(Swedish)

WANETA (wah-NAY-tah) Native
American: "the charger." Also a
short form of Wannetta, "little
pale one."

WANITA (wah-NEE-tah)
Hawaiian form of the Spanish
Juanita, a form of Jane, "God is
gracious." *Wanika* (Hawaiian)

WEDNESDAY Old Norse:
"born on Wodin's day," referring
to Odin, the chief Norse god.

WENDY Invented by J. M.
Barrie for his play *Peter Pan*. The
story goes that Barrie thought of
the name when he heard a child
chant the phrase, "friendly-
wendy." Now also considered
a nickname for Wanda
("wandering one"). *Wendi,
Wendie* (English)

WENONA (weh-NOH-nah)
Native American: "first-born
daughter."

WHITLEY Middle English: "white wood." A surname now used as a girls' name, probably due to its use on the TV series *A Different World*.

WHITNEY Old English: "white island." Originally a boys' name, now immensely popular for girls. Made well known worldwide by singer Whitney Houston. *Whitnee, Whitni, Whitnie, Whitny* (English)

WILHELMINA Old German: "unwavering protector." A favorite in Germany and Scotland. The feminine form of Wilhelm, or William. *Billi, Billie, Helma, Helmine, Min, Mina, Minna, Minni, Minnie, Minny, Valma, Velma, Wiletta, Wilette, Wilhelmine, Willa, Willamina, Willi, Willie, Willy, Wilma, Wilmette, Wylma* (English); *Vilma* (Czech, Hungarian, Russian, Swedish); *Mini, Valma* (Finnish); *Guilette, Mimi, Minette, Wilhelmine* (French); *Helmine, Mina, Minchen, Minna* (German); *Mina, Minka* (Polish); *Williamina, Wilma* (Scottish); *Guillerma, Guillermina, Guilla, Ilma, Mina, Mini, Vilma* (Spanish)

WILLA (WILL-ah) Arabic: "continuation" or "unbroken succession." A child whose birth signals the continuation of a family line or tradition. Also a pet form of Wilhelmina.

WILLOW Middle English: "the willow tree" or "freedom." In Romania, among the Gypsies of Transylvania, the willow was believed to have the power to grant mothers easy delivery and to give the sick and old renewed vitality.

WINDA (WEEN-dah, or Anglicized, WIN-dah) Swahili: "hunt."

WINEMA (we-NEH-mah) Miwok: "woman chief."

WINIFRED Welsh: "holy reconciliation." More popular in England than the United States. *Freda, Freddi, Freddie, Winefred, Winefride, Winie, Winifrin, Winn, Winnifred, Winnifride, Wynifred, Wynn, Wynne* (English)

WINNA (WIN-nah) Kele, Africa: "friend"; or Arabic: "relaxed."

WINONA (wih-NOH-nah) Sioux: "first-born daughter." Made familiar worldwide by actress Winona Ryder. *Wenona* (English, Sioux)

WISIA (VEE-shuh, or Anglicized, WI-shuh) Polish form of Victoria, "victory."

WYANET (wee-AH-net) Native American: "beautiful."

WYNNE Old Welsh: "fair one." *Winne, Winnie, Winny, Wyn, Wynn*

XANDRA (ZAN-drah) Spanish version of Alexandra, "helper and defender of mankind."

XANTHE (ex-AHN-thuh or ZAN-thuh) Greek: "golden yellow."

XAVIER (ex-AY-vee-er or ZAYV-yer) Arabic: "brilliant"; or Spanish Basque: "one who owns a new house." A boys' name now gaining popularity in this country for girls. *Javier, Xaviera* (English)

XENIA (ZEN-ee-ah) Greek: "hospitable." *Xena, Zena, Zenia, Zina* (English, Greek); *Chimene* (French)

XUXU (SHOO-sha) Portuguese nickname for Susan ("lily"), made well known in some countries by the hostess of a popular children's TV show in Brazil.

YACHI (yah-chee) Japanese: "eight thousand." Round numbers were once considered good-luck charms in Japan, and although the superstition has virtually vanished, many number names remain. *Yachiko, Yachiyo* (Japanese)

YACHNE (YAHK-ne) Hebrew: "gracious." A favorite among Lithuanian and Polish Jews.

YALUTA (yah-LOO-tah) Miwok: "women out on a flat telling one another there is a lot of farewell-to-spring seed."

YAMKA (YAHM-kah) Hopi: "flower budding."

YANABA (yah-NAH-bah) Navaho: "she meets the enemy."

YARKONA (yahr-KO-nah) Hebrew: "green." May refer to the yarkona bird, with its greenish-gold feathers, found in the southern part of Israel.

YARMILLA (YAHR-mil-luh) Slavic *yarmarka:* "trader in the marketplace."

YASMEEN (YAHS-meen) Arabic: "the jasmine flower." *Jasmeen, Jasmin, Jasmine, Yasiman, Yasmine* (English)

YASU (yah-soo) Japanese: "the peaceful" or "the tranquil." *Yasuko, Yasuyo* (Japanese)

YELENA (ye-LAY-nah) Russian form of Helen, "light" or "torch." See Helen.

YEMINA (ye-MEE-nah) Hebrew: "right hand." The name connotes strength.

YEPA (YAY-pah) Native American: "the snow maiden."

YEVA (YEH-vah) Russian form of Eva, "life-giving." See Eva.

YIN (yeen) Chinese: "silver."

YNES (ee-NEZ) Spanish form of Agnes, "pure." *Ynez* (Spanish)

YOKI Native American: "bluebird on the mesa."

YOKO Japanese: "positive child," "ocean child," "female." The last implies the dualism of the Eastern concept of the universe. In the beginning, the female principle, Yo, is said to have coexisted with the male principle, In. Yo and In lay dormant in the chaotic egg until it eventually split into heaven and earth. This name was popularized worldwide by singer Yoko Ono, wife of the late John Lennon.

YOLA (YOH-lah) Hausa, Africa: "firefly."

YOLANDA Greek: "the violet flower." The violet is the flower of Aquarius and the month of February. *Eolanda, Eolande, Iolanda, Iolande, Iolanthe, Yolande, Yolane* (English); *Jolan, Jolanka, Joli* (Hungarian); *Jola, Jolanta* (Polish); *Yola, Yoli* (Spanish)

YOLUTA (yo-LOO-tah) Native American: "the farewell-to-spring seed."

YONINA (yo-NEE-nah) Hebrew: "dove." Feminine form of Jonas. *Jona, Jonati, Jonina, Yona, Yonit, Yonita* (English, Hebrew)

YORI Japanese: "the trustworthy." *Yoriko* (Japanese)

YOSHI Japanese: "the good" or "the respectful." *Yoshie, Yoshiko, Yoshio, Yoshiyo* (Japanese)

YOSHINO (YO-shee-no) Japanese: "good field" or "fertile field." The suffix *-no,* meaning "field," is often attached to Japanese names. Other examples: *Kikuno* ("chrysanthemum field"); *Kurano* ("storehouse field"); *Orino* ("weaver's field"); *Umeno* ("plum-tree field"); and *Urano* ("shore field").

YOVELA (yo-VAY-lah) Hebrew: "rejoicing."

YSABEL (EE-sah-bell) Spanish form of Isabel, "dedicated to God."

YU (YOO) Chinese: "jade."

YUKI (yoo-kee) Japanese: "snow" or "lucky." *Yukie, Yukiko, Yukiyo* (Japanese)

YUMI (yoo-mee) Japanese: "arrow." A variation is *Yumiko,* "arrow child" (Japanese)

YURIKO (yoo-ree-koh) Japanese: "lily child" or "village-of-birth child." *Yuri* (Japanese)

Japanese Virtue Names

✦ ✦ ✦

The practice of giving a baby a name denoting a special virtue is common among parents in many cultures. But nowhere is this practice more popular than in Japan. Typical Japanese virtue names for girls include: *Jin* ("gentle"); *Jun* ("obedient"); *Kazuko* ("obedient child" or "self-disciplined child"); *Masa* ("honest"); *Misao* ("loyal"); *Shina* ("loyal" or "faithful"); *Shizu* ("quiet," connoting a calm, peaceful nature); and the ever-popular *Yoshi* ("good").

YVETTE (ee-VETT) Contemporary French-sounding development of the older name Yvonne ("yew bow").

YVONNE Old French: "yew bow." *Evon, Evonne, Yvette, Yvone* (English); *Iwona, Iwonka* (Polish); *Ivone* (Portuguese); *Ivona* (Russian)

Z

ZADA (ZAH-dah) Arabic: "lucky one." Popular in Syria. *Zadah, Zaida, Zayda* (English, Arabic)

ZAHIRA Spanish form of Zara ("princess" or "the brightness of dawn.") *Zaharita* (Spanish)

ZAHRA (ZAH-rah) Swahili: flower."

ZAIDA (zah-EE-dah, or Anglicized, ZAY-dah) Arabic: "prosperous." *Zadam, Zaidah, Zayda* (English)

ZAIDEE (ZAY-dee, rhymes with Sadie) A French form of Sara, "princess" or "one who laughs."

ZAIRA (zah-EE-rah, or Anglicized, ZAIR-ah, to rhyme with Sara). Contemporary American or Arabic form of Zara "princess" or "the brightness of dawn."

ZALIKA (zah-LEE-kah) Swahili: "one who's well-born." *Zuleika* (Arabic)

ZALTANA (zahl-TAH-nah) Native American: "high mountain."

ZANA (ZAH-nah) Arabic: "quick, alert, and merry."

ZANDRA (ZAHN-drah or ZAN-drah) Short form of Alexandra, "helper and defender of mankind."

ZANNA (ZAH-nah) Contemporary Latvian form of Jane, "God is gracious." See Jane.

ZARA Arabic: "princess"; or Hebrew: "the brightness of dawn." *Zaira* (English, Arabic); *Zahira, Zahirita* (Spanish)

ZARIFA (zah-REE-fah) Arabic: "graceful."

> **"***Good name in man and woman is the immediate jewel of their souls.***"**
>
> —WILLIAM SHAKESPEARE

ZARINA (zah-reen-ah) Persian: "golden one" or "a golden vessel." An exotic name used in India.

ZAYIT (zigh-EET) Hebrew: "olive." Also used in Israel as a boys' name. *Zeta, Zetana* (Hebrew)

ZEA (ZAY-ah) Latin: "grain." Name appropriate to give to a girl born under one of the earth signs: Capricorn, Taurus, or Virgo.

ZEL Persian: "a cymbal"; or Turkish: "a bell."

ZELDA Short form of the older name Griselda, "a gray battle maiden."

ZELENKA (zeh-LEHN-kah) Czech: "little green one." Implies the child is innocent and fresh.

ZELLA (ZEL-ah) Bobangi, Africa: "lacking nothing" or "one who knows the path." *Zela, Zellah* (Bobangi)

ZERA (ZAY-rah) Hebrew *zera'im:* "seeds."

ZERDALI (zair-dah-LI) Turkish: "wild apricot."

ZERLINDA Contemporary American creation from Hebrew and Spanish, "beautiful dawn."

ZHANE (zhah-NAY) An exotic contemporary American creation that appears to be based on the French name René. *Zanay, Zhana* (English)

ZHAVONNE (zhah-VONN) Another recent creation, probably modeled after Yvonne, "yew bow" or the Irish Siobhan, a form of Jane ("God is gracious").

ZHEN (zhen, to rhyme with Jen, or in Chinese, cheng) Chinese: "a treasure."

ZIGANA (ZEE-gawh-nah) Hungarian: "gypsy girl."

ZIHNA (ZHEE-nah) Hopi *zynanta:* "spinning." Given by the Hopis to a child fond of spinning tops.

ZINA (ZEE-nah) Nsenga, Africa: "name." Zina refers to a child's secret spirit name, known only to her family.

ZITA (ZEE-tah) Greek: "to seek." Also a popular Spanish form of Rosita, "little rose." See Rose.

ZIZI (ZEE-zee) Hungarian form of Elizabeth, "dedicated to God." See Elizabeth.

ZODY (ZOH-dee) Congo, Africa: "beloved" or "desired."

ZOE Greek: "life."

ZOFIA (zoh-FEE-ah) Czech, Polish, and Ukrainian form of Sofia, "wisdom." See Sofia.

ZOHERET (zoh-HAIR-et) Hebrew: "she shines."

ZOHRA (ZOH-rah) Arabic: "the blooming." Also a name for the planet Venus, which governs Taurus, the bull.

ZORA Hausa, Africa: "a bargain." Also a form of Zorina. *Zorra* (Hausa)

ZORINA (SAW-re-nah, or Anglicized, zo-REE-nuh) Slovak: "golden dawn." *Zora, Zorah, Zorana, Zori, Zorie, Zory* (English)

ZURI (ZOO-ree) Swahili: "beautiful."

ZUZA (ZOO-zah) Czech form of Susan, "lily" or "graceful lily."

ZYTKA (ZET-kah) Polish name used as a short form of many girls' names ending in *-ita,* including Brigita, Margarita, and Rosita. *Zyta* (English, Polish)

Gender-Free Names

✳ ✳ ✳

Due largely to the women's movement, many names have crossed gender barriers and are now used for both boys and girls. Here are some current names that have increasingly become "gender-neutral."

AUSTIN	COREY	JORDAN	PAGE
BAILEY	CORY	KAMERON	REGAN
BLAINE	DACEY	KELLY	ROBIN
BLAIR	DAKOTA	KELSEY	ROYCE
BRADY	DALLAS	KENDALL	SHANNON
BRESLIN	DANA	KILLIAN	SHEA, SHAY
BRICE	DARBY	KIRBY	SHELBY
BROOKE	DARCY	KYLE	SHERIDAN
BRYN	DARYL	LOREN	SLOANE
CAGNEY	DEMPSEY	MACKENSIE	STEVIE
CAMERON	DEVIN	MADISON	SYDNEY
CAMPBELL	DEVLIN	MAGEE	TAYLOR
CARSON	DOLAN	MAGILL	TEAGUE
CARTER	HARPER	MALLORY	TERRY
CASEY	HOUSTON	MARLOWE	TIERNEY
CASSIDY	HUNTER	MERLE	TYSON
CHANNING	GLENN	MORGAN	WALKER
CHARLIE	GORDON	MURPHY	WALLACE
COLBY	JAMIE	NEVADA	ZANE

BOYS' NAMES

A

AARON Hebrew: "lofty" or "exalted." A popular variation—*Aron*—is used in this country as well as the Czech Republic, England, France, Germany, Israel, Norway, Poland, Russia, and Sweden and other countries. Aaron was the brother of Moses, and this is one of the most popular names in the world. *Aron* (English); *Haroun, Harun* (Arabic); *Aron* (Czech, Hungarian, Scandinavian); *Aronne* (German); *Aharon* (Hebrew); *Aranne, Aronne* (Italian); *Arek, Aron, Aronek* (Polish); *Aarao* (Portuguese); *Aron, Aronos* (Russian); *Aaran, Aren, Ari, Arin,* *Aron, Ron, Ronnie, Ronny* (Spanish)

ABAN (AY-bahn) Irish Gaelic: "a little abbot." Name of a sixth-century Irish saint. *Abban* (Irish)

ABASI (ah-BAH-see) Swahili: "stern." The Indian equivalent is Abbas, "stern of countenance," referring to one of the ninety-nine attributes of God listed in the Koran. Both forms are popular among Moslems.

ABDUL (ahb-DOOL) Arabic: "servant of," implying the child is a servant of God. A favorite among Moslems, Abdul is used as an element in many names. Examples: *Abdul Karim,* "servant of the generous One," and *Abdel Nasser,* "servant of the victorious

One." *Abdel, Abdullah* (Arabic); *Abdalla* (Swahili)

ABEL (AY-bel) Hebrew: "breath"; or Assyrian: "son." The second son of Adam and Eve.

ABI Turkish: "elder brother." Comes originally from Turkey, where it's given to a first child when the parents plan to have other children.

> **"***As long as time endures, there will always be royally enthroned the names of Abraham, Moses, Isaiah.***"**
>
> —FROM A 19TH-CENTURY JUDAIC TEXT

ABRAHAM Hebrew: "father of a mighty nation" or "father of the multitude." *Abe, Abi, Abie, Abram* (English); *Ibrahim* (Arabic); *Avram* (Bulgarian, Greek, Romanian); *Bram* (Dutch); *Abram* (Hebrew); *Abrahamo, Abramo* (Italian); *Abrao* (Portuguese); *Abrahamo, Abrahan, Abramo, Abran, Ibrahim* (Spanish); *Arram* (Swedish); *Avram, Avrum* (Yiddish)

ABRAM Hebrew: "the lofty One is the Father." Popular shortened form of Abraham, used not only in this country but in France, Poland, Russia, and Spanish-speaking countries.

ACAR (uh-KAHR) Turkish: "bright."

ACE Latin: "unity."

ADAIR (ah-DARE) Scottish Gaelic: "one from the oak-tree ford."

ADAL (AH-dahl, or Anglicized, ah-DAHL) German: "noble."

ADAM Hebrew: "earth" or "man of the red earth." As name of the first man God created, Adam is a popular name worldwide. *Ad, Ade* (English); *Adamec, Adamek, Adamik, Adamko, Adamok, Damek* (Czech); *Adi, Adrien* (Hungarian); *Adhamh* (Irish); *Adamo, Adan* (Italian); *Adomas* (Lithuanian); *Adamek, Adas, Adok* (Polish); *Adao* (Portuguese); *Adamka, Adas* (Russian); *Adhamh, Keady, Keddie, Keddy* (Scottish); *Adamo, Adan, Adao, Addis, Addy, Adnon* (Spanish); *Adem* (Turkish); *Adi* (Yiddish)

ADAN (ah-DAHN) Yoruba, Nigeria: "a large bat," from the proverb "If you do not have a large bat, you sacrifice a small one." In other words, you simply do your best. The same name is also a Spanish form of Adam.

ADAR Syrian: "ruler" or "prince." Derived from the twelfth month of the Babylonian calendar. Also Hebrew: "fire," from the sixth month of the Jewish calendar.

ADDISON Old English: "Adam's son." Originally a last name, now also used as a first name. *Addisen, Adisen, Adison* (English)

ADEBEN (ah-deh-BEHN) Akan, Ghana: "twelfth-born son."

ADEL (ah-DALE or ah-DELL) Teutonic: "noble." Adel is used as an element in many names, including *Adelar* ("noble eagle"), *Adelard* ("nobly resolute"), *Adelbern* ("noble bear"), and *Adelhart* ("nobly firm").

ADEN (AY-den) A form of Aiden, "little and fiery."

ADIN (AY-din) Hebrew: "an ornament."

ADIR (ah-DEER) Hebrew: "majestic" or "noble."

ADIV (ah-DEEV) Hebrew: "pleasant" or "gentle."

ADLER Old English: "eagle."

ADLI (ahd-LEE) Turkish: "just."

ADMON (ahd-MOHN) Israeli: "a red peony flower." Refers to a flower that grows in the upper Galilee.

ADNAN (AHD-nahn) Arabic: "to settle." An ancient Arabic name held by one of Ismail's descendents.

ADOM (ah-DOHM) Akan, Ghana: "help from God."

ADRI (AH-dree) Hindi: "rock." Adri is a minor god in Hindu mythology who protected mankind and once rescued the

Did You Know...

✱ ✱ ✱

At one time or another, about one-third of all young people wish their parents had given them a different name. Here are a few names children would often rather be without: Augustus, Callister, Julian, Miles, and even Andrew, Charles, and John. Surprisingly, in one study British researchers found "the relatively inoffensive name 'Richard' seemed almost universally unpopular."

sun from evil spirits who tried to extinguish it.

ADRIAN Latin: "dark one." Popular today in this country as well as South America and Spain. *Hadrian* (English); *Adrien* (French); *Adi, Adorjan* (Hungarian); *Adriano* (Italian, Spanish); *Adrik, Andreian, Andreyan, Andri, Andrian, Andriyan* (Russian); *Hadrian* (Swedish)

ADRIEL (AY-dree-ell) Hebrew: "God's majesty" or "belonging to God's congregation." *Adri, Adrial* (Hebrew)

ADWIN (AD-win) Ghana, Africa: "creative one."

AGNI (AHG-nee) Hindi: "god of fire." In Hindu lore, Agni is depicted with three heads, four or seven arms, and seven tongues (each with its own name) for lapping up the butter offered during sacrifices. He often has a ram at his side and rides in a glorious chariot driven by a red-limbed, golden-haired charioteer. The chariot's wheels are the seven winds.

AGUSTIN (ah-GUS-tin or, in Spanish, ah-goo-STEEN) Latin: "belonging to Augustus, the exalted one." Commonly used in Spanish-speaking countries. *Augustus* (English)

AHANU (ah-HAH-noo) Native American: "he laughs."

AHARON (AHR-on) Hebrew form of Aaron, "lofty" or "exalted." See Aaron.

AHDIK (AH-dik) Native American: "caribou" or "reindeer."

AHIR (uh-HEER) Turkish: "end" or "last." Bestowed in Turkey on the last child a mother intends to bear.

AHMED (ah-HMED, or Anglicized, AH-med) Arabic: "the most praised." This name was occasionally used by Muhammad and is one of the more than five hundred names for the Prophet. An old Moslem saying holds that angels pray in every house where an Ahmad or Muhammad lives. *Ahmad* (Arabic)

AHMIK (AH-mik) Native American: "the beaver." In many Native American legends, the beaver epitomizes skill.

AHREN Old German: "eagle." In astrology, the eagle is one symbol of Scorpio.

AIDEN, ADEN (AY-den) Irish Gaelic: "little and fiery."

AILIN (AY-lin) Irish form of Allen, "handsome" or "cheerful."

AINMIRE (AHN-meer) Irish Gaelic: "great lord." A traditional name in Ireland borne by a sixth-century Irish king.

AKANDO (ah-KAHN-do) Native American: "ambush." The name may have originally been bestowed to commemorate a great feat the child's father performed.

AKAR (ah-KAHR) Turkish: "flowing" or "running," referring to water.

AKASH (ah-kash) Hindi: "sky."

AKEMI (ah-KEH-mee) Japanese: "beautiful dawn."

AKIL (ah-KEEL) Arabic: "intelligent," "thoughtful," or "one who uses reason." *Ahkeel, Akeel* (English, Arabic)

AKIM (ah-KEEM) Russian form of the Hebrew Jehoiakim, "God will establish."

AKIN (ah-KEEN) Yoruba, Africa: "brave" or "heroic." *Ahkeen, Akeen* (English, Nigerian)

AKIO (ah-kee-oh) Japanese: "bright boy." *Akira* (Japanese)

AKIRA (ah-kee-rah) Japanese: "intelligent; smart."

AKRON Ochi, Ga, Africa: "ninth-born son." *Akan* (Ochi, Ga)

AKULE (ah-KOOL) Native American: "he looks up." Possibly indicates one of the first things the baby did at birth.

ALA (ah-LAH) Arabic: "glorious."

ALAIN (ah-LANE) French form of Alan.

ALAN Irish Gaelic: "handsome" or "cheerful." *Aland, Alen, Allan, Allen, Allyn, Alyn* (English); *Alain, Allain* (French); *Ailin* (Irish); *Alano* (Italian, Spanish); *Alao* (Portuguese); *Ailean* (Scottish); *Alun* (Welsh)

ALASTAIR Greek: "one who avenges." Also a Scottish form of Alexander, "helper and defender of mankind." *Al, Alaster, Allaster, Alister, Allister* (English); *Alastar* (Irish); *Alasdair, Alisdair, Alistair, Allaster, Aly* (Scottish)

ALBEN Latin: "blond, fair one." *Al, Alban, Albin, Alby* (English); *Albin, Albinek, Aubin, Binek* (Czech); *Aubin* (French); *Albins* (Latvian); *Albino* (Italian, Portuguese, Spanish); *Albek, Albinek, Binek* (Polish)

ALBERT Old English: "noble and brilliant." Became extremely popular after Queen Victoria married Prince Albert of Germany in 1840. Albert Einstein and Albert Schweitzer kept the name in the limelight in the twentieth century, but it has currently fallen out of style. *Adelbert, Al, Albie, Bert, Berty, Burt, Elbert* (English); *Alberik, Ales, Berco, Berti, Bertik, Berty* (Czech); *Aubert* (French); *Albrecht, Bechtel, Bertchen* (German); *Alvertos* (Greek); *Alberto, Aliberto, Berto* (Italian,

Portuguese, Spanish); *Alberts* (Latvian); *Albek, Bertek* (Polish)

ALBIE Contemporary American creation from Albert, "noble and brilliant."

ALBIN Russian form of Alvin, "everyone's friend."

ALDEN Old English: "old friend" or "wise protector."

ALDER Old English: "from the alder tree." Commonly used today in Germany.

ALDO Old German: "old and wise." Popular in Italy. The feminine form is Alda.

ALDRICH Old English: "an old and wise ruler." *Al, Aldric, Aldridge, Eldredge, Eldridge,*

Elric, Rich, Richie, Richy (English); *Audric* (French)

ALEC Pet form of Alexander now used independently. Made known worldwide by British actor Sir Alec Guinness.

ALEIN (ah-LIGHN) Yiddish: "alone."

ALEX Popular short form of Alexander, "helper and defender of mankind." *Alec, Alek, Alik, Alix* (English)

ALEXANDER Greek: "helper and defender of mankind." *Alec, Alek, Aleks, Alex, Alexis, Alic, Alik, Aliks, Alix, Lex, Lexi, Sande, Sander, Sandy, Saunders, Sawnie* (English); *Alekko, Aleksandur, Sander* (Bulgarian); *Ales, Leksik, Lekso* (Czech); *Aleksander, Leks* (Estonian); *Alexandre* (French);

> **"There's a wonderful family**
> **called Stein—**
> **There's Gert, and there's Epp,**
> **and there's Ein;**
> **Gert's poems are bunk,**
> **Epp's statues are junk,**
> **And nobody understands Ein."**
>
> —ANONYMOUS

Alik, Axel (German); *Alekos, Alexandros* (Greek); *Alexandre, Elek, Sandor, Sanyi* (Hungarian); *Alsandair, Alsander* (Irish); *Alessandro* (Italian); *Aleksander, Olek, Oles* (Polish); *Alexio* (Portuguese); *Alek, Aleksandr, Aleksei, Alexandr, Alexei, Les, Oleksandr, Oles, Olesko, Sanya, Sasha, Sashenka, Sashka, Shura, Shurik, Shurka* (Russian); *Alasdair, Alastair, Alister* (Scottish); *Alejandro, Alejo, Alesandre, Alesandro, Alesandros, Alesi, Alesio, Alesis, Alessandro, Alic, Alik, Jandino, Jando, Sander, Sandro* (Spanish); *Aleksander* (Yiddish)

ALEXIS (ah-LEX-iss) Form of Alexander ("helper and defender of mankind") still bestowed on boys, but more common for girls.

ALF Old Norse: "elfin." A favorite in Norway. See Alvin.

ALFONSO (ahl-FON-zoh) Old German: "ready and noble" or "ready for battle." Used frequently by Spanish royalty. Also common in Italy and Sweden. *Alfie, Alphonse* (English); *Alphonse* (French); *Alfons* (German); *Alphonsus* (Irish); *Alfio, Lanzo* (Italian); *Affonso, Afonso* (Portuguese); *Alfie, Alfo, Alfonzo, Alonzo, Alphonso, Fonzi, Fonzo, Lonzo* (Spanish)

ALI Arabic: "Jehovah," "the highest," or "the greatest." Popular among Moslems in many Arabic

countries, as well as in the United States. Ali was a son-in-law of the Prophet Mohammad, married to his daughter Fatimah.

> **"*Bossom? What an extraordinary name. Neither one thing nor the other!*"**
>
> —Sir Winston Churchill, referring to Sir Alfred Bossom

ALIM (ah-LEEM) Arabic: "wise" or "learned." *Aleem, Alem* (Arabic)

ALISTER Popular Scottish form of Alexander, "helper and defender of mankind." See Alexander and Callister.

ALLEN A variation of Alan, "handsome" or "cheerful."

ALMIRON (ahl-mee-ruhn) Hindi: "clothes basket." Naming children after common household objects is traditional in India because the Hindus believe God is manifested in everything. Hence, each time you say the child's name, you are pronouncing the name of God, which is considered a step toward salvation. The feminine form is Almira. *Miron* (Hindi)

ALMON (ahl-MOHN) Hebrew: "forsaken" or "a widower."

ALON (AL-lon) Hebrew: "oak tree." A nature name from Israel. *Allon* (Hebrew)

ALONZO (ah-LAHN-zoh) A favorite Spanish form of Alfonso, "ready and noble" or "ready for battle." The name of a protagonist in Cervantes's famous Spanish novel *Don Quixote. Lonzo* (Italian)

ALRIK Old German: "ruler of all." Popular in Sweden.

ALROY Spanish: "the king."

ALTAIR (ahl-tah-EER or ahl-TAYR) Arabic: "the flying eagle." Also refers to a first-magnitude star in the constellation Lyra.

ALTON Old English: "one who lives in the old town or estate." *Alten, Altin* (English)

ALVIN Old German: "everyone's friend" or "noble friend." *Al, Alvan, Alvie, Alwin, Alwyn, Elvin* (English); *Aloin, Aluin* (French); *Alwin* (German, Portuguese); *Alvino* (Italian); *Albin* (Polish, Russian); *Aluino* (Spanish); *Alwyn* (Welsh)

ALVIS (AHL-vis) Old Norse: "all-knowing." The name of a dwarf in Norse mythology who fell in love with Thor's daughter.

ALYN Contemporary American spelling of Alan, "handsome" or "cheerful."

AMADO (ah-MAH-do) Latin: "loving deity" or "loved by the divine." Name of a saint popular in Spanish-speaking countries.

AMAL (ah-mahl) Hindi: "clean" or "pure." A traditional Hindu name from India.

AMBROSE (AM-brohz) Greek: "immortal." In the fourth century, St. Ambrose was a bishop of Milan, Italy. *Ambrosius* (Dutch, German, Swedish); *Ambroise* (French); *Ambrus* (Hungarian); *Ambrogio, Ambrosi* (Italian); *Ambrosio* (Spanish)

AMEER (ah-MEER) An Anglicized form of Amir, "prince."

AMIEL (ah-mee-AYL) Hebrew: "Lord of my people." Currently popular in Israel. *Ami* (Hebrew)

AMIL (ah-meel) Hindi: "inaccessible," in the sense of being so exalted as to be unattainable.

AMIN (AH-min) East Indian: "faithful." *Ameen, Amitan, Amnon* (East Indian)

AMIR (ah-MEER) Arabic: "prince" or "one who commands or rules." A favorite Arabic name. *Ameer* (English)

AMON (AY-mon) Hebrew: "related to the sun." Name for a boy born under Leo, ruled by the sun.

AMORY Old German: "divine, famous ruler." Has connotations of success and wealth. *Amery, Amor* (English)

AN (ahn) Vietnamese: "peace" or "security."

ANDERS Scandinavian form of Andrew, "strong and manly."

ANDRE (ahn-DRAY) French form of Andrew. Currently used in this country as well as France and Portugal, where it's pronounced AHN-dray.

ANDREW Greek *andreas:* "strong and manly." *Andi, Andie, Andy, Drew* (English); *Andrei, Andres, Andrey* (Bulgarian); *Andrej, Bandi, Ondro* (Czech); *Anders* (Danish, Norwegian, Swedish); *André* (French); *Andreas* (German); *Andreas, Evagelos* (Greek); *Andi, Andor, Andras, Andris, Bandi, Endre* (Hungarian); *Aindreas* (Irish); *Andrius* (Lithuanian); *Aniol, Jedrek, Jedrus* (Polish); *Andrei, Dela* (Romanian); *Andrey, Andreyka, Andrik* (Russian); *Kendrew* (Scottish); *Andras, Andi, Andres, Andris, Necho, Nesho* (Spanish); *Andras* (Welsh)

ANDY Short form of Andrew, used today as a full given name. *Andi, Andie* (English)

ANGEL (ahn-HEL, or anglicized, AYN-jel) Latin: "angel" or "messenger." Still used more for boys than for girls in this country. *Angell* (English); *Angelo* (Greek, Italian); *Angelino* (Spanish)

ANGELO A favorite in Italy, Greece and many other countries as a form of Angel, "angel" or "messenger."

> **"** *Every man has three names: one his father and mother gave him, one others call him, and one he acquires himself.* **"**
>
> —ECCLESIASTES 7: 1–3

ANIL (ah-nil) Hindi: "child of the air or wind." A Hindu name originally from India.

ANKA Turkish: "the legendary phoenix" or "will-o'-the-wisp."

ANLON (AHN-lun) Irish Gaelic: "great hero." English version of an Irish name. *Anluan* (Irish)

ANNAN (ah-NAHN) Ochi, Ga, Africa: "fourth-born son."

ANOKI (ah-NO-kee) Native American: "actor."

ANSEL Old French: "connected with or related to a nobleman"; or Old German: "divine helmet." Made well known by photographer Ansel Adams. *Ancel, Ancell, Ansell, Ansil, Ansill* (English); *Amselmo, Ancelmo, Anselino, Anselm, Anselmo, Anzelmo, Enselmo, Selmo, Semo* (Spanish)

ANSIS Latvian form of John, "gracious gift of God" or "God is gracious." See John.

ANTAINE (ahn-TAYN) Traditional Irish form of Anthony, "inestimable" or "priceless."

ANTHONY Latin: "inestimable" or "priceless." A favorite variation—*Anton*—is used not only in this country but also in Bulgaria, the Czech Republic, Germany, Norway, Romania, Russia, and Sweden. A Christian name of deep spiritual significance popularized throughout Europe by St. Anthony the Great and Franciscan friar St. Anthony of Padua, in whose names God performed miracles for the ill and poor. *Antony, Toni, Tony* (English); *Anton* (Bulgarian); *Antek, Anton, Antonin, Tonda, Tonik* (Czech); *Antoine* (French); *Anton* (German); *Andonios, Andonis, Tonis* (Greek); *Akoni* (Hawaiian); *Antal, Anti, Tonese, Toni* (Hungarian); *Anntoin, Antaine, Antoin, Antoine* (Irish); *Antonio, Toni, Tonio* (Italian, Portuguese, Spanish); *Antons* (Latvian); *Antavas, Tavas* (Lithuanian); *Antek, Anton, Antoni, Antonin, Antos, Tolek, Tonek* (Polish); *Anton* (Romanian); *Antin, Antinko, Anton, Tosya, Tusya* (Russian); *Anders, Anton* (Scandinavian); *Toni* (Slavic)

ANTOINE (an-TWAHN) A French and Irish form of Anthony, "inestimable" or "priceless." Fashionable in this country and throughout Europe.

ANTONIO (an-TOH-nee-oh) Popular Italian and Spanish form of Anthony, "inestimable" or "priceless." *Toni, Tonio* (Italian, Spanish)

ARALT (ar-ahlt) Traditional Irish form of Harold, "army ruler." See Harold.

ARCHER Old English: "a bowman or archer."

ARCHIBALD Old German *ercanbald:* "genuine, simple, and bold." *Arch, Archie, Archy* (English); *Archaimbaud, Archambault* (French); *Archibaldo* (Spanish)

ARDAL (AR-dahl) Irish Gaelic: "highly courageous." A traditional Irish name. *Ardghal, Artegal, Arthgallo* (Irish)

ARDON (AHR-don) Hebrew: "bronze."

AREL (ah-RAYL) Hebrew: "lion of God." The lion is the symbol of the astrological sign Leo. *Areli* (Hebrew)

AREN Norse: "eagle" or "rule." Originally from Norway and Denmark, where it's frequently used.

ARI Hebrew: "lion." Also a short form of Aristotle, "seeking the positive (or best) results," and a Spanish short form of Aaron. *Arie, Arri* (English)

ARIC Old English: "a holy ruler." An older form of Richard now used as a given name. *Arek, Areck, Arick, Ric, Rick, Ricky* (English)

ARIEL (AYR-ree-ayl) Hebrew: "lion of God." A Biblical name now more common for girls than boys. In Jewish mythology, Ariel is a demon water spirit and medieval spirit of the air. *Ariell* (English)

ARIF (ah-REEF) Turkish: "wise and intelligent." *Areef* (English)

ARISTOTLE Greek: "seeking the positive (or best) results." *Ari, Arie, Arri* (English); *Arri* (Greek)

ARKIN Norwegian: "the eternal king's son."

ARLEN Irish Gaelic: "a pledge." *Arlan, Arland, Arlend, Arlin, Arlind* (English)

ARLEY Old English: "the bowman or hunter" or "from the rabbit meadow." For a boy born under Sagittarius, the archer.

ARLO Spanish: "barberry." Made well known by singer Arlo Guthrie.

ARMAND Old German: "armed" or "army man." *Arman, Armin, Armon, Armond, Ormond* (English); *Armando* (Italian); *Armands* (Latvian); *Arek, Mandek* (Polish); *Arman, Armen* (Russian); *Arman, Armande, Armando, Armin, Armon, Armond, Armonde, Armondo, Mando* (Spanish)

ARMINO (ar-MEE-noh) A favorite Italian form of Herman, "army man; soldier" or "of high rank."

ARMON Hebrew: "castle" or "place." *Armani, Armoni* (English)

ARMSTRONG Old English: "man with a strong arm in battle."

ARNE (ahrn or AHR-nee) A contemporary form of Arnold, "power of an eagle." One of the most popular names in Norway, also used in Sweden and Denmark. A favorite form in Iceland is Arni.

ARNEL (ahr-NEL) A contemporary American and Spanish form of Arnold, "eagle."

ARNOLD Old German: "power of an eagle." Once considered an "old" or "staid" name, Arnold has enjoyed a revival as a "power" name due to its association with actor Arnold Schwarzenegger. *Arne, Arnel, Arney, Arni, Arnie, Arny* (English); *Arnauld* (French); *Arnd* (German); *Arni* (Icelandic); *Arne* (Scandinavian); *Arnaldo, Arnel, Arni, Wado* (Spanish)

ARNON (AHR-non) Hebrew: "rushing stream," implying the child is energetic.

LEGENDS & LORE

According to ancient belief in many cultures, if someone knew your true name it gave them power to work evil magic against you. The fear of being harmed if one's name were revealed may be the hidden reason behind the simple English nursery rhyme still occasionally recited on American playgrounds:

> "What's your name?
> Pudding and tame,
> If you ask me again,
> I'll tell you the same."

In India, a child asked his or her name may give a similarly evasive reply: "Khato Pito" (one who eats and drinks).

ARON Form of Aaron used in many parts of the world besides the United States, including the Czech Republic, Poland, Russia, and Scandinavia.

ARPIAR (ahr-pee-AHR) Armenian: "sunny" or "of sunshine."

ARRI (AIR-ee) Contemporary Greek and American form of Aristotle, "seeking the positive (or best) results." *Ari* (English, Greek)

ARRIO (ah-REE-oh) Spanish: "warlike."

ARSENIO (ar-SAY-nee-oh) Greek: "masculine and viral." A favorite Hispanic name made well known by actor and TV personality Arsenio Hall. *Arcenio, Arsanio, Arsemio, Eresenio* (Spanish)

ARSHAD (ar-shahd) Sanskrit: "devout" or "pious." A spiritual name from India.

ARSLAN (ar-SLUN) Turkish: "lion," the symbol of the astrological sign Leo.

ART Short form of Arthur ("a bear" or "noble one") and Artemus.

ARTEMUS Greek: "belonging to Artemis." Artemis was the Greek goddess of the hunt. *Art, Artie, Artimas, Artimis, Tamus, Taymus, Tim* (English)

ARTHUR Celtic *artos:* "a bear"; or Welsh: "noble one." *Art, Arte, Artie, Arty* (English); *Artis* (Czech); *Arto* (Finnish); *Anthanasios, Thanasis, Thanos* (Greek); *Artur* (Irish); *Arturo* (Italian, Spanish); *Artek* (Polish); *Artair* (Scottish); *Atur* (used in many countries, including Bulgaria, Estonia, Hungary, Ireland, Norway, Poland, Romania, Russia, and Sweden)

ARUN (AH-run or ah-roon) Cambodian: "sun"; or Sanskrit: "reddish-brown-haired." A name for a child born under the sign of Leo, ruled by the sun.

ARVAN (ahr-vahn) Hindi: "horse." Taken from Hindu mythology and refers to one of the horses of the moon, a fabulous half-horse, half-bird, on which the gods are said to ride.

ARVE (AHR-ve) Scandinavian: "inheritor of property" or "heir." Especially popular in Norway.

ARVID Scandinavian: "man of the people." Popular in Sweden and Norway.

ASA (AY-sah) Hebrew: "physician, healer." The name of Judah's third king. Made well known most recently by British soccer player Asa Hartford.

ASAD (ah-SAHD) Arabic: "lion." Designates the constellation and astrological sign of Leo, the lion. *Aleser, Alisid, Asid, Assid* (English)

ASADEL (ah-sah-DEL) Arabic: "most prosperous one."

ASH Short form of Asher, Ashley, and other male names starting with *Ash*. According to an old superstition, the ash brings good luck.

LEGENDS & LORE

One legend had it that a sprig of ash worn on the breast would give one prophetic dreams, and ash sap given to a newborn would frighten away evil spirits. Another superstition was that if the first parings of a child's nails were buried beneath an ash tree, he'd become a fine singer.

ASHER Hebrew: "lucky," "blessed," or "happy." *Ash, Ashur* (English)

ASHLEY Old English: "one from the ash-tree meadow." Rapidly becoming exclusively a girls' name. *Ash* (English)

ASHLIN Old English: "from the pool surrounded by ash trees." Name for a boy born under one of the water signs of Cancer, Pisces, or Scorpio. *Ash, Ashlen* (English)

ASHON (ah-SHOHN) Ochi, Ga, Africa: "seventh-born son."

ASHTON Old English: "from the ash-tree farm." Also used for girls. *Ash, Ashe, Ashtin* (English)

ASHUR Swahili: "born during the Moslem month of Ashur"; or eastern Semitic: "warlike." Also a form of Asher, "lucky," "blessed," or "happy."

ASIEL (ah-see-AYL) Hebrew: "God has created him." A traditional Jewish name also used in Israel.

ASIM (ah-SEEM) Arabic: "protector" or "defender." *Aseem* (English)

ASWAD (ahs-WAHD) Arabic: "black."

ATALIK (AHT-ah-leek) Tartar: "like a father." A favorite in Hungary.

ATMAN (AHT-mun) Hindi: "the self."

ATWAN (ah-TWAHN) Ibo, Nigeria *atuanya:* "we throw the eyes." Loosely translated, the name from which this is derived means "unexpected" and is given in Africa to a son born when a daughter was expected. *Atuan* (English)

AUBIN French form of Alben, "blond, fair one."

AUBREY (AU-bree) Old German: "elf ruler" or "elf spirit." Originally a boys' name now bestowed more often on girls. *Aubary, Aubery, Aubri, Aubrie, Aubry* (English)

AUDRIC A French form of Aldrich, "an old and wise ruler."

AUDUN (OW-doon, or Angli-cized OW-dun) Scandinavian: "deserted" or "desolate." Currently popular in Norway. The feminine form is Aud. *Auden, Audon* (English)

AUREK (AW-rek) Latin: "golden-haired." Modern Finnish form of the older, seldom used name Aurelius. *Aurel* (Czech); *Aurele* (French); *Aurelius* (German); *Aurelio* (Italian); *Aureli, Elek* (Polish); *Aurelian* (Romanian), *Avrel, Avreliy* (Russian)

AUSTIN Latin: "venerable one." A trendy contemporary form of Augustine, also used in Scotland. *Austen, Aystyn, Osten, Ostin* (English); *Agoston* (Hungarian)

AVEL Modern Greek: "breath." Connotes man's mortality.

AVERIL Middle English: "born in the month of April." Averil is an ancient Anglo-Saxon word for

Israeli Holy Names

✶ ✶ ✶

Many Israeli names contain references to religion or God. The prefix *"Avi-"* frequently appears in such contemporary names. Several examples include: *Avidan* ("God is just" or "Father of justice"); *Avidor* ("Father of a generation"); *Aviel* ("God is my Father"); *Avital* ("Father of dew"); *Avner* ("Father of light"); and *Avniel* ("My Father is my rock" or "My Father is my strength").

April. *Averel, Averell, Averill, Avril, Avrill* (English)

AVERY Old English: "elfin ruler."

AVI (ah-VEE) Hebrew: "Father," referring to God.

AVIV (ah-VEEV) Hebrew: "spring," "freshness," or "youth." Comes originally from Israel, where it's frequently used.

AWAN (AH-wahn) Native American: "somebody."

AXEL Scandinavian: "divine reward." Also a Scandinavian form of Absalom, "father of peace." A favorite in Sweden and Norway. *Axell* (English)

AZAD (uh-ZUHD) Turkish: "free" or "born free."

AZI (ah-ZEE) Nigerian: "the youth," implying energy.

AZIM (ah-ZEEM) Arabic: "defender," referring to one of God's ninety-nine qualities in the Koran. *Azeem* (English)

AZIZ (ah-ZEEZ) Arabic: "powerful and beloved." Another of the 99 attributes of Allah.

AZRIEL (ahz-ree-AYL) Hebrew: "God is my help."

B

BADAR (bah-dahr) Arabic: "full moon." A Hindu name from India for a child born under the astrological sign of Cancer, ruled by the moon.

BAILEY Old French: "a steward or bailiff." *Bail, Bailie, Baillie, Baily, Bayley* (English)

BAINBRIDGE Old English: "a bridge over rapids." Probably originally bestowed on a child born near a bridge over white waters. Many people characterize this name as aristocratic. *Bain, Bridger* (English)

BAIRD (baird) Celtic: "poet" or "a traveling ballad singer." A popular Scottish clan name that has become a given name for boys. *Bard* (English, Scottish)

BAL (bahl) Tibetan, Sanskrit *bal-bala:* "wool-hair." English Gypsy name for a child born with lots of hair.

BALDER Old Norse: "god of light" or "white god." In Norse mythology, Balder was the son of the god Odin and was killed when touched by a sprig of mistletoe. His astrological sign corresponds to Gemini, the twins. *Baudier* (French); *Baldur* (Scandinavian)

BALDWIN Old German: "bold friend" or "bold protector."

BALIN (BAH-lin) Hindi: "mighty soldier." In Hindu mythology, Balin is a monkey king. A notorious tyrant, he is said to have the power to extract half the strength from anyone who challenges him. *Bali, Valin* (Hindi)

BANAN (BAWN-an) Irish: "white." A traditional boys' name in Ireland.

BANE (BAH-neh) Hawaiian form of Barney, "son of prophecy or consolation." Given to a child after much praying and waiting by parents. See Barney.

BARAM (bah-RAM) modern Israeli: "son of a nation." Derived from Abraham, "father of a mighty nation" or "father of the multitude."

BARNEY Greek, Hebrew: "son of prophecy" or "consolation." Modern American form of the older name Barnabas. *Barn, Barnaby, Barnie, Barny* (English); *Barnabe* (French); *Bane* (Hawaiian); *Barna* (Hungarian); *Barnebas, Bernabe* (Spanish)

A New Naming Trend?

✷ ✷ ✷

As if choosing the perfect first and middle names for your baby weren't enough, many parents now wonder what to use as their baby's *last* name. To reflect equality in the marriage, shouldn't the mother's and father's names be hyphenated, making the baby's last name something like Johnson-Smith or Jackson-Schwartz? Yet on the other hand, should a child really be saddled with such a complicated name to spell in first grade? Struggling with this problem, one New York City couple came up with a creative solution: His last name is Flaherty, hers is Silverman. So when they married, they simply combined their two names to produce Flaherman. Similarly, a Washington State couple named Tribbett and Orwell gave their children the last name Tribwell.

BARON Old English: "a warrior or baron." *Barron* (English); *Baran* (Russian)

BARRET Old German: "mighty as a bear." *Barrett* (English)

BARRY Irish Gaelic: "pointed or like a spear"; or Old French: "a form or barrier." Also a popular short form of Bernard. *Barri, Barrie* (English)

BARTH Hebrew: "a farmer" or "son of the earth." Contemporary short form of Bartholomew. *Bart, Bartel, Bat* (English); *Bartek, Barto, Bartz* (Czech); *Bardo* (Danish); *Barthelmy, Bartholome, Bartholomieu* (French); *Bartel, Barthel, Bartol, Bertel* (German); *Barta, Bartalan, Bertalan, Berti* (Hungarian); *Parthalon* (Irish); *Barnaby, Bartek, Bartos* (Polish); *Parlan* (Scottish); *Jerney* (Slovenian); *Balta, Bario, Barolo, Bartoleme, Bartoli, Toli* (Spanish); *Barthelemy* (Swedish)

BARUCH modern Greek: "doer of good."

BASIL (BAZ-il) Latin: "kingly" or "magnificent"; or Irish Gaelic: "war or strife." *Bas, Bazil, Brasil, Bresal, Vas, Vasily* (English); *Vasil* (Bulgarian); *Bazil, Vasil* (Czech); *Bale, Basile* (French); *Basle* (German); *Vasilis* (Greek); *Bazel, Vazul* (Hungarian); *Breasal* (Irish); *Basilio* (Italian, Spanish); *Bazek* (Polish); *Vasile* (Romanian); *Vas, Vasilek, Vasili, Vassily, Vasya,*

Vasyl (Russian); *Basilius, Basle* (Swedish)

BASIR (buh-SEER) Turkish: "intelligent and discerning."

BAUL (bahl) English Gypsy: "snail."

BAVOL (BAH-vohl) English Gypsy: "wind" or "air."

BAY (BY, or Anglicized, BAY) Vietnamese: "seventh-born child." Also given to a child born on Saturday or in July, the seventh lunar month.

BEACAN (BEH-gawn) Irish Gaelic: "tiny one." The name of a sixth-century Irish saint, this is a favorite in Ireland. *Beagan, Bec, Becan* (English); *Beag, Beccan* (Irish)

BEAU (boh) Old French: "handsome" or "a dandy." Made well known most recently by actor Beau Bridges.

BECK Middle English: "a brook." A common surname in Switzerland.

BEDRICH (BED-rik) Czech form of Frederick, "peaceful ruler."

BELDON Old English: "child of the unspoiled, beautiful glen." *Belden, Beldin* (English)

BELEN (BEL-en) Greek: "an arrow." Name for a boy born

under the sign of Sagittarius, the Archer.

BELLO (BAY-loh) Fultani, Africa, *ballawo bini:* "the helper (or promoter) of the Islamic religion."

BEM (behm) Tiv, Nigeria: "peace."

BEN Arabic and Hebrew: "son" or "son of." Frequently used as part of longer Arabic names. Also short form of Benjamin ("son of my right hand"), Bennett ("blessed"), Benedict, and other names starting with *"Ben-." Benji, Benjy, Benn, Bennie, Benny* (English)

BENEDICT Latin: "blessed." *Ben, Bendix, Benedick, Bennet, Bennett, Bennie, Benny, Dick* (English); *Benedikt* (Bulgarian, Czech, German); *Benoist, Benoit* (French); *Bence, Benci, Benedek, Benedik, Benek, Benke* (Hungarian); *Benedetto, Betto* (Italian); *Bendik* (Norwegian); *Bendek, Benek* (Polish); *Benedicto, Bento* (Portuguese); *Benedikt, Benedo, Venedict, Venedikt, Venka, Venya* (Russian); *Benditto, Benedetto, Benedicto, Benedito, Beni, Benitin, Benito, Bento* (Spanish); *Bengt* (Swedish)

BENNETT Latin: "blessed." A contemporary form of the older name Benedict. *Ben, Benet, Benett, Bennet, Bennie, Benny* (English); *Benoit* (French);

Did You Know...

✴ ✴ ✴

Whenever you sign a check, letter, or library card, your name may reveal more than you think. A Wesleyan University psychologist found that the higher a person's social status, the larger his or her signature. One college freshman always wrote his name in a very tiny space. By the time he had earned his Ph.D. and was teaching in college, his signature size had ballooned nearly 500%.

Benedetto (Italian); *Bendito, Benedetto, Benedicto, Benedito, Beni, Benito, Bento* (Spanish)

BENOIT (ben-WAH) A French form of Bennett, "blessed." Common in France and gaining popularity in the United States.

BENON (BEN-on) Irish Gaelic: "from a good family" or "well-born." An English form of Beanon, a traditional name from Ireland.

Ben, Benen (English); *Beanon, Beinean, Beineon, Binean* (Irish)

BENTLEY Old English: "from the bent-grass clearing or meadow," referring to a type of weedy, course grass. Has a rich, upper class feel due to its association with the Bentley automobile. *Ben, Benny, Bently* (English)

BENTON Middle English: "from the place where the bear grass grows." A last name now used as a given name for boys. *Ben, Benten, Bentin* (English)

BENZI Hebrew *Ben Zion:* "excellent son."

BERCAN (BER-kan) Irish Gaelic: "little spear." Five Irish saints bear this name. English variation of the traditional Irish name Bearchan (BAR-han).

BERDY (BAIR-dee) Russian and Slavic form of Hubert, "brilliant mind" or "brilliant spirit."

BERG German: "mountain." Originally a surname for a family from the mountains. Used in many parts of the world besides Germany, including Holland, Israel, Sweden, and the United States.

BERK Turkish: "solid, firm, or rugged." Also a spelling variation of Burke, "one who lives at the fortress or stronghold."

BERKELEY Old English: "from the birch forest." Also used for girls. *Berk, Berke, Berkley* (English)

BERIN (BAIR-in) Origin unclear, but may be Latin: "blond" or "fair." A deeply spiritual name. St. Berin was a seventh-century Catholic bishop in whose name many miracles took place. It is said that he once walked on the sea. *Birin, Birinus* (English)

BERNARD Old German: "brave as a bear." A truly international name, used in Bulgaria, the Czech Republic, France, Norway, Poland, Romania, Russia, and the United States. Saints have had this name. One, for whom the St. Bernard dog was named, is the patron saint of mountain climbers. *Barn, Barney, Barnie, Barny, Barry, Bern, Bernarr, Bernie, Berny, Burnard, Burnie, Burny* (English); *Bernek, Berno* (Czech); *Bernardin* (French); *Beno, Berend* (German); *Vernados* (Greek); *Bernat* (Hungarian); *Bearnard* (Irish, Scottish); *Bernard, Bernardino, Bernardo* (Italian); *Berngards, Bernhards* (Latvian); *Bernardas* (Lithuanian); *Benek, Bernardyn* (Polish); *Berngards* (Russian); *Björn* (Scandinavian); *Bernal, Bernardel, Bernardito, Bernardo, Nardo* (Spanish)

BERSH English Gypsy: "one year." *Besh* (English)

BERTIN (BARE-tin, or Anglicized, BERT-in) Spanish: "distinguished friend." Made popular by Saint Bertin.

BERTO (BAIR-toh) Spanish short form of Alberto, "noble and brilliant." See Albert.

BERTY Czech development of Albert, "noble and brilliant. Also an American nickname for Albert.

BERWIN Middle English: "friend of the harvest." Name for a boy born under one of the earth signs of Capricorn, Taurus, or Virgo.

BEVAL (BAY-vahl) English Gypsy: "like the wind."

BEVAN (BEV-un) Welsh: "son of Evan." Sometimes used when a child's father is named Evan but the parents want to avoid having an Evan Jr.

BILLY Nickname for William ("unwavering protector") now used independently for both boys and girls. *Bill, Billie* (English)

BIRK Old English: "at the birch tree"; or North English: "from the island of birch trees." Once a nickname for such names as Birkett and Birkey, but now more commonly used as an independent name.

BJORN (byorn) A popular Scandinavian form of Bernard ("brave as a bear") and currently one of the more common names in Norway and Iceland. See Bernard.

BLAINE Irish Gaelic: "one who serves St. Blaan," referring to a seventh-century Scottish saint. *Blain, Blane, Blayne* (English)

BLAIR Scotch-Irish Gaelic: "from the flat or level place" or "child of the fields." Originally a Scottish surname, now used for both boys and girls. Also a name given for a boy born under one of the earth signs of Capricorn, Taurus, or Virgo.

BLAISE (blayz) An older version of the name Blaze ("a stammerer"), now coming back into vogue. St. Blaise (also called St. Blasius) was a Catholic martyr thought to have lived in the fourth century. According to legend, he was a doctor capable of miraculous cures, and his intercession was sought to cure illness. For other variations, see Blaze.

BLAKE Old English: "blond, fair-skinned one" or "dark."

BLANE Irish Gaelic: "thin and lean." *Blain, Blaine, Blayne* (English)

BLAZ Serbo-Croatian form of William, "unwavering protector." See William.

BLAZE Latin: "stammerer." May have originated as a nickname for an older child who stammered. *Blaise, Blase* (English); *Blaise, Blaisot* (French); *Blasi, Blasius* (German); *Balas, Ballas, Balasz* (Hungarian); *Biagio* (Italian); *Blazek* (Polish); *Braz* (Portuguese); *Vlas* (Russian); *Blas* (Spanish)

> **"Fate tried to conceal him by naming him Smith."**
>
> —OLIVER WENDELL HOLMES JR.

BO Old Norse: "householder." A traditional Scandinavian name made well known for boys by athlete Bo Jackson. In China, this name means "precious." *Bosse* (Swedish)

BOAZ (BOH-ahz) Hebrew: "swift and strong." As the name of several Biblical figures, including one of Christ's direct ancestors, this name was a favorite among the Puritans.

BOBBY A pet form of Robert ("shining with fame"), now used as an independent name for both boys and girls.

BODIL (BOH-deel) Scandinavian: "commanding." Used most frequently in Norway and Denmark.

BODUA (boh-DOO-ah) Akan, Ghana: "an animal's tail." Bodua is the ruling spirit of the Akan day corresponding to our Sunday, and the name is given to a child born on that day.

BOHDAN (BOH-dahn) Ukrainian form of Donald, "world ruler." Popularized in the Ukraine in the seventeenth century by Cossack leader Bohdan Chmelnyckyj. See Donald. *Bogdan, Bogdashka, Danya* (Russian)

BOND Old English: "tiller of the soil." Used in Canada as well as Great Britain, Iceland, and the United States. *Bonde, Bondon, Bonds* (English)

BORG Norse: "one who lives in a castle." Originally from Scandinavia.

BORIS Slavic: "battler" or "stranger." A favorite in Hungary and Russia, but seldom used in this country, possibly because of its association with the monsters typically played by actor Boris Karloff. Another famous namesake is Boris Pasternak.

BOTAN (boh-tahn) Japanese: "peony." In Japan, the peony is the flower of June.

BOUREY (boo-rey) Cambodian: "county."

BOWEN Gaelic: "small, victorious one"; or Old Welsh: "the well-born or youthful one's son." *Bow, Bowie* (English)

BOYCE Old French: "son of the forest."

BRAD Old English: "a broad or wide place." Frequently used independently or as a short form of Bradford ("from the wide river crossing"), as well as other names starting with *"Brad-." Bradd* (English)

BRADBURN Old English: "from the broad brook." *Bernie, Berny, Brad, Burn, Burnie, Burny* (English)

BRADEN (BRAY-den) Old English: "from the wide valley." Originally a last name, now used as a first or middle name for boys. *Bradan, Bradin, Bradon, Bray, Braydan, Brayden, Braydin, Braydon, Braydun* (English)

BRADFORD Old English: "from the wide river crossing." A common English place-name that's been adopted as a first name for boys. *Brad* (English)

BRADLEY Old English: "from the wide or broad meadow." *Brad, Bradlee, Brady, Lee* (English)

BRADSHAW Old English: "large, virginal forest." *Brad, Shaw* (English)

BRADY (BRAY-dee) Old English: "from the wide island." Also occasionally used for girls. *Brad, Bradi, Bradie, Braedy* (English)

BRAM Dutch form of Abraham, "father of a mighty nation" or "father of the multitude." Made well known by Bram Stoker, author of the original *Dracula.* See Abraham.

BRANDEIS (BRAN-dice) Czech: "dweller on a burned clearing." Popular in the Czech Republic, Germany, and the Republic of Slovakia. *Brand, Brandt, Brandy, Brant* (English)

BRANDON Old English: "one from the beacon hill." *Bran, Brand, Brandan, Branden, Brandun, Brandy, Brannon* (English)

BRANDUFF (BRAN-duf) Irish Gaelic: "the black raven." Name of a medieval king in Ireland, as well as an Irish saint. This is a favorite in Ireland, where it's often spelled *Brandubh.*

BRANNON A variation of Brendan, "prince." *Bran, Branon* (English)

BRANT Old English: "a firebrand." Also a short form of Brandeis ("dweller on a burned clearing"). A contemporary American name gaining in popularity. *Brandt* (English)

BREDE (BREH-deh) Scandinavian: "glacier." A favorite in Norway and Denmark.

BRENCIS Latvian form of Lawrence, "crowned with laurel." See Lawrence.

BRENDAN Irish Gaelic: "prince." Name of an Irish saint in the sixth century. Made well known by Irish playwright Brendan Behan. Currently quite trendy. *Brandon, Brannon, Branon, Bren, Brenden, Brendon, Brennan, Brenon* (English); *Breandan* (Irish)

BRENNAN A contemporary American variation of Brendan, "prince."

BRENT Old English: "from the steep hill" or "burnt," in terms of having an ancestor who was a criminal. *Brendt, Brenten, Brenton* (English)

BRETT Celtic: "from Brittania." First made well known in the nineteenth century by writer Bret Harte. Popular in Australia as well as the United States. *Bret, Bretton* (English)

A Martyr Named Briant

✳ ✳ ✳

The most famous Briant in history was probably the sixth-century Jesuit priest and English martyr, Alexander Briant. Born in Somersetshire, the son of a yeoman, he was so handsome he earned the nickname "the beautiful youth." At age 25, only 3 years after he'd been ordained a priest, he was executed for refusing to divulge information that would lead to the arrest of his dear friend and tutor, Father Robert Persons. Although Briant was subjected to inhuman tortures, from the rack and starvation to needles forced under his nails, he confided in one of his last letters that he had felt absolutely no pain during the tortures, noting that whether this was a miracle or not, only "God knowth." According to *The Catholic Encyclopedia*, "His face is said to have been strikingly beautiful even up to his death."

BRIAN, BRYAN Celtic: "strong, virtuous, and honorable." Brian Boru (A.D. 926–1014) was the most famous of the Irish kings. A favorite today in Ireland as well as the United States. *Briant, Brien, Brion, Bryant, Bryon* (English); *Briano* (Italian)

BRIDGER Contemporary short form of Bainbridge, "a bridge over rapids." See Bainbridge.

BRISHEN (BREE-shen) English Gypsy: "born during a rain."

BROCK Old English: "a badger" or "brook"; or Old French: "a young deer."

BRODERICK A form of Roderick, "famous ruler." Made well known worldwide by actor Broderick Crawford. See Roderick.

BRODNY (BROHD-nee) Slavic: "one who lives near a shallow stream crossing."

BRODY (BROH-dee) German: "man with an unusual beard"; Russian: "man from Brody in Russia"; Scottish: "man from the muddy place." A name from varied sources with many meanings. Originally a surname. *Brodie* (English)

BRON (brohn) Afrikaans: "source."

BRONE (brohn) Irish Gaelic: "sorrow." Spiritual name borne by an Irish saint. *Bron* (Irish)

BRONSON Old English: "son of the brown one." Originally a last name. Has a strong, masculine ring, possibly because of its association with the action heroes typically played by American actor Charles Bronson. *Bron, Bronsen* (English)

BROOK Old English: "dweller by the brook." As a girl's name, it is more commonly spelled *Brooke.* Now bestowed more often on girls than boys. *Brooke, Brooks* (English)

BROSNAN (BRAHZ-nun) Irish Gaelic: "one from Brosna in Ireland" or "dweller near the Brosna River." A suave-sounding first name, possibly inspired by actor Pierce Brosnan.

BRUNS (broons) German: "dark" or "brown-haired."

BRYCE, BRICE Celtic: "strong and brave." *Brycen, Bryson, Bryston* (English)

BRYN (brin) Welsh: "from the hill." A favorite in Wales, where a longer form is *Brynmor,* "from the great hill." *Brin, Brinn* (English)

BUD Old English: "friend or companion." Short for Buddy, which in turn may have originated as an illiterate or childish pronunciation of "brother." *Budd, Buddy* (English)

BURKE Old French: "one who lives at the stronghold or fortress." *Berk, Berke, Birk, Birke, Burk* (English)

BURR Scandinavian: "youth."

BURT Old English: "shining and glorious." Also a short form of Albert and other names ending in *"-bert." Bert, Berty, Burty* (English)

BYRON Old English: "from the place of cow sheds" or "cattle herder"; or Old French: "from the country estate or cottage." Made famous by English poet George Gordon, Lord Byron.

C

CADAO (kad-YOW) Vietnamese: "folk song" or "ballad."

CADE Middle English: "cask" or "barrel," or "large and lumpy." Currently trendy. *Caid, Caide, Cayde, Kade, Kaid, Kaide, Kayde* (English)

CAESAR (SEE-zar or SEE-zer) Latin: "long-haired." Over time the name has taken on the meaning of "emperor." *Cesar, Cesare,*

Seasar, Sezar (English); *Casar, Cezar, Kaiser* (Bulgarian); *Arek, Cezar, Cezary, Cezek* (Polish); *Kesar* (Russian, Ukranian); *Cecha, Cesar, Cesareo, Cesario, Sarito* (Spanish)

CAFFAR (KAF-fer) Irish Gaelic: "one with a helmet." A traditional name in Ireland, where it's often spelled *Cathbharr.*

CAHIL (kah-HIL) Turkish: "young, inexperienced, and naive."

CAIN (kayn) Hebrew: "a spear," "a smithy," or "possessed." The name of Adam and Eve's first son, who murdered his brother Abel.

CAL Welsh form of Gaius, "to rejoice." Also a short form of names starting with *"Cal-,"* such as Caleb and Calvin.

CALDWELL (KAWLD-wel) Old English: "cool, clear spring." Originally a surname. *Cal, Calder* (English)

LEGENDS & LORE

If you want someone to think of you, call his or her name three times.

CALE (kayl) Irish Gaelic: "thin; slender." *Calen, Calin, Kail, Kale, Kalen, Kayle* (English)

CALEB (KAY-leb) Hebrew *kaleb:* "bold and impetuous" or "a dog," implying faithfulness. In the Bible, Caleb was with Moses as he and his people wandered in the wilderness. After Moses died, Caleb became a leader of Israel. Popular among seventeenth-century Puritans, this spiritual name has once again become trendy. *Cal, Cale, Kale, Kaleb* (English); *Kalb* (Arabic); *Kaleb, Kalev* (Hebrew)

CALLAHAN Irish Gaelic: "small, belligerent one." *Cal, Callaghan, Kalahan, Kallahan* (English); *Ceallachan* (Irish)

CALLISTER Irish Gaelic: "the son of Alexander ('helper and defender of mankind')." A contemporary variation of Alister. *Al, Ali, Cal, Calli, Callie, Cally* (English)

CALLUM (KAL-um) A Scottish nickname for Malcolm, "St. Columba's servant." See Malcolm. *Calum, Kallum, Kalum* (English)

CALVIN Latin: "bald." *Cal, Kal, Kalvin* (English); *Calvino* (Italian, Spanish)

CAM (kahm) English Gypsy: "beloved." The name actually refers to the sun, which governs the sign of Leo.

CAMERON (KAM-er-un) Scottish Gaelic: "one with a wry or crooked nose" or "from the crooked stream." Popular in Australia, Canada, and Scotland, as well as the United States. Used most often as a a boys' name, but occasionally given to girls. *Cam, Camaron, Camron, Kam, Kamaron, Kameron, Kamron* (English)

CAMLO (KAHM-loh) English Gypsy: "lovely" or "amiable"; or Vietnamese: "sweet dew." One dark-skinned Gypsy band uses this as part of their tribal name— Kaulo Camloes—which translates as "the beautiful blacks."

CAMPBELL Scottish Gaelic: "a crooked mouth." A well-known Scottish clan name used as a first name for both boys and girls. *Cam, Camp* (English)

CAPPI (KAP-ee) English Gypsy: "good fortune" or "profit."

CAREY (KAYR-ee) Old Welsh: "one who lives at the castle"; or Latin: "dear, costly." *Cary* (English)

CARL Short form of Charles ("strong and manly") and names starting with *"Carl-"*. *Karl* (English). See Charles.

CARLIN Irish Gaelic: "small champion." *Carl, Carling* (English)

CARLISLE (KAHR-lighl) Old English: "from the castle tower." *Carl, Carlyle* (English)

CARLOS (CAR-lohs) A favorite Spanish form of Charles ("strong and manly"). See Charles. *Carlito, Carlo, Carloto* (Spanish)

CARLTON Old English: "from the peasants' homestead." Originally an English place-name and surname. *Carleton* (English)

CARR Old Norse: "from the marsh." *Karr, Kerr* (English)

CARSON Middle English: "son of the dweller at the mossy place"; or Welsh: "a fort." Also used for girls, familiarized as a first name by twentieth-century American writer Carson McCullers.

CARSWELL Old English: "child from the watercress spring." Many people believe Carswell "sounds like a butler." Name for a boy born under one of the water signs of Cancer, Pisces, or Scorpio. *Caswell* (English)

CARTER Old English: "a cart driver." Originally a surname, now used as a first name for both boys and girls, especially if the mother's maiden name is Carter.

CARVEL Manx (Celtic): "a song"; or Old French: "from the marshy estate." *Carvell* (English)

CARY Form of Carey, "one who lives at the castle" or "dear, costly." Popularized by actor Cary Grant.

CASE Latin: "from the home or dwelling place." Also a pet form of Casey. *Cayce, Cayse* (English)

CASEY (KAY-see) Irish Gaelic: "brave, valorous, and watchful." Originally an Irish family name, Casey has been popular in this country as a first name for nearly a century. *Cace, Case, K.C., Kace, Kacey, Kase, Kasey* (English)

CASIMIR Old Slavic: "he announces or commands peace." Popular in Poland because of Casimir the Pacific, Poland's renowned eleventh-century monarch. *Casimer, Cass* (English); *Kazimir* (Bulgarian, Czech, German, Russian); *Kazmer* (Hungarian); *Kazek, Kazik, Kazio* (Polish); *Cachi, Cashi, Casimiro* (Spanish)

Did You Know...

✱ ✱ ✱

Many parents now give their children initials like K. C. or J. R. instead of full names. In Georgia, this trend is so popular that A., C., and J. all recently made the state's list of top 100 baby names.

CASPER Greek: "precious stone"; or Persian: "master of the treasure." *Caspar, Cash, Cass, Gaspar, Gasper, Jasper* (English); *Kaspar* (Czech, German); *Jasper, Gaspard* (French); *Gaspar, Gazsi* (Hungarian); *Gaspar* (Portuguese, Russian, Spanish)

CASS Contemporary form of Casper, "precious stone" or "master of the treasure." Also a nickname for Casimir.

CASSIDY Irish Gaelic: "curly-haired" or "ingenious and clever." An Irish boys' name now used more often in the United States for girls. *Cass, Cassady, Kass, Kassady, Kassidy* (English); *Caiside* (Irish)

CASSIUS (KASH-us) Latin: "vain one." Made well known around the globe by heavyweight boxer Cassius Clay, who changed his name to Muhammad Ali.

CASTEL (kah-STEHL) Latin: "belonging to the castle." Most often used in Spanish cultures.

CATON (kah-TOHN) Latin: "knowledgeable, wise." Originally from Spain and Latin and South America. *Cato* (English)

CEMAL (ke-MAHL) Arabic: "handsome." A favorite in Turkey. *Kamal* (English, Arabic).

CESAR (SAY-sahr) A Spanish form of Caesar ("long-haired") made well known to Americans of all cultures by farmworker activist Cesar Chavez.

CHAD Old English *cadda:* "warlike one," or "related to Mars." *Chadd* (English)

CHAIM (Khighm, to rhyme with *time*) Hebrew: "life." *Hyam* (Hebrew); *Chaimek, Haim* (Polish); *Khaim* (Russian)

CHAL (chahl) English Gypsy: "lad," "boy," or "son."

CHAM (chahm) Vietnamese: "hard worker."

CHAN (chahn) Vietnamese: "correct" or "true," implying a child is on his true path.

CHANCE Middle English: "good fortune." Also a contemporary form of the older and now extremely rare Chauncey, "a church official" or "chancellor." *Chaunce* (English)

CHAND (chahnd) Sanskrit: "the moon." An astrological name from India for a child born under the sign of Cancer, ruled by the moon. A variation is *Chandran,* meaning "moonlight."

CHANDAN (chahn-dahn) Sanskrit: "the holy sandalwood tree." A deeply spiritual Hindu name from India. *Chan, Chand, Chandie, Chandy* (English)

CHANDLER Old French: "candlemaker." *Chan, Chane, Shandler* (English)

CHANE (CHAH-neh, or Anglicized, CHAIN) Swahili: "weaving leaf." Refers to a strip of tough leaf used for weaving either mats or a bundle. The connotation is one of sturdy dependability.

CHANEY (CHAH-nee or CHAY-nee) Old French: "oak wood." *Cheney* (English)

CHANG (chang) Chinese: "free or unimpeded." A free spirit.

CHANNING Old English: "child of Cann's people"; or Irish Gaelic: "little wolf cub." Originally a last name, now used for both boys and girls. *Chane, Chann, Channe, Channon* (English)

CHARLES Latin *carolus,* "strong and manly." This name has been popular around the globe for centuries. One of the most famous bearers was Charlemagne (Charles the Great), who was crowned Holy Roman Emperor on Christmas Day in A.D. 800. *Carl, Carlton, Cary, Chad, Charley, Charlie, Charlton, Chas, Chaz, Chick, Chip, Chuck* (English); *Karl* (Bulgarian, German, Russian, Scandinavian); *Karel,*

> **"**. . . *there never was a person named Charles who was not an open, manly, honest, good-natured and frank-hearted fellow, with a rich, clear voice that did you good to hear it, and an eye that looked you straight in the face, as much to say: 'I have a clear conscience myself, am afraid of no man, and am altogether above doing a mean action.'***"**
>
> —EDGAR ALLAN POE IN HIS STORY *THOU ART THE MAN,*
> IN WHICH CHARLES WAS LATER REVEALED AS THE MURDERER

Karlik, Karol (Czech); *Kalle* (Finnish, Swedish); *Kalman,* (German); *Carolos* (Greek); *Kale* (Hawaiian); *Karcsi, Kari, Karoly* (Hungarian); *Carlus, Cathal* (Irish); *Carlino, Carlo, Carolo* (Italian); *Karlen, Karlens, Karlis* (Latvian); *Karol, Karolek* (Polish); *Karlen, Karlin* (Russian); *Carlo, Carlos* (Spanish)

CHARLIE Nickname for Charles ("strong and manly") also used independently. Well-known Charlies include actor Charlie Sheen and comedian Charlie Chaplin. *Charley* (English)

CHARLTON (CHARL-ton) Old English: "from Charles's home"; or Old English: "farmers' town." Also a form of Charles ("strong and manly"). *Carleton, Carlton, Charleton* (English)

CHASE Old French: "hunter." Name for a boy born under the sign of Sagittarius, the archer.

CHASKA (CHAHS-kah) Sioux: "first-born son."

CHAU (chah-oo) Vietnamese: "a pearl," indicating that a child is precious.

CHAZ Originally a pet form of Charles ("strong and manly"), now used independently. *Chas, Chick, Chuck* (English)

CHE (chay) Colloquial Spanish pet form of Joseph, "God will increase." See Joseph.

CHEN Chinese: "vast" or "great." One story is told of a boy who was about to receive a fate name when his father dreamed that a god appeared and wrote the character Chen, proclaiming, "Give him this name." The boy, Chang Chen (surname first), grew up to become a minister of state. Fate names, once kept secret, are now used freely in China, particularly by the well educated.

CHESLAV (ches-LAHF) Russian form of Chester, "living at a fortified army camp." See Chester.

CHESMU (CHEHS-moo) Native American: "gritty."

CHESTER Old English: "living at a fortified army camp." *Ches, Cheston, Chet (English);* Cheslav (Russian)

CHET A contemporary form of Chester. Originally a nickname, now given as a full name.

CHEVALIER (cheh-VAL-yay) French: "knight." Originally a surname, now also used as a first name. *Chev, Chevi, Chevy* (English)

CHEVY Old French: "a knight," implying courage and honor. A contemporary short form of the last name Chevalier. Made well

Nigerian "Chi" Names

✳ ✳ ✳

In Nigeria, the god Chi plays an important role in naming babies. An individual's Chi, his personal god, is believed to come into being when a baby is born, follow the child throughout life, and cause both success and misfortune. Among the many Chi names are *Chike* ("power of Chi"); *Chileogu* ("Chi is our protector" or "Chi is our defender"); *Chinelo* ("thought of Chi"); *Chinua* ("Chi's own blessing"); *Chioke* ("gift of Chi"); *Cinese* ("Chi is protecting"); and *Cis* (another spelling of Chi).

known by actor-comedian Chevy Chase.

CHI (chee, or Anglicized, kigh) Ibo, Nigeria: "God." In Nigeria, this name refers to a kind of personal guardian angel.

CHICO (CHEE-koh) Spanish form of Francis ("free man" or "Frenchman"), now also used as a first name. See Francis.

CHIK English Gypsy: "earth."

CHIM (kim) Vietnamese: "bird."

CHRIS Short form of Christopher ("Christ-bearer") and Christian ("believer in Christ, the anointed one"), used also for girls. See Christian and Christopher.

CHRISTIAN Greek: "believer in Christ, the anointed one." Ten Danish kings have been called Christian, and the name has dozens of variations around the world. *Chris, Christen, Christy, Kris, Kristian,* (English); *Jaan, Kristian, Kristjan, Krists* (Estonian); *Krischan* (German); *Christianos, Kristos* (Greek); *Kerestel, Keresztyen* (Hungarian); *Christiano* (Italian); *Krists* (Latvian); *Krist* (Norwegian); *Chrystian, Crystek, Krys, Krystek, Krystian* (Polish); *Cristao, Cristiano* (Portuguese); *Cristian* (Romanian); *Kristian* (Russian); *Cristi, Cristian, Cristianito, Cristiano, Cristino* (Spanish); *Krista, Krister, Kristian* (Swedish)

CHRISTOPHER (KRIS-toh-fer) Greek *Christoforos:* "Christ-bearer," in the sense of one who carries Christ in his heart. One of the most popular names in the world. Many people envision a Christopher as ambitious, confident, popular, healthy, and good-looking. *Chris, Cris, Kit, Kris, Kriss, Kristofer, Kristopher* (English); *Christofer, Kristof* (Czech); *Christoffer* (Danish); *Risto* (Finnish); *Christophe* (French); *Christoforus, Christoph, Kriss, Stoffel* (German); *Kristo* (Greek); *Kristof* (Hungarian); *Christoforo* (Italian); *Kriss, Krisus* (Latvian); *Cristovao* (Portuguese); *Christof, Christofer* (Russian); *Cris, Cristi, Cristo, Cristobal, Tobal, Tobalito* (Spanish); *Kristoffer, Kristofor* (Swedish)

CIARAN (KEER-an) Irish Gaelic: "little black one" or "little black-haired one." A traditional Irish name. *Keeran, Kieran* (English)

CICERON Spanish form of Cicero, "chickpea."

CILOMBO (chee-LOHM-boh) Umbundu, Africa: "roadside camp," a welcome sight to weary travelers in Africa. Hence, the implied meaning is "a sight for sore eyes." The name is a great favorite in Africa and is often given to girls as well as boys.

CIRO (SEE-ro) Spanish form of Cyrus, "the sun," which governs the sign Leo.

CLANCY Irish Gaelic: "son of the ruddy-skinned warrior." An Irish last name used as a first name in the United States. *Clance, Clancey* (English)

CLARK Old French: "a scholar." *Clarke* (English)

CLAUS (klaus) Short form of Nicholas ("victorious army" or "victorious people") often used in Germany, Holland, and Scandinavian countries.

CLAY Old English: "mortal" or "of the earth." Also a short form of Clayton.

CLAYTON Old English: "dweller at the farm built on clay" or "mortal." *Clay, Clayten, Claytin* (English)

CLEAVON (KLEE-von) Contemporary U.S. coinage of uncertain origin, especially popular in Afro-American communities. *Clevon, Kleavon, Klevon* (English)

CLEMENT Latin: "gentle" or "kind." *Clem, Clemens, Clemmie, Clemmons, Clemmy* (English); *Kliment* (Bulgarian); *Klema, Klement, Klemo* (Czech); *Clemens* (Danish); *Klemens, Menz* (German); *Kelemen* (Hungarian); *Clemente, Clemenza* (Italian); *Klemens, Klimek* (Polish); *Kelmet, Klim, Kliment, Klimka, Klyment* (Russian); *Cleme, Clemen, Clemente, Clemento* (Spanish)

CLEVELAND Old English: "from the hilly district." Originally a last name, brought into use as a first name in the 1800s after the election of United States president Grover Cleveland.

CLIFF Pet form of Clifford, now used independently.

CLIFFORD Old English: "from the ford near a slope." Originally a place-name in England. *Cliff* (English)

CLINT A short form of Clinton made internationally known by actor Clint Eastwood.

CLINTON Old English: "from the settlement near a hill." A first name drawn from a common place-name. Associated world-wide with United States president Bill Clinton. *Clint, Clinten, Clintin* (English)

CLIVE (klighv) Old English: "from the clive." A literary name, which first gained wide usage after William Thackery's hero in the novel *The Newcomers*.

CODY Old English: "a cushion." This name skyrocketed in popularity in the 1990s, possibly due to its association at the time with Cody, the son of TV hostess and singer Kathie Lee Gifford. *Codi, Codie, Kodi, Kodie, Kody* (English)

COLBY Old Anglo-Norse: "from the coal-black settlement" or "black-haired." Currently gaining popularity in the United States. *Cole, Coleby, Kolby, Koleby* (English)

COLE Old English: "dark-skinned"; or Old Irish: "a fellow hostage" or "a pledge." In ancient Ireland, children were once exchanged between warring clans as "pledges of peace." Also a nickname for Nicholas ("victorious army" or "victorious people"), as well as names starting with *Col-*. The traditional Irish form is *Comghhall*.

COLIN (KOHL-in or KAHL-in) Irish Gaelic: "young and manly." *Colan, Cole, Collin, Collins, Colyn* (English); *Coilin* (Irish); *Colino* (Italian); *Cailean* (Scottish)

COLLEY Old English: "swarthy" or "black-haired." *Collis* (English)

COLMAN Icelandic: "head man" or "charcoal maker"; or Irish Gaelic: "little dove." *Cole, Coleman* (English)

COLT Old English: "a frisky young male horse." Also a pet form of Colter and Colton. *Kolt* (English)

COLTER Old English: "one who cares for the colt herd." *Cole, Colt, Kolt, Kolter* (English)

COLTON Middle English: "from the homestead on the Cole

River." An English place-name now used for boys. *Cole, Colt, Colten, Coltin, Kole, Kolt, Kolten, Koltin, Kolton* (English)

COMAN (koh-MAHN) Arabic: "noble."

CONALL, CONNELL (KOHN-ahl) Celtic: "mighty." A favorite in Ireland, where it's known as the name of several saints, a great Ulster hero, and two medieval kings. *Congal* (Irish)

CONLEY Irish Gaelic: "prudent fire." A traditional, saintly Irish name for boys. *Conel, Connelly, Konel, Konley, Konnelly* (English); *Conlao, Connlaodh* (Irish)

CONNERY Irish Gaelic: "child of the hunting-dog keeper." Originally an Irish surname, now used as a first name in the United States. Made well known worldwide by actor Sean Connery. *Conary, Conray, Conrey, Conroy, Conry* (English); *Conaire* (Irish)

CONNOR Irish Gaelic: "strong-willed," "meddlesome," or "strongly wise" are some of the meanings contained in this complex Irish name. *Conner, Connors, Conor* (English)

CONRAD Old German: "bold counselor." Spelled *Konrad,* this name is used not only in the United States, but in many other countries, including the Czech Republic, Germany, Hungary, Russia, and Sweden. *Con, Conn, Conni, Connie, Cort, Curt, Kurt* (English); *Conrade* (French); *Conny, Konni, Konrad, Kurt* (German); *Conrado* (Italian, Spanish); *Conrao* (Portuguese)

CONROY Irish Gaelic: "hound of the plain." Also a short form of Connery, "child of the hunting-dog keeper." *Konroy, Roy* (English)

CONWAY (KON-way) Welsh: "from the holy river," referring to the river Conway in North Wales. Also Scottish: "noisy, stormy one"; and Irish Gaelic: "from the sign of the yellow hunting dog." Originally a last name, now used as a given name for boys. *Konway* (English); *Conwy* (Welsh)

CORBIN (KOHR-bin) Old French: "a raven." *Corban, Corben, Corbet, Corbett, Corby, Corbyn, Korbin, Korby, Korbyn* (English)

CORDELL (kohr-DELL) Old French: "a small rope" or "a small rope maker." *Cord, Cordel, Cordelle, Kord, Kordel, Kordell* (English)

COREY, CORY (KOHR-ee) Irish and Scottish: "he lives by a hollow (or misty) pool." Also used today for girls. *Cori, Correy, Corry, Cory, Korey, Kori, Korrey, Korry, Kory* (English)

CORNELL (kohr-NEL) Latin: "horn-colored" or "like a horn"; or Greek: "the cornel tree." *Cornall, Cornel* (English)

CORRIGAN (KOHR-i-gun) Irish Gaelic: "little spear." *Cori, Corigan, Corrie, Corry, Cory, Kori, Korigan, Korrie, Korrigan, Korry, Kory* (English)

COWAN (KOW-un) Irish Gaelic: "a twin" or "hillside hollow." Name sometimes bestowed on a boy born under Gemini, the twins.

CRAIG Scottish Gaelic: "from the crag." *Kraig* (English)

CRAMER (KRAY-mer) Teutonic: "shopkeeper." The cramer was a traveling tradesman who carried butter, cream, and eggs to market in a pack—or cram—on his back. *Kramer* (English)

CRISPUS Latin: "curly-haired one." Famous namesake: Crispus Attucks, a black seaman and probably an escaped slave, who was the first American to die in the Boston Massacre. *Cris, Crispin* (English); *Krispin* (Czech, German, Hungarian, Slavic); *Crepin* (French); *Crispino* (Italian); *Crispo* (Spanish)

CRISTO (KREES-toh) Greek: "the anointed one." A popular Spanish name referring to Jesus of Nazareth. *Criston, Cristos* (Spanish)

CROSBY Old Norse: "from the place with a public cross." *Crosbey, Crosbie* (English)

Naming Customs ...

✳ ✳ ✳

Celebrities like Cher and Frank Zappa may seem ultra-trendy when giving their kids names like Chastity and Moon Unit. But our American tradition of creating original names for children has a history so long it even predates the *Mayflower*. In 1609 in Sussex, England, a Puritan man named Kill Sin Pimple served on a jury. His fellow jurers, *Time* magazine reports, included Fly Debate Roberts, More Fruit Fowler, God Reward Smart, Be Faithful Joiner, and Fight the Good Fight of Faith White.

CULLEN (KUL-un) Irish Gaelic: "holly"; Old English: "dweller near a holly tree"; or Scottish Gaelic: "from the little nook." *Cullan, Cullin, Cully* (English)

CURRAN Irish Gaelic: "hero or champion." *Currey, Currie, Curry, Kurran, Kurrey, Kurrie, Kurry* (English)

CURT Popular short form of Curtis ("courteous") and Conrad ("bold counselor"). *Kurt* (English)

CURTIS (KUR-tiss) Old French: "courteous." *Curt, Kurt, Kurtis* (English); *Curcio* (Spanish)

CY (sigh) A short form of Cyril and Cyrus, now used as an in independent name. *Sy* (English)

CYD (sid) A short form of Sidney, "from the city of St. Denis, France." *Syd* (English)

CYRIL (SIGH-rihl) Greek: "lordly." *Cy, Cyrill* (English); *Kiril* (Bulgarian); *Cyrille* (French); *Cirillo* (Italian); *Kirill, Kiryl* (Russian); *Cirilo, Ciro* (Spanish)

CYRUS (SIGH-rus) Old Persian: "the sun." Name sometimes bestowed on a boy born under the sign of Leo, ruled by the sun. *Cy, Russ* (English); *Kir, Kiril* (Bulgarian); *Ciro* (Italian, Spanish)

D

DABIR (dah-BEER) Algerian, Egyptian: "secretary" or "teacher."

DACEY Irish Gaelic: "a Southerner." Also used for girls. *Dace, Dacy* (English)

DACK (dak) Old Norse: "day." Made well known by actor Dack Rambo.

DAG Old Norse: "day" or "brightness." A favorite today in Norway because of its distinctively Norse sound. The feminine form is Dagny. Popularized around the world by former United Nations Secretary General Dag Hammarskjold.

DAGAN (DAY-gahn) Hebrew: "corn" or "grain"; eastern Semitic: "earth"; or Babylonian: "little fish," referring to the Babylonian god of fish and agriculture. Name for a boy born under one of the earth signs of Capricorn, Taurus, or Virgo. *Daegan, Daegen, Dagen, Dagin, Dagon, Daygan, Daygen, Daygin, Daygon* (English)

DAKOTA Sioux: "a friend." On the rise in popularity for both boys and girls.

DALAL (dah-LAHL) Sanskrit: "a broker." A name from India denoting the bearer's or father's occupation.

DALE Old English: "one who lives in the valley." *Dal, Daley, Daly* (English); *Dalibor* (Czech)

DALFON (DAHL-fon) Hebrew: "raindrop." Comes to this country from Israel. *Dalphon* (Hebrew)

DALLAS Scottish Gaelic: "from the waterfall field." Originally a place-name in Scotland, but through modern usage more associated with the city in Texas.

DALLIN (DAY-lin or DAL-in) Old English: "a proud people." *Dalan, Dalen, Dalin, Dallan, Dallen, Dallon, Dalon, Daylan, Daylen, Daylin, Daylon* (English)

DALTON (DAHL-tun) Old English: "from the hamlet in the valley." *Dallton, Dalten* (English)

DAMAN (DAY-mun) Irish form of Damian, "a tamer of men" or "gentle."

DAMEK (DAH-mek) Czech form of Adam, "earth" or "man of the red earth." See Adam.

DAMIAN, DAMIEN (DAY-mee-en) Greek: "a tamer of men" or "gentle." Used worldwide. *Damion, Damon* (English); *Damek, Damjan* (Hungarian); *Daman* (Irish); *Damiano* (Italian); *Damian, Damyan, Dema, Demyan* (Russian)

DAMON (DAY-mun) A form of Damian used not only in this country but also in England, Greece, and Portugal.

DAN Hebrew: "judge." Popular familiar form of Daniel ("God is my judge") now bestowed as a full name.

DANA (DAY-nuh) Old English: "one from Denmark." Also a Hebrew form of Daniel, "God is my judge." See Daniel.

DANE Old English: "a Dane." Also a Dutch and Lithuanian form of Daniel. *Dain, Daine, Dana, Dayne* (English)

DANI (DAN-ee, or Anglicized, DA-nee) Modern Israeli and Slavic development of Dan, "judge." Also popular in Hungary.

DANIEL Hebrew: "God is my judge." A favorite not only in the United States but also in Germany, Israel, Norway, Romania, Spain, Sweden, and many other countries. *Dan, Dannie, Danny* (English); *Danil* (Bulgarian); *Dano, Danko* (Czech); *Dane* (Dutch); *Taneli* (Finnish); *Donois* (French); *Dana* (Hebrew); *Dacso, Daneil, Dani* (Hungarian); *Daineal, Dainial, Donal* (Irish); *Daniele* (Italian); *Daniels* (Latvian); *Dane, Danukas* (Lithuanian); *Danek* (Polish); *Daniela, Danila, Danilka, Danya, Danylets, Danylo* (Russian); *Dusan* (Serbo-

Croatian); *Dani* (Slovenian); *Danilo, Nelo* (Spanish)

DANIOR (DAH-nee-or) English Gypsy: "born with teeth."

DANLADI (dahn-LAH-dee) Hausa, Africa: "born on Sunday."

DANNY Pet form of Daniel ("God is my judge"), now used as an independent name.

DANTE (DAHN-tay) Latin: "enduring or lasting." A pet form of Durante that became prominent after Italian writer Durante Alighieri used it as his pen name for his *Divine Comedy.*

DANYA (DAHN-yah) Russian form of Daniel, "God is my judge."

DAR Hebrew: "pearl" or "mother-of-pearl."

DARBY (DAR-bee) Old Norse: "one from the deer estate"; or Irish Gaelic: "a free man." *Dar, Darb, Derby* (English); *Diarmaid* (Irish)

DARCY (DAR-see) Irish Gaelic: "a dark man"; or Old French: "dweller in the fortress." *Dar, Darce, Darcey, Darse, Darsell, Darsey, Darsy* (English)

DAREN (DAIR-en) Hausa, Africa: "born at night." Also a contemporary form of Darren, "small and great" or "wealthy."

DARIUS (DAIR-ee-us) Greek: "rich." Darius the Great was a king in ancient Persia. *Dario, Darrius, Derry* (English); *Dareios* (Greek); *Daroosh* (Iranian)

DARNELL (dahr-NEL) Old English: "from the hidden or secret nook." *Dar, Darnal, Darnall, Darnel* (English)

DAROLD (DAIR-ohld) Contemporary American creation, probably a blend of Darryl ("small, dear, or beloved") plus Harold ("army ruler"). *Darrald, Derald, Derrold* (English)

DARRELL, DARRYL (DAIR-ul) Old French: "small, dear, or beloved." Now also used for girls. *Darel, Darrel, Darryl, Daryl, Derril, Derryl, Deryl* (English)

DARREN (DAIR-en) Irish Gaelic: "small and great"; or Greek: "wealthy." *Daran, Dare, Daren, Darien, Darin, Daron, Darran, Darrin, Darron, Darun, Daryn* (English); *Dario* (Italian, Portuguese, Spanish)

DARRICK (DAIR-ik) A variant spelling of Derek, "ruler of the people." See Derek.

DARSHAN (dahr-shahn) Sanskrit: "perceptive one" or "one with vision." A Hindu name used today in India.

DARWIN Old English: "a beloved friend." *Dar, Derwin* (English)

DASAN (DAH-sahn or Anglicized DAY-sun) Pomo: "leader." In Pomo Indian creation legend, Dasan and his father were leaders of a bird clan who brought civilization with them from the waters.

DATHAN (DAY-thun) A contemporary American coinage, probably an English version of Daithin, an Irish form of David ("beloved"). See David. *Daithan, Dathin, Dathon, Daython* (English)

DAUDI (dah-OO-dee) Swahili: "beloved one."

DAVE Short form of David, "beloved." *Daivi* (Irish)

DAVID Hebrew: "beloved." This all-time worldwide favorite is recognized and used in virtually every European country. *Dave, Davie, Davy* (English); *Davidek* (Czech); *Davide* (French); *Davey, Davi, Davy, Tavi* (Hebrew); *Daibhead, Daibhi, Daibhidh, Daith, Daithi, Daithin* (Irish); *Davidde, Davide* (Italian); *Davidas* (Lithuanian); *Dawid* (Polish); *Davi* (Portuguese); *Danya, Daveed, Dodya* (Russian); *Daibidh* (Scottish); *Davi, Davin, Davis, Davito* (Spanish); *Dew, Dewey, Dewi, Dafydd, Dai* (Welsh) *Dawid, Dowid* (Yiddish)

DAVIN (DAH-vin) Old Scandinavian: "brightness of the Finns," who were once thought to be the most intelligent people of the North. Originally from Scandinavia, where it's still popular.

DEAN Old English: "from the valley." *Deane, Dene* (English)

DEANDRE (dee-AHN-dray) A contemporary American creation using the prefix *"De-"* plus *André* (the French form of Andrew). *D'Andre, DeAndre* (English)

DEANGELO (dee-AN-jel-oh) Contemporary American blend of the prefix *"De-"* + *Angelo* ("angel" or "messenger").

DEEPAK (dee-pak) Sanskrit: "lamplike" or "shining brightly." A Hindu name made well known in this country by best-selling author Deepak Chopra.

DEJUAN (dee-WAHN) Contemporary American creation from the prefix *"De-"* + *Juan,* the Spanish form of John. *Dajuan, Dujuan, Jujuan* (English)

DEKEL (DAY-kel) Arabic: "palm tree" or "date palm." Originally from Israel, where it's still used today.

DEL English Gypsy: "he gives." Also a short form of names beginning with *"Del-."*

Where Middle Names Began

✷ ✷ ✷

The origins of many naming customs have been lost through the ages. For all we know, the very first names ever bestowed in primitive societies could have been a growl, a grunt, a howl, a click, a whistle, or even a purr. Luckily, though, we are able to trace the European custom of giving a child a middle name.

The Spanish were giving middle monikers as early as A.D. 1000. The Germans picked up on the custom about the time Columbus discovered America. The British, however, considered the practice of giving a child two baptismal names almost sacrilegious. When nobleman Sir Edward Cook declared a person should never have two Christian names, the British passed a law banning middle names. "Rebellious" though they were, not one Pilgrim on the *Mayflower* had a middle name.

The first recorded middle name in America belonged to Edwin Maria Wingfield, a male member of the Jamestown Colony. But the idea of giving a baby three names didn't really catch on here until the mid-1800s, possibly because by then many Germans with three names had immigrated to this country and were influencing their friends and neighbors.

The most unusual middle name ever bestowed? In his marvelous *Treasury of Name Lore,* Elsdon C. Smith tells of the liberal parents who decided to let each of their children choose her own middle name. In 1965, at the age of thirteen, their daughter Mary fell in love with the folk song, "Don't Ya Weep, Don't Ya Mourn" and insisted upon naming herself Mary Dontyaweepdontyamourn Schulz.

DELANEY Irish Gaelic: "the challenger's descendent." *Del, Delan, Delane, Delaine, Delainey, Lane, Laine* (English)

DELANO Irish Gaelic: "healthy black man"; or Old French: "from the nut-tree place." *Del, Delann* (English)

DELBERT Old English: "bright day" or "sunny day." *Bert, Bertie, Berty, Del* (English)

DELMAR Latin: "of the sea." *Del, Delmer* (English)

DELSIN Native American: "he is so." *Del, Delsie, Delsy* (English)

DEMARCO (de-MAHR-koh) A modern coinage, created by combining the prefix *"De-"* with *Marco* ("warlike one"). *Demarko* (English)

DEMARIO (de-MAH-ree-oh) Another contemporary American creation. This one is a blend of the prefix *"De-"* + *Mario* ("manly").

DEMETRIUS (de-MEE-tree-us) Greek: "belonging to Demeter," the Greek goddess of fertility. A classical name now making a comeback. *Demeter, Demetri, Demitri, Demitrius, Demitry, Dimitri* (English); *Dimitr* (Bulgarian); *Demetre* (French); *Demetri, Demetrios, Dimitrios, Dimos, Mimis, Mitros, Mitsos, Takis* (Greek); *Demeter, Dometer,*

Domotor (Hungarian); *Demetrio* (Italian, Spanish); *Dymek, Dymitry, Dyzek* (Polish); *Dima, Dimitre, Dimitri, Dmitri, Dmitrik* (Russian)

DEMOTHI (de-MOH-tee) Native American: "talks walking." Probably originally bestowed on a child who talked as he walked.

DENIZ (de-NIZ) Turkish: "sea," implying huge waves or a storm. Common in Turkey. Falls into the unusual-but-not-too-unusual category in the United States, as it sounds much like the familiar name Dennis.

DENNIS Greek: "the god of wine." From Dionysus, the god of wine and vegetation. *Den, Denis, Denney, Denny, Deon, Dion* (English); *Denis, Denys, Dione* (French); *Dionysus* (German); *Denes, Dennes* (Hungarian); *Denis, Donnchadh* (Irish); *Dionigi, Dionisio* (Italian); *Denis, Denka, Denya, Denys* (Russian); *Dionis, Dionisio, Nicho* (Spanish)

DENVER Old English: "place where the Danes crossed." A first name for boys borrowed from the city of Denver, Colorado.

DENZEL (den-ZEL) Cornish: "from a place in Corwall." Any further definition remains obscure. An unusual name made well known by American actor Denzel Washington. *Denzell, Denzil* (English)

DER (dair) Short form of Derek, "ruler of the people."

DEREK (DAIR-ek) Old German *dietrich:* "ruler of the people." See Dietrich and Theodoric. *Darick, Darik, Darrek, Darrick, Darrik, Der, Derec, Dereck, Derk, Derrec, Derreck, Derrick, Derrik, Dirk, Rick, Ricky* (English)

DEROR (deh-ROHR) Hebrew: "freedom," "free-flowing," or "a swallow." Originally from Israel and traditionally Jewish. *Derori* (Israeli)

DERRY Irish Gaelic: "red-haired." *Dare, Darrey, Darrie, Dary* (English)

DESHAD (deh-shahd) Hindi: "country" or "nation." A Hindu name from India. *Deshal, Deshan* (Hindi)

DESHAWN (de-SHAWN) Contemporary American blend of *"De-"* + *Shawn* (an Irish form of John). *Desean, Deshane, Deshawne* (English)

DESHI (deh-UH-shee, sure to be Anglicized by a child's classmates to DESH-ee) Chinese: "morally upright." A virtuous child.

DESI (DEZ-ee) Latin: "the desired one." A short form of the Spanish name Desiderio. Made familiar in this country in the twentieth century by bandleader-actor Desi Arnaz, who co-starred in the popular television series *I Love Lucy. Desito* (Spanish)

DESMOND (DEZ-mund) Irish Gaelic: "child from South Munster," now a province but once an ancient kingdom in Ireland. Made well known worldwide by Bishop Desmond Tutu. *Deasun* (Irish)

DESTON (DES-ton) Latin: "destined" or "fated." Appears to be a contemporary American creation from the word "destiny," but may be influenced by its sounding similar to the popular Dustin.

DEVAL (DAY-vahl) Sanskrit: "god-like; divine."

DEVEN (DAY-ven, or Anglicized, DEV-en) Sanskrit: "god-like." Another name for Indra, the Hindu god of heaven, thunder, lightning, storms, and rain. *"Dev-"* is a common element in many Hindu names. Other examples include *Devraj* ("ruler of the gods") and *Devmani* ("divine jewel").

DEVIN (DEV-in) Irish Gaelic: "a poet." Also trendy for girls. *Deavon, Dev, Devan, Deven, Devlin, Devon, Devron, Devy, Devyn* (English)

DEWAYNE (de-WAIN) Contemporary American blend of *"De-"* + *Wayne* ("a wagon-maker"). *Dewain, Dewane* (English)

DEWEY (DEH-wee, or anglicized, DEW-ee) Old Welsh: "beloved." Originally a Welsh form of David. See David for variations.

DEWI (Anglicized DEW-ee or in Wales pronounced DEH-wee) A Welsh form of David, "beloved." *Dew* (Welsh)

DEXTER Latin: "right-handed," implying a child is dexterous. *Deck, Dek, Dex* (English)

DICHALI (dee-CHAH-lee) Native American: "he speaks often."

DIDI (DEE-dee) Israeli diminutive of the older name Jedidiah, "loved by the lord." Also used for girls. *Deedee, Dee Dee* (English)

DIEGO (dee-AY-go) Spanish form of Jacob, "the supplanter." See Jacob.

DIETRICH (DEE-trik) Old German: "ruler of the people." The original German name that was the source for the English Derek and all its variations. Dietrich is still favored in Germany. *Dedrick, Dedrik, Detrik* (English); *Dierck, Dieter, Dieterich, Dietz* (German)

DILLON Irish Gaelic: "faithful." *Dilan, Dillen, Dylan* (English)

DIMA (DEE-mah) Russian nickname for Vladimir, which is a form

of Walter, "powerful warrior" or "ruler of an army." See Walter.

DIMITRI (dih-MEE-tree) A form of Demetrius ("belonging to Demeter") used in Russia as well as the United States.

DINESH (dih-nesh) Sanskrit: "day lord" or "sun god." A popular Hindu name in India.

DINH (din) Vietnamese: "mountain summit" or "crest."

DINOS Latin: "firm and constant." Originally a Greek form of Constantinos, this name has surpassed its longer form in popularity. Dinos and Kostas are among the most popular boys' names in Greece today. *Costa, Konstandinos, Konstantinos, Kostas, Kostis, Kostos* (Greek)

DION (DEE-ohn) Contemporary form of Dennis, "the god of wine." *Deion, Deon* (English); *Dione* (French)

DIRK A short form of Derek, "ruler of the people," which in turn is a form of Theodoric.

DOBRY (DOH-bree) Polish: "good."

DOHOSAN (doh-HOH-sahn) Kiowa: "a small bluff." *Dohasan* (Kiowa)

DOMINGO (doh-MEEN-goh) A favorite Spanish and Italian form of Dominick, "belonging to the Lord" or "born on Sunday."

DOMINICK (DOM-in-ik) Latin: "belonging to the Lord" or "born on Sunday." *Dom, Domenic, Domenick, Nick, Nickie, Nicky* (English); *Domek, Dominik, Dumin* (Czech); *Dominique* (French); *Deco, Domi, Domo, Domokos, Domonkos* (Hungarian); *Domenico, Domingo, Menico* (Italian); *Dominik, Donek, Niki* (Polish); *Domingos* (Portuguese); *Chuma, Chumin, Chuminga, Domicio, Domingo, Mingo* (Spanish)

DON A pet form of Donald ("world ruler") and other names beginning with *"Don-"*. Frequently used independently. *Donn, Donni, Donnie, Donny* (English)

DONAHUE Irish Gaelic: "dark warrior." *Don, Donnie, Donny, Donohue* (English)

DONALD Irish Gaelic: "world ruler." *Don, Donal, Donnie, Donny* (English); *Tauno* (Finnish); *Donaldo* (Italian); *Donalt* (Norwegian); *Donaldo* (Spanish); *Bogdan, Bohdan, Donya* (Ukrainian)

DONAT Form of Donato ("a gift") used not only in this country, but also France, Hungary, Poland, and Russia.

DONATO Latin: "a gift," implying the child is a gift from

God. *Donat, Donatus* (English); *Donat* (French, Hungarian, Russian); *Donatello, Donati, Donato* (Italian); *Dodek, Donat* (Polish)

> **"A man lives a generation; a name to the end of all generations."**
>
> —Ancient Japanese proverb

DONNAN (DUN-nahn, or Anglicized, DON-nun) Irish Gaelic: "small, brown-haired one." A name traditionally used in Ireland. *Donn* (English, Irish)

DONNELLY (DON-e-lee) Celtic: "brave, dark, or black man." *Don, Donely, Donnel, Donnell* (English)

DONOVAN Celtic: "dark or brown-haired warrior." *Don, Donnie, Donny, Donovon, Dunavan, Van* (English)

DOR Hebrew: "a generation" or "a home."

DOREK (DOH-rek) Polish form of Theodore, "God's gift."

DORIAN Greek *dorios:* "child of the sea." Name possibly for a boy born under one of the water signs of Cancer, Pisces, or Scorpio.

DORRAN (DOHR-un or doh-RAN) Celtic: "strange"; or Greek: "a gift." *Doran, Dorein, Doren, Dorin, Doron, Dorren, Dorrin* (English)

DOTAN (doh-TAHN) Hebrew: "law." Originally from Israel, where it's still used. *Dothan* (Israeli)

DOUG Short form of Douglas ("from the dark or black water"), now used as an independent name.

DOUGLAS Scottish: "from the dark or black water." Famous Scottish clan name. *Doug, Douglass, Dugald* (English)

DOV (dahv) Yiddish: "a bear." Also a short form of the Hebrew name Dovev.

DOVEV (doh-VAYV) Hebrew: "to whisper" or "to speak quietly." *Dov* (English, Hebrew)

DOYLE Celtic: "black stranger" or "dark stranger."

DRAKE Middle English: "one who owns the 'Sign of the Dragon' Inn." Once an occupation name, referring to a common trademark (the dragon) often used on hostelries or shops.

DRENG Norwegian: "hired farmhand" or "brave man."

DREW Short form of Andrew, "strong and manly." See Andrew.

DU (yoo, or Anglicized, dyoo) Vietnamese: "playful," "flattery," or "the elm tree."

DUANE, DWAYNE (dwain) Irish Gaelic: "small and dark." *Duwayne, Dwain, Dwaine, Dwane, Dwayne* (English)

DUC (duk) Vietnamese: "virtuous" or "moral." *Duy* (Vietnamese)

DUDLEY Old English: "one from the people's meadow." Made well known in the twentieth century by actor Dudley Moore. *Dudd, Dudly* (English)

DUFF Celtic: "dark-faced."

DUGAN (DOO-gun) Irish Gaelic: "small and dark." *Doogan, Dugann, Dugun* (English)

DUKE Old French: "a leader." Also a short name for Dukker.

DUKKER (DOOK-kuhr) English Gypsy: "to bewitch" or "to tell fortunes." *Duke* (English)

DUMAKA (doo-MAH-kah) Ibo, Nigeria: "help me with hands." This short-sentence name from Africa expresses the father's plan to put the boy to work.

DUMAN (DOO-mun) Turkish: "smoke" or "mist."

DUNCAN Scottish Gaelic: "a swarthy child" or "dark-skinned warrior." *Dun, Dune, Dunn* (English)

DUNHAM (DUN-um) Celtic: "dark or black man." *Dun, Dunam* (English)

DUR Hebrew: "to pile up" or "to encircle."

DURAN (der-AN) Latin: "durable or long-lasting." *Durand, Durant, Durante, Durrant* (English)

DURRIKEN (DOO-ree-ken) English Gypsy: "a fortune-teller."

DURRIL (DOO-reel) English Gypsy: "the gooseberry." *Dur* (English)

DUSAN (doo-SAHN) Serbo-Croatian form of Daniel, "God is my judge." See Daniel.

DUSTIN Old German: "a fighter"; or Old Norse: "Thor's stone." Dustin has become popular in recent years and originally seems to have been brought to attention by actor Dustin Hoffman. *Dust, Dustie, Dusty* (English)

DWADE (dwaid) Contemporary creation, probably a blend of *Duane* ("small and dark") +

Wade ("from the river crossing"). *Duade, Dwayde* (English)

DWAYNE A variation of Duane, "small and dark."

DWIGHT Old Dutch: "blond or white."

DYAMI (dee-AH-mee) Native American: "an eagle."

DYLAN Old Welsh: "son of the wave or of the sea." In Welsh mythology, Dylan the Dark was the son of the sea. Famous name-sakes are poet Dylan Thomas and singer Bob Dylan.

DYRE (dighr) Norse: "dear" or "precious." Very popular in Norway.

E

EARL Old English: "nobleman; count." *Earle, Erl, Erle* (English); *Jarl* (Scandinavian)

EBEN (EB-en or EE-ben) Hebrew: "a stone." *Eban, Even* (Hebrew)

EDAN Celtic: "fire." Name possibly for a boy born under one of the fire signs of Aries, Leo, or Sagittarius.

EDDY Scandinavian: "unresting." Also a short form of Edward, "wealthy guardian," or Edgar, "wealthy spearman."

EDGAR Old English: "wealthy spearman." *Ed, Eddie, Eddy, Ned, Neddy, Ted, Teddy* (English); *Edko, Edus* (Czech); *Edgard* (French, Hungarian, Russian); *Edgardo* (Italian, Spanish); *Edgars* (Latvian); *Edek, Garek* (Polish)

EDIK Russian form of Edward, "wealthy guardian."

EDISON Old English: "Edward's son." *Ed, Eddie, Eddy, Edisen, Edson* (English)

EDMOND Old English: "wealthy protector." Also used in France, Germany, Poland, Romania, and Russia. *Ed, Eddie, Eddy, Edmon, Ned, Neddy, Ted, Teddy* (English); *Esmond* (French); *Odi, Odon* (Hungarian); *Eamon, Eamonn* (Irish); *Edmondo* (Italian); *Edmunds* (Latvian); *Mundek* (Polish); *Edmon, Edmond* (Russian); *Edmundo, Mundo* (Spanish)

EDWARD Old English: "wealthy guardian." The most popular form of this name in the world is *Eduard,* used in Canada, the Czech Republic, England, Estonia, Germany, Holland, Poland, Romania, Russia, and the Republic of Slovakia, as well as the United States. *Ed, Eddie, Eddy, Ned, Neddy, Ted, Teddy* (English); *Edko, Edo, Edus, Edvard* (Czech); *Edvard* (Danish, Swedish) *Edouard* (French); *Edvard* (Hungarian); *Eadbard, Eadbhard* (Irish); *Edoardo, Eduardos* (Italian); *Ed, Edek, Edzio* (Polish); *Duarte, Eduardo* (Portuguese); *Edgard* (Romanian); *Edik* (Russian); *Duardo, Edrardo, Eduardo, Eduarelo, Euardo, Guayo* (Spanish);

EDWIN Old English: "prosperous friend." *Ed, Eddie, Eddy, Edwinn, Edwyn* (English)

EFRAIN (ef-rah-EEN, or Anglicized, EE-frun) A Spanish form of the Hebrew name Ephraim, "extremely fruitful."

EGAN (EE-gun) Irish Gaelic: "small, fiery one." An English form of the traditional Irish name Aodhagan. *Egon* (Irish)

EIJI (ee-jee) Japanese: "second-born son."

EINAR (EYE-nar) Old Norse: "individualist" or "lone warrior." The *einherjar* in Norse legend were the ultimate warriors who were rewarded for their valiant deaths by being sent to Valhalla, the heroes' paradise. One of the most popular names in Norway and Iceland. *Inar* (English); *Ejnar* (Danish)

ELAN (EE-lahn) Native American: "friendly."

ELDRIDGE Old German: "mature counselor"; or Anglo-Saxon: "fearful and terrible."

ELEK (EL-ek) Short Hungarian form of Alexander, "helper and defender of mankind." Also a Polish variation of Aurek, "golden-haired."

ELI (EE-ligh) Hebrew: "Jehovah" or "the highest One." *Eloy, Ely* (English)

ELIA (ay-LEE-ah, or Anglicized, ee-LIGH-ah) Zuni form of Elijah, "Jehovah is my God." See also Ellis.

ELIAS (ee-LIGH-us) A form of Hebrew *Elijah,* "Jehovah is my God." Used in many parts of the world, including Germany, Greece, Holland, and Spanish-speaking countries as well as Canada, England, and the United States.

ELIJAH (ee-LIGH-jah) Hebrew: "Jehovah is my God." The Jewish prophet Elijah ascended into heaven in a chariot of fire. *Eli, Elias, Ellis* (English). See Ellis for variations.

ELKAN Hebrew: "he belongs to God."

ELLERY Middle English: "from the island of the elder trees." *Ellary, Ellerey* (English)

ELLIOTT Hebrew, French: "Jehovah is my God." *Eliot, Eliott, Elliot* (English)

ELLIS Hebrew: "Jehovah is my God." Contemporary form of the older name Elijah. *Elias, Elis* (English); *Elias, Elya, Ilya* (Czech); *Elie, Elihu* (French); *Elias* (Dutch, German, Hungarian, Portuguese, Spanish); *Elias, Ilias* (Greek); *Elia* (Italian); *Elek, Eliasz* (Polish); *Eelia, Eelusha, Ilya* (Russian); *Elihu* (Swedish); *Eli, Elias, Elihu, Elija* (Yiddish); *Elia* (Zuni)

ELLISON Old English: "the son of Ellis." *Elison, Elson, Elyson* (English)

ELMAN German: "like an elm tree." *Elmen, Elmon* (English)

ELON (ay-LON or ee-LON) Contemporary American creation, possibly from the French word *"élan,"* meaning "self-assured, vigorous, and spirited."

ELRAD (ELL-rud) Hebrew: "God rules." *Rad, Radd* (English)

ELSU (EL-soo) Miwok: "falcon flying," as in "falcon circling in the air."

ELTON Old English: "from the old estate" or "from the old town." Made well known worldwide by singer Elton John.

ELVIS Old Norse: "all-knowing" is one popular explanation, although the exact origin is unclear. May also be a variation of Alvis, the name of a British car.

Will be forever linked in many people's minds with twentieth-century rock king Elvis Presley.

EMAN (AY-mahn) Czech form of Manuel, "God be with us." See Manuel.

EMERY Old German: "hardworking ruler." *Emerson, Emmery, Emory* (English); *Imrich* (Czech); *Imre, Imrus* (Hungarian)

EMIL (ay-MEEL) Gothic: "industrious"; or Latin: "flatterer." Used in many countries, including Canada, England, Germany, Hungary, Norway, Poland, and Sweden, as well as the United States. *Emilek,*

Milko, Milo (Czech); *Emile* (French); *Amal* (German); *Emilio* (Italian, Portuguese); *Emils* (Latvian); *Emilian* (Polish); *Emielo, Emileo, Emiliano, Emilio, Hemilio, Imelio, Melo, Milo, Miyo* (Spanish)

EMILIO (ay-MEE-lee-oh) Italian, Portuguese, and Spanish form of Emil, "industrious" or "flatterer." Made well known by actor Emilio Estevez. See Emil.

ENEAS (eh-NAY-us) Spanish form of the Greek *Aeneas*, "the praised one."

ENGELBERT Old German: "as bright as an angel." Made well known around the world by two Engelbert Humperdinks—one a singer and the other a composer. *Bert, Bertie, Berty, Englebert, Ingelbert, Inglebert* (English)

ENLAI (en-ligh) Chinese: "one who appreciates." Made internationally known by twentieth-century Chinese premier Zhou Enlai.

ENLI (EN-lee) Athabascan: "here below dog" and implies "that dog over there." Originally the name may have referred to a dog the father or mother spotted shortly after the child was born.

ENOCH (ay-NOHK, or Anglicized, EE-nuk) Hebrew: "educated" or "dedicated."

ENRIC (AHN-rik) Romanian form of Harold, "army ruler."

ENRIQUE (en-REE-kay) A favorite Spanish form of Henry, "ruler of a home or estate," "heir," or "a person of high rank." See Henry for other Spanish forms.

EPHRAIM (EE-frah-im, or Anglicized, EFF-ram) Hebrew: "extremely fruitful." *Efraim, Efrayim, Efrem, Ephrayim, Ephrem, Ephrim* (English, Hebrew); *Efrasha, Efrem, Rema* (Russian); *Efrain, Efren* (Spanish)

ERAN (EE-rahn) Hebrew: "the wide-awake one" or "watchful." A conventional Jewish name. In the

LEGENDS & LORE

Plant a tree and name it for a person. If the person for which the tree is named loves you, the tree will live.

Bible, Eran was one of Ephraim's grandsons. *Er* (English)

ERIC, ERIK Old Norse: "ever powerful" or "eternal ruler." One of the most popular names in Denmark and Sweden as well as the United States. Also used in Russia. *Erek, Erick, Ric, Ricki, Ricky* (English); *Erich* (Czech, German); *Erico* (Italian, Portuguese); *Eriks* (Latvian, Russian)

ERNEST Old English: "earnest one." Famous namesake was writer Ernest Hemingway. *Ernie, Erny* (English); *Ernst* (German, Norwegian, Swedish); *Earnan* (Irish); *Ernestino, Ernesto, Neto* (Spanish)

ERROL Origin unknown, but possibly a form of Earl, "nobleman; count." Made famous worldwide in the early twentieth century by actor Errol Flynn.

ERWIN Old English: "friend of the sea" or "white river." *Ervin* (Czech); *Ervins* (Latvian); *Erwinek, Inek* (Polish)

ESAU (EE-saw) Hebrew: "hairy" or "rough." In the Bible, Esau was Rebecca's twin son who sold his birthright to his brother. *Esaw* (English)

ESBEN (ESS-ben) Old Norse: "holy bear." Popular in Scandinavia. *Esbern, Esburn* (Danish); *Asbjörn, Esbjörn* (Norwegian)

ESSIEN (eh-see-EHN) Ochi, Ga, Africa: "sixth-born son."

ESTEBAN (eh-STAY-bahn) A favorite Spanish form of Stephan or Steven, "crowned." See Stephan.

ETHAN (EE-thun) Hebrew: "firm and strong." *Etan* (English)

ETU (ay-too) Native American: "the sun." In astrology, the sun governs Leo, the lion.

EUGENE Greek: "noble" or "born of good family." Also used in Ireland. *Gene* (English); *Eugen, Zenda* (Czech); *Eugen, Eugenios, Eugenius, Evgenios* (German); *Jano, Jenci, Jeno, Jensi* (Hungarian); *Egen* (Norwegian, Swedish); *Genek, Genio* (Polish); *Evgeni, Geka, Genya, Yevgeniy, Zheka, Zhenka* (Russian); *Eugenio, Gencho* (Spanish); *Owain* (Welsh)

EVAN Old Welsh: "young warrior" or "young bowman." Also a Welsh form of John, "gracious gift of God" or "God is gracious." *Ev, Evin, Ewan, Owen* (English); *Eoin* (Irish)

EZRA Hebrew: "help." Many Biblical names are derived from this source, including Azariah, Azrikam, Azur, and Ezri. *Esdras* (French, Spanish); *Esra* (German); *Ezera* (Hawaiian)

EZRI (EZ-ree) Hebrew: "my help." A contemporary Israeli form of Ezra ("help").

F

FABER (FAY-ber) German form of Fabian, "bean grower."

FABIAN Latin: "bean grower." *Fabyan* (English); *Fabert, Fabien* (French); *Faber* (German); *Fabiano, Fabio* (Italian); *Fabius* (Latvian, Lithuanian); *Fabek* (Polish); *Fabi, Fabiyan* (Russian); *Fabio* (Spanish)

FABIO (FAH-bee-oh) Spanish form of Fabian ("bean grower"), made familiar worldwide by model and author Fabio.

FADEY (FAH-dee) Ukrainian form of Tad or Thad, "father" or "praiser" or "courageous and stouthearted."

FADIL (fah-DEEL) Arabic: "generous." *Fadeel, Fahdeel* (English)

FAHIM (fah-HEEM) Arabic: "intelligent and learned" or "one who understands." *Faheem* (English)

FAINE (fain) Middle English: "joyful" or "glad." *Fane, Faniel* (English)

FAIRLEIGH Old English: "from the bull meadow" or "from the ram meadow." *Fairlay, Fairlee, Fairlie, Farlay, Farlee, Farley, Farly, Lee, Leigh* (English)

FAISAL (FIGH-sahl) Arabic: "a good judge," in the sense that he can separate right from wrong. *Faisel, Faisil, Faisl, Faizal, Fasil, Faysal, Faysul, Fayzal, Fayzel* (English)

FARID (fah-REED) Arabic: "unique." A favorite in many Arabic countries. *Fareed* (English)

FARRELL (FAIR-el) Irish Gaelic: "a superior man" or "heroic." *Farell, Farrall, Farril, Ferrell* (English)

FARUQ (fah-ROOK) Arabic: "one who can distinguish lies from the truth." *Farook, Farooq, Farouk* (English)

FATH (fahth) Arabic: "victory."

FAXON Teutonic: "long hair."

FEDOR (FAY-dohr, or Anglicized, feh-DOHR) Russian form of Theodore, "God's gift," or Francis, "free man" or "a Frenchman."

FELIKS (FE-lix) Russian form of Felix, "fortunate" or "lucky." Also used in Bulgaria and Poland.

FELIPE (feh-LEE-pay, or Anglicized, fah-LEEP) A favorite Spanish form of Phillip, "lover of horses." See Phillip.

FELIX Latin: "fortunate" or "lucky." *Feliks* (Bulgarian, Polish, Russian); *Fela* (Czech); *Bodog* (Hungarian); *Felic* (Irish); *Felex, Felixiano, Felizano, Feliziano* (Spanish)

FERNANDO (fair-NAHN-doh) Popular Spanish form of Ferdinand, "bold traveler" or "peace." *Ferando, Ferdenando, Ferdi, Ferdino, Fernandeo, Ferni, Hernando, Nando, Nano* (Spanish)

FERRIS (FAIR-iss) Irish Gaelic: "rock."

FIDEL (fee-DEL) Latin: "faithful and serene." Associated worldwide with Cuban leader Fidel Castro.

FILIP (FEE-leep or FIL-ip) Popular form of Phillip ("lover of horses") used in Bulgaria, the

Czech Republic, Lithuania, Norway, Poland, Romania, Russia, the Republic of Slovakia, and Sweden. For other forms, see Phillip.

FINAN (FIN-ahn) Irish Gaelic: "little and fair." A traditional Irish name usually spelled *Fionan* in Ireland. *Finn, Finnin, Fintan, Finton* (English); *Fionn, Fionntan* (Irish)

FINLEY Irish Gaelic: "small, fair-haired, brave one" or "sunbeam." *Fin, Findlay, Findley, Finlay, Finn* (English)

FINN Old German: "from Finland" or "fair-haired, fair-skinned one." Also a short form of Finley.

FISK Middle English: "fish" or "a fisherman." In the zodiac, the fishes symbolize Pisces. *Fiske* (English, Swedish)

FITZ Old English: "son." Also a short form of names starting with *"Fitz-."*

FITZGERALD Old English: "son of the spear-mighty" or "son of the ruler with a spear." *Fitz, Gerald, Gerrie, Gerry, Jerry* (English)

FLAVIO (FLAH-vee-oh) Latin: "blond" or "tawny." A favorite in Italy.

FLETCHER Middle English: "arrow featherer." Refers to an

archer's skill in putting feathers on his arrow. In the zodiac, the sign of Sagittarius is symbolized by the archer. Sometimes associated with Fletcher Christian, leader of the mutiny in *Mutiny on the Bounty. Fletch* (English)

FLINT Old English: "a stream." The name has come to mean "hard as flint stone" and has a strong, rugged feel about it.

FLYNN Irish Gaelic: "son of the red-haired one." *Flin, Flinn, Flyn* (English)

FOLKE (folk) Old Norse: "of the people." A traditional Scandinavian name. *Folk* (English); *Folki* (Danish, Norwegian, Swedish)

FONTAINE (fon-TAYN) French: "from the spring"; or Middle English: "one who lives near a spring or pool." *Fontayne* (English)

FONZI (FOHN-see) Spanish pet form of Alfonso, "ready and noble" or "ready for battle."

FORBES Irish Gaelic: "prosperous one" or "owner of fields."

FORD Old English: "from the shallow river crossing." *Forde* (English)

FORDEL (FOR-del) English Gypsy: "forgiving."

Did You Know . . .

✱ ✱ ✱

Anyone who suspects Americans have gotten *too* creative with our names should consider the crisis in China. There, 350 million people share only 5 last names: Chen, Li, Liu, Wang, and Zhang. The Lis alone would make up the ninth largest country in the world, outnumbering the populations of Australia, Canada, and South Africa combined. In one particular town, literally thousands of people are called Zhang Li. The confusion has gotten so great that banks have trouble keeping their accounts straight, and hospital surgeons increasingly find themselves operating on the wrong patient.

FORREST Middle English: "forest protector." To many people, this name has a strong and outdoorsy, yet sophisticated ring. *Forest, Forester, Forster, Foster* (English)

FRANCESCO (frahn-CHES-koh) A favorite Italian form of Francis, "free man" or "a Frenchman." See Francis.

FRANCIS Latin: "free man" or "Frenchman." Popular worldwide. *Fran, Frank, Frankie, Franky* (English); *Franc* (Bulgarian); *Frants* (Danish); *Frans* (Finnish); *François, Franchot* (French); *Franz, Franzl* (German); *Palani* (Hawaiian); *Proinnsias* (Irish); *Francesco* (Italian); *Frans,*

Franzen (Norwegian, Swedish); *Franio, Franus* (Polish); *Chicho, Chico, Chilo, Chito, Cisco, Currito, Curro, Farruco, Francisco, Frasco, Frascuelo, Paco, Pacorro, Panchito, Pancho, Paquito, Quico* (Spanish)

FRANCOIS (frahn-SWAH) The French form of Francis, "free man" or "a Frenchman." Recently made well known around the globe by French president François Mitterrand.

FRANK Old French: "free man." Also a short form of Francis. *Franki, Frankie* (English); *Franc* (Bulgarian, French); *Frans* (Finnish); *Franz, Franzl* (German); *Ferenc, Feri,* (Hungarian); *Franco*

(Italian); *Franek, Franio, Franus* (Polish); *Cisco, Franco, Paco* (Spanish)

FRANKLIN Middle English: "a free landowner." *Frank, Frankie, Franklyn* (English)

FRASER, FRAZIER (FRAY-zher) Old English: "curly-haired"; or Old French: "a strawberry." *Frase, Frasier, Fraze, Frazer* (English)

FRED A short form of names containing *"fred,"* such as Alfred, Frederick, etc.

FREDERICK Old German: "peaceful ruler." With its many forms, this has been one of the most popular boys' names in the world for some two hundred years. In several studies, this name has been typified as manly and successful. *Fred, Freddie, Freddy, Frederic, Fredrick, Fredrik, Fritz, Ric, Rick, Rickey, Rickie, Ricky* (English); *Bedrich, Fridrich* (Czech); *Riki* (Estonian); *Fredi, Friedel, Friedrich, Fritz, Fritzchen* (German); *Frides, Fritzi* (Hungarian); *Federico, Federigo* (Italian); *Fredek* (Polish) *Fridrich* (Russian); *Federico, Federoquito, Lico, Rico* (Spanish); *Frederik, Fritz* (Swedish)

FRITZ A short form of Frederick, "peaceful ruler," used in many countries. See Frederick.

FYNN Ghanaian, Africa: "the river Offin." Many Ghanaian names come from rocks, rivers, mountains, trees, animals, and other elements in nature.

G

GABI (GAH-bee or GAY-bee) Hebrew: "God's hero" or "God is my strength." A contemporary Israeli form of Gabriel.

GABRIEL Hebrew: "God's hero" or "God is my strength." Popular not only here but also in the Czech Republic, France, Germany, and Spanish-speaking countries. Many people see Gabriel as a warm, successful name, a strong person with integrity. Name associated with the Biblical archangel Gabriel, the football player Roman Gabriel, and South American novelist Gabriel Garcia Marquez. *Gab, Gabby, Gabe, Gabie, Gaby* (English); *Gavril* (Bulgarian, Russian); *Gabko, Gabo, Gabris, Gabys* (Czech); *Gabi, Gabor* (Hungarian); *Gaby* (Israeli); *Gabriele, Gabrielli, Gabriello* (Italian); *Gabian, Gabiel, Gabirel, Gabrial, Riel* (Spanish)

GADI (GAH-dee) Arabic: "my fortune." Originally from Israel. *Gadiel* (Israeli)

GALE Old English: "gay and lively": or Irish Gaelic: "stranger."

Also used for girls. *Gael, Gail, Gayle* (English)

GALEN (GAY-len) Irish Gaelic: "little bright one"; or Greek: "healer; peace." *Gale, Gayle* (English); *Galeno* (Spanish)

GALT (gahlt) Old Norse: "high ground." Originally from Norway, where it's a favorite.

GALVIN (GAL-vin) Irish Gaelic: "a sparrow" or "brightly white." *Gal, Galvan, Galven* (English)

GAN (gahn) Vietnamese: "to be near"; or Chinese: "adventurous."

GANESH (gah-NESH) Sanskrit: "god of the multitude," referring to Ganesa, the Hindu god of good luck and wisdom.

GANNON (GAN-un) Irish Gaelic: "fair-skinned" or "fair-haired." A name used in Ireland. *Gan, Ganen, Ganin, Ganon, Gannie, Ganny* (English)

GARAI (GAH-rah-ee) Mashona, Rhodesia: "to be settled."

GARRET (GAIR-et) A medieval pronunciation of Gerald, "spear brave" or "spear strong." Now gaining in popularity, and especially popular in Ireland. *Garet, Garett, Garrett, Garritt, Gerard, Gerrit, Gerritt* (English); *Gearoid* (Irish)

GARRICK (GAIR-rik) Old German: "spear ruler." The name has an air of success about it, possibly because of its association in many Americans' minds with newscaster Garrick Utley. *Garek, Garick, Garik, Garreck, Garrek, Garrick, Garrik, Gerek, Gerick, Gerreck, Gerrek, Gerrick, Gerrik* (English)

GARRIDAN (GAIR-i-dun) English Gypsy: "you hid."

GARRISON (GAIR-i-sun) Old English: "the son of Garret, or Gary." *Gair, Gare, Gari, Garri, Garrie, Garry, Gary* (English)

GARRON (GAIR-rohn) French: "son of Gary (a spearman)." Sometimes used as a contemporary form of Gary. *Garan, Garen, Garin, Garion, Garon, Garrion, Geron* (English)

GARTH Old Norse: "enclosure," "protection," or "from the garden." Trendy in Scandinavia as well as the United States.

GARVAN (GAR-vun) Irish Gaelic: "little, rough one." An English version of the traditional Irish name *Garbhan. Garv, Garvey, Garvy* (English)

GARY Old English *gari:* "a spearman." A likable name that many people see as strong, robust, and cheerful. *Garey, Gari, Garri, Garry* (English)

GASPAR (gahs-PAHR) A Spanish form of Casper, "master of the treasure."

GAVIN (GAV-in) Old Welsh: "white hawk" or "from the hawk field." *Gav, Gavan, Gaven, Gawain, Gawen* (English); *Gavino* (Italian)

GAVRIL (gahv-REEL) Russian form of Gabriel, "God's hero" or "God is my strength."

GAYLEN (GAY-len) Greek: "calm" or "a healer." Contemporary spelling of the older name Galen. *Gail, Gailen, Gale, Galen, Gay, Gayle* (English)

GENE A pet form of Eugene ("noble" or "born of good family"). See Eugene.

GEOFFREY A spelling variation of Jeffrey, "divinely powerful one," "traveler of peace," or "pledge of peace." See Jeffrey. *Geof, Geoff* (English)

GEORGE Latin: "farmer" or "land worker." *Georgi, Georgie, Georgy, Jorge* (English); *Georg, Georgi* (Bulgarian); *Durko, Jiri, Jur, Juraz, Jurik, Jurko, Juro* (Czech); *Jorn* (Danish); *Juri* (Estonian); *Georges* (French); *Jeorg, Juergen, Jurgen* (German); *Georgios, Giorgis, Giorgos, Gogos* (Greek); *Gyorgy, Gyuri, Gyurka* (Hungarian); *Jurgis* (Lithuanian); *Georg, Goran, Joergen, Jorgen* (Norwegian, Swedish); *Jurek* (Polish); *Egor, Georgiy, Jurgi, Yegor, Yura, Yurchik, Yuri, Yurik, Yurko, Yusha, Zhorka* (Russian); *Jorge, Jorje, Xorge* (Spanish)

> **"***I shall write a book some day about the appropriateness of names. Geoffrey Chaucer has a ribald ring, as is proper and correct; and Alexander Pope was inevitably Alexander Pope. Colley Cibber was a silly little man without much elegance and Shelley was very Percy and very Bysshe.***"**
>
> —JAMES JOYCE

GERALD Old German: "spear brave" or "spear strong." *Gerard, Gerhard, Gerrard, Gerry, Jerry* (English); *Geralde, Gerard, Geraud, Giraud, Girauld* (French); *Gerhard, Gerhart* (German, Norwegian, Swedish); *Gellart, Gellert* (Hungarian); *Geraldo, Giraldo* (Italian); *Gerek* (Polish); *Garald, Garold, Garolds,* (Russian); *Gerado, Geraldo, Gerardo, Herrado, Jeraldo* (Spanish)

GERALDO (hay-RAHL-doh) Spanish form of Gerald, "spear brave" or "spear strong." Associated closely in many people's minds with TV talk-show host Geraldo Rivera. For other Spanish forms, see Gerald.

GERARD (zhay-RAHR, or Anglicized, jeh-RARD) Old High German: "spear brave" or "spear strong." A French form of Gerald popularized worldwide by French actor Gerard Depardieu. *Jerard* (English)

GERARDO (hay-RAHR-doh) A popular Spanish form of Gerald, "spear brave" or "spear strong." See Gerald.

GERHARD (GAIR-hart) A form of Gerald ("spear brave" or "spear strong") popular in Germany and Scandinavia.

GERIK (GAIR-ik) Polish form of Edgar, "wealthy spearman."

GIACOMO (JAHK-oh-moh, or Anglicized, gee-ah-KOH-mo) Italian form of Jacob or James, "the supplanter." See Jacob and James.

GIAMO (JAH-mo) Italian form of James, "the supplanter."

GIAN (jahn) Short form of Giovanni, an Italian form of John ("gracious gift of God" or "God is gracious"). *Gianni* (Italian)

GIBOR (gee-BOHR) Hebrew: "strong." Contemporary name from Israel.

GIDEON Hebrew: "a destroyer" or "feller of trees." In the Bible, Gideon was a judge who delivered the Israelites from captivity and ruled Israel for forty years. Has a strong spiritual feel to it due to its association with the Gideon Bible. *Gedeon* (Bulgarian, French); *Gideone* (Italian); *Hedeon* (Russian)

GIL Spanish form of Giles, "young goat" or "youthful, downy-bearded one."

GILAD (gill-ad) Arabic: "a camel hump." Especially trendy in Israel. *Giladi, Gilead* (English)

GILBERT Old German: "a famous or bright pledge." *Bert, Gib, Gibb, Gil, Gill* (English); *Giselbert* (German); *Gilberto* (Italian, Spanish); *Gibbon, Gilibeirt* (Irish); *Gibby, Gilleabart* (Scottish)

GILES Greek: "young goat"; or Old French: "youthful, downy-bearded one." Saint Giles was the patron saint of beggars. *Egidius* (Dutch, German); *Gilles* (French); *Gil* (Spanish)

GILL Irish Gaelic: "a servant." The older Irish name is *Gialla*. *Gil, Gilley* (English)

GILLIE English Gypsy: "a song."

GINO (JEE-noh) Short form of Eugenio, which in turn is a form of Eugene, "noble" or "well-born," especially popular in Italy.

GINTON (geen-TOHN, or Anglicized, GIN-tun) Hebrew: "a garden." Contemporary Israeli form of the original Hebrew name Ginson.

GIOVANNI (joh-VAHN-nee, or Anglicized, jee-oh-VAHN-nee) A favorite Italian form of John, "gracious gift of God" or "God is gracious." See John.

GIVON (gee-VOHN) Hebrew: "hill or heights." A favorite in Israel.

GLENN Irish Gaelic: "a narrow mountain valley." Well-known Glenns include American actor Glenn Ford and singer Glen Campbell. Also now used for girls. *Glen, Glyn* (English, Irish)

Naming Customs . . .

✳ ✳ ✳

Many formerly masculine names like Brook(e), Glenn, Jordan, Madison, and Payton have crossed gender lines and are also bestowed on girls. Now that these names are considered gender-free, will parents keep giving them to boys? If patterns from the past hold true, probably not. In one study reported in the journal *Names*, researchers concluded that gender-free names tend to travel in only one direction: first the name is given to boys, then girls are given the name and eventually the name is no longer used for boys. Past boys' names now used almost exclusively for girls include Courtney, Evelyn, Leslie, and Shirley.

GOEL (go-AYL, or Anglicized to rhyme with *Joel*) Hebrew: "the redeemer."

GORAN (GOR-ahn) Scandinavian form of George, "farmer" or "land worker." Often used in Sweden.

GORDON Scottish: "from the spacious hill" is the best guess, although the origin is unclear. Also a Scottish clan name frequently used as a given name in Canada, Ireland, and Scotland, as well as in the United States. Sometimes now used for girls. *Gordan, Gorden, Gordie, Gordy* (English)

GORMAN Irish Gaelic: "little, blue-eyed one" or "man of clay."

GOSHEVEN (goh-SHAY-ven) Native American: "the great leaper."

GOWON (GOH-wohn) Tiv, Nigeria: "rainmaker." In Africa, where this name originated, the name is given to a child born during a storm.

GOZAL (goh-SAHL) Hebrew: "a bird." Originally from Israel.

GRADY (GRAY-dee) Irish Gaelic: "noble, illustrious one." Used in Ireland. *Gradey* (English, Irish)

GRAHAM Old English: "dweller in the gray land or gray

LEGENDS & LORE

The next time you go fishing, spit on your hook and give it the name of someone you love. If the person loves you back, you will catch a fish.

---

home." *Graeham, Gram, Gramm* (English)

GRANT Middle English: "great." Many people envision a Grant as strong, good looking, successful, well liked, and sexy. A very popular name.

GRAY Trendy short form of Grayson, "bailiff's son," frequently used independently.

GRAYSON Middle English: "bailiff's son." *Gray, Grey, Greyson* (English)

GREG Short form of Gregory ("watchful one"), now used independently. *Gregg* (English)

GREGORY Latin: "watchful one." In many people's minds, this name has connotations of wealthy sophistication. *Greg,*

Gregg, Greggory (English); *Grigoi, Grigor* (Bulgarian); *Gregoire* (French); *Gregorios, Grigorios* (Greek); *Gregorio* (Italian, Portuguese, Spanish); *Gregors* (Latvian); *Gries* (Swedish)

GUIDO (GHEE-doh, or Anglicized, GWEE-doh) Italian: "a guide" or "leader." Also a Spanish and Italian form of Guy ("life" or "a warrior").

GUILLERMO (ghee-YAIR-moh) A popular Spanish form of William, "unwavering protector." See William.

GUNNAR (GOON-er) Old Norse: "warrior" or "battle army." *Gun, Guntar, Gunter, Gunthar, Gunther* (English); *Gunter* (French); *Guenter, Guenther, Gunter* (German); *Gunnar* (Icelandic, Norwegian); *Guntero* (Italian)

GUR (goor) Hebrew: "lion cub." Many Israeli names come from this root, including *Guri* ("my lion cub"), *Guriel* ("God is my lion" or "God is my strength and protection"), and *Gurion* ("a lion"), connoting strength. In astrology the lion is the symbol of the sign Leo.

GUS Greek form of Constantine, "firm and constant." Also a short form of Gustave or Gustaf.

GUSTAF (goo-STAHF) Old Norse: "staff of the Goths"; or Old

German: "God's staff." Trendy in Sweden. *Gus, Gussie, Gussy, Gustave, Gustus* (English); *Gustav, Gusti, Gustik, Gusty* (Czech); *Gustaff* (Dutch); *Kosti* (Finnish); *Gustav* (French, German, Romanian, Swedish); *Gustavo* (Italian); *Gustavs* (Latvian); *Gustavo, Tabo, Tavo* (Spanish)

GUSTAVO (goo-STAH-voh) This form of Gustaf is especially common in Italy and Spain.

GUY Latin: "life"; or Old German: "a warrior." *Guyon* (English); *Gui, Guy, Vitus* (French); *Guido* (Spanish, Italian)

GUYAPI (goo-YAH-pee) Native American: "candid."

GYAN (GUY-an, rhymes with *Ryan*) Sanskrit: "filled with knowledge." A traditional Hindu name from India.

GYASI (JAH-see) Akan, Ghana: "wonderful child." *Jahsee, Jaysee* (English)

H

HABIB (hah-BEEB) Arabic: "beloved." A favorite in Syria, Tunisia, and other Moslem countries.

HACKMAN Old German: "shopkeeper"; or Old English:

"woodcutter." Made well known by actor Gene Hackman.

HADAD (hah-DAHD) Arabic: "the Syrian god of virility." *Adad, Haddad* (Arabic, English)

HADAR (hah-DAHR) Hebrew: "glorious."

HADDEN Old English: "child of the heather-filled valley" or "child from the heather hill." *Haddan, Haddon* (English)

HADI (hah-DEE) Arabic: "calm, quiet one" or "one who guides," referring to a religious leader.

HADLEY Old English: "child from the heather meadow." *Hadlee, Hadleigh, Lee, Leigh* (English)

HADRIAN Popular Swedish form of Adrian, "dark one." See Adrian.

HAFIZ (hah-fiz) Arabic: "a guardian." A traditional Moslem name.

HAGAN (HAH-gahn) Old Norse: "a chosen son or descendent." Originally from Germany, where it's still used.

HAGEN (HAY-gen) Irish Gaelic: "small and young." *Hagan, Haggan* (English)

HAHNEE (HAH-nee) Native American: "a beggar." May have originally been bestowed by Native Americans to fool evil spirits into thinking a child was unloved and hence not worth bothering with.

HAIDAR (HIGH-dahr) Arabic: "lion." A strong Muslim name also used in India.

HAIG (hayg) Old English: "one from the hedged enclosure." Originally a place-name in England.

HAJI (HAH-jee) Swahili: "born during the hajj," referring to a pilgrimage to Mecca every devout Moslem is expected to make at least once in a lifetime.

HAKAN (hah-KAHN) Native American: "fiery."

HAKEEM (HAH-keem or hah-KEEM) Arabic: "wise." One of the ninety-nine qualities of God listed in the Koran. *Hakim* (English, Arabic)

HAKEM (HAH-kem) Arabic: "ruler." In Afghanistan, Algeria, Iran, Iraq, Jordan, Saudi Arabia, Yemen, and many other countries, Hakem is also a title name meaning "governor."

HAKIM (hah-keem) Ethiopian: "doctor."

HAKON (HAH-ken) Old Norse: "of the high or exalted race." Many Norwegian kings have had

Arabic Occupation and Title Names

✴ ✴ ✴

Many Arabic names have religious significance. All those associated with Muhammad and the members of his family are prime examples. Other Arabic names, however, denote a father's occupation. Among these occupation names are:

Dabir: "secretary"

Ferran: "baker"

Haddad: "smith"

Kateb: "writer"

Khatib: "religious minister"

Khoury: "priest"

Samman: "grocer"

Wakil: "lawyer"

Title names are also common. Among them:

Amid: "general"

Arif: "corporal"

Fariq: "lieutenant general"

Rais: "captain"

Wazir: "minister"

Zaim: "brigadier general"

---

this name. *Haakon, Hako* (Norwegian)

HAL A pet form of Harold ("army ruler") or Henry ("ruler of a home or estate," "heir," or "a person of high rank").

HALDEN (HAHL-den) Old Norse: "half a Dane," referrring to a child who is half Danish. A contemporary version of the older Scandinavian name *Halfdan*, the name of many

Norwegian rulers and characters in Norse legend. *Hal, Haldan, Haldane* (English); *Halfdan, Halvdan* (Scandinavian)

HALE Old English: "from the hall" or "a healthy hero." Also a Hawaiian form of Harold, "army ruler." See Harold.

HALIAN (hah-lee-AHN) Zuni: "belonging to Julius." *Julian* (English)

HALIL (hah-LIL) Turkish: "intimate friend."

HALIM (hah-LEEM) Arabic: "mild," "gentle," or "patient." Popular in Egypt, Iran, Jordan, Saudi Arabia, Turkey, and other Moslem countries.

HALL Short for Hallan, "servant in the hall or manor house" and other names starting with *"Hal-".*

HALLAM (HAL-lum) Old English: "dweller in the remote valley." *Halam, Hallum* (English)

HALLAN (HAW-lin) Old English: "servant in the hall or manor house." *Halan, Hale, Hall, Hallen, Hallin* (English)

HALLEY (HAW-lee) Old English: "from the hall in the grove" or "from an open place in the woods." *Haley, Hall* (English)

HAMAL (HAH-mal or hah-MAHL) Arabic: "lamb." Hamal is also a bright star in the constellation Aries, the ram.

HAMID (hah-mid) Favorite form of Muhammad in Iran and other Moslem countries.

HAMILTON Old English: "from the proud or home-lover's estate." *Hamel, Hamil, Hamill, Tony* (English)

HAMISH (HAYM-ish) Scottish Gaelic form of Jacob and James, "the supplanter." Well known in Scotland, where the more traditional Gaelic spelling is *Sheumais*.

HAMISI (hah-MEE-see) Swahili: "born on Thursday." *Hanisi* (Swahili)

HAMLIN Old English: "lover of home."

HAMMET (HAM-et) Old Franco-German: "from the hamlet or home." A contemporary version of *Hamlet,* which was immortalized by the Shakespearean play of the same name. *Ham, Hamet, Hamlin, Hamlyn, Hammett* (English)

HAMMOND (HAM-und) Middle English: "chief protector" or "protector of the home." *Ham, Hamand, Hammand, Hamond, Hamund* (English)

HAMZA (HAHM-zah) Arabic: "strong or powerful." This was the name of Muhammad's uncle, renowned for his strength and bravery in battle.

HAN (hahn) Vietnamese: "ocean." *Hai* (Vietnamese)

HANAN (hah-NAHN) Hebrew: "God is gracious" or "gracious gift of God." A contemporary Israeli form of John.

HANBAL (HAHN-bahl) Arabic: "pure." Hanbal was the founder of an Islamic school of thought.

HANIF (HAH-neef or hah-NEEF) Arabic: "true believer (in the Moslem religion)." *Haneef* (English, Arabic)

HANK A familiar form of Henry, "ruler of a home or estate," "heir," or "a person of high rank."

HANLEY Old English: "from the high-wood clearing." *Handley, Hanleigh* (English)

HANS Scandinavian and German form of John ("gracious gift of God" or "God is gracious") has a strong, trustworthy, masculine air about it. The name also has friendly, cheerful connotations, possibly due to its association with storyteller Hans Christian Andersen. See John.

HANSEN Scandinavian: "son of Hans, or John." A Danish, Norwegian, and Swedish last name now occasionally used as a first name for boys and sometimes girls, too. *Hansan, Hanson, Hanssen* (English)

HANUMAN (hah-noo-MAHN) Hindi: "the monkey chief." A Hindu monkey chief and one of the favorite characters in Hindu literature, Hanuman could fly, and many stories are told about his fantastically long tail. Once Hanuman was sent by the god Rama to fetch some healing herbs from a mountain before the moon rose. When the monkey god could not find the herbs, he carried the whole mountain back to his master. Uprooting the mountain took him so long, he could not finish the job before the moon came up, so Hanuman ate the moon and coughed it up again when he replaced the mountain.

> **"*Titles are but nicknames, and every nickname is a title.*"**
>
> —THOMAS PAINE

HARB (hahrb) Arabic: "war."

HARDEEP (hahr-DEEP) Punjabi: "one who loves God" or "dedicated to God." *Harpreet* (Punjabi)

HARDY Old German: "courageous and robust." *Hardee, Hardey, Hardie* (English)

HAREL (HAIR-el) Hebrew: "God's mountain." Originally from Israel.

HARI (HAH-ree) Hindi: "tawny." Another name for the Hindu god Vishnu, the protector in the Hindu triad. A common variation is *Haridas*, the *-das* suffix indicating humility and complete subjection to Hari.

HARISH (har-ish) Sanskrit: "the lord Vishnu," a popular Hindu name. *Haresh* (Sanskrit)

HARITH (HAHR-ith or hah-REETH) Arabic: "plowman" or "good provider." *Harithah* (Arabic)

HARLAN Old German: "from the army land."

HARLEY Teutonic: "archer" or "deer hunter"; or Old English: "from the rabbit pasture." Appropriate name for a child born under the sign of Sagittarius, the archer.

HARMAN A variation of Herman, "army man" or "of high rank."

HARO (hah-roh) Japanese: "first son of the wild boar." *Haroko, Haroku* (Japanese)

HAROLD Old Norse: "army ruler." Used not only in this country but also in Bulgaria, France, Germany, Hungary, and Norway. Spelled *Harald,* this trustworthy and reliable name is also popular in Denmark and Sweden. *Hal, Harry* (English); *Jindra* (Czech); *Hale* (Hawaiian); *Aralt* (Irish); *Araldo, Aroldo, Arrigo* (Italian); *Haralds* (Latvian); *Haroldas* (Lithuanian); *Heronim, Hieronim* (Polish); *Haroldo* (Portuguese); *Enric* (Romanian); *Garald, Garold, Gerahd, Kharald* (Russian); *Harailt* (Scottish); *Haraldo* (Spanish)

HAROUN (hah-ROON) Arabic form of Aaron, "lofty" or "exalted." See Aaron. *Harun* (English)

HARPER Old English: "harp player," referring to someone who played a harp at festivals in the Middle Ages. Now also a favorite for girls.

HARRISON Old English: "Harry's son." A strong, successful name made well known most recently by actor Harrison Ford. *Harris, Harrisen* (English)

HARRY Once a pet form of Harold ("army ruler") or Henry ("ruler of a home or estate," "heir" or "a person of high rank") now used independently.

HARSHAL (har-shall) Sanskrit: "delightful" or "joyous one." A traditional Hindu name from India. *Harshad, Harshil, Harshul* (Sanskrit)

HART Old English: "stag." Short form of the older name *Hartley* ("stag-wood" or "stag hill"), made well-known by early twentieth-century American writer Hart Crane. *Harte* (English)

HASAD (huh-SAHD) Turkish: "harvest" or "reaping."

HASANI (hah-SAH-nee) Arabic: "beautiful" or "handsome." A Swahili name originally from East Africa. *Hassani, Husani* (Swahili)

HASHIM (HAH-shim) Arabic: "broker" or "destroyer (of evil)." Hashim was a descendant of the Prophet Muhammad. Popular among Moslems.

HASIM (HAH-seem) Arabic: "decisive one." *Haseem* (English)

HASIN (hah-SEEN) Hindi: "laughing."

HASKEL (HAHS-kel) Hebrew: "wisdom" or "understanding." Also a short form of Ezekiel, "strength." *Haskell* (English); *Chaskel, Haskell, Heskel* (Hebrew)

HASSAN (hah-SAHN or HAH-san) Arabic: "handsome." Among traditional Moslems, children of the same family often receive similar names. Hence, one family might have a Hassan, Husain; Khalid, Khallad; Makhlad, and Muhassan; all of which come from the word *salima,* "to be safe." The Hausa of Nigeria give this name to a first-born male twin; the second twin, if a boy, is named Husseini.

HASSEL Teutonic: "a man from Hassall (the witches' corner)" or "one who lives near a hazel tree." *Hassal, Hassall, Hassell*

HASTIN (hah-steen) Hindi: "elephant." The name refers to a legendary hero in Hindu mythology who was born in an elephant lake.

HATIM (HAH-tim) Arabic: "determined" or "decisive one." A traditional Muslim name. *Hateem, Hatem* (English)

HAU (how) Vietnamese: "longed for" or "desired."

HAWK Contemporary American name from Old Norse: "a falcon," or "bird of prey." *Hawke, Hawkeye* (English)

HAYDEN Old English: "son of the rose-hedged valley."

HAYES (hayz) Old English: "from the hedged enclosure." *Hays* (English)

HEARN (hern) Irish: "horse lord"; or Middle English: "from the stony place or the corner." *Hearne, Herne* (English)

HEDEON (heh-DAY-on) Russian form of Gideon, "a destroyer" or "feller of trees." See Gideon.

HEINMOT (hee-in-mot, or Anglicized, HINE-mot) Nez Perce: "thunder." A common name element among the Nez Perce Indians, this name was often combined with others to create combinations like *Heinmot Ilppilp* ("red thunder") or *Heinmot Tooyalakekt* ("thunder traveling to higher mountain peaks").

HELAKU (heh-LAH-koo) Native American: "sunny day."

HELKI (HEHL-kee) Miwok, *hele:* "to touch." The connotation is "jacksnipe digging into the ground with its bill."

HELMUT (HAYL-moot) Teutonic: "brave or spirited protector." A popular German name. *Helmuth* (German)

HEMAN (HAY-man) Hebrew: "faithful."

HENDERSON Old English: "Henry's son." Originally a last name, now used as a first name for boys.

HENLEY (HEN-lee) Old English: "from the high wood" or "from the woods filled with wild birds." An ecological nature name.

HENRY Old German *heri-mann:* "ruler of a home or estate" or "heir"; or Latin *hermi-nius:* "a person of high rank." *Hagan, Hal, Hank, Harry, Hendrik, Henri* (English); *Henri, Henrim* (Bulgarian); *Hinrich, Jindra, Jindrich* (Czech); *Riki* (Estonian); *Henrik* (Finnish, Hungarian); *Henri* (French); *Heine, Heinrich, Heinz, Hinrich* (German); *Bambis, Enrikos, Haralpos, Khambis, Kharlambos, Lambos* (Greek); *Heneli* (Hawaiian); *Arrigo, Enrico, Enzio* (Italian); *Anraoi, Enri, Hanraoi* (Irish); *Heniek, Henier, Honok* (Polish); *Henrique* (Portuguese); *Enric*

(Romanian); *Anrique, Enrique, Enriquillo, Henrico, Henriko, Inriques, Kiko, Quico, Quinto, Quique* (Spanish); *Hersz* (Yiddish)

> **"*A name pronounced is the recognition of the individual to which it belongs. He who can pronounce my name aright is entitled to my love and service.*"**
>
> —HENRY DAVID THOREAU

HERMAN Old German: "army man; soldier"; or Latin: "of high rank." *Harman, Harmon, Herm, Hermie* (English); *Hermann* (Danish, German); *Armino, Ermanno* (Italian)

HERRICK (HAIR-ik) Old German: "army ruler." *Herick, Herrik* (English)

HERSCH, HERSH (hursh) Yiddish: "a deer." Used today in Israel as well as the United States.

Herchel, Hirsch, Hirschel, Hirsh (English); *Hertz, Hertzel, Hertzl, Herz, Heschel* (Yiddish)

HEVEL (HEH-vel) Hebrew: "breath." A Hebrew form of Abel that comes to this country from Israel. *Abel* (English)

HEWITT (HYOO-it) Old Franco-German: "little Hugh." In England, this name has aristocratic connotations. More frequently used as a middle name in the United States. *Hewett, Hewlett, Hewson* (English)

HIDEO (hee-DEH-o) Japanese: "excellent male child."

HIEN (heeng) Vietnamese: "good-natured and sweet."

HIEU (hyoo, pronounced much like the English *Hugh*) Vietnamese: "respected" or "admired."

HILARY Latin: "cheerful." Originally a boys' name, now used mostly for girls. *Hilery, Hillary, Hillery* (English); *Vidor* (Hungarian)

HILEL (hil-EL) Arabic: "the new moon." Arabic nature name. In astrology the moon governs the sign of Cancer, and the moon card in the tarot deck corresponds to the sign of Pisces.

HILLIARD (HIL-yerd) Middle English: "from the enclosure on the hill"; or Old German: "brave in battle."

HILMAR (HIL-mar) Old Norse: "famous noble." Originally from Scandinavia.

HILTON Old English: "from the town or estate on the hill."

HIMESH (hih-mesh) Hindi: "lord of the snow." Another name for the Hindu god Shiva.

HINTO (HEEN-toh) Dakota, Native American: "blue."

HINUN (hee-NOON) Native American: "god of clouds and rain."

HIROSHI (hee-ro-shee) Japanese: "generous."

HISHAM (hih-SHAHM) Arabic: "one who crushes or smashes," connoting generosity. The name originally referred to a generous caravan driver who returned from his travels with bread to "crush" and share with his tribe.

HISOKA (hee-soh-kah) Japanese: "secretive" or "reserved."

HO Chinese: "the good."

HOANG (hwahng) Vietnamese: "completed."

HOC (hwok) Vietnamese: "studious one."

HOD Hebrew: "vigorous" or "splendid." A Jewish name originally from Israel.

HODIAH (hoh-DIE-ah) Hebrew: "Jehovah is my splendor." *Hodia, Hodiya* (Hebrew)

HOGAN (HOH-gun) Irish Gaelic: "youthful one."

HOLDEN Old English: "from the hollow valley." A place-name brought into familiar use as a first name after novelist J. D. Salinger named his main character Holden in *The Catcher in the Rye*.

HOLIC (HOH-lik) Czech: "barber." A Czech occupation name.

HOLLEB (HALL-eb) Teutonic: "like a dove" or "one who lives at the sign of the dove," a symbol of peace. *Holley, Hollub, Holub, Holly* (English)

HOLLIS Icelandic: "of the great hall" or "island man"; or old English: "from the grove of holly trees."

HOLMES Middle English: "dweller near a holly tree" or "from a river island." Most frequently used as a middle name in the United States.

HOLT Old English: "son of the unspoiled forests."

HONDO (HAHN-doh) Shona, Africa: "warrior."

HONON (HOH-non) Miwok: "bear."

HONOVI (hoh-NOH-vee) Native American: "strong."

HOSYU (hoh-syu) Japanese: "conservative."

HOTOTO (hoh-TOH-toh) Native American: "the whistler."

HOUSTON Scottish Gaelic: "from Houston (Hugh's town)." A strong-sounding contemporary American name associated with the city in Texas. Also bestowed on girls. *Huston* (English)

HOWARD Old German: "brave heart"; Old English: "sheep herder"; or Old Norse: "chief guardian." Has aristocratic associations in Great Britain, and moral, trustworthy connotations in the United States. *Howie* (English); *Haoa* (Hawaiian)

HOWE Middle English: "hill"; or Old German: "high or eminent one."

HOWELL Old Welsh: "eminent" or "little and alert." Also a variation of Hugh, "spirit, mind, heart." *Hywel, Hywell* (Welsh)

HOWI (HOW-ee) Miwok: "turtledove."

HOWIN (HOH-win) Chinese: "a loyal swallow." Chinese nature name.

HOYT Old Norse: "descended of the mind or spirit." A last name now occasionally used as a first name for boys. *Hoyte* (English)

HU (hoo) Chinese: "tiger."

HUANG (hwang) Chinese: "wealthy" or "an emperor." Frequently used in China as an element in compound names, such as *Huang-Fu* ("wealthy future").

HUBERT Old German: "brilliant mind" or "brilliant spirit." Most closely associated in many Americans' minds with twentieth-century vice president

Hubert Humphrey. *Bert, Bertie, Berty, Hobart, Hubbard, Hube, Huber, Hubie, Huey, Hugh, Hugo* (English); *Berty, Hubert, Hubertek* (Czech); *Berdy* (Russian, Slavic); *Berto, Huberto, Hubi, Uberto* (Spanish)

HUGH Old English: "spirit, mind, heart," implying intelligence. Also a short form of Hubert. *Howell, Huey, Hughie* (English); *Hugo* (Danish, Dutch, German, Spanish, Swedish); *Hewe, Hugin, Hugolino, Hugon,*

The Longest Name in the United States

✹ ✹ ✹

Elsdon Smith, author of *Treasury of Name Lore*, reports the longest name in the United States belonged to a Philadelphian named *Hubert Blaine Wolfeschlegelsteinhausenbergerdorff*. Actually, this is a short version of his name. If pressed, Hubert would explain that his full name was *Adolph Blaine Charles David Earl Frederick Gerald Hubert Irvin John Kenneth Lloyd Martin Nero Oliver Paul Quincy Randolph Sherman Thomas Uncas Victor William Xerxes Yancy Zeus Wolfeschlegelsteinhausenbergerdorffvoralternwarengewissenhaftschaferwessenshafswarenwohlgefutternundsorgfaligkeitbeschutzenvorangriefendurchihrraubgierigfeinds, Senior*. Imagine trying to squeeze that on a birth certificate.

Hugues, Huguito, Ugo, Ugolino, Ugone (Spanish); *Huw* (Welsh)

HUI (hwee) Chinese: "wise; intelligent." Also used for girls. In China, Hui-nan was an important Buddhist leader.

HUMBERTO (oom-BAIR-toh) Teutonic: "a Hun," or "famous bear cub." A traditional Spanish name. *Umberto* (Italian); *Humbaldo, Hunfredo, Hunfrido* (Spanish)

HUMPHREY (HUM-free) Old German: "warrior of peace" or "house peace." Made known worldwide by twentieth-century actor Humphrey Bogart. *Humfrey, Humfry, Hump, Humph* (English); *Humfried* (Dutch, German); *Onfroi* (French); *Onofredo* (Italian); *Hunfredo, Onofre* (Spanish); *Humfrid* (Swedish)

HUNT Old English: "the hunt." Also a short form of all boys' names beginning with *Hunt-*.

HUNTER Middle English: "hunter." A rugged, masculine name now also given to girls. *Hunt* (English)

HUNTINGTON Old English: "the hunters' estate." *Hunt, Hunton* (English)

HUNTLEY Old English: "from the huntsman's forest." *Hunt, Huntleigh, Huntly* (English)

Did You Know...

✹ ✹ ✹

A child's name is central to his or her identity, especially in the early elementary school years. In one classic study, more than 25% of 6- and 7-year-olds felt they wouldn't be the same person if their name were taken away. By age 8 or 9, however, only 5% of kids felt this way.

HURLEY Irish Gaelic: "child of the sea and tides." Appropriate name for a boy born under one of the water signs of Cancer, Pisces, or Scorpio. *Hurlee, Hurleigh* (English)

HUSAIN (hoo-SAYN) Arabic: "little beauty." Hussein was a descendant of the Prophet Muhammad. A favorite among Moslems. *Hossein, Husain, Husayn, Hussain, Hussein* (English, Arabic)

HUSAM (hoo-SAHM) Arabic: "sword."

HUSLU (HOO-sloo) Miwok: "bear with lots of hair."

HUSNI (HUS-nee) Arabic: "handsome" or "good." A favorite in the Middle East, borne by Egyptian president Husni Mubarak.

HUTCHINSON Middle English: "the son of little Hugh." A last name now used as a first name for boys. *Hutch, Hutchens, Hutchins, Hutchison* (English)

HUTE (HOO-te) Native American: "star." Indian name for a star in the handle of the constellation Ursa Major, better known as the Big Dipper.

HUTTON Middle English: "from the village on the spur of the hill." *Hut, Hutch, Hutten, Huttin* (English)

HUXLEY Old English: "from Hugh's meadow." *Hux, Lee* (English)

HUY (hwee) Vietnamese: "glorious" or "radiant as sunlight."

HUYU (hoo-yoo) Japanese: "born in winter."

HY (high) Vietnamese: "hope" or "wish." Also a short form of Vietnamese names starting with *"Hy-"* or *"Hi-"*, such as Hien and Hieu.

I

IAN (EE-un or IGH-un) Scottish form of John, "gracious gift of God" or "God is gracious." Currently trendy.

IBRAHIM (ih-brah-HEEM) Arabic form of the Hebrew Abraham, "father of a mighty nation" or "father of the multitude." One of the most popular Moslem names in Arabia, Egypt, India, Iran, Jordan, and Turkey. The patriarch appears in both the Old Testament and the Koran.

IGASHO (ee-GAH-shoh) Native American: "a wanderer."

IGNACIO (eeg-NAH-see-oh) Latin: "fiery one." A common Spanish name borne by several saints, including St. Ignatius of Loyola, who founded the Jesuits. *Ignace, Ignatius, Ignatz* (English); *Ignatius* (Dutch); *Ignaz* (German, Hungarian); *Ignazio* (Italian); *Egnacio, Hignacio, Ignacius, Ignasio, Ignatio, Ignazio, Ignocio, Nacho, Nacio, Nas, Ygnasio, Ygnocio* (Spanish)

IKE A short form of Isaac, "he will laugh." Famous namesakes are American president Dwight ("Ike") Eisenhower and singer Ike Turner.

ILIAS (ee-LEE-ahs) Contemporary Greek form of Elijah, "Jehovah is my God." See Elijah.

ILOM (ee-LOHM) Ibo, Nigeria: "my enemies are many." Ilom is an abbreviated form of the longer name Ilomerika.

ILYA (EELL-yah) Russian short form of Elijah, "Jehovah is my God." See Elijah.

IMMANUEL (i-MAN-yoo-ell) A Yiddish form of Emanuel, "God be with us." See Manuel.

INCE (EEN-tseh) Latin: "innocent one." A Hungarian name borne by thirteen Catholic popes.

INGER Old Norse: "son's army." Comes from Scandinavia, where it's frequently used. *Ingar* (English)

INGMAR Old Norse: "famous son." Popular in Scandinavia, especially Sweden, this name has a distinctively Nordic flavor. Associated worldwide with filmmaker Ingmar Bergman. *Ingamar, Ingemar* (English)

INGRAM (ING-grum) Old German: "angel-raven." Originally an English last name.

INGVAR (ING-var) Old Norse: "warrior," referring to Ing, the fertility god in Norse mythology. A Scandinavian favorite. *Ing* (English); *Inge, Yngvar, Yngve* (Danish, Norwegian, Swedish)

INIKO (ee-NEE-ko) Efek, Ibo, Nigeria: "time of trouble." In Africa, this name is given to a child born during a time of civil war, invasion, or other disaster.

INTEUS (een-TAY-oos) Native American: "he shows his face." In other words, he is not ashamed.

IOAKIM (ee-yoh-AH-keem) Russian form of the Hebrew name Joachim, "God will judge." *Akim, Iov, Jov, Yov* (Russian)

IRA Hebrew: "watchful one" or "descendants." A traditional Jewish name. Well-known Iras have included lyricist Ira Gershwin and novelist Ira Levin, author of *The Boys from Brazil.*

IRVING Old Welsh: "white river"; Irish Gaelic: "handsome"; or Old English: "a sea friend." Famous Irvings include composer Irving Berlin and writer Irving Stone. *Ervin, Erwin, Irvin, Irvine, Irwin, Irwyn* (English); *Eireamhon* (Irish)

ISAAC Hebrew: "he will laugh." Issac was the most popular Jewish name during the twelfth century. Its popularity gradually dwindled until it was seldom used, though these days the name is appearing more frequently again. *Ike, Ikey, Ikie* (English); *Isak* (Bulgarian, Hungarian,

Norwegian, Russian, Swedish); *Izak* (Czech); *Isaak* (German, Greek); *Aizik, Isaak, Izik, Yitzhak* (Yiddish)

ISAIAH (eye-ZAY-ah) Hebrew: "salvation of the Lord." Isaiah was one of the great Hebrew prophets. *Isa, Issa* (Hebrew)

ISAK Form of Isaac ("he will laugh") used in many countries. Also said to be a magical name meaning "identical point," used in incantations to invoke the powers of God.

ISAS (ee-sahs) Japanese: "meritorious one."

ISI (ee-see) Japanese: "like a rock."

ISMAEL (ees-mah-EL) Hebrew: "God hears." A favorite Spanish name from the Bible. Abandoned in the desert, Ismael was saved by God and became the patriarch of the Arabs. *Ishmael* (English); *Ismail, Ismeal, Ismeil* (Arabic); *Esmael, Isamel, Ishmael, Ismeal, Ysmael* (Spanish)

ISRAEL Hebrew: "wrestling with God." This was the name God gave Jacob after he had spent three days struggling in prayer with an angel. Also refers to the Jewish nation and to the twelve tribes who were descended from Jacob's twelve sons. *Issy, Izzy* (English, Hebrew)

ISTU (EES-too) Miwok: "sugar-pine sugar."

IVAN (EYE-vun) Popular in Russia as a form of John, "gracious gift of God" or "God is gracious." See John. *Vanya* (Russian)

LEGENDS & LORE

Among some of the Plains Indians, an astrologer would place grains of rice in a child's mouth, then name the child for the ruling planet at that time and whisper the name to the father and in the baby's ear. This secret "rice name" would never actually be used or even spoken aloud for fear a sorcerer might overhear it and use it to work evil.

IVAR (EE-vahr) Old Norse: "yew-bow army." A favorite in Sweden. *Iver, Ivor* (English); *Yvor* (Russian)

IVES Old English: "son of the yew bow" or "little archer." Name for a boy born under the sign of Sagittarius, the archer. *Yves* (French)

IVON (EE-von) Teutonic: "archer." *Yvon* (English)

IVORY Middle English: "elephant ivory." A modern American coinage used for both boys and girls.

J

JABARI (jah-BAHR-ee) Swahili: "brave one."

JACINTO (hah-SEEN-toh, or Anglicized, jah-SIN-toh) Spanish: "hyacinth." The feminine form is Jacinta.

JACK Originally a cheerful pet form of John ("gracious gift of God" or "God is gracious") or Jackson ("Jack's son"), Jack has been used as a given name since the mid-nineteenth century. *Jackie, Jacky* (English)

JACKSON Old English: "Jack's son." *Jack, Jackey, Jackie, Jacky, Jakson* (English)

> **❝Names are not always what they seem. The common Welsh name Bzjxxllwcp is pronounced Jackson.❞**
>
> —MARK TWAIN

JACOB (YAH-kohb, or Anglicized, JAY-kub) Hebrew *Ya'aqob:* "the supplanter." A classic name with deep spiritual connotations. In the Bible, Jacob impersonated his hairy brother Esau at his blind father's deathbed by putting a goatskin over his hands, thereby receiving the blessing meant for Esau. The meaning "supplanter" refers to someone who takes another's place by trickery. *Cob, Cobb, Jake, Jakie, Jakob, Jock* (English); *Ikov* (Bulgarian); *Jakub, Jokubas, Kuba, Kubes, Kubik, Kubo* (Czech); *Jacques, Jacquet* (French); *Jacob, Jakob, Jockel* (German); *Iakobos, Iakov, Iakovos* (Greek); *Jakab, Kobi*

(Hungarian); *Giacobbe, Giacomo, Giacopo* (Italian); *Jeks, Jeska* (Latvian); *Jecis, Jekebs, Jokubas* (Lithuanian); *Jakub, Jakubek, Jalu, Kuba, Kubus* (Polish); *Jaco, Jaime* (Portuguese); *Jakiv, Jakov, Jasha, Yakov, Yanka, Yashko* (Russian); *Jakob* (Scandinavian); *Hamish* (Scottish); *Diego, Jacobo* (Spanish)

JACQUES (zhahk) An internationally recognized French form of Jacob, "the supplanter."

JACY (JAY-cee) Native American: "the moon." In Tupi-Guarani legend, Jacy, the moon, was the creator of all plant life. The name can also refer to the planet Venus. *Jaycee, J. C.* (English)

JADRIEN (JAY-dree-en) Contemporary American blend of Jay ("the jaybird," "a chatterer," or "victory") + Adrien ("dark one"). One of the many popular names starting with *"Ja-"* that have been recently coined by inventive American parents. Others include: *Jabin, Jacan, Jadon, Jamar, Jamarr, Jaray, Jaron,* and *Jarone.*

JAEGER (YAY-ger or JAY-ger) German: "a huntsman." Originally a last name, recently adopted as a first name for boys.

JAEL (yah-AYL) Hebrew: "mountain goat." Used in Israel for both boys and girls.

JAFAR (jah-FAHR) Arabic: "a little stream."

JAGGER North English: "to carry things in a cart" or "carter."

JAHAN (jah-HAHN) Sanskrit: "the world." A name from India.

> **"***I don't care what you say about me, as long as you say* something *about me, and as long as you spell my name right.***"**
>
> —GEORGE M. COHAN,
> SPEAKING TO A NEWSPAPERMAN

JAHI (JAH-hee) Swahili: "dignity."

JAIME (JAY-mee, or in Spanish, HIGH-may) One of the most popular names in Portugal and Spanish-speaking countries, as well as currently in the top 150 names for boys in the United States. A form of James or Jacob, both meaning "the supplanter." The spelling *Jamie* is used more frequently for girls. See Jacob.

JAKE A robust contemporary form of Jacob, "the supplanter."

JAKEEM (ya-KEEM) A contemporary American form of Yakim ("God will establish"). *Jakim, Yakim* (Hebrew)

JAKOB (YAHK-ohb) A form of Jacob that's a favorite with Danish parents. Also used in Germany, Norway, and Sweden, as well as the United States. See Jacob.

JAL English Gypsy: "he goes." Referring to a wanderer.

JALEN (JAY-len) A contemporary American creation, possibly as a rhyming form of Galen, "little bright one" or "healer; peace." One of the trendy new *"Ja-"* names recently created by American parents. See Jadrien. *Jaylen* (English)

JAMAL (jah-MAHL) Arabic: "handsome." Popular in the Middle East and made well known worldwide by Egyptian president Jamal Abd-al Nasir. Most recently kept in the limelight by basketball player Jamal Wilkes. *Jahmal, Jamaal, Jamael, Jamahl, Jamall, Jameel, Jamel, Jamiel, Jamil, Jamile* (English); *Gamal* (Arabic); *Cemal* (Turkish)

JAMES Hebrew: "the supplanter." Originally an English form of Jacob. One of the most popular names in the world. For

---

New England "Trends"
✳ ✳ ✳

Long known for its sense of history and tradition, New England is the least likely place to find trendy names. Research by geographer Wilbur Zelinsky several years back confirmed this: the 3 most popular baby boys' names in New England — James, John, and William — were also the top three in 1790.

---

other forms, see Jacob. *Jaimie, Jaymie, Jim, Jimmie, Jimmy* (English); *Seamus, Seumas, Shay* (Irish); *Giacomo, Giamo* (Italian); *Diago, Jaco, Jaime, Jayme, Tiago* (Portuguese); *Hamish* (Scottish); *Chago, Chango, Chanti, Diego, Jaime, Jaimito, Jayme, Santiago, Tiago* (Spanish)

JAMIE Once a nickname for James, now popular as an independent name. Also common for girls.

JAMIL (jah-MEEL) Arabic: "handsome." *Jamal, Jameel* (English)

JAN (yahn) Slavic and Dutch form of John, "gracious gift of God" or "God is gracious." One of the most common Christian names in Slavic countries. A unisex name in the United States, now more often used for girls. See John.

JARED (JAIR-ed) Hebrew: "the decendant" or "heir." Currently trendy. *Jarod, Jarred, Jarrod, Jerrod* (English)

JAREK (YAH-rek, or Anglicized, JAIR-ek) Polish form of Janus, "born in January."

JARELL (ja-RELL or JAIR-ul) Contemporary blend of *"Ja-"* + Darnell ("from the hidden or secret nook") or Darrell ("small, dear, or beloved"). *Jarel, Jarrel, Jarrell, Jaryl, Jaryll, Jerrel, Jerrell* (English)

JARETH (JAIR-eth) Contemporary American creation of uncertain origin. May be a form of the trendy Jared, "the descendent" or "heir."

JARL (yarl) A Scandinavian form of Earl, "nobleman; count." In Norse mythology, Jarl was the father of soldiers and noblemen.

JARON (YAH-rohn, or Anglicized, JAIR-un) Hebrew: "to cry out" or "to sing."

JAROSLAV (YAHR-oh-slaf, or Anglicized, JAIR-o-slav) Slavic: "glory of spring." One of the most popular names in the Czech Republic and the Republic of Slovakia.

JARRED (JAIR-ed) A spelling variation of Jared, "the descendent" or "heir."

JARVIS Old German: "keen with a spear" or "a leader in war." *Jervis* (English)

JASON Greek: "a healer." In the Bible, Jason was the author of the book Ecclesiastes and a kinsman of St. Paul. Some translators believe Jason is a Greek form of Joshua or Jesus. *Jayson* (English)

JASPER Old French: "the jasper stone" or a form of Casper, "master of the treasure."

JAVAN (YAH-vun) Hebrew: "one from Greece." In the Bible, Javan was Japheth's son. *Javin, Javon* (English)

JAVAS (JAH-vahs) Sanskrit: "swift" or "quick." Used in India as well as the United States.

JAVIER (hah-vee-AIR) Spanish (Basque): "owner of the new house"; or Arabic: "bright."

JAVIN (jah-VEEN or JA-vin) English form of the Hebrew name Yarin, "to understand."

JAWHAR (jaw-har) Arabic: "jewel" or "essence."

Naming Customs...

★ ★ ★

People in all cultures base nicknames on a child's physical characteristics. In this country, red-haired boys and girls are commonly tagged Red or Rusty, whereas small kids get called Pipsqueak, Shorty, and Squirt. Spanish-speaking cultures have similar crosses to bear. Here's a sampling of common Spanish nicknames along with their translations.

El Apache — the dark one

El Bebe — baby-faced

El Bizco — crosseyed

El Colorado — red-haired

Chato — pug-nosed

Chico — small

El Cuajo Largo — the big eater

Elefante — "big ears" or "fatso"

El Falcon — the one with a hooked nose

JAY Old French: "the jaybird," "a chatterer"; or Sanskrit: "victory." In India, this name is commonly used in compound names, such as *Jayakrishna* ("victorious Krishna). *Jaye, Jey, Jeye* (English)

JAYCEE (jay-see) Contemporary American name that appears to be a spelling out of the initials J. C., *Jaycey, Jaycie, Jaysey, Jaysie* (English)

JAYME (HIGH-may, or Anglicized, JAY-me) Hispanic form of James, "the supplanter."

JAYSON (JAY-sun) A contemporary spelling of Jason, "a healer." *Jace, Jaison, Jase, Jasen, Jayce, Jaycen, Jaysen* (English)

JEAN (zhahn) French development of John, "gracious gift of God" or "God is gracious." This was once by far the most popular boys' name in France. Frequently used as the first element in a combination name like *Jean-Luc* or *Jean-Paul.*

JED Arabic: "the hand." Also a modern short form of Jedediah, "beloved of the Lord." *Jedd* (English)

JEDEDISH (jed-e-DEESH) A contemporary American creation, probably derived from Jedidiah.

JEDIAH (je-DIGH-ah) An eclipsed contemporary form of Jedidiah.

JEDIDIAH (jed-i-DIGH-uh) Hebrew: "beloved of the Lord." *Jed, Jedadiah, Jedd, Jedediah, Jediah* (English)

JEDREK (YED-rik, or Angli–cized, JED-rik) Polish form of Andrew, "strong and manly." See Andrew.

JEFF Contemporary short form of Jeffrey, "divinely powerful one," "traveler of peace," or "pledge of peace." *Geof, Geoff* (English)

JEFFREY Old French: "divinely powerful one," "traveler of peace," or "pledge of peace." *Geoffrey, Jeff, Jefferey, Jeffry, Jeffy* (English); *Geoffroi, Geoffroy, Jeoffroi* (French); *Friedl, Gottfried* (German); *Frici, Gottfrid* (Hungarian); *Sheary, Sheron* (Irish); *Geofredo, Giotto* (Italian); *Gotfrids* (Latvian); *Fred, Gotfryd* (Polish); *Geofri, Godoired*

(Romanian); *Gotfrid* (Russian); *Bogomir* (Serbian); *Fredo, Godofredo, Gofredo* (Spanish); *Sieffre* (Welsh)

JEKS (jayks) Contemporary Latvian form of Jacob, "the sup-planter." See Jacob.

JENS (jens) Danish, Norwegian, and Swedish form of John, "gracious gift of God" or "God is gracious." See John.

JERARD (je-RAHRD) A trendy variation of Gerard, "spear brave" or "spear strong."

JEREMIAH (jair-eh-MIGH-ah) Hebrew: "appointed by Jehovah" or "Jehovah is high." For other forms, see Jeremy.

JEREMY (JAIR-eh-mee) Hebrew: "appointed by Jehovah" or "Jehovah is high." A contem-porary form of Jeremiah. *Jem, Jemmie, Jemmy, Jer, Jerr, Jerrie, Jerry* (English); *Jeremias* (Dutch, Finnish, German, Portuguese, Spanish); *Jereme, Jeremie* (French); *Ember, Jeremiah, Katone, Nemet* (Hungarian); *Geremia* (Italian); *Jeremija, Yeremey, Yerik* (Russian); *Jeremia* (Swedish)

JERMAINE (jer-MAIN, or French, zher-MAIN) Latin: "the German," which in turn comes from Celtic for "the shouter." When this name is used for girls, the first letter is typically a "G," as

LEGENDS & LORE

Through the ages, certain names have been thought to bring illness or healing. As recently as the nineteenth century in some parts of America, it was believed that you could cure a baby of whooping cough by putting knots in a white ribbon and saying, "Jesus, Mary, and Joseph."

in Germaine. *Jamaine, Jermain, Jermane, Jermayne, Jerr, Jerrie, Jerry* (English)

JEROME Latin: "holy name." In the fifth century, St. Jerome translated the Bible into Latin. Legend has it that he removed a thorn from the paw of a lion, who then became his devoted companion. *Gerome, Gerrie, Gerry, Jerrie, Jerrome, Jerry* (English)

JERONE (jeh-RONE) Contemporary American creation, possibly a variation of Jerome, "holy name," or a blend of Jerry + Tyrone ("sovereign one" or "from Owen's land"). *Jeron* (English)

JERRICK (JAIR-ik) Another contemporary American coinage, probably derived from either Eric ("ever powerful" or "eternal ruler") or Derrick ("ruler of the people").

JERROD (JAIR-ud) Contemporary American form of Jared, "the descendent" or "heir." See Jared.

JERRY A short, friendly form of Gerald, Jeremy, or Jerome. *Jere, Jerrie* (English)

JESSE Hebrew: "wealthy one." *Jess, Jessie, Jessy* (English)

JESUS (hay-SOOSS) Hebrew: "God is salvation" or "helper of God." Though English-speaking Christians seldom use this first name out of respect for Jesus Christ, the name is extremely popular among Spanish-speaking Christians, who pronounce it hay-sooss and see it as giving a child special protection. *Hesus, Jesu, Jesuso, Jezus* (Spanish)

JETT Contemporary American coinage. Originally from Middle English: "to throw," but in contemporary usage refers to the jet plane. May also come from Greek: "jet-black," referring to a hard, lustrous type of coal from Asia Minor, used to make jewelry. A good name for a boy who's a real go-getter. This is the name of actor John Travolta's son. *Jet* (English)

JEVIN (JEV-in) Contemporary American creation, possibly based on Kevin ("lovable and gentle") or Devin ("a poet"). *Jevan, Jevon* (English)

JI (jee) Chinese: "continuity."

JIBBEN (JIB-ben) English Gypsy: "life." Similar is the English Gypsy name Jivvel, "he lives."

JIM, JIMMY Short, confident, assertive forms of James ("the supplanter"), frequently used independently. There have been many well-known Jims and Jimmys, including football star Jim Brown, writer Jimmy Breslin, and the late actor Jimmy Stewart. *Jimi, Jimmie* (English)

JIN Chinese: "gold." This name is occasionally used by Chinese astrologers if a child's horoscope is found to have too many wood influences. It is thought such names can overcome the evil in the stars because metal conquers wood.

JING (jing) Chinese: "pure" or "a capital city." An element in the

> ❝When I was a kid back in Connecticut, I used to love U.S.C. backfields. You had to be fascinated. I remember rolling the names off my tongue. Morley Drury. Homer Griffith. Grenville Landshell. Gaius Shaver. Irvine Warbyton. Orville Mohler. You read them and felt like going out and throwing rocks at your mother and father for calling you Jim.❞
>
> —SPORTSWRITER JIM MURRAY

city name Beijing, also used as a first name for boys.

JIRO (jee-ROH) Japanese: "the second male."

JIVAN (jih-vahn) Hindi: "to give life." A traditional Hindu name gaining popularity in the United States. *Jeeven, Jeven, Jiven, Jivin* (English)

JO Japanese form of the Biblical Joseph, "God will increase."

JOAB (JOH-ahb) Hebrew: "praise the Lord."

JOAQUIN (wah-KEEN) Hebrew: "God will judge." A favorite Spanish form of the Hebrew Joachim.

JOBEN (joh-ben) Japanese: "one who enjoys cleanliness."

JOCK A familiar short form of Jacob ("the supplanter") or John ("gracious gift of God" or "God is gracious"). *Jocko* (English)

JOE A strong, manly pet form of Joseph, "God will increase." Some of the many famous Joes include boxer Joe Louis and football greats Joe Namath and Joe Montana. *Joey* (English)

JOEL Hebrew: "God is willing" or "Jehovah is the Lord." In the Bible, Joel was a Hebrew prophet. Many people envision a Joel as ambitious, intelligent, caring, and creative.

JOHAN (YO-hahn) One of the most popular names in Scandinavia, this is a form of John. *Johann, Johannes* (Germany)

JOHAR (jo-har) Hindi: "jewel."

JOHN Hebrew *Yohanan:* "gracious gift of God" or "God is

Did You Know...

★ ★ ★

Until about 700 years ago, most people in medieval England had only one name—their first. Ten or 20 of the 100 people in a village might have been called Mary or John. To avoid confusion, villagers began describing each person precisely (Mary the daughter of the blacksmith; John the brownhaired). Eventually, the names were shortened—Mary Smith, John Brown—and passed on from parent to child.

gracious." Though John is no longer number one in the United States, it's still the most common first name in the Western world. It owes its immense popularity to the fact that two men with this name—John the Baptist and John the Apostle—were associated with Christ. *Jack, Jacki, Jackie, Jock, Johan, Johnie, Johnnie, Johnny, Jon, Jonni, Jonnie, Jonny, Sean, Shaun, Shawn, Zane* (English); *Hovhannes* (Armenian); *Iban* (Basque); *Johan* (Bavarian); *Jan, Jehan* (Belgian); *Ioan, Ivan* (Bulgarian); *Hanus, Honza, Ianos, Jan, Janco, Janek, Jano, Jenda* (Czech); *Hans, Jan* (Danish); *Jan* (Dutch); *Johan* (Estonian); *Hannes, Hannu, Janne, Juhana, Juho, Jukka, Jussi* (Finnish); *Jean, Jeannot, Jehan* (French); *Haensel, Hans, Hansel, Hansl, Johann, Johannes* (German); *Giannis, Giannos, Gioannes, Ioannes, Ioannis, Yannis* (Greek); *Jancsi, Jani, Janika, Janko, Janos* (Hungarian); *Eoin, Sean, Seann, Shane, Shawn* (Irish); *Gian, Gianetto, Gianni, Giannini, Giovanni, Vanni* (Italian); *Joba, Jofan* (Lapp); *Ansis* (Latvian); *Jonas, Jonelis, Jonukas, Jonutis* (Lithuanian); *Jens, Johan* (Norwegian); *Jehan* (Persian); *Ignac, Iwan, Jan, Janek, Jankiel, Jas, Jasio* (Polish); *Joanico, Joao* (Portuguese); *Iancu, Ioan, Ionel* (Romanian); *Ioann, Ivan, Ivanchik, Ivano, Ivas, Vanek, Vanka, Vanko, Vanya, Yanka* (Russian); *Ian* (Scottish); *Jovan* (Slavic); *Juan, Juanch, Juancho, Juanito* (Spanish); *Hans, Hansel, Hasse, Hazze, Jan, Jens, Johan, Jonam* (Swedish); *Ohannes* (Turkish); *Ieuan, Ifan, Jone, Sion, Sionym* (Welsh); *Yochanan* (Yiddish)

JOJI (Joh-ji) A Japanese form of George, "farmer" or "land worker."

JOLON (JO-lohn) Native American: "valley of the dead oaks."

JON Contemporary short form of John or Jonathan.

JONAH Hebrew: "dove," the symbol of peace. In the Bible story, Jonah was swallowed by a whale. *Jonas* (English, French, Icelandic, Spanish, Swedish); *Giona, Guiseppe* (Italian); *Iona, Yona* (Russian); *Yunus* (Turkish)

JONATHAN Popular in the United Sates, from Hebrew, "gracious gift of God" or "God is gracious." See John. *Johnathan, Johnathon, Jon, Jonathon* (English)

JONE Welsh form of John, "gracious gift of God" or "God is gracious."

JONTE (JAHN-tay) Contemporary American creation, perhaps a combination of John ("gracious gift of God" or "God is gracious") + Dante ("enduring or lasting"). Hence, the appealing connotation is "a lasting gift from God." *Jontay* (English)

JORDAN Hebrew: "descendant," or "flowing downward." *Jori, Jory* (English); *Jourdain* (French); *Giordano* (Italian)

JORELL (johr-ELL) A contemporary American name that seems to have been inspired by the fictional character Jor-el, Superman's father. *Jorel, Jorrel, Jorrell, Jurell, Jurrell* (English)

JORGE (HOR-hay) A common Spanish form of George, "farmer" or "land worker." See George.

JORI (JOR-ee or YOR-ee) Contemporary American and Hebrew form of Jordan, "descendant" or "flowing downward."

JORN (yohrn) A Danish form of George, "farmer" or "land worker."

JORY (JOR-ee) Originally a nickname for Jordan ("descendant" or "flowing downward"), growing in popularity as an independent name. Also used for girls. *Joree, Jorey, Jori, Jorie, Jorrie, Jorry* (English)

JOSE (hoh-ZAY) An immensely popular form of Joseph in the Spanish-speaking world. See Joseph, below.

JOSEPH Hebrew: "God will increase," in the sense that "He shall add to His powers." A

powerful Biblical name, a Joseph is often seen as a man who's very warm, stable, caring, and honest. Well-known Josephs include mythologist Joseph Campbell, writer Joseph Conrad, tycoon Joseph Kennedy, and actor Joseph Cotten. *Jodi, Jodie, Jody, Joe, Joey, Jojo* (English); *Yazid, Yusef* (Arabic); *Iosif, Yosif* (Bulgarian); *Josef, Joza, Jozef, Jozka, Pepa, Pepik* (Czech); *Joosef, Jooseppi* (Finnish); *Josephe* (French); *Beppi, Josef, Jupp, Peppi, Sepp* (German); *Iosif* (Greek); *Joska, Joszef, Jozsef, Jozsi* (Hungarian); *Iosep, Ioseph, Seosamh, Seosap, Seosaph* (Irish); *Giuseppe, Pino* (Italian); *Jo* (Japanese); *Jazeps* (Latvian); *Josef* (Norwegian, Swedish); *Josef, Jozio, Juzef, Juziu* (Polish); *José, Josef, Zeusef* (Portuguese); *Iosif, Osip, Osya, Yeska, Yesya, Yusif, Yusup, Yuzef* (Russian); *Josep, Josip, Joze, Jozef, Jozhe, Jozhef* (Serbian); *Che, Cheche, Chepe, Chepito, Jobo, José, Josecito, Joseito, Joselito, Pepe, Pepillo, Pepin, Pepito, Pipo* (Spanish); *Yusuf* (Swahili); *Osip* (Ukrainian); *Josef, Yousef* (Yiddish)

JOSHA (JO-shuh) East Indian: "satisfaction."

JOSHUA Hebrew *Yoyoshua:* "God of salvation." In the Bible, Joshua was Moses' successor. Currently trendy, the name has a warm, trustworthy, caring air about it. *Josh* (English); *Josue* (French); *Josua* (German); *Josua,*

Jozsua (Hungarian); *Giosia* (Italian); *Joaquim* (Portuguese); *Iosua* (Romanian); *Joaquin, Josue* (Spanish); *Josua* (Swedish); *Yehoshua, Yeshua* (Yiddish)

JOSIAH (joh-SIGH-ah) Hebrew: "Jehovah saves, supports, or heals." Name of an upright king of Judah who led his followers back to God. *Josias, Josie, Josy* (English)

JOTHAM Hebrew: "God is perfect."

JOV (yohv) Short form of the Russian Ioakim, "God will establish."

JOVAN (joh-VAHN) A Slavic form of John, "gracious gift of God" or "God is gracious."

JUAN (hwahn or wan) An immensely popular Spanish form of John, "gracious gift of God" or "God is gracious." In one recent survey, Juan was the fourth most popular boys' name in California.

JUDD Hebrew: "praised." A modern development of Judah.

JUDE Hebrew: "praised." Contemporary Israeli form of Judah. *Juda, Judas, Judd* (English)

JULES A short form of Julius, used in both the United States and France. Made internationally familiar by cartoonist Jules Feiffer

and writer Jules Verne, author of *20,000 Leagues Under the Sea.*

JULIAN Latin: "one belonging to Julius." Common in Spanish-speaking countries is *Julio. Halian* (Zuni)

> ❝*No, Groucho is not my real name. I'm breaking it in for a friend.*❞
>
> —GROUCHO MARX
> (BORN JULIUS MARX)

JULIUS Latin: "youthful" or "downy-bearded." *Jule, Jules* (English); *Julio* (Spanish)

JUMAH (JOO-mah) Swahili: "born on Friday," the holy day in the Muslim religion. *Jimoh, Juma* (English)

JUN (joon) Chinese: "truth"; or Japanese: "obedient." Also used as a girls' name.

JURI (YOO-ree) Estonian form of George, "farmer" or "land worker." See George.

JUSTIN Old French: "upright and just." Popular not only in this country, but also in the Czech Republic, France, and Germany. *Justen, Justis* (English); *Iustin*

(Bulgarian); *Jusa, Justyn* (Czech); *Just, Justus* (German); *Guistino* (Italian); *Justins, Justs* (Latvian); *Justas, Justinas, Justukas* (Lithuanian); *Justinus* (Norwegian, Swedish); *Inek, Justek, Justyn* (Polish); *Iustin, Ustin, Yusts, Yustyn* (Russian); *Justino, Justo, Tuto* (Spanish)

K

KABIL (kah-BEEL) Turkish: "possessed." The English form is Cain.

KABIR (kah-bir or kah-BEER) Hindi: "in honor of St. Kabir," referring to a saint who preached brotherhood and tried to unite the Moslems and Hindus under a single faith in one God.

KACEY (KAY-see) A trendy contemporary spelling of Casey, "brave, valorous, and watchful." See Casey.

KADAR (KHAH-dahr) Arabic: "powerful." *Kedar* (English)

KADE A popular variation of Cade, "cask" or "barrel" or "large and lumpy." See Cade.

KADIN (khah-DEEN, or Anglicized, KAY-din) Arabic: "friend," "companion," or "confidante." *Kadeen* (English)

KADIR (KHAH-deer) Arabic: "green" or "green crop (of grain)," connoting freshness and innocence. *Kadeer* (English)

KAGA (KAH-gah) Native American: "writer" or "chronicler."

KAI (kigh) Hawaiian: "sea" or "seawater." Name also used for girls.

KAKAR (KAH-kuhr) Todas, India: "grass."

KALA (KAH-lah) Hindi: "black" or "time." One of the many names for the Hindu god Siva.

KALB (kahlb) Arabic form of Caleb, "dog." The name is rarely used in the Arabic world today unless a family has lost many children and is trying to make the evil spirits believe the child is worthless to them. *Kilab* (Arabic)

KALE (KAH-le, or Anglicized, kayl) Hawaiian form of Charles, "strong and manly."

KALEB (KAY-leb) Another spelling of Caleb, "bold and impetuous" or "a dog." See Caleb.

KALIL (khah-LEEL) Arabic: "good friend." In Israel the same name means "crown" or "wealth." *Kahlil, Khaleel, Khalil* (English)

KALIQ (KHAH-leek) Arabic: "creative." Refers to a quality of God.

KALKIN (kahl-KEEN, or Anglicized, KAHL-kin) Hindi: "the god Kalkin." In Hindu mythology, Kalkin is the tenth incarnation of the god Vishnu and will come during the Age of Darkness. Some Hindu scholars say Kalkin is yet to come, others say he is already here. It is believed that Vishnu as Kalkin, or Kalki, will appear riding a white horse.

KALLE (KAH-le) Form of Charles, "strong and manly." A favorite in Scandinavia, particularly in Finland and Sweden. See Charles.

KALLUM (KAL-um) Another spelling of Callum, which in turn is a nickname for Malcolm, "St. Columba's servant." See Malcolm.

KALMAN (KAWL-mahn) German form of Charles, "strong and manly."

KALOOSH (kah-LOOSH) Armenian: "blessed coming" or "blessed advent."

KALVIN (KAL-vin) A modern American spelling of Calvin, "bald."

KAMAL (khah-mal) Sanskrit: "lotus." The Hindus associate the lotus with the birth of Brahma, and Hindu dieties often sit enthroned on its petals. In Arabic, this name is pronounced kah-MAHL and means "perfect."

KAMALI (kah-MAH-lee) Shona, southern Rhodesia: "the kamali spirit." Among the Mashona people, Kamali is a spirit believed to help a newborn baby live when other children in the village are ill.

KAMDEN (KAM-den) Anglo-Gaelic: "one from the winding or crooked valley." *Cam, Camden, Kam* (English)

KAMERON (KAM-er-un) Another spelling of Cameron, "one with a wry or crooked nose" or "from the crooked stream." One of the many trendy names in which the letter "C" has been replaced by a "K." See Cameron for other forms.

KAMI (KAH-mee) Hindi: "loving." Another name for Kama, the handsome black Hindu god of love. Kama is said to ride a parrot and carry a bow of sugarcane strung with bees and flower-tipped arrows.

KAMIL (khah-MEEL) Arabic: "perfect." One of the ninety-nine qualities of God listed in the Koran. Popular Moslem name. *Kameel* (English)

KANE Japanese: "golden"; Hawaiian: "man" or "the eastern sky"; or Irish: "son of Cathan." *Kaine, Kayne* (English)

KANG (kahng) Chinese: "healthy" or "well."

KANGI (KAN-gee, or Japanese, kahn-jee) Japanese: "tin"; or Sioux: "raven." *Kangee, Kanjee* (English)

KANIEL (kah-nee-AYL, or Anglicized, to rhyme with *Daniel*) Hebrew: "stalk" or "reed." *Kan, Kani, Kanny* (English)

KANTU (kahn-too) Hindi: "happy." Another name for Kama or Kami, the Hindu god of love. See Kami.

KARDAL (KHAHR-dal) Arabic: "mustard seed."

KAREEM (khah-REEM) Arabic: "generous, friendly, precious, and distinguished," often interpreted as simply "generous." Generosity is one of the ninety-nine qualities of God listed in the Koran. The name is a favorite among Moslems and gaining popularity in the United States, possibly because of retired basketball player Kareem Abdul-Jabbar. *Karim* (English)

KARL Popular German form of Charles, "strong and manly." Also used in Bulgaria, Russia, and Scandinavia.

KARMEL (kahr-MELL) Hebrew: "vineyard," "garden," or "farm." Originally from Israel, this name is used for both boys and girls.

KASEKO (kah-SAY-koh) Shona, southern Rhodesia: "to mock" or "to ridicule." A Mashona woman who has been scorned because she has no children may proudly name her first-born son Kaseko.

KASIB (KHAH-sib or khah-SEEB) Arabic: "fertile." *Kaseeb* (English)

KASIM (khah-SEEM) Arabic: "divided." *Kaseem* (English)

KASIMIR (KAH-se-mer) Old Slavic: "commands peace."

KASPER Greek: "precious stone;" or Persian: "master of the treasure." Especially popular in Germany. See Casper.

KASS German: "blackbird-like." A familiar name in Germany. *Kaese, Kasch, Kase* (English)

KASSIDY (KASS-i-dee) A variation of the currently popular Cassidy, "curly-haired" or "ingenious and clever." A gender-free name now used most often for girls. See Cassidy.

KAVI (KAV-ee) Sanskrit: "a poet." Used in India as well as the United States.

KAYIN (kay-YEEN) Yoruba, Africa: "celebrated." Used by the Yoruba for a long-hoped-for child.

KAZUO (kah-ZOO) Japanese: "first-born."

KEAHI (ke-AH-hee) Hawaiian: "fire." Also a girls' name.

KEANDRE (kee-AHN-dray) A combination of *"Ke-"* plus Andre ("strong and manly"). Contemporary American creation that sounds slightly French. A similar-sounding but truly French name is *Leandre*.

KEANE (keen) Irish Gaelic: "son of the warrior"; or Middle English: "quick and sharp." *Kean, Keen, Keene* (English)

KEANU (kee-AH-noo) A contemporary American name of uncertain origin, made familiar by actor Keanu Reeves.

KEATON (KEE-ton) Middle English: "from the estate of the Kesteven people (in England)." Originally a surname, now used as a first name for boys.

KEB Egyptian: "the Egyptian god Keb." A mystical name. Keb was an ancient earth god upon whose back grew the world's trees and plants. He is sometimes pictured with a goose on his head, and is often called the great cackler because he supposedly laid the egg from which the world sprang.

KEDAR (keh-DAHR) Hindi: "mountain lord." One of the 1,008 names of the Hindu god Siva. Also a variation of the Arabic Kadar, "powerful."

KEDDY Scottish variation of Adam, "earth" or "man of the red earth." See Adam. *Keady, Keddie* (English)

KEDEM (KEE-dem) Hebrew: "ancient," "old," or "from the east."

KEDRICK (KED-rik) A trendy American form of the older British name Cedric, invented by Sir Walter Scott for a character in *Ivanhoe.*

KEEFE (keef) Irish Gaelic: "grandson of the good-looking one," sometimes translated simply as "handsome, noble, or lovable." Originally a surname, now used as a first name for boys. Also short for Kiefer. *Keeffe* (English)

KEEGAN Irish Gaelic: "little fiery one." Name for a boy born under one of the fire signs of Aries, Leo, or Sagittarius.

KEENAN (KEE-nahn) Irish Gaelic: "little, ancient one." Can also be translated as "grandson of the little, ancient one." *Keen, Kienan* (English); *Cianan* (Irish)

KEIR (KEER) Celtic: "dark-skinned."

KEITH Irish Gaelic; "one from the battle place"; or Old Welsh: "from the forest." Has an athletic, confident, friendly feel about it.

KEKOA (ke-KOH-uh) Hawaiian: "the fine-leafed koa tree on the beautiful green ridges of the Koolau (mountains)." A short form of the long Hawaiian name *Kekoalauliinopalihauli-uliokekoolau.*

KELAN (KEL-un) Irish Gaelic: "tiny and slender." A contemporary American version of the popular Irish name *Caolan. Kealan, Kelen, Kelin* (English)

KELBY Old German: "from the farm by the spring." *Keelby, Kelbee, Kelbie, Kellby* (English)

KELE (kel) Hopi: "sparrow hawk." Used by Hopis in the rattlesnake cult. *Kelle* (English)

KELEMEN (KEL-e-men) Hungarian form of Clement, "gentle" or "kind."

KELII (ke-LEE-ee) Hawaiian: "the chief."

KELL Old Norse: "from the spring." Name for a boy born under one of the water signs of Cancer, Pisces, or Scorpio.

KELLEN (KEL-en) Irish Gaelic: "a mighty warrior." *Kalin, Kelin, Kellan, Kelle, Kellin* (English)

KELLY Irish Gaelic: "a warrior." A gender-free name now more commonly given to girls. *Kele, Kellen, Kelley* (English)

KELSEY (KEL-see) Old English: "victory ship" or "from Ceol's Island (the high island in the marsh)"; or Irish Gaelic: "war-

rior." A gender-free name made well known by actor Kelsey Grammer. *Kelci, Kelcie, Kelsi, Kelsie, Kelsy* (English)

KELVIN (KEL-vin) Scottish Gaelic: "from the narrow stream." Though it's not readily apparent, this is actually a nature name. The Kelvin is a river in Scotland. *Kelvan, Kelven* (English)

KEM English Gypsy: "the sun." In astrology, the sun rules the sign of Leo.

KEN A short, manly form of Kenneth, "a royal oath" or "handsome."

KENDALL Old English: "from the valley of the river Kent." Also one of the trendy gender-free names for girls. *Ken, Kendal, Kendale, Kendel, Kendell, Kenny* (English)

KENDREW (KEN-droo) A Scottish form of Andrew, "strong and manly."

KENDRICK (KEN-drik) Old Welsh: "chief hero"; or Old English: "royal ruler." *Ken, Kendric, Kendrik, Kendrix, Kenerick, Kenric, Kenrik, Kerrick, Kerrik* (English)

KENJI (ken-jee) Japanese: "bright; second-born son."

KENN Old Welsh: "clear, sweet water."

KENNEDY Irish Gaelic: "ugly head" or "helmeted head." A Scottish and Irish clan name occasionally used as a name for boys. *Cinneidid* (Irish)

KENNETH Old English: "a royal oath"; or Irish Gaelic: "handsome." For many people, this name contains connotations of success, ambition, good cheer, and intelligence. British Shakespearean actor Kenneth Brannagh has helped keep this name in the limelight. *Ken, Kenney, Kenny* (English); *Kenya, Kesha* (Russian)

KENNY A friendly pet form of Kendall ("from the valley of the river Kent"), Kendrick ("chief hero" or "royal ruler"), or Kenneth ("a royal oath" or "handsome"). Now used as an independent name.

KENT Old Welsh: "brightly white." A short, easy-to-spell, all-American name.

KEREL (keh-REL) Afrikaans: "young man."

KEREM (keh-REM) Turkish: "noble and kind."

KEREY (KAIR-ee) English Gypsy: "homeward bound." *Keir, Ker, Keri* (English)

KERN English variation of the Irish Kieran, "little black one." See Kieran.

KERR (kur) Irish Gaelic: "dark one" or "a spear."

KERRIL (kurl) An ancient Irish name of uncertain origin. A favorite in Ireland. *Kerill* (English); *Coireall* (Irish)

KERRY Irish Gaelic: "son of the black one" or simply "black one." *Keary* (English)

KERS (kurz) Todas, India: "the wight plant." The name refers to a plant native to India.

KERSEN (CURE-sen) Indonesian: "cherry."

KERWIN Irish Gaelic: "little jet-black one." Used in Ireland as well as this country. *Kerwen, Kerwinn, Kirwin* (English)

KESAR (keh-SAHR) Russian form of Caesar, "long-haired." Also used in the Ukraine. See Caesar.

KESIN (keh-SEEN) Hindi: "long-haired beggar." A title name in India.

KESSE (KEH-se) Fanti or Ashanti, Africa: "fat at birth."

KEVIN Irish Gaelic: "lovable and gentle." A current favorite which for many parents contains connotations of open friendliness and popularity. *Kev, Kevan, Keven, Kevvy* (English)

KHANG (khahng) Vietnamese: "robust, hearty one."

KIAN (KEE-ahn) Irish Gaelic: "ancient" or "one from the past." An English form of the old Irish name *Cian* (keen), this name is gaining popularity in the United States. *Kean, Keane, Keen, Keene* (English)

KIBBE (KEEB-beh) Nayas, Native American: "the night bird."

KIEFER (KEE-fer) May be a German variation of Cooper, "barrel maker." Given worldwide recognition by actor Kiefer Sutherland. *Keefe, Keifer* (English)

KIEL (kighl) Variation of Kyle, "crowned with laurel" or "one from the strait."

KIENAN (KEE-nahn) Irish Gaelic: "little and ancient" or "small one from the past." *Kanin, Kenan* (English)

KIERAN (KEER-ahn) Irish Gaelic *ceirin:* "little black one" or "little black-haired one." An Irish name currently trendy in this country. There are many Irish saints with this name, but the most celebrated is St. Kieran of Clonmacnoise. *Kearn, Kearne, Keeran, Kern, Kerne* (English); *Cianon, Ciaran* (Irish)

KIJIKA (kee-YEE-kah, or Anglicized, ki-JEE-kah) Native American: "walks quietly."

KILLIAN (KEEL-yan, or Anglicized, KIL-ee-un) Irish Gaelic: "small and warlike." English form of the traditional Irish name *Cillian* or *Cillin,* borne by an Irish missionary who was martyred. *Kilian, Killie, Killy* (English)

KIM Vietnamese: "gold" or "metal"; or Old English: "ruler." In Vietnam, this name is sometimes given to restore the balance of metal and wood influences in a child's horoscope.

KIMBALL Old English: "royal and bold"; or Old Welsh: "war chief." In Rudyard Kipling's novel *Kim,* the lead character's full name was Kimball. *Kim, Kimbell, Kimble* (English)

KIN Japanese: "golden."

KINGSLEY Old English: "one from the king's meadow." *King, Kingsly, Kinsley* (English)

KINGSTON Old English: "from the king's estate." *King, Kinston* (English)

KIPP Old English: "one from the pointed hill." *Kip, Kipper, Kippie, Kippy* (English)

KIRAL (ki-RAHL) Turkish: "king."

KIRAN (kir-an) Sanskrit: "a light ray." A traditional Hindu name from India.

KIRBY Old Norse: "one from the church village." Also used for girls. *Kerby* (English)

KIRI (kee-ree) Cambodian: "mountain summit," implying a child is at the peak of perfection.

KIRIL (KI-ril) Bulgarian form of Cyril, "lordly."

KIRITAN (keer-ee-tahn) Hindi: "wearing a crown." Another name for the Hindu gods Vishnu and Indra.

KIRK Old Norse: "from the church." Associated worldwide with "Captain Kirk" of *Star Trek*. *Kerk, Kirklan, Kirklen, Kirklin, Kyrk, Kyrksen* (English)

KIRWIN (KER-win) Irish Gaelic: "small and jet-black." *Kerr, Kerwin, Kirr* (English)

KISTUR (KEE-stoor) English Gypsy: "a rider."

KIT Short form of Christopher, "Christ-bearer." Now used as an independent name. *Kitt* (English)

KITO (KEE-toh) Swahili: "jewel." Implies the child is precious.

KIVI (KEE-vee) Hebrew: "supplant" or "protected." Also used today in Israel. *Akiba, Akiva, Kiva* (Hebrew)

KIYOSHI (kee-yoh-shee) Japanese: "quiet," an admirable Japanese virtue. *Yoshi* (Japanese)

Native American Nature Names

✱ ✱ ✱

N ative Americans have created some of the most detailed and intriguing of all nature names. The very meanings of these names reveal how closely they have observed the natural world. Among these colorful names are *Kalmanu* ("lightning striking a tree"); *Nikiti* ("round and smooth like an abalone shell"); *Siwili* ("long tail of the fox which drags along the ground"); *Tiktcu* ("jacksnipe bird digging wild potatoes"); *Wenutu* ("sky clearing after being cloudy"); and *Yotimo* ("the yellow jacket carrying pieces of meat from a house to its nest").

KIZZA (keez-SAH) Uganda, Africa: "born after twins."

KLIMENT Russian form of Clement or Clemens, "gentle" or "kind." See Clement.

KNOX (nox) Old English: "one from the hills."

KNUT, KNUTE (noot) Old Norse: "knot." Popular in Norway and Sweden and made well known in the United States by American football coach Knute Rockne. *Canute* (English); *Knute* (Danish)

KODY (KOH-dee) Contemporary American spelling of Cody, "a cushion."

KOI (KOH-ee) Chocktaw: "a panther."

KOJI (ko-jee) Japanese: "little one" or "child."

KOLBY (KOHL-bee) Another spelling of Colby, "from the coal-black settlement" or "black-haired." See Colby.

KOLTON (KOHL-tun) A contemporary American variation of Colton, "from the homestead on the Cole River (in England)." See Colton.

KOLYA (KOLE-ya) Russian pet form of Nicholas, "victorious army" or "victorious people."

KONANE (koh-NAH-ne) Hawaiian: "bright as moonlight."

KONNI (Anglicized, KON-ee) German form of Conrad, "bold counselor." See Conrad for other forms.

KONO (KOH-noh) Miwok: "a tree squirrel biting through the middle of a pine nut."

KONRAD A form of Conrad ("bold counselor") used in many countries.

KONTAR (KOHN-tahr) Akan, Ghana: "only child."

KORBIN (KOHR-bin) A variation of Corbin, "a raven." See Corbin. *Korb, Korban, Korben* (English)

KORDELL (kor-DELL) Variation of Cordell, "a small rope" or "small rope maker."

KORRIGAN (KOR-i-gun) A variant of Corrigan, "little spear." *Kori, Korigan, Korrie, Korry, Kory* (English)

KORUDON (koh-ROO-don) Greek: "helmeted one" or "crested one." *Corydon, Coryrell* (English)

KORY (KOHR-ee) A modern spelling of Cory, "he lives by a hollow (or misty) pool." See Corey.

KOSTAS (KOH-stahs) Contemporary Greek form of Constantine, or Constantinos "firm and constant." See Dinos.

KOSTI (KOH-stee) A pet form of Gustaf, "staff of the Goths," from Finland. See Gustaf.

KOVAR (KOH-vahr) Czech: "smith."

KRAIG (krayg) A contemporary spelling of Craig, "from the crag." See Craig.

KRISPIN Czech, German, Hungarian, and Slavic form of Crispus, "curly-haired one." See Crispus.

KRISS Contemporary American and Latvian form of Christopher, "Christ-bearer." See Christopher.

KRISTER (KREE-ster) Swedish form of Christian, "believer in Christ, the anointed one." See Christian.

KRISTIAN Form of Christian popular in Russia and Sweden as well as the United States. See Christian.

KRISTO (KREE-s-toh) Contemporary Greek form of Christopher, "Christ-bearer." See Christopher.

KRISTOPHER A modern spelling of Christopher, "Christ-bearer." See Christopher for pet forms and other variations.

KRUIN (KROO-in) Afrikaans: "top of a tree" or "mountain peak."

KUMAR (koo-MAHR) Sanskrit: "a son." Originally from India, where it's still used today.

KUPER Yiddish: "copper." For a boy with reddish hair.

KURT An athletic-sounding German form of Conrad, "bold counselor." See Conrad.

KURTIS A modern spelling of Curtis, "courteous." See Curtis.

KUZIH (KOO-zih) Athabascan, Carrier Indian: "great talker."

KWAKU (KWAH-koo) Akan, Ghana: "born on Wednesday."

KWAM (kwahm) Zuni form of Juan, which in turn is a Spanish form of John, "gracious gift of God."

KWAME (KWAH-me) Akan, Ghana: "born on Saturday." The feminine form is Ama.

KWAMIN (KWA-men) Ga, Africa: "born on Saturday."

KWESI (KWEH-see) Ochi, Africa: "born on Sunday."

KYLE Yiddish: "crowned with laurel," a victory symbol; or Irish Gaelic: "one from the strait." A gender-free name connoting confident good looks, but still more popular for boys than girls. *Kiel, Kile, Kiley, Ky, Kylie* (English)

L

LABAN (LAY-bahn) Hebrew: "white."

LADD Middle English: "an attendant." *Lad, Laddie, Laddy* (English)

LADO (LAH-doh) Bari, southern Sudan: "second-born boy." Common among the Bari people of southern Sudan, Lado is often used for a second-born male twin, along with Ulan ("first-born male twin").

LAIS (lace) East Indian: "lion." Common among the Moslems in India. In astrology, the lion symbolizes Leo.

LAL (lahl) Hindi: "beloved." Another name for Krishna. See Krishna.

LAMAR (lah-MAHR) Latin: "close (or related) to the sea"; Old French: "dweller by a pool"; or Old German: "land famous." *LaMar, LaMarr, Lamarr* (English)

LAMONT (lu-MONT) Old Norse: "lawman." *Lammond, Lamond, Lamonte* (English)

LANCE Old German: "land." A strongly masculine name originally associated with Sir Lancelot of Arthurian legend. *Lancelot, Launce, Launcelot* (English)

LANDON Old English: "from the open, grassy meadow." *Landan, Landen* (English)

LANE Middle English: "one from the narrow road." *Laine, Layne* (English)

LANG Old Norse: "tall man." Popular in Scandinavia.

> **"Name not proper, child's words not accepted; his words not accepted, he cannot achieve anything."**
>
> —Confucius

LANGDON Old English: "from the long hill." *Lang, Langsdon* (English)

LANGLEY Old English: "from the long meadow or forest." *Lang, Langly* (English)

LANGSTON Old English: "from the tall man's town or estate." A literary name associated with poet Langston Hughes. *Lang, Langsdon* (English)

LANGUNDO (lahn-GOON-doh) Native American: "peaceful."

LANI (LAH-nee) Hawaiian: "sky." This is also a common element in many longer Hawaiian names (see box, page 143.)

LANU (LAH-noo) Miwok: "people passing one another at the *pota* ceremony when running around the pole." Refers to a tribal custom.

LANZO (LAHN-zoh) Italian short form of Alfonso, Alonzo, "ready and noble."

LARAMIE (LAIR-ah-mee) Old French: "from Aramis in France." By usage, has become associated with Laramie, Wyoming.

LARNELL (lahr-NEL) This modern invention appears to be a blend of Larry ("crowned with laurel") + Darnell ("from the hidden or secret nook"). *Larnel* (English)

LARRY Nickname for Lawrence ("crowned with laurel"), now used as an independent name. *Lary* (English)

LARS Scandinavian form of Lawrence, "crowned with laurel."

Has a strong masculine feel and is one of the most popular names in Norway. See Lawrence.

LASALLE (lah-SAL) Old French: "one who lives or works in the large room or hall." A surname now also used as a given name for boys.

LASHI (LAH-shee) English Gypsy form of Louis, "a famous warrior." *Lash, Lasho* (English)

LATHAN (LAY-thun) Contemporary American creation of uncertain origin. May be a rhyming variation of the popular Nathan, "a gift."

LATHROP (LAY-thrup) Old English: "from the barn farmstead." *Lathe, Lathrope, Lay* (English)

LAVI (LAH-vee) Hebrew: "lion." In astrology, the lion is the symbol of Leo. *Leib, Leibel* (English)

LAWRENCE Latin: "crowned with laurel." First popularized by St. Laurence, a third-century martyr. For many Americans, this name connotes sophisticated success. Kept in the limelight in the twentieth century by Sir Laurence Olivier and the enigmatic Lawrence of Arabia. *Larrance, Larrence, Larry, Lary, Lauren, Laurence, Laurie, Lawrance, Lon, Lonnie, Lonny, Loran, Loren, Lorence, Lorin, Lorn, Lorne, Lorrie, Lorry*

(English); *Lauritz, Lorens, Lorenz* (Danish); *Laurens* (Dutch); *Lauri* (Finnish); *Laurent* (French); *Lorenz* (German); *Lenci, Lorant, Lornic* (Hungarian); *Labhras, Lochlainn, Lorcan* (Irish); *Lorenzo, Loretto, Renzo* (Italian); *Brencis, Labrencis* (Latvian); *Raulas, Raulo* (Lithuanian); *Lars, Larse, Laurans, Lorens* (Norwegian, Swedish); *Inek, Lorenz* (Polish); *Laudalino, Laurencho, Lorenco, Lourenco* (Portuguese); *Labrentsis, Larka, Larya, Lavr, Lavrik, Lavro* (Russian); *Labhruinn* (Scottish); *Chencho, Laurencio, Lencho, Lorenzo* (Spanish)

LAWTON Old English: "from the town or estate on the hill." *Laughton, Law* (English)

LEANDER (lee-AN-der) Greek: "like a lion." In Greek mythology, the youth Leander swam the Hellespont nightly to visit his beloved Hero. One night a tempest arose and he was drowned; upon learning of his fate, Hero also cast herself into the sea. *Leon* (English); *Leandre* (French); *Leandro* (Italian, Spanish)

LEANDRE (lay-AHN-dray) A French form of Leander ("like a

The Most Unpopular Names in This Country

✳ ✳ ✳

Lists of most popular names abound, and the entries keep changing from year to year. But what about the most *unpopular* names in the United States? According to Stephen Pile's *Book of Heroic Failures*, the following names—all used between 1838 and 1900—have fallen into "spectacular neglect."

ABISHAG	DESPAIR	MINNIEHAHA
AMOROUS	DOZER	MURDER
BABBERLEY	ENERGETIC	SALMON
BRAINED	FEATHER	STRONGITHARM
BUGLESS	HAM	TRAM
CLAPHAM	LETTUCE	UZ

lion") gaining popularity in the United States. See Leander.

LEBEN (LAY-ben) Yiddish: "life."

LEE Irish Gaelic: "a poet"; or Old English: "from the meadow." Also a short form of names containing *"lee." Leigh* (English)

LEIF (layf) Old Norse: "beloved." Popular in Norway. Strongly associated in many people's minds with explorer Leif Erickson. *Lief* (English, Scandinavian)

LEIGHTON (LAY-ton) Old English: "one from the meadow farm." *Lay, Layton, Leigh* (English)

LEL (layl) English Gypsy: "he takes."

LELAND (LEE-lund) Old English: "from the fallow land or the untilled field."

LEMAR (leh-MAR) Possibly a modern American variation of Lamar, "close (or related) to the sea," "dweller by a pool," or "land famous." See Lamar.

LEN Hopi: "flute." From the Hopi flute cult. Also shortened form for all names containing *"len."* The Hopis often combine this name with other words to create new names, such as *Lenmana* ("flute maiden") and *Len-hononoma* ("standing

flute"), referring to the flute ceremony.

LENCI (LEN-tsee) Hungarian development of Lawrence, "crowned with laurel." See Lawrence.

LENN A familiar form of Leonard, "brave as a lion." See Leonard.

LENNO (LEHN-no) Native American: "man."

LENNOR (LEN-ohr) English Gypsy: "spring" or "summer."

LENNOX (LEN-ux) Scottish Gaelic: "from the place of the elm trees." *Len, Lenn, Lenox* (English)

LENNY Nickname for Leonard ("brave as a lion"), now used as an independent name. See Leonard.

LENSAR (LEN-sahr) English Gypsy: "with his parents." The variation *Lendar* means "from his parents."

LEO Latin: "lion." Name for a boy born under the sign of Leo. *Lio* (Hawaiian)

LEON French: "like a lion." Used in France, Germany, Poland, Romania, and Spanish-speaking countries as well as the United States. Also a form of Leonard. *Leo, Leosko, Lev* (Czech); *Leonidas* (Greek); *Leone* (Italian); *Leonas, Liutas* (Lithuanian);

Leos, Levnek (Polish); Leao, Leonardo (Portuguese); Lev, Leva, Levka, Levko, Levya (Russian)

LEONARD Old Frankish: "brave as a lion." Used in many countries. Lee, Len, Lenard, Lenn, Lennard, Lennie, Lenny, Leo, Leon, Lon, Lonnie, Lonny (English); Lienard (French); Leonhard (German); Leonardo (Italian, Portuguese, Spanish); Leonhards, Leons (Latvian); Leonards (Lithuanian); Lennart, Lenne, Nenne (Norwegian, Swedish); Linek, Leonek, Nardek (Polish); Laya, Leongard, Leonid (Russian)

LEONARDO (lay-oh-NAR-doh) Italian, Portuguese, and Spanish form of Leonard, "brave as a lion." See Leonard.

LEOR (leh-OHR) Hebrew: "I have light." Originally from Israel. Also used as a girls' name.

LERON (leh-ROHN) Hebrew: "song is mine." A modern Israeli name. Lerone, Liron, Lirone (English)

LERONE (le-ROHN) A contemporary American blend of Lee ("a poet" or "from the meadow") + Tyrone or Ron (a short form of Ronald). LeeRon, LeeRone, Leron (English)

LES Short form of Lester ("from the chosen camp") or Leslie ("from the gray fortress").

LESHAWN (le-SHAWN) Many contemporary American names have been created by combining the prefix "Le-" with a familiar name, in this case Shawn, a variation of John ("gracious gift of God" or "God is gracious").

LETROY (le-TROY) Another "Le-" name recently created by inventive parents. The "Troy" syllable in this name means "a foot soldier" or "from the curly-haired people's region."

LEV Czech and Russian form of Leo ("lion") or Leon ("like a lion").

LEVI (LEE-vigh) Hebrew: "joined to" in the sense of being joined with God. Originally from Israel. Has a strong, sturdy quality to it. Lev, Levey, Levy, Lewi (Israeli)

LEWAYNE (le-WAIN) A contemporary blend of the prefix "Le-" + Wayne ("a wagon maker").

LEWIS Form of Louis, "a famous warrior." See Louis for other variations.

LEX Short form of Alexander, "helper and defender of mankind." See Alexander.

LI (lee) Chinese: "mighty and strong." Frequently used as an element in compound Chinese names, such as Li-Liang ("excellent strength"). Lee (English)

LIAM (LEE-um) One of the most popular names in Ireland and now trendy in the United States, Liam is a short form of William, "unwavering protector." Made popular recently by actor Liam Neeson. *Uilliam* (Irish)

LIANG (lee-AHNG) Chinese: "good" or "excellent."

LIEM (lim, or Anglicized, LEE-em) Vietnamese: "honest one."

LIKO (lee-koh) Chinese: "Buddhist nun." This unusual Chinese name is given to boys to suggest to the demon world that the child is of little value and protected by Buddha.

LINCOLN Old English: "from the poolside colony." Often bestowed to honor Abraham Lincoln, sixteenth president of the United States, this name has high connotations of trustworthiness and success. *Linc, Link* (English)

LINFRED Old German: "gentle peace." More common in Germany than the United States.

LIO (LEE-oh) Hawaiian development of Leo, "lion."

LIONEL Old French: "a young lion." Made known worldwide by British actor Lionel Barrymore and singer Lionel Richie. *Lionell, Lonell, Lonnell* (English); *Leonel* (Spanish)

LISE (LEE-se) Miwok: "salmon's head just coming out of the water." According to one legend, the salmon were once locked away from the Indians by two old demons. The coyote, who was talkative and polite in those days, tricked the demons into giving him the key to the lock, and freed the salmon and the river for the Indians.

LIU (LEE-oo) Ngoni, African: "voice." Used by the people of Nalawi.

LIWANU (lee-WAH-noo) Miwok: "bear growling."

LLOYD Old Welsh: "gray-haired" or "holy." *Floyd, Loyd* (English); *Llwyd* (Welsh)

LOE (LOH-eh) Hawaiian form of Roy, "king."

LOGAN Scottish Gaelic: "from the little hollow." Originally a Scottish clan name. *Login* (English)

LOKNI (LOHK-nee) Miwok: "rain coming through a small hole in the roof." Possibly given to a boy born during a rainstorm.

LOMAN (LOH-mahn) Serbo-Croatian: "delicate"; or Irish Gaelic: "little and bare." A traditional Irish name borne by four Irish saints.

LON Irish Gaelic: "fierce and strong." Also a short form of Lawrence, "crowned with laurel." *Lonnie, Lonny* (English)

LONATO (lo-NAH-to) Native American: "flint."

LONNIE Irish Gaelic: "little, strong, and fierce." Rapidly becoming a girls' name, but still used for boys. *Lon, Lonne, Lonny* (English)

LONO (LOH-noh) Hawaiian: "god of peace and agriculture."

LONZO (LAHN-zoh) Short for Alonzo, a Spanish form of Alfonzo or Alphonso, "ready and noble" or "ready for battle." See Alfonso and Alonzo.

LORANT (LO-rawnt) Hungarian form of Lawrence, "crowned with laurel." See Lawrence.

LORCAN Irish form of Lawrence, "crowned with laurel." See Lawrence.

LOREN (LOR-en) A short form of Lawrence, "crowned with laurel." Used about equally for boys and girls. See Lawrence.

LORENS Form of Lawrence popular in Denmark, Norway, and Sweden.

LORENZO (loh-REN-zoh) An assertive Italian form of

> ## Did You Know...
> ✶ ✶ ✶
> A study published in *Psychological Reports* found that you're slightly (8%) more likely to marry someone with a first name that begins with same letter as your own first name than someone whose name begins with a different letter. Given a choice between two equally attractive men—Adam and Louis—Angela will be slightly more likely to marry Adam.

Lawrence, "crowned with laurel." Also popular in Spanish cultures. See Lawrence.

LORNE A modern form of Lawrence, "crowned with laurel." *Lorn* (English)

LOTHAR German form of Louis, "famous warrior."

LOUDON Teutonic: "from the low valley." *Lowden* (English)

LOUIS Old German: "a famous warrior." *Lew, Lewes, Lewis, Lon, Lou, Louie* (English); *Lude, Ludek, Ludko, Ludvik* (Czech); *Ludirk* (Finnish); *Clovis, Louis* (French); *Lothar, Ludwig* (German); *Ludovici, Luigi* (Italian); *Ludis* (Latvian); *Ludvig* (Norwegian, Swedish); *Ludwik, Lutek* (Polish); *Luis* (Portuguese, Spanish); *Ludis* (Russian)

LOWELL (LOH-el or lohl) Old French: "wolf cub"; or Old English: "little and beloved." *Lovel, Lovell* (English)

LUCAN (LOO-kun) An Irish form of Luke, "light" or "bringer of light or knowledge." See Luke.

LUCAS (LOO-kus) An internationally popular form of Luke, "light" or "bringer of light or knowledge." See Luke for other forms.

LUIS (loo-EES) A favorite Spanish and Portuguese form of Louis, "a famous warrior."

LUISTER (loo-EES-tair) Afrikaans: "a listener."

LUKE Latin: "light" or "bringer of light or knowledge." Biblical name popular worldwide due to St. Luke. Especially well-used in Germany and the United States. *Lucas, Lucian, Lucien, Lucius, Luck, Lucky* (English); *Lukas* (Czech, Irish, Swedish); *Luce, Lucien, Lucius* (French); *Lucius,*

Lukas (German); *Loukas* (Greek); *Lukacs* (Hungarian); *Lukass* (Latvian); *Lukasz* (Polish); *Lucas, Lucio* (Portuguese, Spanish); *Luchok, Luka, Lukash, Lukasha, Lukyan* (Russian); *Lusio* (Zuni)

LUNT Old Norse: "from the grove." Originally from Scandinavia.

LUONG (loong) Vietnamese: "large bamboo," implying a child is morally straight and strong.

LUTHERUM (LOO-ther-um) English Gypsy: "slumber." Given by the Gypsies to child who sleeps a lot.

LUYU (LOO-yoo) Miwok *luyani:* "to shake the head," the connotation being "dove shaking its head sideways."

LUZ (loos, rhymes with *loose*) Spanish: "light." Short for Maria de la Luz (Mary of the Light), referring to the Virgin Mary. Also a girls' name.

LYLE Old French: "from the island." *Ly, Lyell* (English)

LYNDON (LIN-dun) Old English: "from the linden-tree or lime-tree hill." Most frequently associated with former United States president Lyndon Johnson. *Lin, Lindon, Lindy, Lynn* (English)

M

MAC Scottish Gaelic: "son of." Also a short form of all boys' names starting with *Mac-*. *Mack* (English)

MACAULEY (mah-KAWL-ee) Scottish Gaelic: "the son of Olaf (an ancestral relic)." Made well known worldwide as a first name by actor Macauley Culkin, famous for his roles in the *Home Alone* films. *Macalay, Maccauley, Macawlay* (English)

MACDOUGAL Scottish Gaelic: "the dark stranger's son." *Mac, Mack, Dougal* (English)

MACKENSIE (mah-KEN-zee) Scottish Gaelic: "fair or handsome" or "child of the handsome one." A name that has a "creative" feel and is also bestowed on girls. *Mac, MacKensie, McKenzie, Kensie, Kenzie* (English)

MACMURRAY Irish Gaelic: "the mariner's son." *Mac, Mack, Murray, Murry* (English)

MADISON Old English: "the mighty warrior's son." A boys' name becoming increasingly popular for girls. *Maddie, Maddy* (English)

MAHESH (mah-hesh) Sanskrit: "great lord." Another name for the Hindu god Shiva.

MAHIR (mah-HEER) Hebrew: "industrious" or "expert."

MAIMUN (MIGH-mun) Arabic: "lucky."

MAJID (mah-JEED) Arabic: "illustrious" or "glorious." Common in India. *Magid, Maj, Majdi, Majeed* (English)

MAKIS (MAH-kis) Modern Greek form of Michael, "Who is like God?" See Michael.

MAKOTO (mah-koh-toh) Japanese: "sincere and honest."

MAKSIM (mahk-SEEM) Russian form of Maximilian, "greatest in excellence." See Maximilian.

MALCOLM (MAL-kum) Scottish Gaelic: "St. Columba's servant." St. Columba was an Irish missionary who helped convert Scotland to Christianity. The most recently famous Malcolms include civil-rights activist Malcolm X and philanthropist and publisher Malcolm Forbes. *Callum, Calum, Kallum, Kalum, Malcom* (English, Scottish)

MALIK (MAH-lik) Arabic: "master." According to some Moslems, the name God dislikes most is Malik Al-Amlak, which means "king of kings."

MALLORY Old German: "an army counselor"; or Old French: "unfortunate and strong." *Mal, Malory, Lory* (English)

MAMO (MAH-moh) Hawaiian: "saffron flower" or "yellow bird." Also a girls' name.

MANCHU Chinese: "pure."

MANCO (MAHN-koh) Inca, Peru: "king."

MANDEK (MAHN-dek) Polish form of Armand, "armed" or "army man."

MANDER (MAHN-der) English Gypsy: "from me."

MANDO (MAHN-doh) Spanish pet form of Armand, "armed" or "army man."

MANIPI (mah-NEE-pee) Native American: "a walking wonder."

MANSA (MAHN-sah) African: "king." In ancient Egypt, the mansa rulers basked in elegance. One mansa was always accompanied by at least three hundred servants and musicians, the latter carrying gold and silver guitars. Another mansa, from Mali, was so extravagant that when he passed through Cairo on a pilgrimage to Mecca, he and his followers threw such a quantity of gold on the market that they undermined the price of the Egyptian dinar.

MANSUR (mah-SOOR) Arabic: "divinely aided." Popular Arabic name.

MANU (mah-NOO) Akan, Ghana: "second-born son." Used by the Ghanaian people for the second boy in a row.

MANUEL (MAN-yoo-el, or Spanish, mahn-WELL) Hebrew: "God is with us." The older form of this name is Emanuel. Used in Portugal, Russia, and Spain, as well as this country. *Immanuel, Mannie, Manny* (English); *Eman, Emanuel* (Czech); *Maco, Mano* (Hungarian); *Emanuele* (Italian); *Emek* (Latvian); *Manoel* (Portuguese); *Emmanuil, Manuil, Manuyil* (Russian); *Mango, Manny, Manolo, Manue, Manuelito, Mel, Minel, Nelo* (Spanish); *Immanuel* (Yiddish)

MANZO (MAHN-zoh) Japanese: "third son, as strong as 10,000 men."

MARAR (mah-RAHR) Wataware, southern Rhodesia: "dirt." *Marara* (African)

MARC A French form of Mark, "warlike one."

MARCEL (mahr-SEL) Latin: "little warlike one," referring to Mars, the Roman mythological god of war. A French pet form of Marc.

MARCUS A variation of Mark used in many countries. See Mark.

Did You Know . . .

✳ ✳ ✳

When people vote in elections but know little about the candidates, they almost always vote for "smooth-sounding" names. In one study, would-be voters preferred a candidate called Mark Fairchild (a made-up name) over George Sangmeister (a real guy) by a margin of 2 to 1. The more voters know about a candidate, however, the less influence a name has.

MARID (MAIR-eed) Arabic: "rebellious."

MARIO (MAH-ree-o) Latin: "manly" is the most likely meaning, although this name (a favorite in Italy and Spanish cultures) may also be connected to Mars, the Roman god of war. Many consider this a masculine form of the feminine Maria, referring to the Virgin Mary. As a result, this name is often bestowed in her honor. Well-known Marios include Peruvian novelist Mario Vargas Llosa; Mexican comedian Mario Moreno, who is also known as Cantinflas.

MARK Latin: "warlike one," from Mars, the mythological Roman god of war. Popular worldwide due to the Biblical St. Mark. *Marc, Marcus* (English); *Marek, Marko, Markus* (Czech); *Markus* (Dan- ish, Dutch, German, Swedish); *Marc, Marcel, Marcellin, Marcus* (French); *Marinos, Markos* (Greek); *Marci, Marcilka, Markus* (Hungarian); *Marco* (Italian); *Markus, Marts* (Latvian); *Marcos* (Portuguese, Spanish); *Mark, Marka, Markusha* (Russian); *Mari, Marko* (Slovenian)

MARLON Old French: "small falcon or hawk"; or Middle English: "from the land on a lake." Popularized worldwide by actor Marlon Brando. *Marlen, Marlin* (English)

MARLOW (MAHR-loh) Middle English: "from the hill by a lake." A surname now used as a first name for boys and girls. *Marlowe* (English)

MARNIN (mahr-NEEN) Hebrew: "one who creates joy" or "one who sings." Currently used in Israel as well as the United States.

MARQUIS (mar-KEE) Latin: "the son of Mark" or "belonging to Mars," the Roman mythological god of war. A French form of the Spanish surname *Marques*.

MARSHALL Old High German: "horse-servant" or "groom." *Marshal, Marshel, Marshell* (English)

MART Turkish: "born during the month of March." Also a short form of Martin, "warlike."

MARTIN Latin *martinus:* "warlike." An international name used in most of Europe and Central and South America, as well as Canada, Russia, and the United States. *Mart, Martan, Marten, Martey, Marti, Martie, Marton, Marty* (English); *Martinka, Tynek, Tynko* (Czech); *Mertin* (French); *Martel* (German): *Martinos* (Greek); *Marci, Marcilki, Martino, Marton* (Hungarian); *Mairtin* (Irish); *Martino* (Italian); *Martins* (Latvian); *Martinas* (Lithuanian); *Marcin* (Polish); *Martino* (Portuguese); *Martyn* (Russian); *Martiniano, Martino, Marto, Tino* (Spanish); *Marten* (Swedish); *Marti* (Swiss)

MARTY Pet form of Martin ("warlike") also bestowed as an independent name.

MARV Old English: "friend of the sea."

MARVIN Origin debatable. May be from Old English: "sea friend" or from Old Welsh: "sea fortress." *Marv, Marvine, Marvyn* (English)

MASATO (mah-sah-toh) Japanese: "justice."

MASKA (MAHS-kah) Native American: "powerful."

MASLIN Old French: "little twin." Might be a name for a boy born under the sign of Gemini, the twins.

MASON Old French: "stoneworker."

MASUD (mah-SOOD) Arabic: "fortunate." Commonly used by Swahili-speaking people in Africa.

MATO (MAH-to) Native American: "brave."

MATOPE (mah-TOH-peh) Mashona, southern Rhodesia: "this shall be the last child."

MATT A short, manly form of Matthew ("gift from Jehovah"), popularly used as a given name.

MATTHEW Hebrew: "gift from Jehovah." One of the most popular names in the world due to its association with St. Matthew, one of Christ's twelve apostles. *Mat,*

Mathew, Mathia, Mathias, Matt, Mattias, Mattie, Matthia, Mattmias, Matty (English); *Matei* (Bulgarian); *Matek, Matus* (Czech); *Matt* (Estonian); *Mathieu, Matthieu* (French); *Mathe, Matthaus, Matthias* (German); *Matthaios* (Greek); *Mate, Matyas, Matyi, Matyo* (Hungarian); *Maitiu, Matha* (Irish); *Matteo* (Italian); *Matteus* (Norwegian); *Matyas* (Polish); *Mateus* (Portuguese); *Matheiu* (Romanian); *Matfei, Matvey, Mayfey, Motka, Motya* (Russian); *Mata* (Scottish); *Mateo, Matias, Matteo, Mattheo, Teo* (Spanish); *Mathias* (Swedish)

MAULI (MOW-lee) Hawaiian: "dark-skinned."

MAURICE (mor-REES or mau-REES) Latin: "dark-skinned" or "Moorish." *Maurie, Mauris, Maury, Mo, Moris, Morrice, Morrie, Morris, Morriss, Morys, Moss* (English); *Maurits* (Dutch); *Muirgheas* (Irish); *Maurizio* (Italian); *Moritz* (German, Hungarian); *Maolmuire* (Scottish); *Mauricio, Maurie, Mauro, Moris* (Spanish)

MAVERICK (MAV-rik) American: "a wild nonconformist" or "an independent free spirit." After Samuel A. Maverick, an American pioneer in Texas who did not brand his calves. Came into use when actor James Garner starred in a TV series called *Maverick*, and Tom Cruise played a daredevil character by the same name in the movie *Top Gun. Mav, Mavrick* (English)

MAX Short for Maximilian ("greatest in excellence") or Maxwell, now used as a given name. *Maxey, Maxy* (English)

MAXIMILIAN Latin: "greatest in excellence." *Mac, Mack, Max, Maxie, Maximillian, Maxy* (English); *Maxi, Maxim* (Czech, French); *Maximalian* (German); *Maks, Makszi, Miksa, Maxi* (Hungarian); *Massimiliano, Massimo* (Italian); *Makimus, Maksymilian* (Polish); *Maximiliao* (Portuguese); *Maksim, Maksimka, Maksym, Sima* (Russian); *Maxi, Maxie, Maximiliano, Maximino, Maximo* (Spanish)

MAXWELL Old English: "important man's spring or pool" or "Maccus's well." Famous twentieth-century Maxwells include playwright Maxwell Anderson and editor Maxwell Perkins. *Max, Maxie, Maxy* (English)

MAYER (MIGH-er, or Anglicized MAY-er) Germanic: "overseer or farmer." One of the commonest names in Austria.

MEAD Old English: "from the meadow." *Meade* (English)

MEHMET (MEH-met) A form of Muhammad particularly popular in Turkey. See Muhammad.

MEHTAR (meh-tahr) East Indian: "prince." Often used in India to indicate noble ancestry.

MELVERN Native American: "great chief."

MELVIN Irish Gaelic: "polished chief"; or Old English: "sword friend" or "council protector." The nickname *Mel* is frequently used independently. *Mel, Melvyn* (English)

MENACHEM (men-ah-kem) Yiddish: "comforter." Famous namesake: Israeli Prime Minister Menachem Begin. *Mendeley* (Yiddish)

> **"***Let us speak plain: There is more force in names than most men dream of . . .***"**
>
> —J. R. LOWELL

MENDEL eastern Semitic *min'da:* "wisdom" or "knowledge."

MENDELEY (men-de-LAY) Yiddish: "comforter"; or Latin "of the mind." Used mostly in Russia. Also a Yiddish form of Menachem.

MERED (meh-RED) Hebrew: "revolt."

MERLE (murl) French: "blackbird." Though not used as a first name in France, it is a given name for both boys and girls in the United States.

MERRICK (MAIR-ik) Welsh: "dark-skinned" or "Moorish." Originally a form of Maurice, now frequently used as an independent name. *Merick, Merik, Merrik, Meyrick* (English)

MERRILL Old French: "small and famous." *Meril, Merill, Merle, Merrel, Merrell, Meryl* (English)

MERRIPEN (MAIR-i-pen) English Gypsy: a paradoxical name that can mean either "life" or "death."

MERRIT (MAIR-it) Old English: "little famous one," a child of merit. *Merit, Meritt* (English)

MESTIPEN (MESS-ti-pen) English Gypsy: "fortune" or "luck."

MEYER (MIGH-er) German: "farmer." A common name in Belgium.

MICAH (MIGH-kah) A variation of Misha, the Hebrew form of Michael, "Who is like God?" Also used for girls. See Michael.

MICHAEL Hebrew: "Who is like God?" In its many variations, this is one of the most popular names in the world. The spelling Michael is used in Germany and Ireland as well as all English-speaking countries. *Mickel, Micki, Mickie, Micky, Mike, Mitch, Mitchel, Mitchell* (English); *Mihail* (Bulgarian); *Michal, Min, Minka, Misa, Miso, Misko* (Czech); *Mihkel, Mikk* (Estonian); *Mikko* (Finnish); *Dumichel, Michau, Michel, Michon* (French); *Makis, Michail, Mihail, Mikhail, Mikhalis, Mikhos* (Greek); *Mica, Micah, Micha, Misha* (Hebrew); *Mihal, Mihaly, Misi, Miska* (Hungarian); *Michele* (Italian); *Mikelis, Miks, Mikus, Milkins* (Latvian); *Mikkel* (Norwegian); *Machas, Michak, Michal, Michalek, Mietek* (Polish): *Miguel* (Portuguese); *Mihail, Mihas* (Romanian); *Michail, Mika, Mikhail, Mikhalka, Mischa, Misha* (Russian); *Micheil* (Scottish); *Micho, Mickey, Miguel, Migui, Miki, Mique* (Spanish); *Mickel, Mihalje, Mikael* (Swedish); *Mihailo* (Ukrainian); *Mihangel* (Welsh); *Michael* (Yiddish)

MICHIO (mee-chee-oh) Japanese: "having the strength of three thousand men."

MIGUEL (mee-GEL) Spanish form of Michael, "Who is like God?" See Michael for many other forms used around the world.

MIKE A favorite short form of Michael ("Who is like God?")

now used independently. See Michael.

MIKI (mee-kee) Japanese: "tree."

MILES Latin: "soldier" or "warrior"; or Old German: "merciful one." *Myles* (English)

MIMIS (MEE-mis) Greek pet form of Dimitri, "belonging to Demeter."

MINCO (min-koh) Choctaw: "chief." *Minko* (English)

MINGAN (MEEN-gahn) Native American: "the gray wolf."

MINH (min) Vietnamese: "luminous and clear," with connotations of a bright light.

MISCHA (MEE-shuh) Russian pet form of Michael, "Who is like God?"

MISU (MEE-soo) Miwok: "rippling water."

MITCH Short form of Mitchell, which in turn is a form of Michael, "Who is like God?"

MITCHELL A form of Michael that's been used since the twelfth century. See Michael. *Mitch, Mitchel* (English)

MOHAN (moh-HAHN) Sanskrit: "attractive," "delightful," or "bewitching." Another name for the much-celebrated Hindu god

Krishna, an incarnation of Vishnu, the lord of creation.

MOHANDAS (moh-HAHN-das) Sanskrit: "servant of Mohan (or Krishna)." Made famous worldwide by Indian leader Mohandas Karamchand Gandhi, known as Mahatma Gandhi.

MONROE Scottish or Irish Gaelic: "from the red swamp," referring to a place near the Roe River in Ireland. *Monro, Munro, Munroe* (English)

MONTAGUE (MON-tah-gyou) French: "from the pointed hill." *Montagu, Monte, Monty* (English)

MONTANA Latin: "from a mountainous region." A rugged-sounding contemporary name associated with the state of Montana. Possibly coined as a first name in the twentieth century due to the popularity of football player Joe Montana.

MONTEL (mon-TEL) Latin: "mountain," implying a child is the summit or peak of excellence. Made well known in the United States by TV talk-show host Montel Williams. *Monteil, Montell* (English)

MONTY A short, snappy form of names containing *mont,* especially Montague.

MORGAN Old Welsh: "seashore" or "great and bright." A

Miwok Water Names

✷ ✷ ✷

Water names were common among the Miwok Indians of California. Examples include *Iskemu* ("water running gently when the creek dries"); *Miltaiye* ("water in waves"); *Uhubitu* ("foul, stinking, stagnant water"); and *Yottoko* "black mud at the edge of the water"). Such names often referred to the way a nearby stream looked when the baby was born.

gender-free name now used more frequently for girls. *Morgen* (English)

MORRIS Latin: "dark-skinned one." A modern English form of Maurice. *Maurey, Maurie, Maury, Morey, Morie, Morrie, Morry* (English)

MORVEN Scottish Gaelic: "child of the sea" or "a mariner"; or Irish Gaelic: "great, fair-skinned one." Name for a boy born under one of the water signs of Cancer, Pisces, or Scorpio.

MOSES Hebrew: "saved (from the water)." *Moe, Mose, Moshe, Moss* (English); *Moisei* (Bulgarian); *Moise* (French); *Moisis* (Greek); *Moise, Mose, Moshe* (Hebrew); *Mozes* (Hungarian); *Moise, Mose* (Italian); *Moze* (Lithuanian); *Moshe, Mosze, Moszek* (Polish); *Moises* (Portuguese); *Moisey, Mosya* (Russian); *Moises, Moshe, Mozes* (Yiddish)

MOSHE (MOH-she) Hebrew form of Moses, "saved (from the water)." An extremely popular Jewish name.

MOSI (MOH-see) Swahili: "first-born."

MOSWEN African: "light in color." From Botswana.

MOTEGA (moh-TEH-gah) Native American: "new arrow."

MUHAMMAD Arabic *hamida:* "the praised one." The Prophet Muhammad universalized this name. With its many variations, this is the most popular boys' name among Moslems and the most common boys' name in the world. A Moslem saying goes, "If you have a hundred sons, name them all Muhammad." Among the more than five hundred variations: *Ahmad, Ahmed, Amad, Amed, Hamdrem, Hamdun, Hamid, Hammad, Hammed,* *Humayd, Mahmud, Mahmoud, Mehemet, Mehmet, Mohamad, Mohamet, Mohammad, Mohammed, Muhammed*

MUNDAN (MOON-dahn) southern Rhodesia: "garden." *Munda* (African)

MURACO (moo-RAH-choh) Native American: "white moon."

> **"Any family in which there's a male named Muhammad will have an angel sent by God every morning and evening to pray for the household."**
>
> —AN ANCIENT MOSLEM BELIEF

MURPHY Irish or Scottish Gaelic: "sea warrior." A common last name in Ireland, now popular in this country as a first name for both boys and girls. *Murph, Murphie* (English)

MURRAY Scottish Gaelic: "mariner," "sea warrior," or "from the place by the sea," referring to a place in Scotland. *Murrey, Murry* (English); *Muirioch* (Irish)

MUSENDA (moo-SEND-ah) Baduma, Africa: "nightmare." Among the Baduma people of Africa, this name is given to a child when the mother has a vivid dream right before the baby's birth.

MYLES (mighlz) A form of Miles, "soldier," "warrior," or "merciful one."

MYRON Greek: "sweet-smelling oil" or "myrrh." This name contains hidden religious meaning, as myrrh was one gift the three wise men brought to the Christ child. *Miron* (English)

NABIL (nah-BEEL) Arabic: "noble."

NAGID (nah-GEED) Hebrew: "ruler" or "prince."

NAHELE (nah-HEH-le) Hawaiian: "forest" or "grove of trees."

NAHMA (NAH-mah) Native American: "the sturgeon."

NALREN (NAHL-ren) Athabascan, Carrier Indian: "he is thawed out."

NAM (nahm) Vietnamese: "child from the south."

NAMID (NAH-meed) Native American: "star dancer." This Indian name probably refers to the vain coyote, who wanted to dance with the stars. One night he asked a star to sail by a mountain and take him by the paw, which she did. The next night, impatient for the star's return, the coyote jumped off the mountain himself, thinking that if the star could fly, so could he. The legend says that he was "ten whole snowfalls in falling, and when he landed, he was squashed as flat as a willow mat."

NAMIR (nah-MEER) Hebrew: "leopard," connoting swiftness. Modern Israeli name.

NANDIN (nahn-deen) Hindi: "destroyer." One of the 1,008 names for the Hindu god Siva, the destroyer.

NAPIER (NAYP-ee-er) Spanish: "of the new city." *Neper* (Spanish)

NARAIN (nah-RAIN) Hindi: "the god Vishnu," another name for Vishnu, the Hindu god said to be the protector and sustainer of the world.

NARD Persian: "the game of chess."

NAREN (nahr-en) Sanskrit: "manly." A popular Hindu name from India.

NARESH (nah-resh) Sanskrit: "king" or "lord." A popular boys' name in India. The feminine form is Naresha.

NARONG (nah-rong) Thai: "battle."

NASSER (NAS-er, or Arabic NAHS-sehr) Arabic: "victorious." A favorite among Moslems, this name refers to one of the ninety-nine qualities of God listed in the Koran. *Nassor* (Swahili)

NATAL (nah-TAHL) Spanish form of Noel, "born on Christmas."

NATHAN Hebrew: "a gift." Now more popular than the longer Nathaniel. Also common in France, Italy, Norway, and Sweden. *Nat, Nate, Nathon, Natt, Natty* (English); *Natan* (Hungarian, Polish, Russian); *Nata, Natan* (Spanish)

NATHANIEL Hebrew: "given by God." *Nat, Nate, Nathan, Nathon, Natt, Natty* (English); *Nathanael* (French); *Nataniele* (Italian); *Natanael* (Spanish)

NAV (nahv) Hungarian *nev:* "name." Coined by the English Gypsies.

NAWAT (NAH-waht) Native American: "left hand."

NAYATI (nah-YAH-tee) Native American: "the wrestler."

NED A familiar form of names beginning with *"Ed-,"* such as Edgar, Edmund, and Edward. Now an independent name.

NEEL Hindu: "sapphire blue." Refers to a Hindu monkey god.

NEHRU (NAY-roo) Sanskrit *nahar:* "canal." The twentieth-century Indian prime minister Jawaharlal Nehru's family was so named because a canal passed by his family's ancestral estates.

NEIL Irish Gaelic: "a champion" or "a cloud." *Neal, Neale, Neill, Neils, Nels, Nial, Niels, Niles* (English); *Nilo* (Finnish); *Niall* (Irish); *Nil, Nilya* (Russian); *Nels, Niels, Nils* (Scandinavian); *Niall* (Scottish)

NELEK (NEL-ek) Polish pet form of Kornelek, "horn-colored" or "like a horn." The English equivalent is Cornel.

NELS A Scandinavian form of Neil, "champion."

NELSON Middle English: "the son of Neil ('a champion')." *Nealson, Nels, Nelsen, Nils, Nilsen, Nilson* (English)

Nicknames:
Insulting or Flattering?

★ ★ ★

Some nicknames are almost impossible to avoid. If your last name were Rhodes, for example, it would be almost impossible for your son to avoid the nickname Dusty. And if your surname were Waters, some wag at school would inevitably call him Muddy Waters. Though some psychologists insist an extremely insulting nickname like "Fatso" or "Stinky" can leave lasting psychological scars on a child, more recent research suggests this may not be so. In fact, a team of Oxford University researchers headed by Rom Harre found that in all cultures, having a nickname—even an insulting one—is better than having no nickname at all. The Oxford researchers concluded that being nicknamed at least entitles a child to *some* social attention, whereas a child with no nickname may be viewed as something of a nonperson.

How can you help your child avoid an unfortunate nickname? You might choose a "good" nickname for your child from the start. If you name your son Benjamin James and then call him "B. J." yourself, chances are his school chums won't name him "Benji" (after the famous dog). Likewise, when your baby is small, avoid cutesy-pie names he or she may later be saddled with. Studies have shown kids especially abhor nicknames like Goo-Goo, Honey-bunch, and Sweetie-pie.

NEN Egyptian: "the spirit of Nen." In Egyptian mythology, Nen personified the inert, motionless primeval waters and was sometimes pictured with a human body and a frog's head.

NERO Latin: "strong" or "stern." *Neron* (Bulgarian, French, Spanish); *Nerone* (Italian)

NESTOR (NES-ter) Greek: "one going or departing." In Greek mythology, Nestor was a long-lived ruler who helped the Greeks win the Trojan War with his wise counsel.

NETO (NEH-toh) Spanish pet form of Ernest, "earnest one."

NEVADA Spanish: "snowed upon" or "snowy." A contemporary coinage from the state of Nevada. Also for girls.

NEVAN, NEVIN (NEV-un) Irish Gaelic: "the saint's worshiper"; or Old German: "nephew." A given name in Ireland. *Nev, Nevins, Niven* (English)

NEVILLE (NEV-il) Old French: "from the new town." A contemporary American name borrowed from a common place-name in France. *Nevil, Nevile, Nevill* (English)

NEWLIN Old Welsh: "son of the new pool." Given to a child whose home is beside a pool. *Newlyn* (English)

NIALL (NEE-ul) One of the most popular names in Ireland, this is a Gaelic form of Neil, "a champion" or "a cloud." See Neil.

NIAN (NEE-ahn) Cambodian: "one who knows," implying a child who is intuitively wise. The more traditional Cambodian spelling is Nhean. *Neeean* (English)

NIBAW (NEE-baw) Native American: "I stand up."

NICABAR (nee-kah-BAHR) Spanish Gypsy: "to take away" or "to steal."

NICANOR (nee-kah-NOHR) Spanish form of Nicholas, "victorious army" or "victorious people."

NICHOLAS (NIK-oh-lahs) Greek: "victorious army" or "victorious people." *Claus, Cole, Nic, Nichol, Nick, Nickey, Nickolas, Nicky, Nicol, Nik, Nikki, Nikky* (English); *Nikita, Nikolas* (Bulgarian); *Nikula, Nikulas* (Czech); *Claus, Nicolaas* (Dutch); *Nikolai* (Estonian); *Colas, Colin, Nicolas, Nicole* (French); *Claus, Klaus, Nickolaus, Nikolaus* (German); *Nikolaos, Nikolos, Nikos* (Greek); *Micu, Miki, Miklos, Niki, Niklos* (Hungarian); *Cola, Niccolo, Nicola* (Italian); *Kola, Niklavs, Nikolais* (Latvian); *Nicolai* (Norwegian); *Mikolai, Milek* (Polish); *Nicolaio, Nicolau* (Portuguese); *Kalya, Kolya,*

Nikolai (Russian); *Nicanor,*
Nicolas (Spanish); *Niklas, Nils*
(Swedish)

NICK A congenial pet form of
Nicholas ("victorious army" or
"victorious people"), now used
independently. See Nicholas.

NIEN (NEE-en) Vietnamese: "a
year."

NIGAN (NEE-gahn) Native
American: "ahead."

NIGEL (NIGH-jel) Latin: "black"
or "dark." *Niguel* (Spanish)

NIKI Polish form of Dominick,
"belonging to God" or "born on
Sunday." Also the Greek form of
the girls' name Nicole, "victorious
army."

NILS A Scandinavian form of
Neil ("a champion") and a
Swedish form of Nicholas
("victorious army" or "victorious
people").

NIRVAN (neer-VAHN) Sanskrit:
literally, "a blowing out." A
spiritual name drawn from the
blissful state of Nirvana, when all
passions, desires, and illusions are
extinct and the soul is in perfect
peace.

NISSAN (NEE-sahn) Hebrew:
"flight."

NISSIM (NISS-im or nee-SEEM)
Hebrew: "sign" or "miracle."

NITIS (NEE-tes) Native American: "friend" or "good friend."
Netis (English)

NNAMDI (NAHM-dee) Nigerian:
"my father is still alive." Given in
Nigeria to a child thought to be
the reincarnation of his father.

NOAH Hebrew: "quiet peace"
or "rest." In the Bible, Noah was
chosen by God to build the Ark
so his family would survive the
flood. Worldwide the most
popular spelling of this name is
Noe, used in the Czech Republic,
France, Greece, Hungary, Ireland,
Italy, Romania, Spain, and many
other countries. *Noi* (Bulgarian);
Noach (Dutch); *Noak* (Norwegian, Swedish); *Noi, Noy*
(Russian); *Noel* (Spanish)

NODIN (NOH-din) Native
American: "the wind." *Knoton,*
Noton (English)

NOEL French: "born on
Christmas." Also a Spanish form
of Noah, "quiet peace" or "rest."
Nowell (English); *Natale* (Italian);
Natal (Spanish)

NOLAN Irish Gaelic: "noble and
famous."

NORMAN Old French: "a
northman" or "Norseman"; or Old
Norse: "Njord's brilliance." In
Norse mythology, Njord was the
god of mariners and the winds.
An old name that regained a
strong, "tough" image in the

1990s due to its association with United States general Norman Schwarzkopf. *Norm, Normie, Normy* (English)

NORRIS Old French: "one from the north," or "a nurse." *Norice, Noris, Norreys, Norrie, Norriss, Norry* (English)

NOWLES (nohlz) Middle English: "from the grassy slope in the forest." Name for a boy born under one of the earth signs of Capricorn, Taurus, or Virgo. *Knolls, Knowles* (English)

NOY Hebrew: "beauty." Originally from Israel.

NUMAIR (noo-MAIR) Arabic: "panther."

NUNCIO (NOON-see-oh) Latin: "messenger" or "announcer." A well-known Spanish name. *Nunzio* (Spanish)

NUREN (NOOR-en) Arabic: "light" or "illumination." A popular Arabic name. *Noor* (Arabic); *Nuru* (Swahili)

NURI (NOOR-ee) Hebrew: "fire." Used today in Israel as well as the United States. *Nur, Nuria, Nuriel* (English, Hebrew)

NUSAIR (noo-SAIR) Arabic pet form of *Nasr,* "vulture."

O

OCTAVIO (ohk-TAH-vee-oh, or Anglicized, awk-TAY-vee-oh) Latin: "eighth-born child." A favorite Spanish name, this was the name of several saints, including one who lived like a hermit in an elm tree. *Octavius, Octavus* (English); *Actavio, Octavianno, Octavino, Octavion, Octovio* (Spanish)

ODELL (oh-DEL) Middle English: "from the wooded hill"; or Scandinavian: "little and wealthy." *Dell, Ode, Odey, Odie, Ody* (English)

ODIN (OH-din) Old Norse: "the god Odin." Odin is the chief god in Norse mythology, source of all wisdom, patron of culture, and champion of heroes.

ODINAN (oh-dee-NAHN) Ochi, Ga, Africa: "fifteenth-born child."

ODION (o-dee-OHN) Benin, Nigeria: "first of twins."

ODISSAN (oh-DEES-sahn) Ochi, Ga, Africa: "thirteenth-born son."

ODON (OH-dohn) Contemporary Hungarian form of Edmond, "wealthy protector," or French form of Otto, "prosperous one." *Odi* (English)

Nigerian Holy Names

✱ ✱ ✱

Like all people around the globe, the Yoruba-speaking people of Nigeria frequently name their babies after gods or spiritual figures. Whereas Christians the world over are fond of the Apostle names Matthew, Mark, Luke, and John, and Moslems favor variations of the name Muhammad, Nigerian parents often name their babies after Ogun, their god of war. Examples are *Ogunkeye* ("Ogun has earned honor"); *Ogunsanwo* ("Ogun gives help"); and *Ogunsheye* ("Ogun has performed honorably"). Other Nigerian baby names referring to God are *Olufemi* ("God loves me"); *Olujimi* ("God gave me this"); *Olukayode* ("my Lord brings happiness"); *Olushegun* ("God is the victor"); and *Olushola* ("God has blessed me").

OGANO (oh-gah-noh) Japanese: "small deer field."

OGDEN Old English: "dweller in the oak valley." *Ogdan, Ogdon* (English)

OGUN (OH-gun) Yoruba, Africa: "god of war." In Yoruba legend, Ogun is the god of war and the son of the river and lake goddess.

OHANKO (oh-HAHN-koh) Native American: "reckless."

OHARA (oh-hah-rah) Japanese: "small field."

OHIN (oh-HEEN) Akan, Ghana: "chief."

OKEMOS (oh-keh-moss) Ojibwa (Native American): "a little chief."

OKO (oh-KOH) Yoruba, Africa: "the god Ogun."

OKON (oh-KOHN) Efik, Africa: "born at night."

OLAF Old Norse *anleifr:* "ancestral relic." A favorite in Norway, this was the name of five Norwegian kings. *Olin* (English); *Olafur* (Icelandic); *Olay* (Norwegian)

OLERY Old German: "ruler of all." A commonly used name in France.

OLES (OH-les) Polish form of Alexander, "helper and defender of mankind." See Alexander.

OLIN An English form of Olaf, "ancestral relic."

OLIVER Old Norse: "kind and affectionate"; or Old French: "an olive tree." *Oli, Olley, Olli, Ollie, Olly* (English); *Olivier* (French); *Oliviero* (Italian, Spanish)

OLIVIER (oh-LIV-ee-ay) A French form of Oliver ("an olive tree") made known worldwide by British actor Sir Laurence Olivier.

OLORUN (oh-loh-ROON) Yoruba, Africa: "belonging to the god Olorun." The supreme god of the Yoruba pantheon, Olorun was born from Olokun, the mighty ocean of the sky. This ancient deity is no longer worshiped, but the name remains.

OMAR Arabic: "first son," "most high," or "the Prophet's follower." *Omer* (English)

ONAN (oh-NAHN) Turkish: "prosperous." Also a Turkish surname.

ONANI (oh-NAH-nee) Ngoni, Malawi: "look!"

ONI (o-NEE or OH-nee) Yoruba, Nigeria: "one born in a sacred place"; or Benin, Nigeria: "the wanted one."

ORBAN (OHR-bahn) A Hungarian form of Urban, "one from the city." See Urban.

ORDANDO (ohr-DAHN-doh) Spanish form of Roland, "from the famous land." *Orlando* (German, Italian, Spanish)

OREN (OHR-en) Hebrew: "a pine tree or ash tree." *Oran, Orran, Orren* (English); *Orin, Orrin* (Hebrew)

ORLANDO (ohr-LAHN-doh) A favorite form of Roland ("from the famous land") used in Italy, Germany, and Spanish-speaking countries, as well as the United States. See Roland.

ORRIN (OHR-rin) Greek: "man of the mountains." Also a Hebrew variation of Oren, "a pine or ash tree." The dramatist Eugene O'Neill is believed to have coined the name Orin from the Greek name Orestes for use in his play *Mourning Becomes Elektra*. See Oren for other forms.

ORSON Latin: "little bear"; or Old English: "the spear man's son." *Sonnie, Sonny, Urson* (English)

ORUNJAN (oh-ROO-jahn) Yoruba, Africa: "god of the midday sun."

OSCAR Old English: "the spear of God." Famous Oscars include Broadway producer-lyricist Oscar Hammerstein II and writer Oscar Wilde.

OSGOOD Old English: "divinely good." *Ozzi, Ozzie, Ozzy* (English)

OSMOND Old English: "a divine protector." *Osman, Ozzi, Ozzie, Ozzy* (English); *Osmanek, Osmen* (Polish); *Osmundo* (Spanish)

OSSIAN (OH-see-un) Irish Gaelic: "a fawn or little deer." An Anglicized form of the traditional Irish name *Oisin. Ossin* (English)

OTADAN (oh-TAH-dahn) Native American: "plenty." *Tadan* (English)

OTTAH (oh-TAH) Urhobo, Africa: "thin one." Used by the people of Nigeria for a child who is thin at birth.

OTTO Old German: "prosperous one." Modern German form of an older name—*Odo*—which was introduced into England by the Normans and was used occasionally in England in the nineteenth century. Otto is now used in many countries, including the Czech Republic, Hungary, Romania, Russia, Sweden, and the United States. *Otik, Oto* (Czech); *Odon, Othon* (French); *Otho, Otfried, Ottocar,*

Ottomar (German); *Othon* (Greek); *Otello, Ottone* (Italian); *Audr, Odo* (Norwegian); *Onek, Otek, Oton, Otton, Tonek* (Polish); *Otilio, Otman, Oto, Oton, Tilo* (Spanish)

OURAY (oh-RAY) Native American: "the arrow." In astrology, the archer is the symbol of Sagittarius.

OWAIN (OH-wen) Old Welsh: "a lamb"; or Irish Gaelic: "young." Also a Welsh form of Eugene, "noble" or "born of good family." Popular in Wales, where a variation is Owen.

OWEN Form of Evan, "young warrior" or "young bowman." See Evan.

OXFORD Old English: "from the place where the oxen cross the river." *Ford* (English)

OZURU (oh-zoo-roo) Japanese: "large stork," the stork being a symbol of longevity.

P

PABLO (PAH-bloh) Spanish form of Paul, "little." See Paul.

PACO (PAH-koh) Native American: "bald eagle." Also a Spanish form of Francis or Frank.

To Each His Own

✳ ✳ ✳

Just before graduating from high school, Californian Peter John Eastman, Jr., legally changed his name to Trout Fishing in America, the title of Richard Brautigan's 1960s cult novel. "You're going to have endless problems and troubles in your life because of this name," the judge warned Trout at his official name-change hearing. Yet, at last report, his new name had only gotten Trout lots of attention, landing him stints on a national TV talk show and *Good Morning America*.

PADDY Contemporary American creation from Patrick, "noble one." Also an Irish form of Patrick.

PADRAIG (PAH-dreek) In Ireland, this is the most often used form of Patrick, "noble one." See Patrick for other variations in Ireland and around the world.

PAGE French: "young attendant." Increasingly used as a girls' name. *Padget, Padgett, Paget, Paige* (English)

PAKI (PAH-kee) South African: "witness."

PAL (pahl) English Gypsy: "brother." Also a form of Paul, "little."

PALANI (pah-LAH-nee) Hawaiian form of Francis, "free man" or "Frenchman."

PALLATON (PAL-ah-ton) Native American: "fighter." *Palladin, Pallaten* (English)

PALMER Old English: "a crusader" or "a pilgrim bearing palms."

PANCHO Spanish form of Francisco, which in turn is a form of Francis, "free man" or "Frenchman."

PARISH (PAIR-ish) Middle English: "one who lives in a parish," referring to an area under the care of a priest. *Parrish* (English)

PARKER Middle English: "protector (or keeper) of the park." *Park, Parke* (English)

PARLAN (PAHR-lun) Scottish form of Barth, "a farmer" or "son of the earth." See Barth.

PARNELL (par-NEL) Old French: "little Peter." In twelfth-century England, this was a feminine form of Peter until it came to mean a promiscuous woman and fell into disfavor. Enjoying a minor revival today as a boys' name. *Parnall, Parnel, Parrnell, Pernel, Pernell* (English)

PASCAL Latin: "pass over" or "born at Easter or Passover." Hebrew name for a child born during the Passover or Christian name for a baby born during the Easter season. *Pace, Pascual, Pasqual* (English); *Paco, Pascalo, Pasco, Pascualo, Pasqul, Pasquel* (Spanish)

PAT Native American: "fish." Also a short form of names beginning with *Pat,* especially a nickname for Patrick, "noble one." In astrology, fishes are the symbol of Pisces.

PATAMON (PAHT-ah-mahn, or Anglicized, PAT-a-mun) Native American: "raging."

PATRICK Latin: "noble one." The name honors St. Patrick, patron saint of Ireland, and is currently popular in Ireland and England as well as the United States. *Paddy, Pat* (English); *Patrice* (French); *Patricius, Patrizius* (German); *Paddy,*

Padhra, Padhraic, Padi, Padraic, Padraig, Paidin, Patraic, Patric, Paxton, Peyton (Irish); *Patrizio* (Italian); *Patek* (Polish); *Patricio* (Portuguese); *Padruig* (Scottish); *Patricio, Ticho* (Spanish)

PATRIN English Gypsy: "leaf trail." This name refers to a trail made by Gypsies from handfuls of leaves or grass thrown along the way to guide those behind.

PATTIN (PAHT-tin) English Gypsy: "a leaf," connoting fresh-ness. Also a form of the name Patton, "from the warrior's estate."

PATTON (PAT-ton) Old English: "from the warrior's estate." *Pat, Paten, Patin, Paton, Patten, Pattin* (English)

PATWIN (PAT-win) Native American: "man." According to Liwaito Indian legend, a great flood covered the Sacramento valley and destroyed all but one man. After an earthquake opened the Golden Gate and drained off the water, this man mated with a crow and repopulated the earth with Patwin, modern man.

PAUL Latin: "little." Often bestowed in honor of St. Paul. *Paulis, Pol* (English); *Pavel* (Bulgarian, Czech); *Poul* (Danish, Norwegian); *Pal, Pali, Palika* (Hungarian); *Pall* (Icelandic); *Pol* (Irish); *Paolo, Paulo* (Italian); *Pauls, Pavils* (Latvian); *Paulin, Pawel* (Polish); *Pasha, Pashka,*

Pavel, Pavlik, Pavlo, Pawl
(Russian); *Oalo, Pablo, Paulino,
Paulo* (Spanish); *Pal* (Swedish);
Pewlin (Welsh)

PAVEL Bulgarian, Czech, and
Russian form of Paul, "little."

PAXTON Old English: "from
the peaceful town." *Pax, Paxon*
(English)

PAYAT (PAY-aht) Native
American: "he is coming." *Pay,
Payatt* (English)

PAZ (pahz) Spanish: "peace."
Also used as a girls' name.

PEDRO (PAY-droh) Italian,
Portuguese, and Spanish form of
Peter, "rock" or "stone." See Peter.

PEPIN Old German: "persever-
ant one" or "one who petitions."
Pepi, Peppie, Peppy, Pippi
(English)

PERRY Old French: "little
Peter"; or Middle English: "a pear
tree."

PETER Latin: "rock" or "stone."
Introduced into England by the
Normans, Peter was associated
with the papacy in Rome and
was a great favorite until Henry
VIII broke with the pope in 1534.
For nearly three centuries the
name was an outcast, considered
rustic and old-fashioned. Peter
came into vogue again in the
early 1900s, with the sudden

enormous popularity of James M.
Barrie's 1904 play *Peter Pan*.
Pete, Petey, Petie (English); *Petr,
Piotr* (Bulgarian); *Piet, Pieter*
(Dutch); *Peet, Peeter* (Estonian);
Pierre, Pierrot (French); *Panos,
Petros, Takis* (Greek); *Ferris,
Peadar* (Irish); *Pedro, Pero, Piero,
Pietro* (Italian); *Petras, Petrelis,
Petrukas* (Lithuanian); *Peder,
Petter* (Norwegian); *Pictrus,
Pietrek, Piotr, Piotrek* (Polish);
Pedro (Portuguese); *Petar, Petru*
(Romanian); *Perka, Petinka,
Petr, Petro, Petruno, Petrusha,
Pyatr, Pyotr* (Russian); *Peadair*
(Scottish); *Pedrin, Pedro, Pequin,
Perequin, Perico, Petronio, Peyo,
Piti* (Spanish); *Per, Peter*
(Swedish)

PEYTON (PAY-ton) Old
English: "from the fighter's
estate." *Pate, Payton* (English)

LEGENDS & LORE

It's bad luck to have thirteen
letters in a name. Some say it's also
bad luck if a child's initials spell a
word (although others believe this
will bring wealth).

PEZI (PEH-zee) Sioux: "grass," connoting freshness.

PHIL Short form of Phillip, often used independently.

PHILLIP Greek *philippos:* "lover of horses." *Phil, Philip, Phill, Phillipp* (English); *Filip* (Bulgarian, Czech, Lithuanian, Norwegian, Romanian, Serbian, Swedish); *Philippe* (French); *Philipp* (German); *Phillipos* (Greek); *Fulop* (Hungarian); *Filip, Pilib* (Irish); *Filippo* (Italian); *Filips* (Latvian); *Fil, Filip, Filipek* (Polish); *Feeleep, Filip, Filipp, Filya* (Russian); *Felipe, Felipino, Filipo* (Spanish); *Fischel* (Yiddish)

PIAS (PEE-ahs) English Gypsy: "fun."

PIERCE (peers, to rhyme with "fierce") Old Anglo-French: "rock or stone." An early form of Peter used before the fifteenth century, Pierce has made a comeback as a strong-sounding contemporary name. Popularized by actor Pierce Brosnan. *Pearce, Piers, Pierse* (English)

PIERRE (pee-AIR) A French form of Peter, "rock" or "stone."

PIERRO (PEER-roh) Greek: "with flaming hair."

PILAR (pee-LAHR) Spanish: "pillar" or "fountain base." Refers to Mary, the mother of Jesus, pillar

of the Christian religion. Also a girls' name.

PILI (PEE-lee) Swahili: "second-born son."

PILLAN (pee-LAHN) Araucanian (Native American): "supreme essence." A major deity among the Araucanian Indians, Pillan is the god of thunder, lighting, and other natural phenomena. *Pilan* (English)

PIN (peen, or Anglicized, pin) Vietnamese: "faithful and true."

PLACIDO (PLAH-see-doh) Latin: "tranquil or calm." A popular Spanish name. *Placedo, Placijo, Plasido, Plasio* (Spanish)

PLATON Spanish: "broad-shouldered."

POL (pohl) Greek: "crown." A shortened form of Pollux, the name of an orange star, the brighter of two first-magnitude stars in the constellation Gemini, the Twins. Also a short modern form of Paul, "little."

PORTER Latin: "a porter" or "gatekeeper."

POV (pohv) English Gypsy: "earth."

POWA (POH-wah) Native American: "rich."

PRAMOD (prah-mod) Sanskrit: "joyous" or "delightful." A Hindu name from India.

PRAVIN (prah-VIN, or Anglicized, PRA-vin) Hindi: "skillful, capable."

PREM (prem) Sanskrit: "lovable or affectionate." A Hindu name from India.

PRENTICE Middle English: "an apprentice." *Prent, Prentise, Prentiss* (English)

PRESCOTT Old English: "from the priest's home." *Prescot, Scot, Scott, Scottie, Scotty* (English)

PRESTON Old English: "from the priest's estate."

PRICE Old Welsh: "the ardent one's son." *Pryce* (English)

PRYOR Latin: "head of the monastery." *Prior, Pry* (English)

PUTNAM Old English: "one who lives by the pond."

QUADE (kwaid) Irish Gaelic: "the son of Walter"; or German: "the cross, ill-tempered one." A

surname now used as a first name for boys. *Quaid, Quaide* (English)

QUENTON, QUINTIN (KWEN-tun, KWIN-tun) Latin: "fifth-born child." *Quent, Quentin, Quenton, Quint* (English); *Quito* (Spanish)

QUICO (KEE-ko) Short form of many Spanish names, including Enrique (a form of Henry, "ruler of a home or estate," "heir," or "a person of high rank") and Francisco (a form of Francis, "free man" or "Frenchman").

QUILLAN (KWIL-un) Irish Gaelic: "cub." Name for a child born under the sign of Leo, the lion.

QUINLIN Irish Gaelic: "strong one." *Quinley, Quinn* (English)

QUINN Irish Gaelic: "intelligent" or "wise." Also a form of Quinlin, Quintin, and other names starting with *Quin-*.

QUIRIN (KEER-in) "The quirin stone." Exact origin unknown. The quirin, also known as the traitor's stone, is a magic stone said to be found in the lapwing's nest. According to legend, when placed on a sleeping person's head, the stone causes him to reveal his innermost thoughts.

QUON (kwahn) Chinese: "bright one."

R

RABI (rah-bee) Arabic: "breeze," connoting the fragrance, for example, of new-mown hay or the earth after a spring rain.

RAD Short contemporary American name, originally a nickname for any name containing *"rad." Radd* (English)

RADBURN Old English: "one from the red stream." *Burnie, Burny, Rad, Radborn, Radborne, Radbourne, Radburne, Radd* (English)

RADCLIFF Old English: "from the red cliff." *Cliff, Racliffe, Rad, Radd* (English)

RADFORD Old English: "from the red ford." *Rad, Radd, Radferd* (English)

RADMAN (RAHD-mun) Slavic: "joy."

RADOMIL (RAHD-o-mill or RAHD-oh-meel) Slavic: "lover of peace." Popular in the Czech Republic and the Republic of Slovakia.

RAFAEL A favorite Spanish form of Raphael, "God cures" or "God has healed." Also used in Romania.

RAFE Short form of Raphael ("God cures" or "God has healed") or Rafferty ("rich and prosperous").

RAFFERTY Irish Gaelic: "rich and prosperous." *Rafe, Rafer, Raff, Raffer* (English)

RAFI (rah-FEE, or Anglicized, RAH-fee) Arabic: "exalting." The Prophet Muhammad objected to this name because it was too proud. Also a familiar form of Raphael ("God cures" or "God has healed").

RAGNAR (RAHG-nahr, or Anglicized, RAG-nahr) Old Norse: "mighty army." Popular in Norway and Sweden. *Ragnor, Rainer, Rainier, Rayner, Raynor* (English)

RAHIM (rah-HEEM) Arabic: "compassionate." A favorite Moslem name based on one of the ninety-nine qualities of God listed in the Koran.

RAHMAN (rah-MAHN) Arabic: "compassionate" or "merciful." Popular Moslem name referring to qualities of God listed in the Koran. A favorite combination is *Abdul Rahman* or *Abd-al-Rahman* ("servant of the Merciful One"), which is considered one of the two Moslem names God loves best. The other is *Abdul Allah* or *Abd-Allah* ("servant of God"). *Rahmet* (Turkish)

RAIDEN (RYE-den or RAY-den) Japanese: "thunder god." Raiden, the thunder god of Japanese legend, is usually depicted as a red demon carrying a drum and having two claws on each foot.

RAINER (RIGH-ner, or Anglicized, RAY-ner) A German form of Raynor, "powerful army." *Rain, Raine, Ray, Reiner* (English)

RAINI (RAY-nee) Native American: "the Creator." In Tupi-Guarani Indian legend, the god Raini created the world by placing it in the shape of a flat rock on another god's head.

RAINIER (RAIN-ee-er) English variation of the Scandinavian

Ragnar, "mighty army." See Ragnar.

RAJAB (rah-jahb) Arabic: "glorified." A child born in the seventh month of the Arabic calendar. *Raj* (English)

RALEIGH Old English: "from the deer meadow." *Lee, Leigh, Rally, Rawleigh, Rawley* (English)

RALPH Old English: "wolf counsel" or "swift wolf." *Rafe, Raff, Raffy, Ralf, Rolf, Rolph* (English); *Raoul* (French); *Raul* (German); *Raol, Raoul, Raul, Raulio, Rulo* (Spanish); *Rolf* (Swedish)

RAMADAN (rah-mah-DAHN) Swahili: "born in the month of

The Long and Short of Presidential Names

✷ ✷ ✷

If you want your child to grow up to be President of the United States, it helps to have a long last name. At least that's one tongue-in-cheek conclusion reported in *Psychology Today*. In 29 of the 38 Presidential elections in which the candidates of the two major parties had last names of different lengths and the popular vote was recorded, the candidate with the longest last name won. At last count, the candidate with the longest last name had won 76% of the time, making the "long-name rule" one of the most powerful predictors of U.S. Presidential elections.

Ramadan," the ninth month of the Moslem year, during which pious Moslems fast from sunrise to sunset.

RAMIRO (rah-MEE-roh) Spanish: "a great judge" or "son of Raymond, a wise protector." The name of a sixth-century Spanish martyr. *Ramirez* (Spanish)

RAMON (rah-MOHN) A favorite Spanish form of Raymond, "wise protector." See Raymond.

RAMSDEN Old English: "ram's valley." In astrology the ram symbolizes Aries.

RAMSEY Old English: "ram's island" or "the raven island." *Ramsay, Ramsy* (English)

RANCE African: "borrowed all"; also a short form of Ransom, "the son of the shield-wolf."

RAND A short form of Randall or Randolph. Means simply "shield."

RANDALL Contemporary American form of Randolph, "shield-wolf." This name, which has come back into vogue only recently, was quite popular in the Middle Ages. *Rand, Randal, Randel, Randell, Randi, Randie, Randy* (English)

RANDOLPH Old English *rand-wulf:* "shield-wolf." Came into vogue in the eighteenth century

as a then "modern" form of Randal. *Rand, Randal, Randall, Randel, Randell, Randi, Randie, Randy* (English)

RANDY A friendly short form of Randall or Randolph, now used as an independent name. *Randi, Randie* (English)

RANON (ra-NOHN) Hebrew: "to sing" or "to be joyous." Modern Israeli name. *Ranen* (Israeli)

RANSOM Old English: "the son of the shield." Originally a surname, now used as a given name. *Rance, Rand, Ransome, Ranson* (English)

RAPHAEL (rah-figh-ELL) Hebrew: "God cures" or "God has healed." Name of one of the seven archangels in the Bible. Used in many countries. *Raf, Rafe, Rafi* (English); *Rafael, Refael, Refi, Rephael* (Hebrew); *Rafaelle, Rafaello* (Italian); *Rafael* (Romanian); *Felio, Rafael, Rafaelo, Rafeal, Rafel, Raffael, Rafito, Raphel* (Spanish)

RAPIER Middle French: "strong as a sword." James T. Rapier (1839–1884) was a black congressman from Alabama who called for strong enforcement of the civil rights legislation passed during Reconstruction. Rapier urged blacks to unite and form labor unions and organized the first conclave of black working men.

Hidden Meanings
in Our Own Names

✳ ✳ ✳

People who don't understand Native American naming customs may smirk at names that translate into English as "sweaty blanket," "running bear," or "rain-in-the-face." But before feeling smug, they should investigate what their *own* names really mean. Here are some famous names from the past and present and their less-than-glittering hidden meanings:

Calvin Klein: "young, small, bald man."

Mary Tyler Moore: "bitter, dark-skinned roofer."

Cecil B. De Mille: "the miller's dim-sighted son."

Claude Debussy: "lame son from the thicket of brush."

Barbara Walters: "foreign army ruler."

Woody Allen: "fierce forest warden."

John Fitzgerald Kennedy: "big-headed gracious gift of God, bastard son of the ruler with a spear."

RASHAD (rah-SHAHD) Arabic: "one who follows the right path." A child with good judgment. *Rashad, Rasheed, Rashid* (English)

RASHAUN (rah-SHAWN) A contemporary American creation. A blend of the prefix *"Ra-"* + Shawn, a variation of John. *Rasean, Rashawn, Rayshawn* (English)

RASHID (rah-SHEED) Swahili *rashidi:* "one of good council"; or Arabic: "rightly guided." Popular modern American name. *Rasheed* (English)

RAUL (rah-OOL) Spanish and German form of Ralph, "wolf counsel" or "swift wolf." A favorite in many Spanish-speaking countries around the world, as

well as the United States. See
Ralph.

RAVI (RAH-vee) Hindi: "confer-
ring." One of the titles of the
Hindu sun god Surya, who is
considered one of the twelve
guardians of the months of the
year. In India the Ravi River is a
tributary of the sacred Indus.
Made well known by sitar player
and composer Ravi Shankar.

RAVIV (rah-VEEV) Hebrew:
"rain" or "dew."

RAY Short for Raymond ("wise
protector") and other names
beginning with *"Ray-."* See
Raymond.

RAYMOND Old German: "wise
protector." Used also in Russia
and France. *Ramond, Raimon,
Raimond, Ray, Raymund*
(English); *Rajmund* (Czech);
Raimund (German); *Reamonn,
Redmond* (Irish); *Raimondo*
(Italian); *Raimundo* (Portu-
guese); *Reimond* (Romanian);
*Monchi, Mondo, Mundo,
Raimondo, Raimundo, Ramon,
Ramone, Ramundo, Raymon,
Raymondo, Raymundo*
(Spanish)

RAYNOR Old German: "powerful army." *Rainer, Rayner* (English, German); *Ranier* (French)

RAZI (RAH-zee) Aramaic: "my
secret." Popular in Israel. *Raz,
Raziel* (English, Israeli)

REDFORD Scottish Gaelic: "from
Redford ('the red river crossing')."
A surname now used as a given
name; has a strong, handsome air,
possibly because of its association
with actor Robert Redford.

REDMOND (RED-mund)
Middle English: "red-haired,"
"protective counsel" or "from the
red-stone place." Also an Irish
form of Raymond, "wise protector." Farrah Fawcett and Ryan
O'Neal have a son named
Redmond. *Redmund* (English)

REECE (rees) Old Welsh:
"ardent" or "rash." *Rees, Reese,
Rhett* (English); *Rhys* (Welsh)

REED Old English: "red-haired"
or "ruddy-skinned." *Read, Reade,
Reid* (English)

REEVE (reev) Middle English:
"a bailiff." *Reave, Reeves* (English)

REGAN (RAY-gan or REE-gun)
Irish Gaelic: "little king." Rapidly
becoming a name used mostly for
girls. *Reagan, Reagen, Regen*
(English)

REGINALD (REJ-ih-nald) Old
English: "powerful counsel"; or
Old German: "ruler of judgment."
*Reg, Reggie, Reggy, Reynold,
Reynolds* (English); *Reinold*
(Dutch); *Reinald, Reinwald*
(German); *Regnauld, Renaud,
Renault, René* (French);
Raghnall (Irish); *Rinaldo*
(Italian); *Naldo, Reinaldo,*

Reinaldos, Renato, Reynaldo
(Spanish); *Reinhold* (Swedish)

REGIS (REE-jis) Latin: "regal."
Made well known in the 1990s
by TV host Regis Philbin.

REMINGTON Old English:
"from the estate of the raven
family." Made well known as a
first name by the 1980s TV series
Remington Steele. Rem, Remy
(English)

RENDOR (REN-dohr)
Hungarian: "policeman."

RENE (re-NAY) French:
"reborn." Also used for girls.

REUBEN (ROO-ben) A form of
Ruben ("behold a son"), used in
France, Germany, and Israel, as
well as Canada, Great Britain, and
the United States. See Ruben.

REX Latin: "king." One famous
Rex who helped make this name
familiar around the globe was
actor Rex Harrison. *Roi* (French);
Rey (Spanish)

REY (ray) Spanish form of Roy,
"king."

RHETT (ret) Possibly a form of
Reece, "ardent" or "rash." Usually
associated with Rhett Butler, the
rakish hero in Margaret Mitchell's
novel *Gone With the Wind.*

RICH Originally a nickname for
Richard and other names begin-

ning with *Rich-*. Now used
independently. See Richard.

RICHARD Old German:
"powerful ruler"; or Old English:
"brave and powerful." Commonly
used in many countries, not only
in the United States but also
Bulgaria, the Czech Republic,
England, France, and Germany.
*Dick, Dickie, Dicky, Ric, Ricard,
Rich, Richerd, Rick, Rickert,
Rickie, Ricky, Ritch, Ritchie,
Ritchy* (English); *Risa* (Czech);
Arri, Juku, Riki, Riks, Rolli
(Estonian); *Reku, Rikard*
(Finnish); *Richart* (German);
Rihardos (Greek); *Riczi, Rikard*
(Hungarian); *Riocard* (Irish);
*Ricardo, Riccardo, Ricciardo,
Ricco* (Italian); *Richards, Rihards*
(Latvian); *Risardas* (Lithuanian);
Rikard (Norwegian); *Rye, Rysio,
Ryszard* (Polish); *Ricardo*
(Portuguese); *Dic* (Romanian);
*Rostik, Rostislav, Rostya, Slava,
Slavik, Slavka* (Russian); *Ricardo,
Richi, Ricky, Rico, Riqui*
(Spanish); *Rickard* (Swedish)

RICKY Short for Richard
("powerful ruler") or Derek
("ruler of the people"). Now used
independently. See Richard.

RICO (REE-koh) Spanish short
form of Ricardo, "powerful ruler"
or "brave and powerful." See
Richard.

RIDA (REE-dah) Arabic: "favor,"
implying the child is in God's
favor.

Naming Customs ...

✳ ✳ ✳

If you worry your child might be given an unpleasant nickname in grade school, it may be comforting to remember that even adults nickname each other. When researchers interviewed men in a large shipbuilding yard in England, here's a sampling of the adult nicknames they found:

Balloon—for a man fond of the phrase, "Don't let me down."

Bungalow—given to a dull-witted man because popular opinion had it there was "nothing upstairs."

The Parson—for a guy who only worked on Sundays, when he could get paid double-time.

Sheriff—given to a foreman who, when he caught men idling, frequently said, "What's the holdup?"

—FROM NICKNAMES: *THEIR ORIGINS AND SOCIAL CONSEQUENCES*

RIDER Old English: "a knight or mounted warrior." Also "a guardian of the forest." *Ryder* (English)

RIKI Estonian form of Fredrick ("peaceful ruler") and Henry ("ruler of a home or estate," "heir," or "a person of high rank").

RILEY Irish Gaelic: "valiant" or "sportive." *Reilly, Reyly* (English)

RIMON (ri-MOHN) Hebrew: "pomegranate." A favorite in Israel.

RINGO Japanese: "apple." The apple is an Asian symbol of peace and this name has the connotation "peace be with you." Made well known by Beatles drummer Ringo Starr.

RIORDEN (REER-den) Irish Gaelic: "royal poet."

RIP Dutch: "ripe" or "full grown." Also a modern short form of Ripley. *Ripp* (English)

RIPLEY Old English: "from the shouter's meadow." *Lee, Rip, Ripp* (English)

ROALD (ROH-ahl, or Anglicized, ROH-ahld) Old Norse: "famous ruler." One of the most popular names in Norway, made well known worldwide by Norwegian polar explorer Roald Amundsen and children's book author Roald Dahl.

ROB Modern short form of Robert, "shining with fame." *Robb, Robbie, Robby* (English)

ROBERT Old English: "shining with fame." Extremely popular worldwide, Robert is used not only in the United States and other English-speaking countries, but also in Bulgaria, the Czech Republic, France, Germany, Hungary, Norway, Poland, and Sweden. The name was made world famous in the fourteenth century by Robert the Bruce, king of Scotland, and has been a favorite ever since. *Bert, Bob, Bobbi, Bobbie, Bobby, Rab, Rob, Robb, Robbi, Robbie, Robby, Robertson, Robin, Robinson, Rupert* (English); *Berty, Bobek, Rubert* (Czech); *Robers, Robin, Robinet* (French); *Rudbert, Ruprecht* (German); *Robi* (Hungarian); *Riobard* (Irish); *Roberto, Ruberto, Ruperto* (Italian); *Roberts* (Latvian); *Rosertas* (Lithuanian); *Robin* (Romanian); *Berto, Bobby, Rober, Roberto, Ruperto, Tito* (Spanish)

ROBI Hungarian nickname for Robert, "shining with fame." See Robert.

ROBIN Contemporary form of Robert, "shining with fame." Also a popular name for girls.

ROCKY Old English: "from the rock" or "rock-like," implying a

> **"I have long had a suspicion that an entire generation of Americans grew up feeling inferior to just the names of the guys on the radio.... There wasn't a Charlie Schmidlap in the lot."**
>
> —JEAN SHEPHERD, AUTHOR OF *IN GOD WE TRUST, ALL OTHERS PAY CASH*

child is firm and steadfast. Gaining popularity in the United States, possibly because of its association with the *Rocky* films starring Sylvester Stallone. *Rock, Rockie* (English)

ROD Contemporary short form of many names, including Roderick, Rodger, and Rodman. Now popular as an independent name. *Rodd* (English)

RODAS (ROH-dahs) Spanish name from the Greek meaning "place of roses."

RODERICK Old German: "famous ruler." *Broderick, Rick, Ricky, Rod, Roddie, Roddy, Roderic, Rodrich, Rodrick, Rory* (English); *Rodrique* (French); *Roderich* (German); *Rodrigo* (Hungarian, Italian, Portuguese); *Rory* (Irish); *Rurich, Rurik* (Russian); *Rurik* (Slavic); *Drigo, Gigo, Rodi, Rodito, Rodrego, Rodrigo, Ruy* (Spanish); *Rhydderch* (Welsh)

RODGER A variant spelling of Roger, "famous spear."

RODMAN Old English: "famous" or "heroic." *Rod, Rodd, Roddie, Roddy* (English)

RODNEY Old English: "from the famous man's island." *Rod, Rodd* (English)

RODRIGO (rah-DREE-goh) A form of Roderick ("famous ruler") used in Brazil, Hungary, Italy, Portugal, and Spanish-speaking countries. For other forms, see Roderick.

ROGER Old German: "famous spear." A favorite in England in the Middle Ages, Roger fell out of favor in the sixteenth century, when it was associated with any vagabond or rogue. Now it has once again become popular. *Rodge, Rodger, Rog, Rutger, Ruttger* (English): *Rudiger* (German); *Rogerios* (Hungarian); *Ruggero* (Italian); *Gerek* (Polish); *Rogelio, Rogerio* (Spanish)

ROHAN (ROH-hahn) Hindi: "sandalwood," connoting the fragrance of sweet incense.

ROHIN (roh-HEEN) Hindi: "on the upward path."

ROI Form of Roy ("king") used today in India.

ROLAND Old German: "from the famous land." *Orland, Rolland, Rollin, Rollins, Rollo, Rolly, Rowe, Rowland* (English); *Orlando, Rudland, Ruland* (German); *Lorand, Lorant* (Hungarian); *Orlando, Rolando* (Italian); *Rolek* (Polish); *Lando, Olo, Orlo, Rolando, Roldan, Rollon, Rolon* (Spanish); *Roland* (Welsh)

ROLF (rohlf) Old German: "swift wolf" or "wolf counsel." Currently popular in Norway and

Sweden. Also a form of Rudolf, "famous wolf." *Rolfe, Rolph* (Scandinavian)

ROLON (roh-LOHN, or Anglicized, RO-lun) Spanish name, originally from Old German, meaning "famous wolf."

ROMAIN (roh-MAIN) A French form of Roman.

ROMAN Latin: "one from Rome." *Romain* (French); *Romano* (Italian); *Romao* (Portuguese); *Mancho, Roman, Romano, Romarico* (Spanish)

ROMNEY Old Welsh: "curving river." Name possibly for a boy born under one of the water signs of Cancer, Pisces, or Scorpio.

RONALD Old Norse: "ruler of judgment" or "mighty power." Although this name has strong connotations of ambition and success, it has currently dropped out of the top boys' names in the United States, falling far below such relative newcomers as Ian, Shane, Travis, and Trevor. *Ron, Ronnie, Ronny* (English); *Raghnall* (Irish); *Rinhaldo* (Portuguese); *Naldo, Rainald, Ranaldo, Raynaldo, Reinaldo, Renaldo, Rey, Reynaldo* (Spanish)

RONAN (ROH-nahn) Irish Gaelic: "a little seal." A favorite in Ireland, borne by a dozen saints as well as a legendary king.

RONI (ROH-nee, or Anglicized, RAHN-ee) Hebrew: "my joy." Modern Israeli variations: *Ron* ("joy" or "song"); *Ronel* ("joy or song of God"); and *Ronli* ("joy or song is mine").

RONNIE A pet form of Ronald ("ruler of judgment" or "mighty power") also used independently. See Ronald.

RORY Irish Gaelic: "red king." Also a modern American and Irish form of Roderick, "famous ruler." *Ruari* (Irish); *Rurik* (Slavic)

ROSH (in Israel, rohsh; or Anglicized, rahsh, to rhyme with *Josh*) Hebrew: "a chief." A short Israeli name that's also easy for Americans to pronounce and remember.

ROSHAN (roh-SHAHN) Persian: "dawn" or "light."

ROSS Scottish Gaelic: "one from the peninsula or cape." *Rosse, Rossie, Rossy* (English)

ROTH Old German: "red-haired or ruddy-skinned." Popular in Germany.

ROURKE (rork) Irish Gaelic: "restless." A trendy, Irish-sounding name, probably a short form of the last name O'Rourke. *Rork, Rorke* (English)

ROWAN (ROH-un) Irish Gaelic: "little, red-haired child." Seldom

Naming Tip

★ ★ ★

When considering what to call your baby, here's another question to ponder: How *flexible* should the name be? The longer names tend to offer plenty of potential. Depending on the name that best suits her personality, for example, a baby girl named Margaret could later be dubbed Megan, Maggie, Marge, Greta, or even Peg.

Though boys' names generally have less flexibility, some are more fluid than others. Call a boy John, and his pals could nickname him John-John, Johnny, or Jack. Call him Cody or Drew, and that's probably the name he will be called.

By playing around with first- and middle-name combinations your options become greater. Christopher Jay could become Chris, C. J., or C. Jay. Jamie Lee could be tagged Jamie, Jaylee, or Jolly.

Clearly, there's no "right" or "wrong" way to go, and the best choice is simply the one you prefer. Some parents understandably want their child's name to be used exactly as they chose it; others prefer keeping their options open.

used in Ireland, but popular as an Irish-sounding name in the United States.

ROY French: "king." *Roi* (French); *Loe* (Hawaiian); *Rey* (Spanish)

ROYCE Old English: "the king's son." Has "rich" connotations, probably due to its association with the Rolls-Royce automobile.

ROYD Old Norse: "from the forest clearing."

ROZEN (ROH-zen) Hebrew: "a ruler." A name from Israel. *Rosen* (English)

RUBEN Hebrew: "behold a son." A name that's easily recognized in France, Russia and Spanish-speaking cultures, as well as all English-speaking regions of the world. The variation *Rubin* is used not only in the United States, but also Israel, Norway, Romania, Russia, and Sweden. *Reuben, Reuven, Rube, Rubin, Ruby* (English); *Reuben* (French, German, Hebrew); *Rouvin* (Greek); *Ruvim* (Russian)

RUDO (ROO-doh) Shona, Zimbabwe: "love."

RUDOLF, RUDOLPH Old German: "famous wolf." The Rudolf spelling, originally Slavic and Scandinavian, is presently surpassing the older Rudolph, although neither enjoys great popularity in the United States. *Dolf, Rodolph, Rolf, Rolfe, Rollo, Rolph, Rudie, Rudy* (English); *Ruda, Rudek, Rudolf* (Czech); *Rodolphe* (French); *Ralph, Rudolf, Rutz* (German); *Rezso, Rudi* (Hungarian); *Rodolfo, Rudolfo* (Italian); *Rudolfs* (Latvian); *Dodek, Rudek* (Polish); *Dolfe, Dolfi, Rude, Rudi* (Slavic); *Rolf, Rolfe, Rolph* (Scandinavian); *Rodolfo, Rolo, Rudi, Rudolfo, Rudy, Rufo* (Spanish)

RUDY (ROO-dee) This short, fun-loving form of Rudolph ("famous wolf") is now used more often than the longer name from which it comes.

RURIK Slavic form of Rory, "red king," or Roderick, "famous ruler."

RUSH Anglo-French: "red-haired" or "ruddy-skinned." Made well known in the United States by conservative commentator Rush Limbaugh. *Rushe* (English)

RUSS Short form of Russell, "red-haired." *Rus, Rust, Rustie, Rusty* (English)

RUSSELL Old French: "red-haired." *Rus, Russ, Russel, Rustie, Rustin, Rusty* (English); *Rosario* (Italian, Spanish)

RUSTON Old English: "from the home in the brushwood" or "from the red-haired one's estate." An English place-name and surname, now also used as a first name for boys. *Russ, Rusten, Rusti, Rustie, Rustin, Rusty* (English)

RYAN Irish Gaelic: "little king." A trendy, athletic-sounding name currently in the top ten on many American and Canadian name lists. Associated most recently with actor Ryan O'Neal and baseball player Nolan Ryan. *Ryon* (English)

RYKER (RIGH-ker) Origin unclear, but may come from Middle English: "son of Ricard" (an early form of Richard). Possibly coined as a first name from the character "Commander Riker" in *Star Trek: The Next Generation*.

S

SABURO (sah-boo-roh) Japanese: "third-born male."

SACHIO (sah-chee-oh) Japanese: "fortunate" or "well-born."

SAGE Latin: "wise and knowing" or "healthy and whole," referring to the herb. Also used for girls.

SAHALE (sah-HAH-leh) Native American: "above."

SAHEN (shah-hehn, or Anglicized, SAH-hen) Hindi: "falcon." Originally from India.

SAKIMA (sah-KEE-mah) Native American: "king."

SALAMAN (SHAH-lah-mun) A Hungarian form of Solomon, "peaceful."

SALIH (SAH-lee) Arabic: "good" or "right."

SALIM (sah-LEEM) Arabic: "peace." Swahili name. In Arabic countries, the name is also pronounced SAH-lim and means "safe." *Saleem* (English)

SALMALIN (sahl-mah-leen) Hindi: "taloned." Another name for Garuda, the half-giant, half-eagle vehicle of the Hindu god Vishnu. Garuda is pictured with the body, arms, and legs of a man; the talons, beak, and head of an eagle; and a white face, red beak, and golden body. According to legend, he was hatched from a monstrous egg five hundred years after his mother laid it.

SALOMON (sahl-oh-MOHN) Spanish form of Solomon, "peaceful."

SALVADOR (SAL-vah-dor) Latin: "the Savior." A Spanish name given to Jesus, the Savior.

SAM A short form of Samuel ("his name is God" or "God has heard") also used as an independent name. *Sammi, Sammie, Sammy* (English)

SAMIR (SAH-meer or sah-MEER) Arabic: "a friend to talk with in the evening."

SAMMON Arabic: "grocer."

SAMSON Hebrew: "like the sun." Used not only in the United States, Canada, and England, but also Bulgaria, France, Romania, and Russia. *Sam, Sammie, Sammy, Sampson, Sanson, Sansum* (English); *Sansone* (Italian); *Sansao* (Portuguese); *Sanson* (Spanish); *Simson* (Swedish)

SAMUEL Hebrew: "His name is God" or "God has heard." This ever-popular name from the Bible is used not only in this country and England, but also the Czech Republic, France, Germany, Hungary, Norway, Poland, Russia, Sweden, and most Spanish-speaking countries. A true whole-world name. *Sam, Sammel, Sammie, Sammy, Sem, Shem* (English); *Samuil* (Bulgarian); *Samko, Samo* (Czech); *Zamiel* (German); *Samouel* (Greek); *Sami, Samu* (Hungarian); *Somhairle* (Irish); *Samuele* (Italian); *Samaru* (Japanese); *Samuelis* (Lithuanian); *Samuil, Samvel* (Russian); *Sawyl* (Welsh); *Schmuel, Shem, Shemuel* (Yiddish)

SANDY Middle English: "sandy-haired." Also a short form of Alexander, "helper and defender of mankind." *Sandee, Sandi, Sandie* (English)

SANI (SAH-nee) Navajo: "old." A child wise beyond his years.

SANJIRO (sahn-jee-roh) Japanese: "admired" or "praised." *Sanji* (Japanese)

SANTIAGO (sahn-tee-AH-goh) Hebrew, Latin: "St. James." A Spanish name that's a blend of *San* ("saint") + *Diego* or *Iago* ("James"). Santiago is the patron saint of Spain. *Antiago, Chago, Chano, Sandiago, Sandiego, Saniago, Tago, Vego* (Spanish)

SANTO (SAHN-toh) Latin: "sacred" or "saintly." A favorite Italian and Spanish name. *Santos* (Spanish)

SARAD (sah-RAHD) Hindi: "born in autumn."

SARNGIN (SARN-geen) Hindi: "archer." Another name for the Hindu god Vishnu, the protector, who carries a bow called the *sarnga*. Name appropriate for a boy born under the sign of Sagittarius, the Archer.

> **❝ *Name your shoe while you're tying it, and you'll have good luck.* ❞**
>
> —AN OLD TENNESSEE LEGEND

SAROJIN (sah-ROH-jeen) Hindi: "lotuslike." The lotus is revered by Hindus because Buddha was born in the center of this sacred flower.

SAUL Hebrew: "asked for," implying the parents asked God to send them a child. In the Old Testament, Saul was the first king of Israel, and in the New Testament, Saul was the original Hebrew name of the apostle Paul. Most famous recent Saul is novelist Saul Bellow. *Sol, Solly* (English)

SAVAN (sah-vahn) Hindi: "the moon." Also refers to the fifth month of the Hindu calendar, and is often given to a boy born during India's rainy season.

SCOTT Old English: "a Scotsman." *Scot, Scotti, Scottie, Scotty* (English)

SEAMUS (SHAY-mus) A traditional Irish form of James, "the supplanter." See James. *Shamus, Shay, Shaymus* (English); *Seumas* (Irish)

SEAN (shawn) Irish form of John currently trendy in the United States. See John. *Shaun, Shawn* (English)

SEBASTIAN (se-BAS-tyun) Latin: "venerable" or "man from Sebastia," referring to a town in Asia Minor. This was the name of a third-century Christian martyr. *Bastion, Seb* (English); *Sebastien* (French); *Sebastiano* (Italian); *Bastiao, Sebastiao* (Portuguese); *Bastian, Bastien, Sebastian, Sebastiano, Sebo* (Spanish)

SEF Egyptian: "yesterday." Name of an Egyptian lion god. In astrology, the lion governs the sign of Leo.

SEGEL (SEE-gehl) Hebrew: "treasure." Derived from the Biblical phrase *Am Segulah*, "a treasured people," often used to refer to Israel.

SEIF (SE-eef) Arabic: "sword of religion."

SEIJI (SAY-jee) Japanese: "lawful and just."

SENON (SAY-nohn) Spanish: "living" or "given by Zeus."

SENWE (SEHN-weh) Baduma, Africa: "a dry stalk of grain." Given in Africa to a frail child who resembles a thin stalk.

SEPP German form of Joseph, "God will increase." See Joseph.

SERGEI (SIR-gay or sair-GAY) Latin: "an attendant" or "servant." A very popular boys' name in Russia. *Serge* (English); *Sergius* (German); *Sergio* (Italian); *Serg, Sergiusz, Sewek* (Polish); *Serge, Sergey, Sergeyka, Sergi, Sergie, Sergo, Sergunya, Serhiy, Serhiyko, Serzh, Syarhey* (Russian); *Cergio, Checho, Checo, Sergeo, Sergio, Serjio, Zergio* (Spanish)

SERGIO (SAIR-jee-oh) A favorite Italian and Spanish form of Sergei, "an attendant" or "servant."

SETH Hebrew: "appointed one." Seth was Adam's third son.

SEVILEN (se-vi-LEN, or Anglicized, SEV-i-len) Turkish: "beloved."

SHAD Origin uncertain, but may be Babylonian, "the sun god Aku's command." In the Bible, Shadrach was one of three devout Jewish men who were thrown into a raging furnace for refusing to worship the Babylonian god. Saved by God, they emerged from the furnace unharmed.

SHAFAN (SHAY-fahn) Hebrew: "a badger" or "a coney," referring to a type of rabbit. A familiar Biblical name in Israel. *Shayfan* (English); *Shaphan* (Hebrew)

SHAKA (SHAH-kah) Zulu, Africa: "first" or "founder." Shaka Zulu founded the Zulu empire. A powerful African name.

SHALOM (shah-LOHM) Hebrew: "peace." *Sholom* (English, Hebrew)

SHAMIR (SHAY-mer or shuh-MEER) Hebrew: "the shamir stone" or "flint-like," with a connotation of strength. A traditional Jewish name that refers to a hard precious stone believed to have been used in building Solomon's temple.

SHANAHAN Irish Gaelic: "wise one." A surname, now also used as a given name. *Shan, Shana, Shane* (English)

SHANDLER Contemporary spelling of Chandler, "candle-maker." *Sandy, Shandy* (English)

SHANDY Old English: "little and rambunctious." *Andy, Shan, Shandie* (English)

SHANE Contemporary Irish form of John, "gracious gift of God" or "God is gracious." *Shaine, Shayn, Shayne* (English)

SHANNON Irish Gaelic: "little, old, and wise." A name viewed as "Irish" in this country, but not actually used in Ireland. Now more frequently bestowed on girls than boys. *Shannan* (English)

SHANON Hebrew: "peaceful" or "secure." Common today in Israel. *Shanan* (English)

SHAQUILLE (shah-KEEL) Arabic: "well-developed" or "handsome." Recently popularized by appropriately named basketball star Shaquille O'Neal. *Shakeel, Shakil, Shaq, Shaquil* (English)

SHARIF (shah-REEF) Arabic: "honest." A popular name in Arabic countries, made well known worldwide by actor Omar Sharif.

SHARONE (shah-ROHN) Contemporary American creation, blending the female Sharon ("princess" or "a plain") + Tyrone ("sovereign one" or "from Owen's land").

SHAUN, SHAWN (shawn) Trendy American variations of John, "gracious gift of God" or "God is gracious." See John and Sean. *Shaughn, Shawn, Shonn* (English)

SHAW Middle English: "dweller near the wood or grove"; or Old Gaelic: "a wolf." A traditional Scottish name.

SHAWNEL (shaw-NEL) Contemporary American name developed by combining Shawn (a form of John, "gracious gift of God" or "God is gracious") with the suffix "*-el.*" Also used for girls. *Shaunel, Shaunell, Shaunelle, Shawnell, Shawnelle* (English)

> **"** *I have said everything when I have named the man.* **"**
>
> —PLINY THE YOUNGER

SHAY A pet form of the Irish Seamus, which in turn is a form of James, "the supplanter."

SHEA (shay) Irish Gaelic: "majestic" or "learned."

SHEEHAN Irish Gaelic: "little, peaceful one." A surname, now also used as a given name.

SHELBY Old English: "from the village where the willows grew," referring to Shelby in Yorkshire, England. *Shel, Shelbey, Shelbi, Shelbie* (English)

SHELDON Old English: "from the ledge-hill," possibly referring to a flat-topped hill. A place-name in England. *Shel, Shelden, Shelley, Shelly, Shelton* (English)

SHEM Yiddish: "name." A short form of the Yiddish Shemuel, "His name is God" or "God has heard." See Samuel.

SHEN Egyptian: "sacred amulet"; or Chinese: "deeply spiritual." This magical name refers to an Egyptian amulet that symbolized eternal life.

SHERBORN Old English: "from the clear, pure brook." An astrological and ecological water name. *Sherborne, Sherburn, Sherburne* (English)

SHERIDAN (SHAIR-i-dun) Irish Gaelic: from two different sources, this paradoxical name can mean either "peaceful" or "wild man." Once exclusively a boys' name, now also bestowed on girls. *Sheridon* (English)

SHERMAN Old English: "wool-cutter." An occupational name in England that originally referred to a shearer of cloth. *Sherm, Shermann* (English)

SHEVI (SHEV-ee, to rhyme with *Chevy*) Hebrew: "return." A name originally from Israel.

SHING (sheeng) Chinese: "victorious."

SHIRO (shee-roh) Japanese: "fourth-born son."

SHODA (shoh-dah) Japanese: "a level field."

SIDNEY Old French: "from the city of St. Denis, France." Spelled Sydney, this name is now more frequently used for girls than boys. *Cid, Cyd, Cydney, Si, Sid, Sidon, Syd, Sydney, Sydny* (English); *Sidonio* (Spanish)

SIGFRID Old German: "peaceful" or "victorious." Especially popular in Germany. *Siegfried, Sig, Sigfried, Singefrid* (English); *Siffre, Sigfroi* (French); *Seifert, Seifried, Siegfried* (German); *Szigfrid, Zigfrid* (Hungarian); *Sigefriedo* (Italian); *Zigfrids* (Latvian); *Sigvard, Siurt* (Norwegian); *Zygfryd, Zygi* (Polish); *Fredo, Siguefredo* (Portuguese); *Zigfrids* (Russian); *Sigfrido, Sigifredo* (Spanish)

SIGURD Old Norse: "victorious guardian." Sigurd was a major hero in Norse mythology, and the name is still a favorite in Scandinavian countries.

SILVAIN (sil-VAYN) Latin: "from the forest." Also used in France. *Silvanus, Sylvain, Sylvester* (English)

SIMEN (SEE-min, but sure to be Anglicized in the U.S. to SIGH-men) English Gypsy: "alike," "equal," or "it is we." The name

implies a resemblance between the newborn baby and his parents.

SIMON Hebrew: "to hear" or "to be heard." *Si, Simeon, Symon* (English); *Samein* (Arabic); *Simeon, Simion* (French); *Sim, Simeon, Simmy* (German); *Semon* (Greek); *Simone* (Italian); *Simao* (Portuguese); *Simion* (Romanian); *Simeon* (Russian); *Sim* (Scottish); *Shimon* (Yiddish)

SINCLAIR (sin-CLAIR) Old French: "from the town of St. Clair" in Normandy, France.

SIVAN (SIGH-vahn) Hebrew: "born in the ninth month," referring to the ninth month of the Jewish calendar, corresponding in astrology to Gemini, the Twins.

SKELLY Irish Gaelic: "a storyteller." *Skelley, Skellie* (English)

SKIP Old Norse: "ship master." *Skipp, Skipper, Skippie, Skippy* (English)

SKYLER (SKY-ler) Dutch: "a schoolmaster." Currently trendy. *Skylar, Skylor* (English)

SLADE Old English: "child from the valley." *Slaid, Slayde* (English)

SLANE Czech: "salty."

SLAVIK (SLAH-vik) Russian pet form of Stanislav, "glorious position." See Stanislav.

SLAVIN (SLAH-vin) Irish Gaelic: "mountaineer." *Slaven, Slevin* (English); *Sleibhin* (Irish)

SLOAN (slohn) Irish Gaelic: "a warrior or fighter." *Sloane* (English)

SOFIAN (SO-fee-ahn) Arabic: "devoted."

SOL Latin: "the sun" or "child of the sun." Name given for a boy born under Leo, the lion, which is ruled by the sun. Also short for Solomon, "peaceful."

SOLOMON Hebrew: "peaceful." *Selim, Sol, Solaman, Sollie, Solly, Solom, Soloman* (English); *Salamun* (Czech); *Lasimonne, Salaun, Salomon* (French); *Salomo* (German, Swedish); *Salaman, Salamon* (Hungarian); *Salomone* (Italian); *Salomonas* (Lithuanian); *Salomon* (Norwegian, Spanish); *Salamen* (Polish); *Shelomoh, Shlomo* (Yiddish)

SONGAN (SOHN-gahn, or Anglicized, SAHN-jun) Native American: "strong."

SONNY Middle English: "little son." Also a short form of names containing the syllable *"son."* Made well known in the late twentieth century as a given name by the late singer-turned-politician Sonny Bono. *Sonni, Sonnie, Sunny* (English)

SOREN (SOHR-en) Latin: "strict or stern." *Soran, Sorin, Sorran, Sorren, Sorrin* (English)

SORLEY (SOHR-lee) Irish Gaelic: "a summer sailor." A traditional name in Ireland, especially if a child has the last name MacDonnell or O'Gormley. *Somhairle* (Irish)

> **"There was a boy called Eustace Clarence Scrubb, and he almost deserved it."**
>
> —C. S. LEWIS, *THE VOYAGE OF THE DAWN TREADER*

SOVANN (so-ven, or Anglicized, so-VAHN) Cambodian: "golden one," implying a child is as precious as gold.

SPENCER Middle English: "dispenser of provisions in a household," possibly referring to a steward or butler. *Spence* (English)

STALLONE (stah-LOHN) Middle English: "a stallion." Use as a first name may come from its association with actor Sylvester Stallone.

STAN A short form of many boys' names containing the syllable *"stan,"* now bestowed as an independent name. Associated in many people's minds with baseball legend Stan "the Man" Musial.

STANCIO (STAHN-see-o) Spanish form of Constantine, "firm" or "constant."

STANE Serbian diminutive of Stanislav, "glorious position."

STANFORD Old English: "from the stony ford." Has a distinguished, educated ring to it, possibly because of its association with Stanford University. *Stamford, Standford* (English)

STANISLAV (STAHN-ih-slav) Slavic: "glorious position." Popular in the Czech Republic, Russia, and the Ukraine. *Stan, Stanislas, Stanislus* (English); *Stana, Stando, Stano* (Czech); *Stanislas* (French); *Stanislau* (German); *Stanislaw, Stasiek, Stasio* (Polish); *Stanislao* (Portuguese); *Slava, Slavik, Slavka, Stas, Stashko, Staska* (Russian); *Stane* (Serbian); *Estanislao, Lao, Tano, Tanix, Tilo* (Spanish)

STANLEY Old English: "from the stony meadow or clearing." *Stan, Stanleigh, Stanly* (English)

STEELE Sanskrit: "he resists"; or Middle English: "hard as steel." *Steel* (English)

STEPHAN, STEVEN Greek *stephanos:* "crowned." Brought into usage worldwide by St. Stephen, the first Christian martyr. A generally popular name connoting self-confidence, friendly good cheer, and success. *Stef, Steffen, Steph, Steve, Stevie, Stevy* (English); *Stefan* (Bulgarian, Czech, Polish, Swedish); *Tapani, Teppo* (Finnish); *Etienne, Tiennot* (French); *Stefan, Steffel* (German); *Stamos, Stavros, Stefanos, Stefos, Stephanos* (Greek); *Isti, Istvan* (Hungarian); *Stefano* (Italian); *Stefans* (Latvian); *Steffen* (Norwegian); *Estevao* (Portuguese); *Stefan, Stenya, Stepan, Stepanya, Stepka* (Russian); *Astevan, Este, Esteban, Esteben, Estefan, Estefon, Estevan, Estiban, Estifa, Estovan, Istevan, Stevan, Teb* (Spanish); *Steffan* (Welsh)

STERLING (STIR-ling) Old English: "a starling," referring to a type of bird. The more contemporary connotation is "precious as sterling silver." *Stirling* (English)

STEVE Nickname for Steven ("crowned") frequently bestowed as an independent given name. See Stephan.

STEWART, STUART Old English: "steward" or "keeper of the pen." The name later came to mean "manager of a household." A favorite Scottish name, borne by the Scottish royal family. *Stew, Stu* (English)

STIGGUR (STEEG-gur) English Gypsy: "gate."

STODDARD (STAHD-erd) Old English: "caretaker of the horses or oxen." *Stodd, Stoddart* (English)

STOFFEL A German form of Christopher, "Christ-bearer."

SUDI (SOO-dee) Swahili: "luck." A favorite in East Africa.

SULLIVAN Irish Gaelic: "black-eyed" or "hawkeyed." *Sullavan, Sullevan, Sullie, Sully* (English)

SULTAN Swahili: "ruler."

SUTTON Old English: "from the southern homestead or village."

SVEN Scandinavian: "youth." One of the most popular names in Norway, in part because of the Scandinavian trend toward choosing more Norse-sounding names. *Svend* (Danish)

SYLVESTER Latin: "from the sylvan forest." Associated in many people's minds with actor Sylvestor Stallone, but also with the cartoon character Sylvester the cat. *Sly* (English); *Silvester* (French); *Silvestio* (Italian); *Silvestre, Silvestro* (Spanish)

T

TAB Old German *tabbert:* "brilliant one among the people"; or Middle English: "drummer."

TABIB (tah-BIB) Turkish: "doctor" or "physician."

TABOR (TAH-bor) "from the camp" or "from the fortified encampment." Used in Hungary and Turkey.

TAD Old Welsh: "father." Also a form of Thad, "praiser" or "courageous and stouthearted." See Thad. *Tadd* (English)

TADASHI (tah-dah-shee) Japanese: "faithful servant."

TADEO (TAHD-ay-oh) Spanish form of Thad, "praiser" or "courageous and stouthearted." See Thad. *Tadd* (English)

TADI (TAH-dee) Omaha (Native American): "wind." The feminine form of this name is Tadewi.

TADZI (TAHD-zee) Athabascan, Carrier Indian: "the loon." A name from the Carrier Indians of Canada.

TAHIR (TAH-heer) Arabic: "pure." A popular Moslem name used in Egypt, India, Jordan, Saudi Arabia, and Turkey, as well as the United States.

TAI (tigh) Vietnamese: "talented one."

TAIT Scandinavian: "cheerful." *Taite, Tate* (English)

TAIZO (tah-ee-zo) Japanese: "third-born son."

TAJ (tahzh) Hindi: "crowned." *Tahj* (Hindi)

TAKEO (tah-kay-oh) Japanese: "strong as bamboo."

TAKESHI (tah-keh-shee) Japanese: "bamboo" or "unbending one."

TAKIS (TAH-kis) Contemporary Greek form of Peter, "rock" or "stone."

TAL (tahl) Hebrew: "dew" or "rain." Used in Israel for both boys and girls. Also short form for names starting with *"Tal-."*

TALBOT Middle English: "woodcutter"; or Old German-French: "valley-bright." *Tal, Talbert, Tallie, Tally* (English)

TALIB (TAH-leeb) Arabic: "seeker." A child who seeks after truth.

TALLI (TAHL-lee) Lenape, Native American: "the leader Talli." In Lenape Indian lore, Talli led the tribe after the great flood to the Snake Land, where they rebuilt civilization.

TALMAN (TAHL-mahn) Aramaic: "to injure" or "to oppress." *Tal, Tallie, Tally, Talmon* (English)

TALOR (TAY-lor) Hebrew: "dew of the morning." Popular in Israel. *Tal* (Israeli)

TALVRIN (TAL-vrin) Old Welsh: "high hill." A modern American spelling of the Welsh name *Tal, Talfryn* (English)

TAM (tahm) Vietnamese: "eighth-born child."

TAMAN (TAH-mahn) Serbo-Croatian: "dark" or "black."

TAMAS (TAH-mahsh) Hungarian form of Thomas, "a twin." See Thomas.

TAN (tahn) Vietnamese: "fresh and new."

TANEK Polish name originally from Greek: "immortal." *Arius* (German); *Atanazy, Atek* (Polish); *Afon, Afonya, Fonya, Opanas, Panas, Tanas* (Russian)

TANI (tah-nee) Japanese: "valley." Also used as a girls' name.

TANJIRO (tahn-jee-roh) Japanese: "precious second son."

TANNER Old English: "a tanner or leather worker." *Tan, Tann, Tanney, Tannie, Tanny* (English)

TANO (TAH-noh) Ghana, Africa: "the river Tano." Many names in Ghana are taken from nature. *Tanno* (Ghanaian)

TARIQ (tah-REEK) Arabic: "one who knocks at the door." *Tareek, Tarick, Tarik* (English)

TARO (tar-ro) Japanese: "first-born male." Loosely translated, Taro means "big boy."

TARUN (tah-roon) Sanskrit: "youthful one."

TAS English Gypsy: "a bird's nest."

TATE Native American: "windy" or "a great talker"; or Middle English: "cheerful one." *Tait, Taite, Tayte* (English)

TAUNO (TAH-noh) Contemporary Finnish form of Donald, "world ruler."

TAVAS (TAV-ahs) Hebrew: "peacock." Also a Lithuanian form of Anthony, "inestimable" or "priceless."

TAVI (TAHV-ee) Aramaic: "good." In Israel, this is also a pet form of David, "beloved."

TAVIS (TA-vis) Scottish form of Thomas, "a twin." See Thomas.

TAVISH Another Scottish form of Thomas. *Tevis, Tevish* (English)

TAVOR (TAY-vor) Aramaic: "misfortune." A familiar Israeli name taken from the name of a mountain in that country. *Tabor* (Israeli)

TAWNO English Gypsy: "small" or "tiny." The feminine equivalent is Tawnie.

TAYIB (tah-YEEB) Arabic: "good" or "delicate." Common in India.

TAYLOR Middle English: "a tailor." This name is also now given to girls. *Tayler, Taylour* (English)

TAYMUS Contemporary short form of Artemus, "belonging to Artemis, goddess of the hunt."

TEAGUE (teeg) Irish Gaelic: "a poet" or "philosopher." Some forms of this name are also gaining popularity for girls. *Teagan, Tegan* (English): *Teige, Teigue* (Irish); *Tadhg, Taogh* (Scottish)

TEB A pet form of Estephan, a Spanish form of Stephan ("crowned").

TED A short form of Theodore ("God's gift") and names beginning with *"Ted-"* or *"Ed-."* *Tedd, Teddie, Teddy* (English)

TEGER (TAY-ger) A contemporary American creation, probably created from Teague ("a poet" or "philosopher"). *Tayger, Teiger* (English)

TELEK (TEL-ek) Polish: "iron cutter."

TELEM (TEH-lem) Hebrew: "ford near a cliff" or "a furrow." The English equivalent is Clifford.

TEM English Gypsy: "country"; or Egyptian: "the Creator god Tem." In ancient Egyptian mythology, Tem was the oldest of the gods and the Creator who lived when "not was sky, not was earth, not were men, not were born the gods, not was death." He dwelled in the celestial waters and thought of the creation of the world. When Tem's ideas were spoken aloud, the world came into being.

TEMAN (TAY-mun) Hebrew: "right side," referring to the south. A modern Israeli name.

TERRIL Old English: "the thunder ruler." English variation of the Old Norse name Thor ("Thunder"). *Terel, Teril, Terrell, Terrie, Terrill, Terry, Teryl, Tirrel, Tyrrell* (English)

TERYL (TAIR-el) Contemporary American creation of uncertain origin; probably a variation of Terril, "the thunder ruler," referring to the Norse god Thor. See Terril.

TESHER (TEH-sher) Hebrew: "a gift." This name comes originally from Israel.

TEVA (TAY-vah) Hebrew: "nature."

TEVIN (TEV-in) Contemporary American coinage, probably a rhyming variation of *Kevin*. Made well known by Tevin Campbell. *Tevan, Teven, Tevon, Tevvan, Tevvin, Tevvon* (English)

THAD Latin: "praiser"; or Greek: "courageous and stouthearted." Contemporary short form of the older name Thaddeus, one of Christ's twelve apostles. Many scholars believe that Thaddeus was also known as St. Jude. *Tad, Tadd, Taddy, Thadd, Thaddy* (English); *Tadeas, Tades* (Czech); *Thadee* (French); *Thaddaus* (German); *Tade* (Hungarian); *Taddeo, Thaddeo* (Italian); *Tadek, Tadzio* (Polish); *Faddei, Fadey, Tadey* (Russian); *Tadeo* (Spanish)

THAI (tigh) Vietnamese: "multiple" or "many."

THANE Old English: "attendant warrior" or "follower." *Thain, Thaine, Thayne* (English)

THANOS (THAN-ohs) Contemporary Greek form of Arthur, "bear man" or "noble one."

THEODORE Greek: "God's gift." Several saints have borne this name. *Ted, Tedd, Teddie, Teddy, Theo, Theodor, Tudor* (English); *Feodor* (Bulgarian); *Bohdan, Fedor, Tedik, Teodor, Teodus* (Czech); *Tewdor, Theodor*

(German); *Tivadar, Todor*
(Hungarian); *Teodoro* (Italian);
*Dorek, Fedor, Teodor, Teodorek,
Teos, Todor, Tolek* (Polish); *Fedar,
Fedinka, Fedir, Fedor, Fedya,
Feodor, Feodore, Teodor, Todor,
Todos* (Russian); *Teodomiro,
Teodoro* (Spanish); *Todor*
(Ukrainian); *Tewdwr* (Welsh)

THEODORIC Old German
theuda-ricja: "ruler of the people." In the thirteenth century the
most common form of this name
was Terry, which is again popular
today. *Derek, Derk, Derrick, Ric,
Rick, Ricky, Ted, Teddie, Teddy,
Terrie, Terry* (English)

THERON (THAIR-un) Greek: "a
hunter." Possible name for a boy
born under Sagittarius, the
archer.

THOMAS Greek: "a twin." With
the spelling *Tomas,* this name is
used in many countries, including
Canada, the Czech Republic,
England, Ireland, Lithuania, Nor-
way, Portugal, Russia, Sweden, and
Spanish-speaking countries. It
owes its worldwide popularity to
St. Thomas. *Tam, Tameas,
Tammany, Tammen, Tammy,
Thom, Tom, Tomm, Tommie,
Tommy, Massey* (English);
Toomas (Estonian); *Tuomas,
Tuomo* (Finnish); *Thumas*
(French); *Thoma* (German);
Tamas, Tomi (Hungarian);
Tomasso, Masaccio (Italian);
Tomelis (Lithuanian); *Tomcio,*

Tomek, Tomislaw, Slawek
(Polish); *Tomas, Tome* (Portu-
guese); *Foma, Fomka* (Russian);
Tavis, Tavish, Tevis, Tevish
(Scottish); *Chumo* (Spanish);
Tomos (Welsh)

THOR Old Norse: "thunder."
From the Old Norse thunder god
Thor, this is one of the most
popular names in Denmark. *Tor*
(English, Norwegian)

THORNTON Old English:
"dweller at the thorny estate."
Made well known worldwide by
American author Thornton
Wilder. *Thorn, Thorne* (English)

THORPE Old English: "dweller
in the village." *Thorp* (English)

THU (too) Vietnamese: "born in
autumn."

TIEN (ting, or Anglicized,
tee-EN) Vietnamese: "the first
one."

TIET (tayt) Vietnamese:
"festival" or "season."

TILDEN Old English: "from the
valley of the good, liberal one."

TILFORD Old English: "from
the ford belonging to the good,
liberal one."

TILTON Old English: "from the
good, liberal one's estate." *Tiltan,
Tilten, Tiltin* (English)

TIMIN (tee-MEEN) Arabic *tinnin:* "sea serpent." In Hindu mythology, Timin is a huge fish. Even bigger is Timin-gila, "swallower of Timin," and bigger still is Timin-gila-gila, who swallows Timin-gila. The sea monster is the Hindu symbol for the lunar month corresponding to our astrological sign Capricorn.

TIMOTHY Greek *timotheos:* "honoring God." The apostle St. Timothy made this name popular in many forms around the world. *Tim, Timkin, Timmie, Timmy, Timon* (English); *Timotei* (Bulgarian); *Timo* (Finnish); *Timothe* (French); *Timotheus* (German); *Timotheos* (Greek); *Timot* (Hungarian); *Tiomoid* (Irish);

Scandinavian Mythology Names

✳ ✳ ✳

Old Norse mythology is the source for many contemporary Scandinavian names. Such names as Siegfried (or Sigvard), Sigmund, and Sigurd are drawn from medieval folktales. Thor, the Old Norse god of thunder, is also the source of many Scandinavian names. Among them are: *Thorbjörn* ("Thor's bear" or "thunder bear"); *Thorleif* ("Thor's beloved"); and *Thorvald* ("thunder ruler"). Many English first and last names secretly commemorate Thor as well, including *Thorald* ("Thor-ruler" or "thunder ruler"); *Thorbert* ("Thor's brilliance"); *Thorburn* ("Thor's bear" or "thunder bear"); *Thorley* ("Thor's meadow"); *Thormond* ("Thor's protection"); *Thurlow* ("from Thor's hill"); and *Thurston* ("Thor's stone or jewel"). As mankind's benevolent friend and protector, Thor is represented as a god of fabulous strength who slays giant demons with a thunderbolt and rides in a goat-drawn chariot, the rolling wheels of which sound like thunder. The English *Thursday,* a day-of-the-week name sometimes given to girls, comes originally from "Thor's day."

Timoteo (Italian, Portuguese, Spanish); *Timoteus* (Norwegian, Swedish); *Tymek, Tymon* (Polish); *Tima, Timka, Timofei, Timofey, Timok, Tisha, Tishka* (Russian)

TIMUR (tee-MOOR) Hebrew: "tall" or "stately."

TINO (TEE-no) Spanish nickname for Augustino, "the exalted one's son."

TITO (TEE-toh) Spanish and Italian form of Titus, "of the giants."

TITUS Greek: "of the giants." In Greek myth the giant Titus was slain by Apollo. Used in Bulgaria and Canada, as well as England, Germany, and the United States. *Tite* (French); *Titos* (Greek); *Tito* (Italian, Spanish); *Titek, Tytus* (Polish)

TIVON (TY-von) Hebrew: "naturalist" or "lover of nature."

TOBAL (toh-BAL) Spanish pet form of Christobal, which in turn is a Spanish form of Christopher, "Christ-bearer." See Christopher.

TOBBAR (TOH-bar) English Gypsy: "road." *Boro tobbar killipin* is the Gypsy term for high toby, or highway robbery.

TOBY Diminutive of the Hebrew Tobias, "God is my good."

A favorite nickname used as a given name, particularly in Ireland. *Tobey, Tobie* (English)

TODD North English: "a fox." Popular modern American name. *Tod* (English)

TODOR (TOH-dor) Used in Hungary, Poland, Russia, and the Ukraine, Todor is a form of Theodore, "God's gift."

TOHON (toh-HOHN) Native American: "cougar."

TOLEK (TOH-lek) A well-known nickname in Poland, used as a short form of Anton (the Slavic form of Anthony, "inestimable" or "priceless") and Todor (the Slavic form of Theodore, "God's gift").

TOMAS The most popular form of Thomas in the world, used in the Czech Republic, Lithuania, Norway, Portugal, Russia, Sweden, and Spanish- and English-speaking countries. See Thomas.

TOMI (TOH-mee) Kalabari, Nigeria: "the people"; or Japanese: "rich." Also a modern Hungarian form of Thomas ("a twin"). This is an example of how the same name can be created and used by what were once widely separated cultures.

TOMLIN Old English: "little twin." A diminutive form of Thomas. Twins are the symbol of the astrological sign Gemini. See Thomas. *Tomkin* (English)

TONI English, Hungarian, and Slavic form of Anthony, "inestimable" or "priceless." See Anthony.

TOPWE (TOHP-way, or Anglicized, TOP-wee) southern Rhodesia: "the topwe vegetable." This is an example of a southern Rhodesian "second name," given when a child reaches maturity, usually at age twelve or fourteen. This particular name suggests a personal quirk, topwe referring to a vegetable the child loved to eat.

TOR Tiv, Nigeria: "king." In Scandinavia the same name is a popular variation of Thor (see box, page 381). See Thor.

TORAO (toh-rah-oh) Japanese: "tiger boy."

TORIN Irish Gaelic: "chief."

TOSHIO (toh-shee-oh) Japanese: "year boy." Popular in Japan. *Toshi* (Japanese)

TOVI (TOH-vee) Hebrew: "my good." A traditional Israeli name. The shorter name *Tov* simply means "good."

TRACE A nickname for Tracey now also used independently. See Tracey, below.

TRACEY, TRACY (TRAY-see) Latin: "bold and courageous"; or Irish Gaelic: "a fighter." This name once had very "strong" connotations, possibly because of its association with actor Spencer Tracy. Now used mostly for girls. *Trace* (English)

Miwok Indian Insect Names

✶ ✶ ✶

Insect names were common among the Miwoks and often reflected these Native Americans' subtle observations of nature. Examples are *Hesutu* ("lifting a yellow jacket's nest out of the ground"); *Momuso* ("yellow jackets piled up in their nest during the winter"); *Muata* ("little yellow jackets in the nest"); *Patakasu* ("small ant biting a person hard"); and *Tiimu* ("black-and-white caterpillar coming out of the ground").

TRAHERN (tra-HERN) Old Welsh: "iron-like," implying strength. Contemporary American development of the older name *Trahaearn,* popular in Wales. *Traherne, Tray* (English)

TRAI (trigh, or Anglicized, tray) Vietnamese: "oyster" or "a pearl," implying a child is precious.

TRAVIS (TRA-viss) Old French: "from the crossroads." Currently one of the top fifty favorite names for boys in this country. *Traver, Travers, Travus* (English)

TREMAIN (tre-MAIN) Celtic: "from the house by the rock." *Tremaine, Tremayne, Trey* (English)

TRENT Latin: "the rapid stream," referring to the Trent River in England. Rapidly gaining popularity in the United States. *Trenten, Trentin, Trenton* (English)

TREVOR (TREH-vor) Irish Gaelic: "wise, discreet one." *Tref, Trefor, Trev, Trevar, Trever* (English)

TREY (tray) Middle English: "third-born." Also a pet form of Tremain, "from the house by the rock."

TRISTAN (TRIS-tun) Old Welsh: "tumultuous" or "riotous." Name of a knight in Celtic legend who drank a love potion meant for the

king and fell in love with Iseult. The legend of Tristan and Iseult is a classic tragic love story in mythology. *Tris, Trist, Tristram, Trys, Tryst, Trystan, Trystram* (English)

TROY Irish Gaelic: "a foot soldier"; or Old French: "from the curly-haired people's region."

TUAN (tung, or Anglicized, twan). Vietnamese: "goes smoothly" or "without complications."

TUKULI (too-KOO-lee) Miwok: "caterpillar traveling headfirst down a tree during the summertime." The name is derived from *tukini,* "to throw oneself endwise."

TULLY (TUL-ee) Irish Gaelic: "people mighty," "living with God's peace," or "devoted to God's will." A traditional Irish favorite. *Tull, Tulley, Tullie* (English); *Tuathal* (Irish)

TUNU (TOO-noo) Miwok: "deer thinking about going to eat wild onions."

TUPI (TOO-pee) Miwok *tupi:* "to pull out" or "to pull up." The elaborate connotation is "throwing a salmon onto the riverbank."

TURI (TOO-ree) Nickname for Arturo, the Spanish form of Arthur, "a bear man" or "noble one."

TURK Slavic: "from Turkey." A contemporary American coinage.

TUYEN (tooing, or Anglicized, TOO-yen) Vietnamese: "angel."

TYEE (TIGH-ee) Native American: "chief."

TYLER Middle English: "tile maker" or "roofer." Currently trendy in the United States. *Ty* (English)

TYRONE Greek: "sovereign one"; or Irish Gaelic: "from Owen's land." *Ty, Tye* (English)

TYSON Middle English: "the son of Ty," which in turn is a form of Dionysus, the Greek god of wine. Also has the meaning "one who kindles mischief or strife." A "tough" name associated in many people's minds with boxer Mike Tyson. *Tie, Ty, Tye, Tysen, Tysone* (English)

U

UDOM (oo-dom) Thai: "absolute."

ULAN (oo-lahn) Bari, southern Sudan: "first-born twin." See also Lado.

ULRIC Old German: "ruler of all" or "wolf-ruler." *Alaric, Ric, Rich, Richie, Richy, Rick, Rickie, Ricky, Ulrich, Ulrick* (English)

UMBERTO (oom-BAIR-toh) Italian form of Humberto, "a Hun" or "famous bear cub."

UPTON Old English: "from the upper town or estate."

URBAN Latin: "one from the city." *Orban, Urbane* (English); *Urbain, Urbaine* (French); *Orban* (Hungarian); *Urbano* (Italian, Portuguese, Spanish); *Urvan* (Russian)

URI (YOOR-ee) Hebrew: "God is my light" or "Jehovah's flame." *Uriah, Urie, Uriel* (English); *Uriano, Urias, Uriel* (Spanish)

URIEL (YOO-ree-el) A longer form of Uri ("God is my light" or "Jehovah's flame"), frequently used in Israel. The name of one of the archangels who dwells near God's throne.

URIEN (yoo-RYE-un) Old Celtic: "from a privileged family"; or possibly Latin: "heavenly one." Popular in Wales. *Urian, Uryan, Yurvan* (English)

UZOMA (OOZ-oh-mah) Ibo, Nigeria: "born during a journey."

V

VADIN (VAH-deen) Hindi: "speaker," implying scholarly or learned discourse.

VALIN (VAH-leen) Hindi: "the monkey king." See Balin.

VAN Dutch: "son of." Originally a nickname, this has now become a given name. Many old Dutch names have this prefix. Van is also a feathered monster or dragon in Armenian myth. *Vann* (English)

VANCE Middle English: "a thresher." *Van* (English)

VARDEN Old French: "from the green hills." *Vardon, Verden, Verdon* (English)

VARTAN Armenian: "rose."

VASILIS (vah-SEE-lees) Greek form of Basil, "kingly" or "magnificent." See Basil.

VASIN (vah-seen) Hindi: "ruler" or "lord."

VASSILY (vah-SEE-lee) Russian form of Basil ("kingly," or "magnificent") or William ("unwavering protector"). See Basil or William.

VAUGHN (vawn) Old Welsh: "small." *Vaune, Vawn, Vawne, Von, Vonn, Vonne* (English)

VENCEL (VEN-tsel) Hungarian: "wreath" or "garland."

VERED (VAIR-ed) Hebrew: "a rose."

VERN A short form of Vernon ("youthful" or "like spring"), now used independently. *Verne, Vernn* (English)

VERNON Latin: "youthful" or "like spring." *Vern, Verne, Vernen, Vernin, Vernn* (English)

VIC Short form of Victor ("a conqueror"), now used in the United States as an independent name. See Victor.

VICTOR Latin: "a conqueror." *Vic, Vick* (English); *Viktor* (Bulgarian, Hungarian, Russian, Swedish); *Victoir* (French); *Vittore, Vittorio* (Italian); *Wiktor, Witek* (Polish); *Vitor* (Portuguese); *Vika, Vitenka, Vitka, Vitya* (Russian); *Victorino, Victorio, Victuriano, Vitin, Vito* (Spanish)

VIDOR (VEE-dor) Hungarian form of Hilary, "cheerful."

VILJO (VEEL-yo) Very popular name in Finland, this is a Finnish form of William, "unwavering protector."

VINCENT Latin: "conquering." *Bink, Vin, Vince, Vinn, Vinnie, Vinny, Vinsent, Vint* (English); *Vincenc, Vinco* (Czech); *Vincenz* (French, German); *Binkentios*

(Greek); *Vinci* (Hungarian); *Enzo, Vicenzo, Vincenzo* (Italian); *Wicek, Wicent, Wicus* (Polish); *Kesha, Vika, Vikent, Vikenti, Vikesha* (Russian); *Chenche, Vicente* (Spanish)

VINSON Old English: "Vincent's son." *Vince, Vinse, Vinsen* (English)

VITO (VEE-toh) Latin: "relating to life." Popular Spanish name. Also a Spanish form of Victor, "a conqueror."

VLADIMIR (VLAHD-i-meer) Old Slavic: "powerful warrior" or "ruler of an army." Form of Walter that's popular in Russia. For variations around the world, see Walter. *Vlad, Vladi, Vlady* (English)

VLADLEN (VLAHD-len) Russian creation from Vladimir + Lenin. Became popular in Russia after Lenin came into power.

WABAN (wah-BAHN) Native American: "the east wind."

WADE Old English: "from the river crossing."

WALDEN Old English: "child of the forest valley." Closely associated in many people's minds

with Thoreau's Walden Pond. *Wald, Waldon* (English)

WALLACE Old English: "a Welshman." *Wallie, Wallis, Wally, Walsh, Welch, Welsh* (English)

WALT Short form of Walter, "powerful warrior" or "ruler of an army." Used today as an independent name. Well-known namesakes are Walt Disney and poet Walt Whitman.

WALTER Old German: "powerful warrior" or "ruler of an army." *Wallie, Wally, Walt* (English); *Valtr, Vladko, Waltr* (Czech); *Gauther, Gautier* (French); *Walli, Walther, Waltili* (German); *Gualtiero* (Italian); *Valter, Valters* (Latvian); *Vacys, Vanda, Vandele, Waldemar* (Lithuanian); *Landislaus* (Polish); *Dima, Dimka, Vladimir, Volya, Vova, Vovka* (Russian); *Gualberto, Gualterio, Gutierre* (Spanish)

WAPI (WAH-pee) Native American: "lucky."

WARD Old English: "a guardian" or "watchman."

WARNER Old German: "the defending army" or "defending warrior."

WATTAN (wah-tahn) Arapaho: "black."

WAYNE Old English: "a wagonmaker." Originally a short form of

Wainwright, but long used as an independent name. *Lewayne* (English); *Vaino* (Finnish)

WEBB Old English: "a weaver." *Web* (English)

WELBY Old English: "from the farm by the spring."

WEMILAT (weh-MEE-laht) Native American: "all given to him." Indian name for a child born to wealthy parents.

WEMILO (weh-MEE-loh) Native American: "all speak to him," implying all respect him.

WEN English Gypsy: "born in winter."

WES Originally a nickname for Wesley ("from the west meadow or woods"), now bestowed as an independent name.

WESH English Gypsy: "from the forest" or simply "woods."

WESLEY (WES-lee or WEZ-lee) Old English: "from the west meadow or woods." *Wes, Wesleigh, Wesly, Wessley, West, Westley, Wezley* (English)

WESTBROOK Old English: "dweller near the west brook." *Brook, Brooke, Wes, West, Westbrooke* (English)

WICENT Polish form of Vincent, "conqueror." See Vincent.

WICHADO (wee-CHAHD-oh) Native American: "willing."

WILANU (wee-LAH-noo) Miwok: "pouring water on acorn flour in a leaching place."

WILDON Old English: "from the wild valley." *Will* (English)

> **❝*Going to call him 'William'? What kind of a name is that? Every Tom, Dick and Harry is called William. Why not call him Bill?*❞**
>
> —FILMMAKER SAM GOLDWYN

WILL Old English: "unwavering and determined." A short form of William and other names starting with *"Wil-,"* used today as an independent name.

WILLIAM Old German: "unwavering protector." *Bill, Billie, Billy, Will, Willi, Williamson, Willie, Willy, Wilson* (English); *Vilhelm* (Bulgarian); *Vila, Vilek, Vilem, Viliam, Vilko,*

Vilous (Czech); *Viljo* (Finnish): *Guillamus, Guillaume* (French); *Wilhelm, Willi, Willy* (German); *Vasilios, Vassos* (Greek); *Vili, Vilmos* (Hungarian); *Liam, Uilliam* (Irish); *Vas, Vasilak, Vasili, Vasiliy, Vaska, Vassili, Vassily, Vasya, Vasyl* (Russian); *Giermo, Gigermo, Gijermo, Gillermo, Guilermon, Guille, Guillelmo, Guillermino, Guillermo, Guillo, Guirmo, Gullermo, Ilermo, Memo, Quillermo* (Spanish); *Vilhelm, Ville, Wilhelm, Willie* (Swedish); *Welfel, Wolf* (Yiddish)

WILNY (WIL-nee) Native American: "eagle singing while flying."

WILTON Old English: "from the farm with a spring." *Will, Willie, Willy, Wilt* (English)

WILU (WEE-loo) Miwok: "chicken hawk calling *wi*."

WINFIELD Teutonic: "friend of the soil" or "friend of the earth." *Field, Win, Winn, Winny, Wyn* (English)

WINGI (WEEN-gee) Native American: "willing."

WINSTON Old English: "from a friend's town." *Win, Winn, Winsten, Wyn, Wynston* (English)

WINWARD Old English: "by friend's (or brother's) forest" or "my brother's keeper." *Ward, Win, Winn, Wyn* (English)

WOLFGANG Old German: "path of the wolf" or "a traveling wolf." A traditional German name recently brought back into vogue by celebrity chef Wolfgang Puck, as well as actress Valerie Bertinelli and musician Eddie Van Halen, who named their son Wolfgang. In Germany, the name is pronounced

❝He was convinced, among other things, that he had been given his commonplace first name [William] because his parents had been too busy to think of anything else (his older brother had the distinctive name of Lessing).❞

—SAID OF WILLIAM ROSENWALD, ONE OF THE SONS OF THE FOUNDER OF SEARS ROEBUCK, FROM STEPHEN BIRMINGHAM'S *THE GRANDES DAMES*

VOLF-gahng. *Wolf* (English); *Wulf* (German)

WOODROW Old English: "from the hedge near the forest." *Wood, Woody* (English)

WOODY Short form of names containing the syllable *wood.* Now used as an independent name. Famous namesakes are singer Woody Guthrie and actor Woody Harrelson.

WORTH Old English: "from the farmstead."

WULITON (WOO-li-tun) Native American: "to do well."

WUNAND (WOO-nand) Native American: "God is good."

WUYI (WOO-yee) Miwok: "turkey vulture soaring."

WYATT Old French: "little warrior." *Wiatt, Wyat* (English)

WYNN Welsh: "fair one." *Win, Winn, Wyn* (English)

XAVIER (ZAYV-yer) Arabic: "bright"; or Spanish: "owner of the new house." Xavier and Javier are both common forms of Spanish names. *Javier*

(English); *Xaver* (German); *Saverio* (Italian)

XENOS (ZEE-nohs) Greek: "a guest" or "a stranger."

XERXES (ZERK-sees) Persian: "ruler." Name of a famous Persian king.

XYLON (ZIGH-lon) Greek: "dweller in the forest."

YADIN (yah-DIN) Hebrew: "God will judge." *Yadon* (Israeli)

YAKECEN (YAH-keh-shen) Athabascan, Carrier Indian: "sky on song."

YAKEZ (YAH-kehz) Athabascan: "heaven." Shortened from the Carrier Indian words *ya kezudzepe,* which mean "within heaven's ears."

YAKIM (YAK-kim) Hebrew: "God will establish." A short form of Yehoyakim now used as an independent name. A traditional Jewish name from Israel.

YALE Old English: "from the slope" or "from the land corner."

YANCY Native American: "Englishman."

Lucky Chinese Names

✱ ✱ ✱

While a girl in China is often given a name to signify beauty, a boy is frequently given a name in the hope it will bring him luck or success. Among these "lucky" boys' names in China are *Chen* ("great"); *Cheng-Gong* ("success"); *Cheung* ("good luck"); *Huang* ("wealthy, an emperor"); *Huang-Fu* ("wealthy future"); *Sheng* ("victory"); *Sheng-Li* ("great victory"); *Wing* ("glory"); and *Zhiyuan* ("ambition").

YANNIS Contemporary Greek form of John, "gracious gift of God" or "God is gracious."

YARB English Gypsy: "herb," implying a fragrant scent.

YARIN (YAR-in) Hebrew: "to understand," implying a child is sensitive and wise. *Jarin* (English)

YASAR (yah-SAHR) Arabic: "wealth." The Prophet Muhammad objected to this name because he considered it too proud. Made known world-wide by PLO leader Yasser Arafat. *Yaser; Yasir; Yasser* (Arabic)

YAZID (YAH-zeed) "he will increase." Arabic name which dates to antiquity and is almost identical in meaning to the Hebrew Joseph, "God will increase," in the sense that power and influence will grow. The difference is that the "he" in the Arabic name refers to the bearer of the name, whereas in the Hebrew, "God" refers, of course, to Jehovah. *Zaid* (Arabic)

YEMON (yeh-mohn) Japanese: "guardian of the gate."

YEN (ing, or Anglicized, yen) Vietnamese: "calm; serene" or "a swallow."

YERIK Modern Russian form of Jeremy, "appointed by Jehovah" or "Jehovah is high."

YIN (ying) Chinese: "silver."

YORK Old Celtic: "from the yew estate"; or Old English: "from the estate of the boar." *Yorke* (English)

YU (yoo) Chinese: depending on the character, this common Chinese name means "shining brightly" or "universal."

YUCEL (YOO-sel) Turkish: "sublime."

YUKIO (yoo-kee-oh) Japanese: "snow boy," implying "boy who goes his own way." *Yuki, Yukiko* (Japanese)

YULE Old English: "born on Christmas." Made well known by actor Yul Brynner. *Yul* (English)

YUMA (YOO-mah) Native American: "the chief's son."

YUNUS (YOO-nus) Turkish form of Jonah, "dove," the symbol of peace.

YURI (YOOR-ee) Popular in Russia as a form of George, "farmer" or "land worker." See George.

YUSEF (YOO-sef) Arabic form of Joseph, "he will increase." Also used today in the Czech Republic, Germany, and Poland. See Joseph. *Yazid* (Arabic)

YUTU (YOO-too) Miwok: "to claw" with the connotation of "coyote making a feint so he can seize a bird with his claws."

YVES (eev) French form of Ives, "son of the yew bow" or "little archer." In astrology, the

Archer is the symbol of Sagittarius. See Ives.

Z

ZACH Short form of Zachary ("Jehovah has remembered") now popular in this country as an independent name.

ZACHARY Hebrew: "Jehovah has remembered." Currently trendy in the United States. *Zach, Zachariah, Zack, Zak* (English); *Sakari* (Finnish); *Zacharie* (French); *Sacharja, Zacharia* (German); *Zacharias, Zako* (Hungarian); *Sakarias, Sakarja, Zakris* (Norwegian, Swedish); *Zacharias* (Portuguese); *Sachar, Zakhar* (Russian); *Zacarias* (Spanish)

ZAHID (zah-HEED) Arabic: "self-denying" or "ascetic."

ZAHUR (zah-HOOR) Swahili: "flower."

ZAID (zah-EED) Shortened Arabic form of Yazid, "he will increase," a development of Joseph. See Yazid.

ZAKI (ZA-kee) Arabic: "intelligent."

ZAMIR (zah-MEER) Hebrew: "a bird" or "a song." Currently a name popular in Israel. *Zemer* (English)

ZANE An English form of John, "gracious gift of God" or "God is gracious." See John.

ZAREB (zah-REB) Sudanese: "protector against enemies."

ZARED (zah-RED) Hebrew: "ambush."

> **"He who steals my purse steals trash; but he that filches from me my good name makes me poor indeed."**
>
> —WILLIAM SHAKESPEARE

ZAREK (ZAH-rek) Polish name derived from Greek and meaning "may God protect the king."

ZEB Hebrew: "to exalt or honor." A short form of the older Hebrew name Zebulon, now used independently. In the Bible, Zeb was Jacob's tenth son by Leah.

ZEEMAN Dutch: "seaman." Name for a boy born under one of the water signs of Cancer, Pisces, or Scorpio.

ZEHEB (zeh-HEB) Turkish: "gold."

ZEKE Aramaic: "spark" or "shooting star." Also a modern short form of Zachariah, "the memory of the Lord."

ZEKI (ze-KEE) Turkish: "intelligent" or "quick-witted."

ZELIMIR (zel-ih-meer) Slavic: "he wishes peace."

ZENON (ZEE-non) Greek: "living" or "given life by Zeus." *Zeno* (French, Greek); *Zewek* (Polish); *Zinon* (Russian); *Cenon, Zenon* (Spanish)

ZENOS Latin: "Jupiter's gift." Name for a boy born under the sign of Sagittarius or Pisces, both ruled by Jupiter.

ZESIRO (zeh-SEE-roh) Luganda, Uganda: "elder twin." Common name in Uganda, Africa.

ZINAN (zee-nan) Japanese: "second-born son."

ZIVEN (ZEE-ven) Slavic: "vigorous and alive." Used especially in the Czech Republic, Poland, the Republic of Slovakia, and Russia. *Ziv, Zivon* (English)

ZORYA (ZOR-ya) Ukrainian: "star."